I0816775

UABB 2015 Catalogue
RE-LIVING THE CITY
城市原点

curated by Aaron Betsky
Alfredo Brillembourg
Hubert Klumpner
Doreen Heng Liu

edited by Gideon Fink Shapiro

TSINGTAO
青島啤酒

理发
电话:13728273612
RE

20%
和其王

TSINGTAO
青島啤酒
青島啤酒

RE-LIVING THE
RE

大玩具
RE-LIVING THE CITY
RE

特价
10元3个
Rice Cooker
Rice Cooker

期已入住

合家歡樂迎
RE-LIVING THE CITY
RE
辣

CONTENTS

RADICAL URBANISM

COLLAGE CITY 3D

PRD 2.0

SOCIAL CITY

MAKER MAKER

ADDITIONAL

FOREWORD: RE-LIVING THE CITY FOR A POETIC FUTURE

Shenzhen Biennale of Urbanism\ Architecture Organising Committee

An Innovative and Open Platform for International Exchange

The Bi-City Biennale of Urbanism\Architecture (UABB) is the one and the only biennale of urbanism and architecture in the world. Over the past decade, UABB has set up an innovative and open platform for international exchange in Shenzhen. Professional leaders from all over the world gather in Shenzhen, sharing their observations and insights on urbanism and enhancing the international exposure of Shenzhen. Nowadays even international exhibitions like the International Architecture Biennale Rotterdam (IABR) and V&A's China Design Now select works from UABB, while the others like the later-launched Istanbul Design Biennial and the Seoul International Biennale on Architecture and Urbanism currently under preparation have shown great interest in sharing the experiences of UABB. In 2014, the year of its 10th anniversary, UABB presented the UABB@Venice program at the China Pavilion, and the exhibition of a roof model, which was created at a UABB workshop based on the twelfth-century Chinese architectural treatise, *Yingzao Fashi* at the Central Pavilion; in addition, it realized an installation entitled *Re-Creation* in collaboration with the Museum of Finnish Architecture based on a design by Alvar Aalto. These projects forged an even more profound connection between UABB and the Venice Biennale in terms of exhibition works and participants, making UABB another platform for joint exploration on urbanism.

In March 2014, UABB launched an international call for proposals to select the curatorial team for UABB 2015. Following a period of application and multiple rounds of reviews by the UABB Academic Committee, curatorial responsibility was awarded to a team including Aaron Betsky, curator, critic and lecturer on art and architecture; Alfredo Brillembourg and Hubert Klumpner, co-principals of Urban Think Tank and Chair of Architecture and Urban Design at ETH Zürich; and Doreen Heng Liu, Adjunct Associate Professor of Chinese University of Hong Kong and Founder and Principal of NODE. Following more than a year of preparation, they now present an innovative exhibition themed *Re-living the City*.

A Public Educational Platform on Urbanism

In the same vein as other significant exhibitions, museums and art galleries around the world, UABB has been exploring the reciprocity and complementarity between professional depth and public enthusiasm. As UABB has accumulated a remarkable appeal and influence in the field of urbanism and architecture since its launch in 2005, while the urban issues are much discussed livelihood topics of the public interests, UABB has been striving for the richness and diversity of the exhibitions.

Following the pattern established over five UABB exhibitions in the past ten years, the exhibition structure of the 2015 Biennale will be: 1) Main Exhibition, 2) Invitational Exhibition of National and Regional Pavilions, 3) Affiliated Exhibitions, 4) Sponsor Display Corner, 5) Collateral or Thematic Exhibitions, and 6) UABB School (Educational Program). Conceived by the curatorial team, the Main Exhibition is centered on the proposed theme, yet encompasses a variety of presentation forms. The Invitational Exhibition of National and Regional Pavilions features prestigious cultural institutions and organizations from around the world who have been invited to participate in the Biennale. Affiliated Exhibitions, a newly incorporated part in UABB 2015, explores innovative possibilities for a selection of traditional architecture. The Sponsor Display Corner offers our long-term partners an opportunity to present their corporate image and social responsibilities through self-designed exhibitions. Collateral Exhibitions are solicited from the public; any interested organization may propose a creative exhibition based on the UABB theme, for review by the UABB Academic Committee, the Chief Curators and the Organising Committee. UABB School aims to integrate the resources and strengthen the role of education. Targeting professional visitors, the general public and family visitors, it serves as a bridge between the professional field and the public by offering a series of free courses and events during the Biennale.

With such exhibition structure and positioning, UABB is committed to creating a global exchange platform that responds to contemporary urban issues in real time. It hosts a convergence of global wisdom and practical examples to explore good urban development modes, involving the whole public in the mission of creating a better life.

Poetic Construction of Urban Future

Over the past few years, Shenzhen in particular and China in general has witnessed the emerging trend of a new type of urbanization. The whole society has been reflecting and reconsidering the impact of blindly rapid growth upon cities, the environment and cultural memory. The urban development of recent decades offers valuable experiences, both positive and negative, and confirms the importance of the spiritual and cultural legacy from both pre-industrial and industrial eras.

As a tribute to this concept, the former Dacheng Flour Factory and No. 8 Warehouse, a representative industrial legacy in Shekou Industrial Zone, were chosen as the main venue for UABB 2015, while a traditional Hakka enclosed house, Xipu House in Longgang, serves as an affiliated venue. In addition, there are collateral exhibitions taking place all over the city that will involve visitors from different regions and fields in urbanism and art-themed events and activities.

UABB, as a cultural catalyst and creative "bonfire," seeks to illuminate the places of all urban dwellers, opening a narrowly-defined niche field into a wider conversation.

The young city of Shenzhen continues to inspire the creativity of architects, planners, commentators, scholars and artists from around the globe. Their original work and thought, presented through multiple media, connect Shenzhen with the world, the general public with the professional realm, and tradition with the future.

INTRODUCTION

Gideon Fink Shapiro

This book presents the exhibits and curatorial visions of UABB 2015. Four originally separate volumes, prepared before and during the Biennale, were combined to create this rich collection of projects and essays.

Re-Living the City, the theme articulated by the curators, sets a markedly different agenda from the more obvious projects of redesigning, rebuilding, or re-planning the city. It lays emphasis on the life of the people in the city, while also attributing a kind of sentience to the city itself. *Living* suggests that the city is an ongoing project that belongs to everyone, every day. It reflects the embodied knowledge of people and places as well as professional expertise in the designed environment. Most of all, the living of the city evokes a shared process of reinvention and reflection that is never complete.

The *re* in *re-living* suggests a return: but to what, where, or when? Certainly this Biennale is no exercise in repetition or restoration. Instead, it experiments with processes for generating a new city out of the existing one. Adaptive reuse and recycling are part of this conversation, but so are other, more figurative metamorphoses. Re-living may signify the return of a memory—one that changes every time it is recalled, colored by new perspectives. Thus the Biennale asks participants and visitors to re-live the city as they bring new potentials to light.

Urbanisation in the world's fastest growing regions today (particularly in Asia, Africa, and Latin America) has a dual character: a bonanza of officially-sanctioned, standardized development shadowed by a second, unregulated or 'informal' city built by disenfranchised migrants. The present Biennale operates between these poles, seeking alternative paradigms to generate more sustainable, equitable, and imaginative urban habitats. It calls for clean air and water, but also wider freedom and power to participate in remaking the city and to express one's place in it. Through experiments and case studies, the curators and participants embrace a hands-on role for designers, makers, and ordinary residents alike.

The projects and essays in this volume show the status quo of architecture and urbanism to be inadequate on many accounts. But they also reject the false dream of designing a perfect city from zero, tabula rasa. Instead, they portray the city as the incremental product of its inhabitants and designers, who make and remake its fabric—through tactical, systemic, improvisational, social, physical, ecological, or other means—without full control or knowledge of all of its parts at once. Even if no single plan or intervention can make the city whole, they can introduce new functions and experiences that have a wider effect.

Each of the curators has charted a different approach to the theme of Re-Living the City. They have contributed not only curatorial essays, but also conceptual or polemical briefs to frame the exhibitions and installations. Aaron Betsky writes that the built environment already has 'enough buildings, enough objects, and enough images.' To inject fresh vigor into worn material and figural fragments, he proposes, architects can selectively reuse and recombine them, either literally or metaphorically, as in early modern collage art. The participating artists and architects in his 'Collage City 3D' exhibition were asked to create adjacent three-dimensional installations to explore the idea of habitable collage. This section also contains guest essays from Jimenez Lai and myself.

Alfredo Brillembourg and Hubert Klumpner, curators of the 'Radical Urbanism' exhibition, call attention to the contributions of ordinary citizens in reshaping the urban fabric to their needs. They trace a brief history of radical urbanism, a concept that asks professional architects and planners to learn from ad-hoc practices. The etymology of *radical* refers to roots, and indeed radical urbanism seeks the roots of urbanism in bottom-up innovations. Guest essays by Pedro Gadanho, Lydia Kallipoliti, and Justin McGuirk lend further critical perspective.

Doreen Heng Liu, curator of 'PRD 2.0', advocates for a more balanced relationship between people, technology, and the environment in Shenzhen and the Pearl River Delta. She contends that this industrious region, which is quite possibly the largest conurbation in the world today, has focused too narrowly on economic growth since the establishment of the first Special Economic Zone in 1980. The catalogue of the PRD 2.0 exhibition is followed by topical essay contributions by Jacob Dreyer and Lori Gibbs.

Renny Ramakers of Droog describes Social City, an online sharing platform and installation at UABB that merges the public with the personal, and the physical with the digital. Like a reflection of the urban unconscious, it allows people to voice their needs and dreams for a better city, while logging their activities, intentions, and affections.

Benjamin Ward, curator of the Maker Maker exhibition, explains how new tools of production are spurring a democratic renewal of craft, turning everyone into a potential maker. Manufactured objects, long seen as units of alienated labor, here express personal and collective inventiveness. Documentation of the national, regional, and thematic pavilions reveals a variety of international perspectives on the future of urbanism and architecture.

As the contents of this volume make clear, Re-Living the City can take many forms. It remains for the reader and exhibition-goer to decide which hold the most promise, and how they might stimulate further experiments.

CURATOR PROFILES

AARON BETSKY

Curator of 'Collage City 3D'

Aaron Betsky is Dean of the Frank Lloyd Wright School of Architecture at Taliesin. He is also a curator, critic, and lecturer on art, architecture and design. In 2008, he directed the 11th Venice International Architecture Biennale, which was at the time the highest attended such event. Between 2006 and 2014, he was Director of the Cincinnati Art Museum, and before that was Director of the Netherlands Architecture Institute (2001-2006) and Curator of Architecture, Design, and Digital Projects at the San Francisco Museum of Modern Art (1995-2001). Trained in the humanities and then as an architect at Yale University, Betsky has also worked as a writer and as an architectural designer for Frank Gehry and Hodgetts & Fung Design Associates. He writes a twice-weekly blog for architectmagazine.com, as well as articles for both professional and general audience publications and lectures regularly around the world. He has published over a dozen books including, most recently, his collected essays, *At Home in Sprawl*, and a survey of modernism in architecture and design, *Making it Modern*.

ALFREDO BRILLEMBOURG & HUBERT KLUMPNER

Curators of 'Radical Urbanism'

Alfredo Brillembourg and Hubert Klumpner head the interdisciplinary design firm Urban-Think Tank. Meeting as graduate students in architecture and urban design in New York, they co-founded U-TT in Caracas, Venezuela, in 1998 to develop prototypical interventions for informal urban environments. Brillembourg and Klumpner co-founded the Sustainable Living Urban Model Laboratory (SLUM Lab) as adjunct professors at GSAPP, Columbia University. Together, they have held a Chair of Architecture and Urban Design at the Swiss Federal Institute of Technology (ETH) in Zurich, Switzerland, since 2010. As coprincipals of U-TT, Brillembourg and Klumpner have received the 2010 Ralph Erskine Award, the 2011 Holcim Gold Award for Latin America, and the 2012 Holcim Global Silver Award for innovative contributions to ecological and social design practices. They have published the books *Informal City: Caracas Case* and *Torre David: Informal Vertical Communities*, and were part of the team awarded the Golden Lion at the 13th International Architecture Exhibition – La Biennale di Venezia for the installation 'Torre David/ Gran Horizonte'. Urban-Think Tank's most notable built work includes the Metro Cable and a series of 'Vertical Gyms' in Caracas. Additional projects are currently underway in Sao Paulo, Barranquilla, and Cape Town.

Production Manager: Andrés Ruiz Andrade
Exhibition Coordinator: José Castrezana López

DOREEN HENG LIU
Curators of 'PRD 2.0'

Doreen Heng Liu, born in Guangzhou, is an architect practicing in China. She received her Masters in Architecture from UC Berkeley and Doctorate of Design at Harvard Graduate School of Design. Her research focuses on contemporary urbanism and architecture in the Pearl River Delta, and the specific impact of urbanization on design and practice in China today. Liu established her own design practice NODE (Nansha Original Design) in Hong Kong and Nansha, Guangzhou in 2004, and opened another studio in Shenzhen in 2009. Her built architectural works include the Value Factory – Main Entrance & Warehouse renovation – in the 2013 Biennial; the Nansha Science Museum and Nansha Bookstore, Guangzhou Times Museum; the Lianzhou Int'l Photography Festival Permanent Site. Her design works have been published in *Architectural Record*, *Domus*, *Abitare*, and *Volume*. She and her studio have also participated in various architectural and art exhibitions in Shanghai, Guangzhou, Venice and Rotterdam. In 2012, NODE was shortlisted, as one of five international emerging architects, for the Audi Urban Future Initiative (AUFI) awards. Liu is Adjunct Associate Professor at the School of Architecture, Chinese University of Hong Kong. In 2014, She was nominated as Curator for the Hong Kong Pavilion for the 14th International Architecture Exhibition – la Biennale di Venezia.

CO-CURATOR PROFILES

RENNY RAMAKERS
Curator of 'Social City'

Co-founder and director of Droog, Renny Ramakers curates design exhibitions, is a judging panelist on various design boards and leads workshops and lectures worldwide. She has served as a member of the Dutch Council of Culture (1995-2001) among other governmental advisory boards. She has contributed to international magazines, books, and catalogues, and has also authored several books. She has been chair of the board of THNK, Amsterdam school for creative leadership. In 2012 she was named one of the '150 Women Who Shake the World' by Newsweek. Ramakers is trained as an art historian, but decided to become a designer herself. She started the program Design+Desires to link the dreams, desires, and needs of citizens to their virtual and real daily experiences. The objective is to find solutions and opportunities that can be implemented daily in the existing environment. The ultimate goal is to upscale these experiments towards a larger infrastructure and to develop a conceptual model for a partly self-organising city. In all her projects, Ramakers focuses on creating interaction with the public, new collaborations, tools, technologies, and systems embedded in community and social context.

JASON HILGEFORT & MERVE BEDIR
Curators of 'Aformal Academy – RE:Learning The City'

Jason Hilgefort is an urbanist and architect who studied at University of British Columbia and University of Cincinnati. He has worked in New York, Los Angeles, Rotterdam, and Bombay. He won Europan 11 (Vienna), and is currently part of Future Urban Research group in the Netherlands. He published an essay in *The Architecture of Knowledge: The Library of the Future*, and contributes regularly to *uncube* magazine. Merve Bedir is an architect and researcher. Currently a Ph.D. candidate at Delft University of Technology, she curated One Architecture Week 2015 (Plovdiv, Bulgaria), and *Vocabulary of Hospitality* (Istanbul). She produced the documentary film *Agoraphobia* and is currently facilitating Bostan, a refugee garden and community kitchen (Gazientep, Turkey). She has worked with or at the Netherlands Architecture Institute (NAI), INTI, Studio X Istanbul, the Swiss Federal Institute of Technology (EPFL), *Archis*, and the African Centre for Cities (Cape Town). She has written for *Volume, MONU, Failed Architecture, Zivot*, and other publications. Hilgefort and Bedir are partners in Land+Civilization Compositions, a Rotterdam/Istanbul/Shenzhen-based studio exploring issues at the ever-expanding edge of urbanism that views city creation as an art forum. Their contribution to UABB School 2015, "Aformal Academy – RE:Learning The City," is developed in cooperation with Ljubo Georgiev and Hristo Stankushev.

BENJAMIN WARD
Curator of 'Maker Maker'

Benjamin Ward currently works as a project manager and production engineer at MakeTime. MakeTime is an online, transactional marketplace where manufacturers connect to buy and sell CNC machine production capacity by the hour. MakeTime seeks to revolutionize manufacturing by making it as easy for entrepreneurs, designers, and makers to purchase manufacturing capacity as to purchase server bandwidth in the cloud. Previously, Ward worked as a project manager and fabrication specialist for Parrish Rash & van Dissel, Parrish Production, and Rash, LLC – all known for producing works for top-level artists, designers and hospitality companies. Additionally, Ward has worked professionally at the offices of Morphosis Architects in Culver City, California, as well as Future Cities Lab in San Francisco, California. Throughout his career, Ward has been directly involved with the digital and physical production of hundreds of projects ranging from large-scale architectural installations to high-precision components for some of the world's most progressive companies in the automotive, robotics and medical manufacturing industries.

Project Manager: Liu Si
Production Manager: Yin Yujun

VENUE MAP

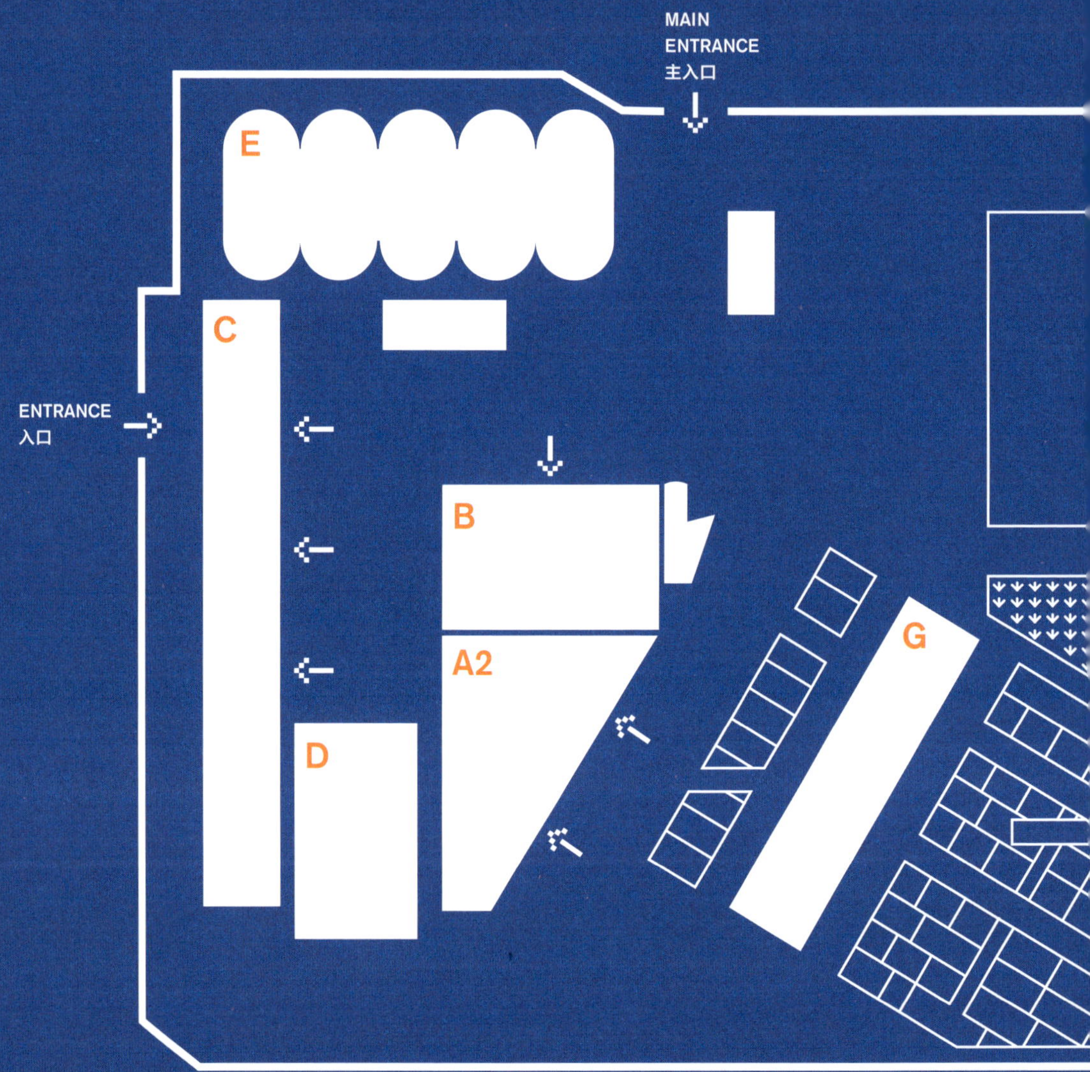

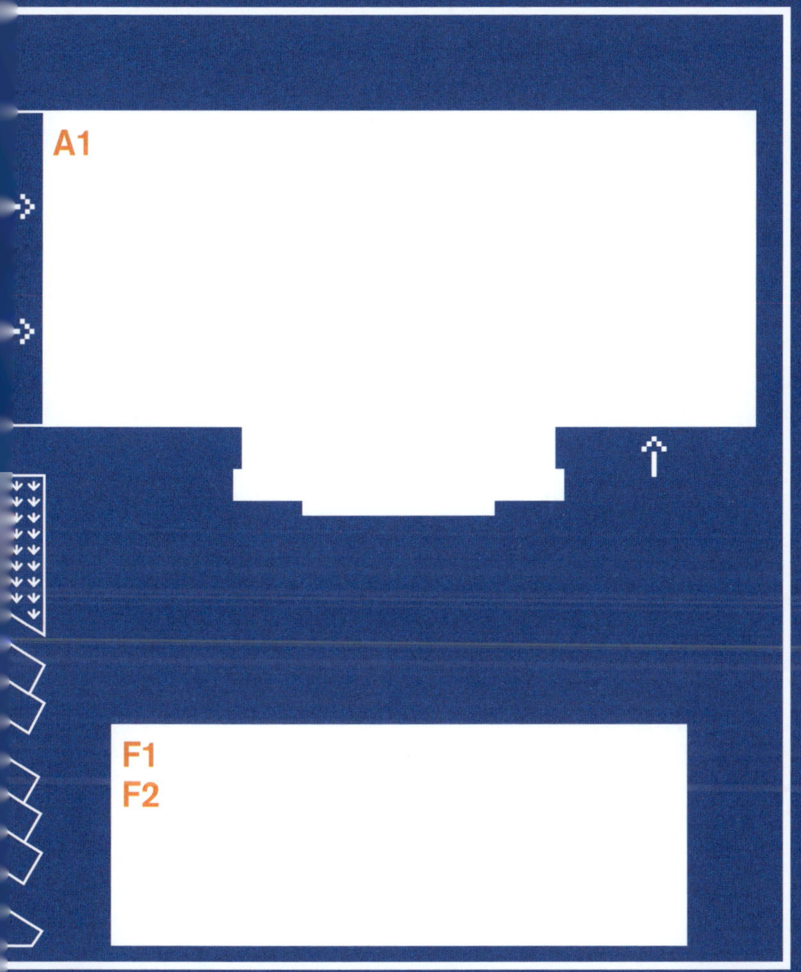

A1
MAIN HALL
主展区

A2
MAIN / MAKER MAKER
主展 / 创客展会

B
INFO + UABB SCHOOL
问询 + UABB学堂

C
MEDIA
媒体区

D
AUDITORIUM
报告厅

E
SILO
筒仓

F1
COLLATERAL EXHIBITION
外围展

F2
SPONSOR EXHIBITION
企业馆

G
SHEKOU ROUND TABLE
蛇口议事

A MANIFESTO

Aaron Betsky

This Biennale makes a simple argument: We have enough stuff. We have enough buildings, enough objects, and enough images.

We certainly have enough cities and built-up areas. We do not need to make or build any more. What we need to do is to reuse, rethink, and reimagine what we already have. Specifically, we need architecture that is not the imposition of an abstract idea on a plot that was either inhabited or natural, which is to say an act of appropriation that uses up non-renewable natural resources in the process. Rather we should think of architecture as the thoughtful gathering together of what we already have to create structures that open us up to new relationships with each other and with our environment. We need to discover the new within what we have and know.

The methods we need to employ in this endeavour are simple and well-known: the reuse of existing buildings and materials; tactical insertions in the grids and closed structures of our cities that open them up to new forms of occupation, new uses, and new vistas; reinterpretations of existing images and forms so that we can both recognise ourselves and our heritage and understand that we can reinvent our world and our roles within the reality we have inherited; and a forceful cutting, slicing, and making our own of the structures that otherwise keep us imprisoned — those whose physical confinement represents and makes real the social, political, and economic control to which we are subject.

There is a history to such tactics as well, although it is one that this Biennale does not examine in detail, as its nature is to be a celebration of current experimentation. It is the history of collage, assemblage, and appropriation; of installations and performance art that breaks the boundaries of what usually defines art and architecture; of the reuse of imagery that used to be part and parcel of the artist's and the architect's practice, and that was briefly resurrected during the period of Post-modernism; and the notion of art as the magical repurposing of existing forms, images, and patterns to imbue them with new significance beyond the conventions out of which the base material arose.

Collage and assemblage, as they emerged as techniques in artmaking starting in the early 20th century, served as counterpoints to pictorial techniques that assumed reality was an illusion, and to art that claimed to understand deeper principles beyond physical and time-based materiality. This abstract and spiritually-oriented approach, steeped in a centuries-long tradition, sought to create a window into a world of pure and ultimately *a*-human and *a*-physical truths, moving the viewer into the realm of ideas and ideals. In architecture, this meant forms that came out of orders and organisational principles that were not bound by time or place, and that reflected the power to impose an institution's, state's, or individual's power over people, resources, and spaces.

Against such an approach, collage and assemblage proposed to gather what was real, emphasising the material's sensual qualities by eschewing anything that was finished, complete, or still functional. The stuff with which collage makers worked was incomplete, damaged, and useless: it was the detritus of human civilisation. It also bore the marks of use, containing within itself the humanity that had made and worn it down. Artists put this material together into compositions that were themselves unstable, often without the central focal point and certainly without the crutches of perspectives or other abstract forms of organisation that transformed material such as paint into the building blocks of an imaginary world. Instead, they created rhythms and patterns, weaving together the fragments into something that cohered, though often barely. These compositions could be read as abstractions — but more importantly as experimental reconfigurations that gave dead material a second life with many potential vectors.

Architects did not pick up on these techniques until the 1980s, and even then in a manner that still showed the central place abstraction and order held and hold in their discipline: they assembled fragments of historical forms and quotations into collages. Though some of them might have looked to 'architecture without architects' or Roman 'spolia', what they produced was not the reassembly of found materials, but an assemblage of references. Combined with the rising fashion of historic preservation, itself guided by the necessity of preserving existing resources, this produced something like collage architecture, though it was a fake one. What was constructed was new in terms of either the image it presented or the material it used, or it was a specious recreation of what existed.

Only with the advent of computer technologies, paired with the replacement of abstraction with scenarios and conceptual projects during the 1990s, did collage architecture come closer to being realised. While industrial and graphic designers finally embraced radical and tactical reuse, architects created stage sets and piled functions on top of each other, mixed existing and new materials, and opened up their buildings to multiple ways of either moving through or interpreting them.

In the last decade architects have embraced the idea of collage, but often only in the limited sense of producing two-dimensional representations (by using software such as Photoshop to virtually assemble buildings from existing images) or by rehabilitating existing buildings for more symbolic and ceremonial purposes such as museums. On a larger field, architects and urbanists have looked at urban situations, proposing the re-appropriation of disused spaces for urban agriculture, guerrilla gardening, or pop-up 'parklets', while using their knowledge and skills to help homeless and powerless people to take over and make use of abandoned structures.

In theoretical projects, some architects and designers have pointed to further possibilities. Since the experimental architecture of the 1980s, these collage architects have proposed ways of making structures and cities out of existing forms and materials, and, more recently, have even developed computer programmes that would facilitate such tactics. These are the architects we have assembled for this Biennale. We have attempted to show the diversity of their tactics, which range from the literal gathering together of junk or used materials, through the appropriation of existing spaces or structures, to the playing out various scenarios through the use of computers and social modelling techniques so that we can imagine other uses of and vistas through existing urban environments.

Such is the scene in which this Biennale operates, and such are its building blocks. The question is what it does with such forms and methods today. This is where we have sought to collect the best work at various scales, in different situations, and in a variety of locations in order to show the viability of architecture that is a gathering and a revealing rather than an invention.

The criteria we use are that the work must, first, be sustainable. This does not mean the addition of technologies that ameliorate the waste of resources inherent in construction. Sustainable architecture does not just harness wind, ground, and solar energy in order to make its environments less wasteful. It does not waste any resources in its very construction and use.

Kurt Schwitters, *Merzbau* [Detail: Great Group], 1933, Hannover. Room installation, various materials, 393 x 580 x 460 cm, destroyed 1943. Photo by Wilhelm Redemann. Kurt Schwitters Archives at the Sprengel Museum Hannover. Repro: Michael Herling / Aline Gwose, Sprengel Museum Hannover © VG Bild-Kunst, Bonn.

Early 20th-century techniques of collage and assemblage served as counterpoints to pictorial techniques steeped in abstract idealism.

Kurt Schwitters, *Merzbau* [Detail: Stairway Entrance Side], 1933, Hannover. Room installation, various materials, 393 x 580 x 460 cm, destroyed 1943. Photo by Wilhelm Redemann. Kurt Schwitters Archives at the Sprengel Museum Hannover. Repro: Michael Herling / Aline Gwose, Sprengel Museum Hannover ©VG Bild-Kunst, Bonn.

Collage makers eschewed anything that was finished or complete, and instead proposed to gather the detritus of human civilisation—fragments of the real, the incomplete, the damaged, and the useless—into compositions that were themselves unstable, to serve as the building blocks of an imaginary world.

This means, furthermore, that all architects have to ask themselves the question, when they are asked to design a new building, whether that is truly necessary. Those who would develop or redevelop properties, potentially commissioning architects, also need to consider alternatives to new construction. To answer the needs of space, identity, and being at home in your living, your work, or your play, you may not need a new building. It might be that you need to redefine who or what you are as an individual or an organisation. If you do need more space, you can usually find it in existing buildings and neighbourhoods. That does not mean that we are calling for historic preservation in the sense of embalming the past, nor do we want what is new about the reused structures or urban environments to be indistinguishable from the structures designers need to open up. We are calling for architecture and urbanism that are radically new in their opening up, reimagination, and repurposing of existing structures.

The shock of the new must come out of a reuse of what is, which will gain it an echo effect: a sense that it is strangely familiar.

Rethinking the underlying values of design will in turn cause designers and architects to rethink aesthetics, and perhaps even to generate a new style. Therefore this Biennale calls for a new style, in the sense of articulating a point of view and making visible the possibilities of collage architecture and urbanism. What is made, even if it is remade, is particular to the maker, the materials, and the situation (in time and space) in which it appears. What we are saying is that this particular architecture, this mode of appearance, this style, is one that consists of editing, curating, composing, and collaging together.

The shock of the new must come out of a reuse of what is, which will gain it an echo effect: a sense that it is strangely familiar.

Collage architecture and urbanism will take their place as part of a wider movement in our culture towards making as remaking: sampling in music and visual arts, repacking, riffing on existing styles and forms; and the Photoshop Aesthetic, in which the work of art is the deformation and reformation of existing images, understood in their malleability and artificiality. Art in this sense is ultimately the revelation of the artifice we have made for ourselves, and an attempt to position ourselves in that position of instability. It places us, but in a manner that recognises our placelessness and timelessness. It is the construction of not understanding some meaning and extension, but seeing and knowing what is right now and here.

In short, we call for:

Architecture that reuses,
reimagines, restages, and repurposes

Architecture that
is an act of opening

Architecture that gathers
together what is into the new

Architecture that breaks
open the boxes in which we live,
work, and play

Architecture that does not use up
natural resources, but makes
them available to all

Architecture that forms
a collage or assemblage

Architecture that works tactically to liberate the city

Architecture that is strangely familiar

Architecture that reveals the artifice of our world

Architecture that is a manner of seeing and knowing our world.

Aaron Betsky

THE EVOLUTION OF RADICAL URBANISM

Alfredo Brillembourg,
Hubert Klumpner,
and Alexis Kalagas

What does it mean to be a radical architect or designer today? Never before have cities mattered as much to the future of humanity.

As David Harvey attests, we have sleepwalked unknowingly into a full-blown 'crisis of planetary urbanization', with acute social, political, and ecological dimensions.[1] Cities are fundamentally places of opportunity – after all, urban migrants continue to be drawn in their millions by the promise of security as well as upward mobility. But cities are too often sites of yawning inequality, where land, housing, infrastructure, and services are transformed into symptoms of exclusionary growth. Faced with contemporary urbanisation patterns, we are forced to question how cities and city-making have traditionally operated. More to the point, as architects and designers we are forced to rethink how we can operate within the city, learning from its emerging intelligence and shaping its outcomes to radical and tactical ends.

The notion of a radical urbanism draws us unavoidably into the realm of the political. Imagining a more equitable and sustainable future involves an implicit critique of the spatial and societal conditions produced by prevailing urban logics. As such, we are not only reminded of Le Corbusier's famous ultimatum, 'architecture or revolution', but its generational echo in Buckminster Fuller's

1 — David Harvey, 'The Crisis of Planetary Urbanization' in Pedro Gadanho, ed., *Uneven Growth: Tactical Urbanisms for Expanding Megacities* (New York: The Museum of Modern Art, 2014), 29.

more catastrophic pronouncement, 'utopia or oblivion'.[2] Both were zero-sum scenarios born of overt social disjuncture, whether the deprivations and tensions of the interwar period, or the escalating conflicts and ecological anxiety of the late 1960s. While the wave of experimental 'post-utopian' practices that emerged in the early 1970s positioned themselves explicitly in opposition to perceived failures of the modern movement, these disparate groups shared a belief – however disenchanted – with their predecessors in the idea that radical difference was possible, as well as a conviction that a break was necessary.[3]

It is precisely this potent mix of idealism and criticality that we wish to explore under the rubric of 'radical urbanism' – utopian dreams tempered by an unflinching engagement with social reality. We are interested in those who advocate for the exceptional while cloaked in the trappings of routine. Those who infiltrate peripheral disciplines, embed themselves as outside observers, and leverage a proximate vantage point to influence decisions and policies. Those who relinquish direct control in favor of distributed autonomy and instrumental feedback. We are interested in projects that seek distance from disciplinary bounds, and from legal, political, and societal norms. That render complicit the immanently possible and the highly improbable, the absolutely necessary and the prohibitively taboo. A radical project does not necessarily view design as a solution, nor as a means to elucidate a question, but as a fundamental restructuring of assumptions in the way we live, and the environments that are necessary to support that life.

The history of architecture and urbanism is littered with individuals, groups, movements, structures, unbuilt work, conceptual projects, research programs, theories, exhibitions, publica-

2 — See Le Corbusier, *Toward an Architecture*, trans. John Goodman (London: Frances Lincoln / Getty Trust, 2007), first published in French as *Vers une architecture* (Paris: G. Cres, 1924); R. Buckminster Fuller, 'Invisible Future', *San Francisco Oracle* 11 (December 1967), 24.

3 — Fredric Jameson, *Archaeologies of the Future: The Desire Called Utopia and Other Science Fictions* (New York: Verso, 2005), 168.

tions, and performances that collectively trace a potent tradition of radical intention. What ties these diverse activities together is not a desire to escape disciplinary boundaries entirely, but instead to redefine the very possibilities of architecture and design as a means to usher in an alternative to the status quo. Though radical urbanism can assume countless forms, one can point to three potential fields of contestation that embody alternative modes of practice, thought, or engagement. The first is by outlining a provocative vision that challenges the normative thinking of the time. The second is by recasting the role of the architect in order to question what is pragmatically possible when intervening in an urban environment. The third is to operate at the vanguard of political change, or, in other words, architecture *as* revolution.

If one accepts the foundational modernist belief that addressing the realities of contemporary life means working in (and through) the city, then architecture and urbanism can represent a radical subversion of established social structures beyond material questions of form and aesthetics.[4] From unrealised visions and plans like Antonio Sant'Elia's La Città Nuova, Yona Friedman's Ville Spatiale, Constant Nieuwenhuys' New Babylon, and Cedric Price's Potteries Thinkbelt, to the avant-garde provocations of Archigram's Plug-In City, Superstudio's The Continuous Monument, and Archizoom's No-Stop-City, the inclusive humanism of the Smithsons, the animist hybridity of Pancho Guedes, the techno-utopianism of the Metabolists, and the politically charged agit-prop of groups like Ant Farm, Utopie, and HausRuckerCo, we can see a shift from the limited understanding of architecture as the design of discrete structures, to an expanded notion that architecture and urbanism can embody a form of cultural critique, or venture even more decisively into the realm of social and political action.

4 — John R. Gold, *The Experience of Modernism: Modern Architects and the Future City, 1928-53* (London: Thomson Science, 2013) 15-16.

A courtyard and one of the inhabitant-modified houses in the experimental Proyecto Experimental de Vivienda (PREVI) project near Lima, Peru, 2011.

An aerial view of Khayelitsha, one of South Africa's largest informal settlements on the outskirts of Cape Town, 2012.

This critique dovetails with a parallel line of thought that views the role of the architect as extending beyond 'pure' design, to support the agency of the individuals and communities whose everyday life shapes the evolving built environment. We see this in the flexible open building concepts of John Habraken, the simple modular housing system of Walter Segal, the self-build and self-management theories of John Turner, the cooperative strategies and 'pragmatic anarchism' of Colin Ward, the *tecnica povera* of Riccardo Dalisi with children from the Traiano Quartiere in Naples, and the 'action planning' of Otto Koenigsberger in India. Besides a common concern with the groups or 'users' most often marginalised or excluded by formal processes of authority and control, these projects are linked by a modesty that contrasts starkly with the heroic projections of the modern movement. It is a radical urbanism characterised by sensitivity to scale and time, an appreciation of context, and a shift from author to enabler.

The third type of radicality emanates from the inside out, where urbanism is adopted as an institutionalised building block prefiguring a new way of life. Though discredited in its most deterministic guise – the hubristic belief in the ability to 'correct society on the drawing board'[5] – this direct alignment of architects and designers with revolutionary governance is perhaps urbanism at its most 'radical'. While the emblematic case remains the 'social condensers' of Mozei Ginsburg and the Russian constructivists, which were consciously designed to induce collectivism, it is echoed in Álvaro Siza's involvement with the 'brigades' of the Serviço de Apoio Ambulatório Local (SAAL) housing program following the Portuguese revolution, the Proyecto Experimental de Vivienda (PREVI) launched in Peru in the brief mid-1960s interlude between military dictatorships, and the peripheral new towns designed by BV Doshi's Vãstu-Shilp Consultants in post-independ-

5 — Meyer Schapiro, 'Architect's Utopia: Review of Architecture and Modern Life', *Partisan Review* 4 (1938) 46, 89-92.

ence India. In tune with emancipatory political agendas, these schemes sought to underpin alternative forms of economic and social development.

Reyner Banham has described dreams of a better world as the true 'ghosts in the machine' of 20th-century architecture, while Tahl Kaminer argues the loss of the 'utopian horizon' means the idea of progress has been rejected as a myth.[6] Does it make any sense then to speak of a contemporary radical urbanism? In short, we are convinced it does. Cities are complex, hybrid spaces where divergent ways of acting, thinking about, and living urban life collide and transform. And in these spaces, a new generation of architects, designers, advocates, artists, sociologists, anthropologists, economists, and activists are collectively reimagining new tactics to tackle critical urban and social issues. The city today is perhaps more radical than those operating within it. It computes unknown possibilities, conducts high-risk experimentation, and telegraphs previously unknowable futures more quickly and more completely than the raft of professionals tasked with its stewardship, analysis, or design.

6 — Reyner Banham, *Theory and Design in the First Machine Age,* 2nd ed. (Cambridge, Mass.: MIT: 1980), 12; Tahl Kaminer, *Architecture, Crisis and Resuscitation: The Reproduction of Post-Fordism in Late-Twentieth-Century Architecture* (New York: Routledge, 2011) 19.

The city today is perhaps more radical than those operating within it. It computes unknown possibilities, conducts high-risk experimentation, and telegraphs previously unknowable futures more quickly and more completely than the raft of professionals tasked with its stewardship, analysis, or design.

A discussion based around concrete and scalable projects is necessary to reframe the term 'radical' and its potentials for design in the 21st century. The 'Radical Urbanism' exhibition in this Biennale brings greater visibility to alternative models of housing, mobility, production, and recreation grounded in the pursuit of social and environmental justice, diversity, and equality. It highlights forms of radical praxis that question the role of the architect and redefine the discipline, claiming new territories, new functions, and new legitimacy for architectural and design thinking. It gives space to projects that are both courageous and provocative – that call attention to game-changing urban agents of tomorrow. It will show how it is possible to develop path-breaking tactics of intervention and engagement while operating legitimately within the blind spots of existing power structures. And it will reaffirm the capacity of architects and designers to articulate empowering, transformative, confronting, and *realisable* visions of our collective urban future.

VENUE RENOVATION: RE-LIVING THE DACHENG FLOUR FACTORY

Doreen Heng Liu

The renovation of the former Dacheng Flour Factory as a public exhibition venue for UABB 2015 demonstrates the principles of 'Re-Living the City'. The 32,780 m^2 mill complex was first opened in 1980 along the bay in Shenzhen's Shekou Industrial Zone and shut down in 2010. Re-activated with new public programs for UABB 2015, the complex marks the continuing transformation of the city from agrarian to industrial and, today, cultural and mixed-use development.

Commissioned by Shekou Industrial Zone, NODE Architecture & Urbanism began developing a flexible and integrated urban design proposal in late 2013, which was selected in 2014 over competing proposals from teams led by Ryue Nishizawa, Jurgen Meyer, and Philip Yuan. The UABB 2015 curators and organising committee agreed upon the Dacheng mill as the main venue for UABB 2015 (Shenzhen). NODE led an accelerated design and construction process from March through October, 2015 to renovate the complex in time for the Biennale opening.

The renovation conserves landmark features such as the grain silos, while adapting the former factory buildings and grounds to accommodate a range of new functions including exhibition, public space, hostel, lecture events, screenings, and urban agriculture. Physical interventions include new circulation routes, cut-outs, inserted volumes, vertical additions, ecological ponds, interior and exterior lighting, and new surfaces for use and decoration. NODE's original design evolved with input from fellow curators, Urban-Think Tank, and UABB and Shekou.

The process was driven not only by the physical requirements of hosting the Biennale, but also by a desire to articulate the cultural memory of the site and open the possibilities for its future. While the former factory was designed to produce a physical commodity, the renovation seeks to re-produce the site itself as a PLACE of PUBLIC LIFE.

大成麵粉
鉄人麵粉

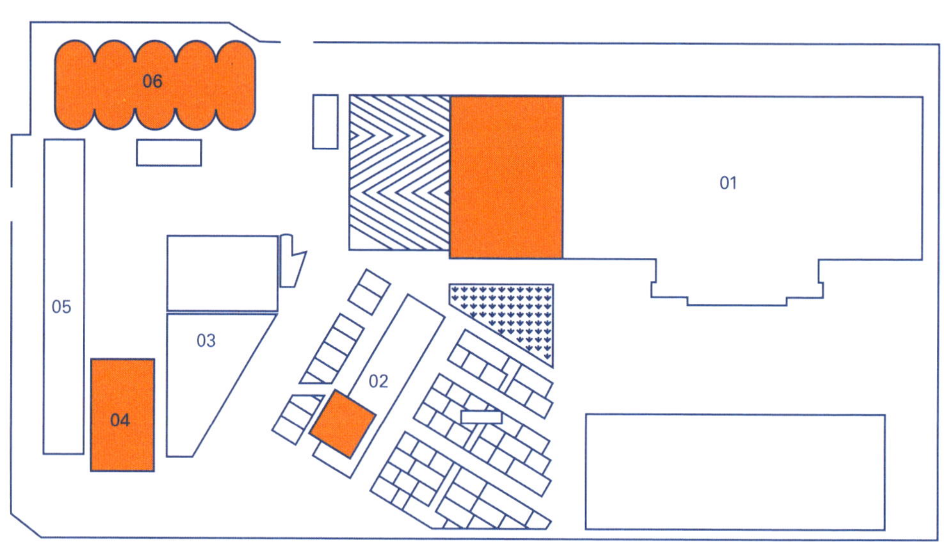

01

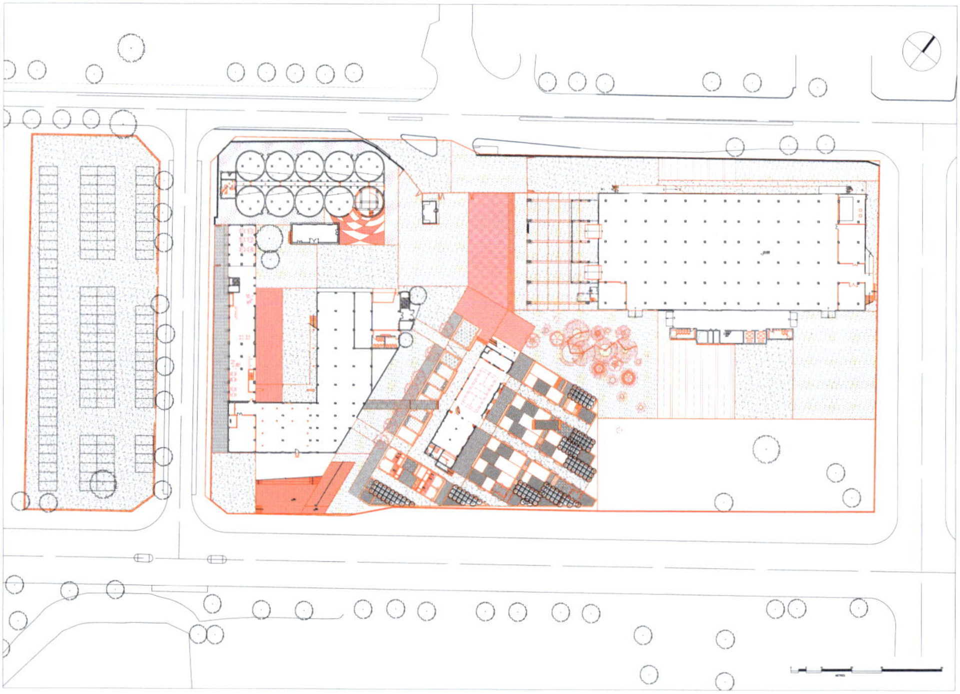

02

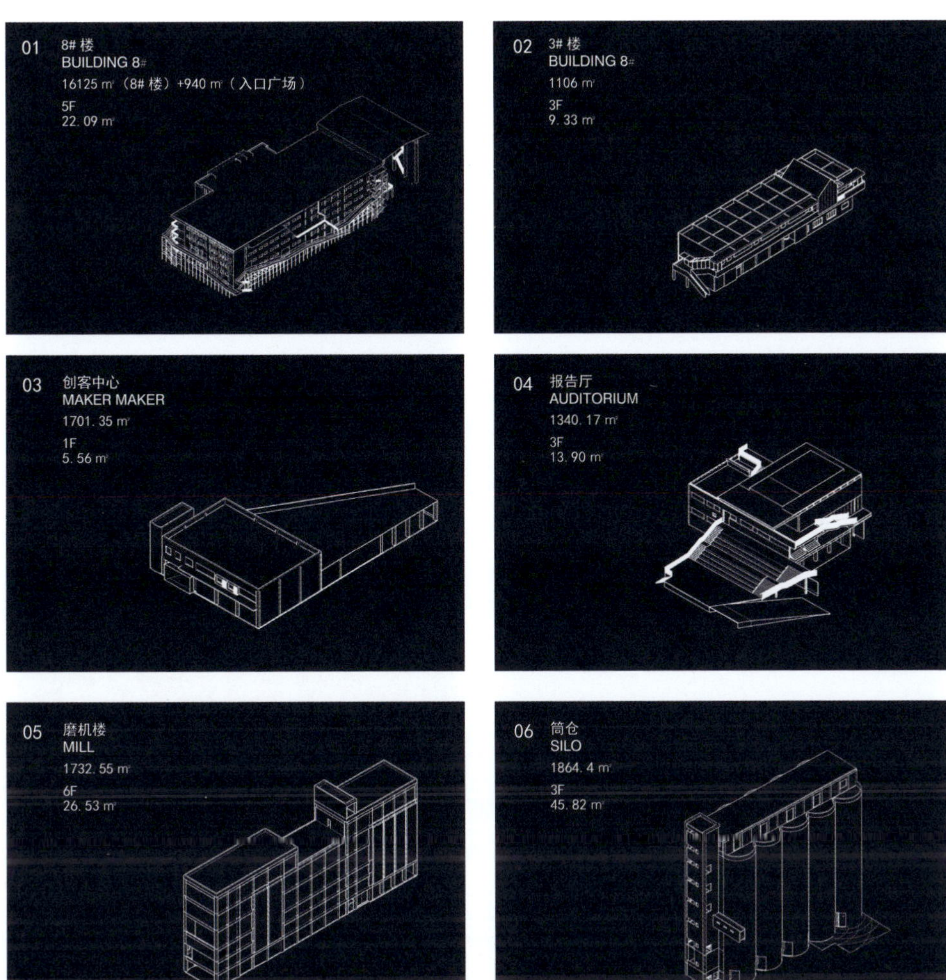

03

01 Master plan of the converted mill complex for UABB 2015. 02 Diagram plan showing the situation of existing buildings with pink tones indicating major renovations and additions. 03 The renovated Dacheng complex consists of six buildings: (1) Building 8, the enormous concrete-slab structure housing the primary exhibitions; (2) Building 3, a simple two-story structure transformed into a multi-use café, kitchen, gallery, workspace, library, and hostel; (3) the wedge-shaped, single-story building given over to the Maker Maker exhibition; (4) the new auditorium space built on top of a nondescript structure, with glass walls and an observation deck overlooking the bay; (5) the former mill building; and (6) the iconic silos, retrofitted to offer a transporting spatial experience.

中国中铁建工集团有限公司
600米

Building 8 – Structure's Last Stand

The reinforced concrete slabs and sturdy columns of Building 8 are less permanent than they look. According to current development plans, a wide new boulevard will cut straight through the site currently occupied by the building—soon it will no longer exist. UABB 2015 may be its last stand. As a humorous expression of the clash between present and future realities, the planned road is collaged onto the façade of the condemned building.

Another highly visible addition to Building 8 is the series of escape stairs and ramps that wrap around the outside of the building. This circulation feature, enlarged to the maximum width, on one hand complies with the fire protection requirements, and on the other hand creates a visually dynamic façade out of an otherwise monotonous elevation. In effect, the sharp diagonal lines of the escape route advertise the Biennale to motorists and pedestrians along the city's trunk road.

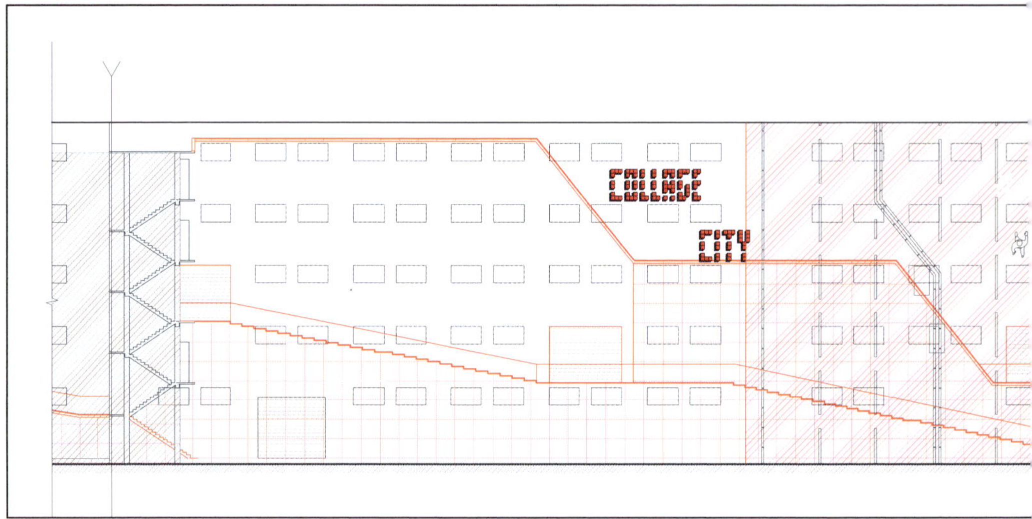

02

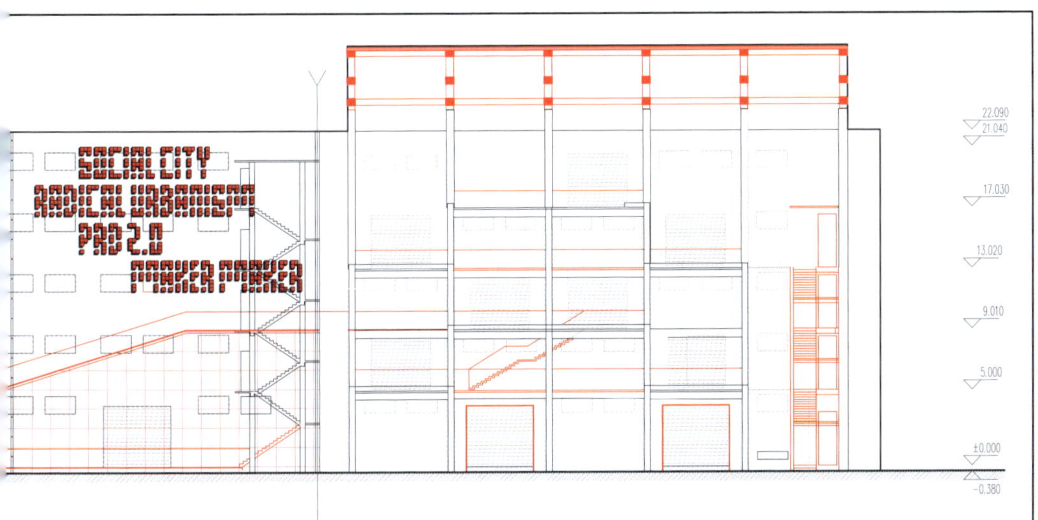

01

03

01 North elevation (left) and west elevation (right) of Building 8, showing the enhanced external circulation system and wall graphics referring to the planned road through the site. 02 The renovated warehouse interior. The utilitarian elegance of the reinforced concrete structure required little intervention beyond upgraded sprinkler and lighting systems. Each pavilion or installation was assigned a module of space within the repeating grid of columns. 03 The main stair along the west elevation, with refurbished circulation and roof canopy. (Courtesy of NODE Architecture & Design)

Building 3 – A Play of Program

Building 3 would seem to be an ordinary frame-structure with few distinguishing features. Yet beneath this mediocre shell lies the possibility of innovative spatial and programmatic combinations inside. To change the mediocre look of the whole building, a small, transparent, slope-roofed house is inserted into the third floor. This sunlit space is conceived as an urban kitchen, an informal meeting and exhibition space, where the mixed uses of the building come together. A more literal response to the urban kitchen concept can be found directly outside Building 3 in the agriculturally-themed 'Floating Fields', a series of stepped ponds evoking the region's mulberry dyke-fish ponds and the broader question of urban ecology.

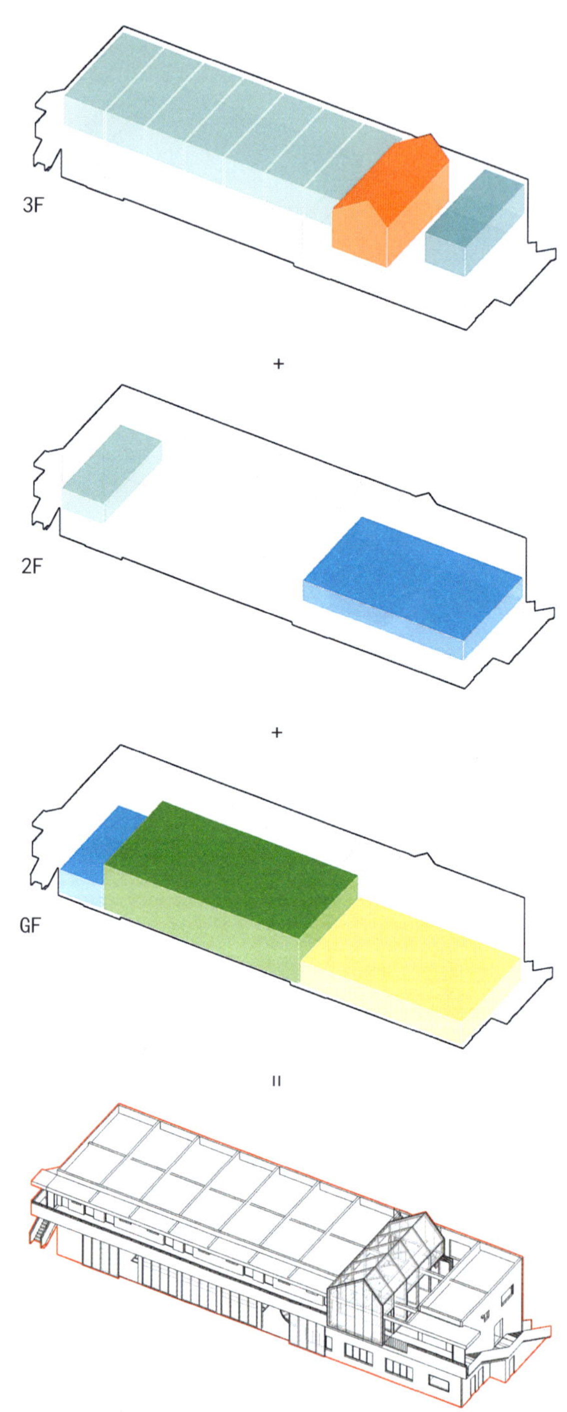

浴室 bathroom
办公 office
咖啡 cafe
教育 education
厨房 kitchen
青旅 youth hotel

01

02

03

01 Program diagram of the renovated Building 3, containing a rich new mixture of uses. The redesigned third floor (3F) is designed as a youth hostel, inspired by its former use as an employee dormitory. Shared kitchen and laundry rooms in the middle of the floor add variety to the residential function and create a social meeting space.
02 The generous space on the ground floor (1F) is redesigned to serve alternately as the education hall and a badminton court, finished with high-performance flooring and rolling furniture on wheels.
03 A cafeteria and offices are implanted within two different levels of the south side of the building. The transparent volume of the urban kitchen, an informal meeting and exhibition space inserted into the third floor.

Auditorium as View Finder

The newly built auditorium, lofted above an older building, is positioned to enjoy views of the Taiziwan Bay to the south, and the impressive grain silos to the north. The north and south glass facades are defined as two gigantic frame finders to bring in attractive views while creating a transparent performance space against the urban backdrop.

Visibly separated from the older base, the new steel-frame structure appears like a glass box resting gently on top of the half-grid platform of the old building. The new volume's lightness and transparency contrast with the squat solidity of the older building below.

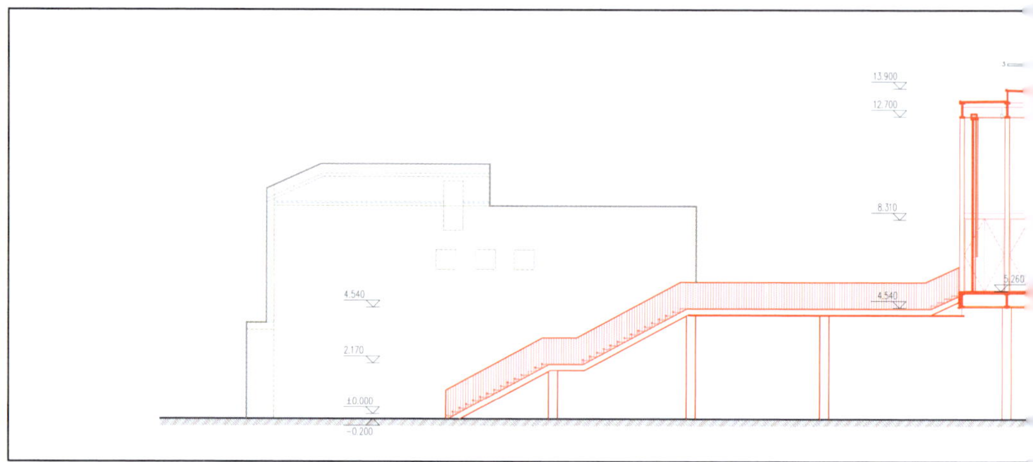

02

01 The ground level is given over the Maker Maker exhibition, while restrooms and meeting rooms occupy the remaining space on 2F. A new leisure bar and terrace is found on 3F, accessible from the lecture hall and the amphitheatre steps. 02 The standard column grid of the older building could not accommodate the large span required for the lecture hall, so its columns were partially truncated at the second level to create a platform on which the lecture hall rests. 03 Rather than producing the expected sense of enclosure, the lecture hall offers a panoramic view of the sea and the site thanks to its terraces, external stairs, and amphitheatre seating.

13.350
12.700
8.410
8.390
8.310
5.260
4.540
4.610
4.610
2.710
2.880
2.880
0.880
±0.000
−0.420
±0.000
−0.450

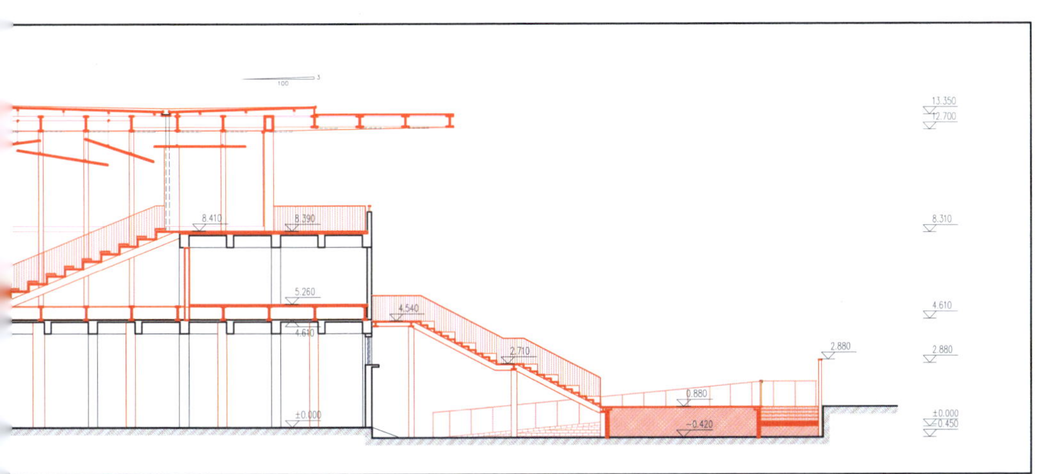

01

03

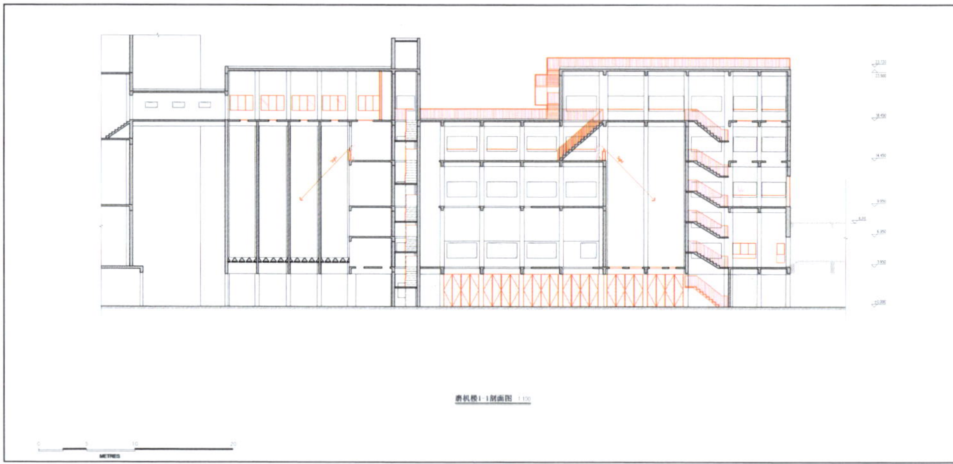

An encounter with the production line

The mill building is a spatial manifestation of the whole process and technology of flour processing. Its form reflects the logic of the operations for which it was built. While renovating the mill building, NODE similarly followed the functionalist principle, but this time with new functions of exhibition, circulation, and symbolic monumental value. Just a few design moves, including selected cut-outs through the slab and new staircases, allow visitors to access the rich space and industrial memory of the mill building.

01

02

01 View of the 46m-tall silos from the street.
02 Contemplative meditation space inside the silos.
03 A newly built stair hugs the inner wall of the silo cylinder, leading to a new platform and walkway that cuts through the walls of the adjacent silos, revealing a variety of textures and spaces.

03

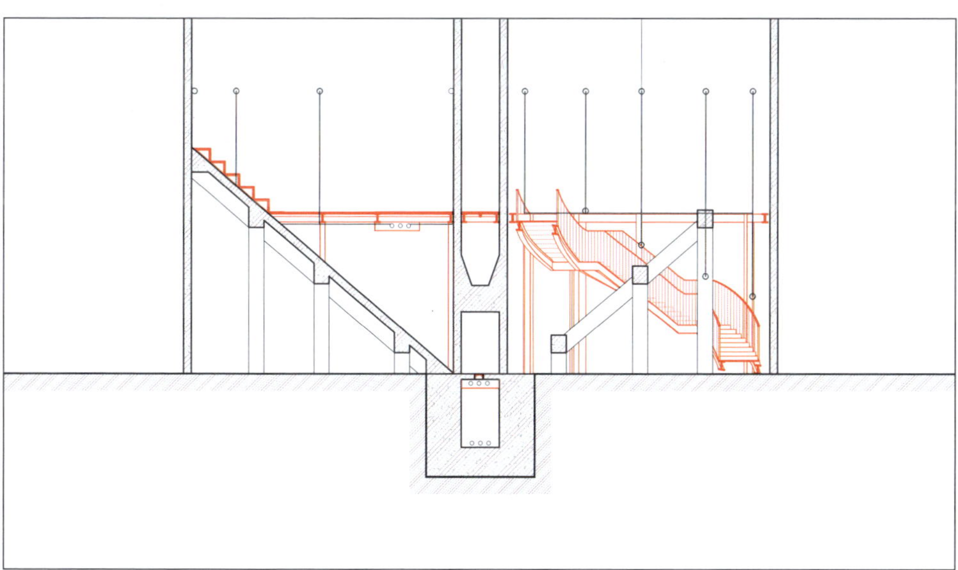

Future of the Silos

After the close of UABB 2015, the renovation of silos for cultural use is expected to continue. The main silo spaces will become an art museum, according to NODE's plan, with different spaces connected by a continuous ribbon stair circling up through the ten silos, bridging from centre to centre. Libraries and full-height meditation rooms are placed now and then along the way to highlight the spiritual attributes of the silos and elevate the visitor experience. A new top floor of the silos will feature glass walls following the undulating plan of the original structure to create a cloud-like profile against the sky. These transparent volumes will house executive office spaces.

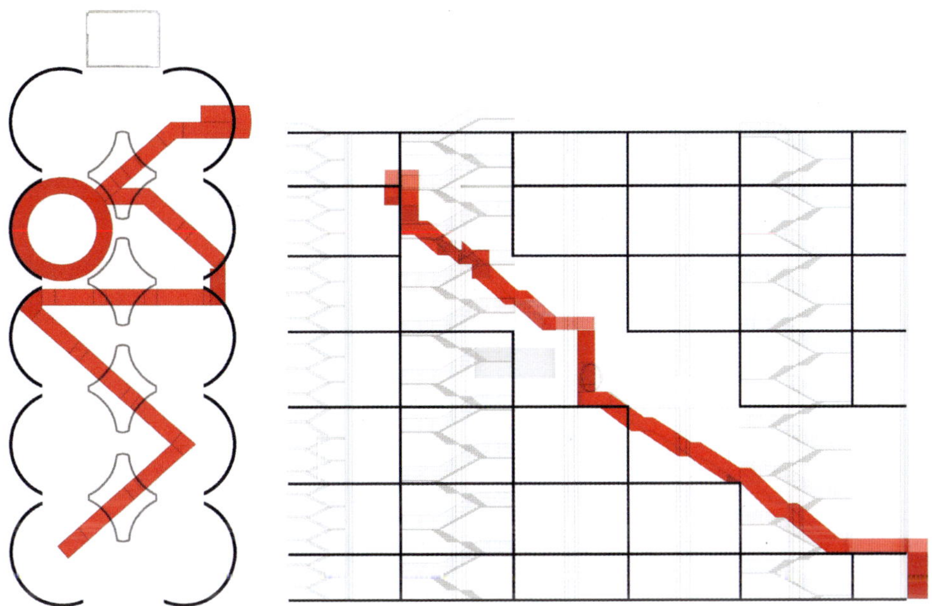

Credits:

Architecture, Urban Design & Landscape
NODE Architecture & Urbanism: Doreen Heng LIU, HUANG Jie-Bin, GUAN Yu-Tao, SHI Xue-Yuan, ZHENG Gui-Tang, WANG Rui, LI Yang-Wen-Zhao, ZHANG Yu

Program & Planning Consultant
Department of Land & Planning, China Merchants Shekou Industrial Zone Co.: Zheng Yu Long

Urban Design Partner
Urban-Think Tank: Hubert Klumpner & Alfredo Brillembourg

Construction Documents
Shenzhen General Institute of Architectural

Design & Research
Landscape Design 'Mulberry Fields & Floating City' School of Architecture, Chinese University of Hong Kong: Thomas CHUNG

Lighting Design Consultant
Shenzhen Lighting Formula

Façade Installation Consultant for Building 8
Yang Yong

RADICAL

Woven textile banner designed by Thonik, suspended at exhibition entrance.

FREE RADICALS

Alfredo Brillembourg,
Hubert Klumpner,
and Alexis Kalagas

However applied, the expression 'radical' is value-laden.

To be a radical is to inspire both admiration and contempt. Radical change is by definition far-reaching and fundamental. In other words, it offers a prospect equally liberating or terrifying depending on your vantage point and stake in the prevailing system. In the expanded field of architecture, the radical repertoire – provocation, agitation, infiltration, subversion, emancipation – is a cyclically recurring phenomenon. Urbanisation generates a shifting landscape of winners and losers, and this dichotomy inevitably gives birth to alternative modes of practice, thought, and action. The 'Radical Urbanism' exhibition in the 2015 Bi-City Biennale explores how research and projects fueled by a potent mix of idealism and critical social engagement can remake our cities as spaces of social and environmental justice, diversity, and equality. That is, it investigates how we can reframe the term 'radical' and its potentials for design in the 21st century.

As we have stressed previously, the city today is perhaps more radical than those operating within it.[1] And nowhere is this as evident than in the unprecedented expansionary zeal of contemporary China. The scale, pace, and intensity of urbanisation in instant metropolises like Shenzhen force us to conceive of

1 — See 'The Evolution of Radical Urbanism' in this volume.

an entirely different kind of 'radical urbanism', moving beyond the idea of guerrilla architects operating as sleeper agents of change to grapple with the far-reaching transformations wrought by the machinery of accelerated economic growth. In a little over three decades Shenzhen has mushroomed from a network of fishing villages into a migrant megacity of over 15 million residents. Throughout the Pearl River Delta region, the mass production of the built environment unleashed by China's top-down rush to embrace a socialist market economy has generated the largest urban area in the world, in both size and population.[2]

We think of countercultural revolutionaries bent on 'blowing up the system' as symbols of radical action. But what if the system in their targets is itself radical? The Chinese state has had a direct and firm hand in the hyper-urbanisation patterns associated with the country's post-1980 role as the 'factory of the world'. Government officials have not only encouraged massive rural-urban migration to promote sustained economic development, but also established the export-led industrial clusters that have acted as magnetic poles of growth.[3] In both conception and execution, the central planning power that has allowed cities like Shenzhen to emerge is the stuff of modernist tabula rasa dreams. As a realised vision of sweeping and elemental change, Shenzhen embodies a certain kind of radical urbanism. As a cautionary tale of the social and ecological challenges of runaway growth, it is also the very embodiment of why the tactics presented in the 'Radical Urbanism' exhibition matter.

Today's Pearl River Delta has been described as a 'maturing mega-urban region'.[4] The breakneck forces of development are compelling designers and decision-makers to recognise the need to reorient towards a more sustainable strategy of

2 — See *East Asia's Changing Urban Landscape: Measuring a Decade of Spatial Growth* (Washington, D.C.: The World Bank, 2015).

3 — Chen Lu et al, 'Driving Force of Urban Growth and Regional Planning: A Case Study of China's Guangdong Province' (2013) 40 *Habitat International* 35, 36.

redevelopment and reuse of the existing urban fabric. This pivot is referenced in the Biennale's title – *Re-Living the City* – and the possibilities of adaptive reuse are also explored in Muck Petzet Architekten's 'Radical Reuse' installation. But the unintended consequences of rapid development encompass more than just questions of land use intensity and environmental stress. As Filip de Boeck points out, the main infrastructural unit or building block of urban space is the human body. It is therefore the 'body itself that creates the city'.[5] While Shenzhen's pre-1980 urban villages are fragments of an evolving social city built by and for people, these remnants are now endangered islands amid a sea of identikit detached high-rises stretching to the horizon.

Whether characterised as 'bottom-up', 'organic', 'self-generated', or 'popular', many of the Radical Urbanism installations are ultimately concerned with how people can achieve greater agency in the transformation of their cities. For Anna Heringer, Martin Rauch, and Mu Jun, rammed earth construction technologies have the greatest potential to reimagine existing forms of city-making. Ecosistemo Urbano offers an accessible catalogue of 'networked urbanism' tools. Recetas Urbanas promotes self-building as a form of empowered critical citizenship. Casting a wider net, the Collective City team documents and collages examples of the sometimes hidden intelligence that lies within existing cities worldwide. And Wolff Architects presents Du Noon township in Cape Town as a bounded case study in how the construction of opportunity is as important as the construction of infrastructure in resource-constrained settings. In each case, the onus is on architects and planners to support the aspirations and needs of residents.

A parallel theme that emerges within the exhibition centres on notions of inclusion and contestation. Atelier Hitoshi Abe,

4 — See Uwe Altrock and Sonia Schoon, eds., Maturing Megacities: The Pearl River Delta in Progressive Transformation (Dordrecht: Springer, 2014), 19.
5 — Filip de Boeck and Marie-Françoise Plissart, *Kinshasa: Tales of the Invisible City* (Leuven: Leuven University Press, 2014) 236.

Masashige Motoe, and Wowlab present the ongoing results of a participatory experiment in 'domestic urbanism' taking place in the Oroshimachi region of Sendai. Interboro Partners uses the battle over beach access in New Jersey to problematise and address wider issues of public space enclosure. MAS Urban Design at ETH Zurich demonstrates how semi-formal settlements in Cairo are an important and innovative source of affordable housing in the post-Arab Spring era, yet remain outside entrenched legal frameworks. Manuel Herz Architects documents the self-administered refugee camps of the Western Sahara, showing how these enduring settlements have evolved into both cities and spaces of emancipation. And Crimson Architectural Historians reminds us how public space around the world continues to be the critical arena where struggles over urban and national governance unfold.

Collectively, the contributions to the 'Radical Urbanism' exhibition also question the role of the architect. They do so primarily by highlighting new ethical terrain and functions for design thinking. For example, the work of Forensic Architecture uses spatial analysis to investigate and intervene in theatres of urban conflict. The Center for Spatial Research examines territories of risk, and AGENCY Architecture proposes a future-focused scenario exploring the collapse or conflation of military and domestic space. A common thread linking these and other installations is a nuanced understanding of architecture as a process, event, or transmitted knowledge, rather than an end in itself. It is fitting that the exhibition takes place in a setting where urbanisation patterns and forms have laid bare the limits of individual and institutional influence. Architects and policy-makers must develop alternative models and free them to take root, seeding a more grounded form of urbanism that may at times escape their direct control.

The idea of 'rewilding', which has its origins in conservation biology, suggests a possible way forward. Advocates of rewilding focus on conserving functional ecosystems and biodiversity through the restoration of ecological processes. This does not reflect a desire to freeze living systems in time, but instead to resist the modern urge to control nature.[6] While the destructive power of urbanisation is no doubt anathema to conservationists, we can nonetheless draw parallels between biological systems and the functioning of urban ecologies. Just as nature inevitably 'finds a way', people in cities display a collective resilience and ability to forge supportive communities in even the most adverse conditions. Overly prescriptive planning and development policies can have the effect of stifling, rather than strengthening, a flourishing urban life. Countless forms of control, separation, and restraint are enacted in the search for order and a sense of guided progress that threatens diversity, vitality, spontaneity, and sustainability in the way we live.

6 — See George Monbiot, Feral: Rewilding the Land, the Sea, and Human Life (Chicago: University of Chicago Press, 2014).

The rewilding of our cities would be a radical act. But no more radical than the policies and plans that treat urbanisation primarily as an economic driver, or cities as networked economic units. The people who breathe life into the built environment, imbuing static urban settings with intangible civic qualities, cannot be relegated to an afterthought. The 'Radical Temporalities' installation by Rahul Mehrotra, Felipe Vera, and Diego Pinochet is testament to the capacity of self-organised groups to erect large-scale ephemeral settlements fit for pilgrimage, play, or political refuge. Equipped with the right tools, backed by more permissive regulatory regimes, and empowered by more flexible spatial models, these same individuals have the potential to contribute in comparatively lasting ways to the social, economic, and environmental sustainability of cities worldwide. 'Re-living' the city means not only reassessing the material utility of what already exists, but also rethinking how urban dwellers inhabit their surroundings.

The following pages: The newly remodelled entrance to People's Park, Chengdu, which originally dates from the early 20th century. / An intersection in the central business district (CBD) of Chengdu, which transformed over the last century from the provincial capital of Sichuan province into Western China's economic center. / Chengdu's urban core hosts small-scale manufacturers working from shopfronts or sidewalks, in addition to hundreds of massive factories around the perimeter of the city. A gardener at People's Park, which is now surrounded by towers. / Large-scale industrial projects, like the extension of a new underground metro station pictured here in 2011, are ever-present as city planners strive to catch up with a growing population. / The entrance to a nightclub at the edge of a new neighborhood. Chengdu's robust middle-class supports a sizeable entertainment and service industry. Photos by Daniel Schwartz/U-TT at ETH.

中央商务
建

锦兴路

畅越起重机
昊建工
中铁十五局
40
转变作风

川投大厦
CRCC
中国铁建
中铁十五局
SUPERPOWER

紫晶演艺
The best partner
Of your business
莎迪女子美容会

乐部
栓
STATION
所

RADICAL URBANISM FLOORPLAN

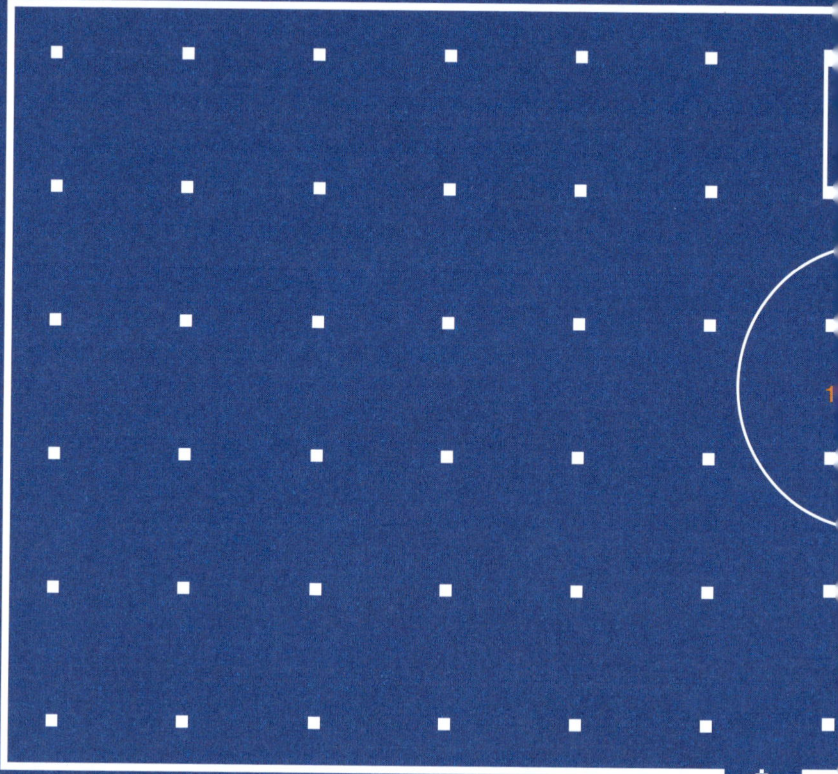

1
Cartographies of Planetary Urbanisation
Neil Brenner, Christian Schmid, and Milica Topalovic

2
Autonomy & Autodigestion
Lydia Kallipoliti, Meg Studer, and Kyong Kim

3
Self-Building Processes as Critical Conscience
Recetas Urbanas

4
Arsenal of Exclusion and Inclusion: The Battle for the Beach
Interboro Partners

5
Radical Cairo: From Agrarian Land to New Urban Forms
Marc Angélil, Charlotte Malterre-Barthes, and Something Fantastic, ETH Zurich

6
Global Grids: Populations at Risk
Center for Spatial Research, Columbia University

7
The Medellín Diagram: Visualisation of the Political
Teddy Cruz and Fonna Forman with Matthias Goerlich and Alejandro Echeverri

8
Radical Reuse
Muck Petzet Architekten

9
Urban Earthworks
Anna Heringer, Martin Rauch, and Mu Jun

10
Collective City
Alexander Eisenschmidt / Visionary Cities Project

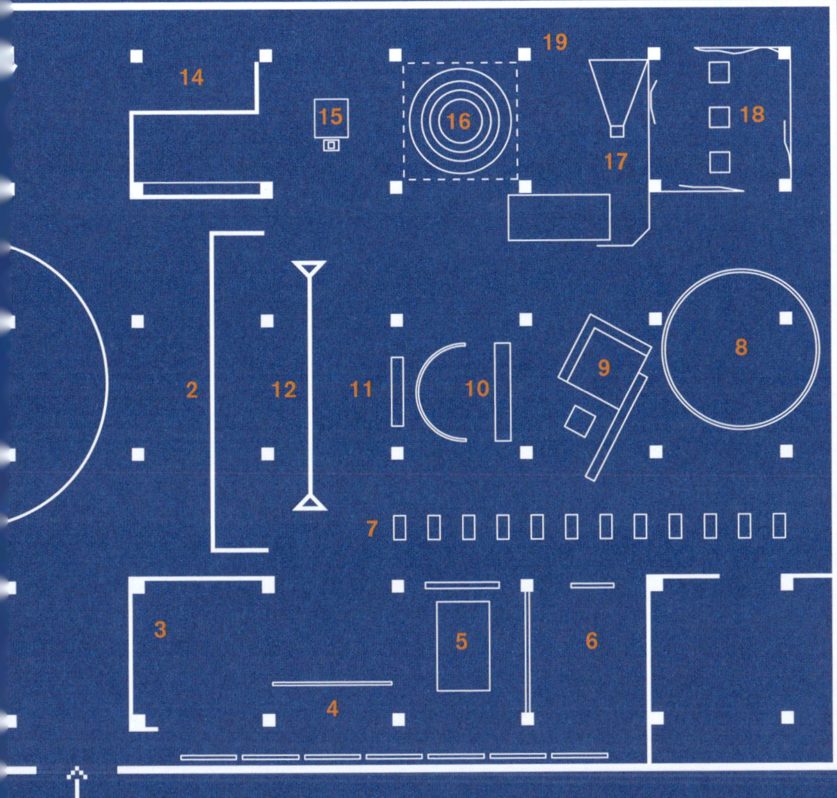

11
Opportunity and Transformation
Wolff Architects

12
Refugee Camps of the Western Sahara
Manuel Herz Architects

13
Do You Hear the People Sing?
Crimson Architectural Historians with Hugo Corbett

14
Networked Urbanism
ecosistema urbano

15
Domestic Urbanism in Oroshimachi, Sendai
Atelier Hitoshi Abe with Masashige Motoe and wowlab

16
Radical Temporalities (The Ephemeral City)
Rahul Mehrotra and Felipe Vera with Diego Pinochet

17
The Urban-Data Complex
Forensic Architecture

18
StereoTypes: Dump, Camp, and Graveyard
AGENCY

19
Moments in-between
Iwan Baan

RADICAL URBANISM EXHIBITS

CARTOGRAPHIES OF PLANETARY URBANISATION

Neil Brenner, Christian Schmid, and Milica Topalovic

Today, urbanisation has become planetary. The boundaries of the urban have been exploded to encompass vast territories far beyond the limits of even the largest megacity regions. Meanwhile, novel patterns of urbanisation are crystallising that challenge inherited conceptions of the urban as a bounded, universal settlement type.

This exhibit proposes a radical rethinking of inherited cartographies of the urban. The popular claim that we now live in an 'urban age' because the world's majority population lives in 'cities' is a deeply misleading basis for understanding the contemporary "urban revolution" theorised by Henri Lefebvre. Cities are not isolated manifestations or universally replicated expressions of the urban condition, but are embedded within wider, territorially uneven and restlessly evolving processes of urbanisation at all spatial scales, encompassing both built and unbuilt spaces, across earth, water, sea, and atmosphere.

In this exhibit, interdisciplinary research teams from the ETH Zürich, ETH Future Cities Laboratory Singapore and the Urban Theory Lab at the Harvard Graduate School of Design present new frameworks for understanding and representing contemporary forms of urbanisation through three interrelated lines of inquiry:

1. Comparative analysis of the urbanisation processes that have transformed Tokyo, Hong Kong/Shenzhen/Dongguan, Kolkata, Istanbul, Lagos, Paris, Mexico City and Los Angeles. We explode the singular notion of the city to explore, in comparative perspective, differing patterns and pathways of urbanisation in some of the world's most dynamically changing urban territories.

2. The extension and thickening of the urban fabric in some of the planet's supposedly most 'remote' or 'wild' zones—the Amazon, the Arctic, the Gobi desert, the Himalayas, the Sahara, Siberia, the Pacific Ocean, and the earth's atmosphere. Even these sparsely populated areas are today experiencing a massive intensification of land use, the construction of new connectivity infrastructures, and accelerated socio-environmental transformation to support the world's major population centres.

3. The transnational hinterland archipelago that supports urbanisation in Singapore, one of the world's most globally networked agglomerations. In contrast to standard representations of cities as self-propelled economic powerhouses, we track the wide-ranging flows

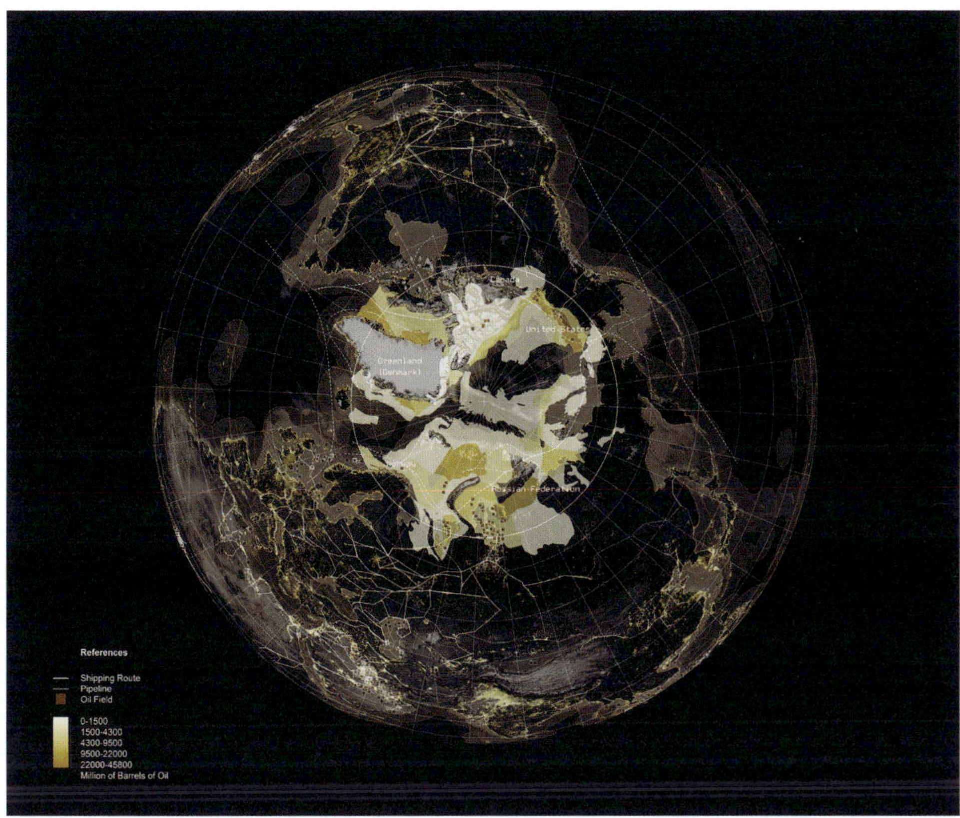

01

of food, water, energy, sand, and labor-power that support this growing, globally strategic urban centre. Instead of the city-state, we propose the cross-border metropolitan region as the new urban paradigm for Singapore.

The exhibition highlights the interplay between (a) the search for new theoretical concepts, (b) territorially grounded studies of specific patterns and pathways of urbanisation, and (c) the use of cartography to decipher new geographies of urbanisation for which we currently lack an adequate analytical or representational vocabulary.

Credits:
Cartographies of Planetary Urbanisation is a group exhibition by three interdisciplinary research teams from ETH Zurich, ETH Future Cities Laboratory Singapore and the Urban Theory Lab at the Harvard Graduate School of Design. Project team leaders are:
Neil Brenner, Urban Theory Lab, Harvard GSD
Christian Schmid, Urban Sociology, Dept. of Architecture, ETH Zurich
Milica Topalovic, Assistant Professor of Architecture and Territorial Planning, Dept. of Architecture, ETH Zurich
Exhibition Design: Architecture of Territory, ETH Zurich
Concept and project lead: Milica Topalovic, Hans Hortig, Fabian Kiepenheuer.
Team: Panos a Coucopoulos, Karoline Kostka, Stefanie Krautzig, Ani Virhervaara, Lukas Wolfensberger
Graphic design: Goda Budvytyte

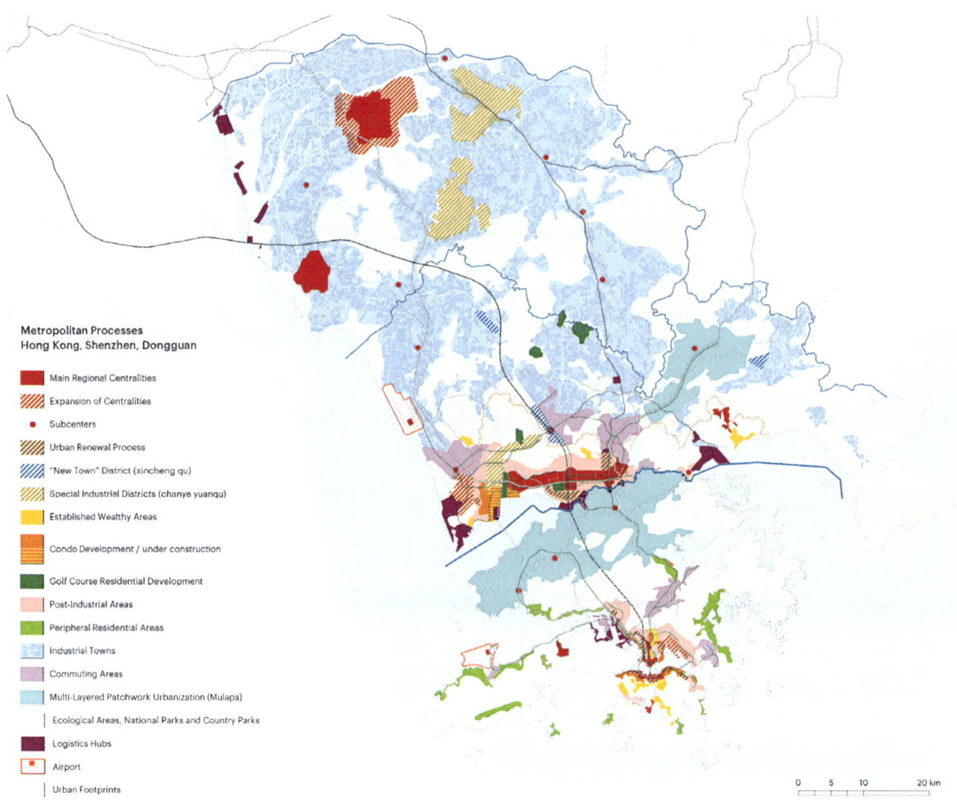

01

01 Joules of the Arctic, Grga Basic, Urban Theory Lab Harvard GSD. 02 Metropolitan Processes: Hong Kong, Shenzhen, Dongguan. Work in progress, November 2015. Urban Sociology, ETH Future Cities Laboratory Singapore: Planetary Urbanization in Comparative Perspective. Ethnographic fieldwork and mapping: Tammy Kit Ping Wong. Map design and editing: Philippe Rekacewicz. 03 Cross-Border Metropolitan

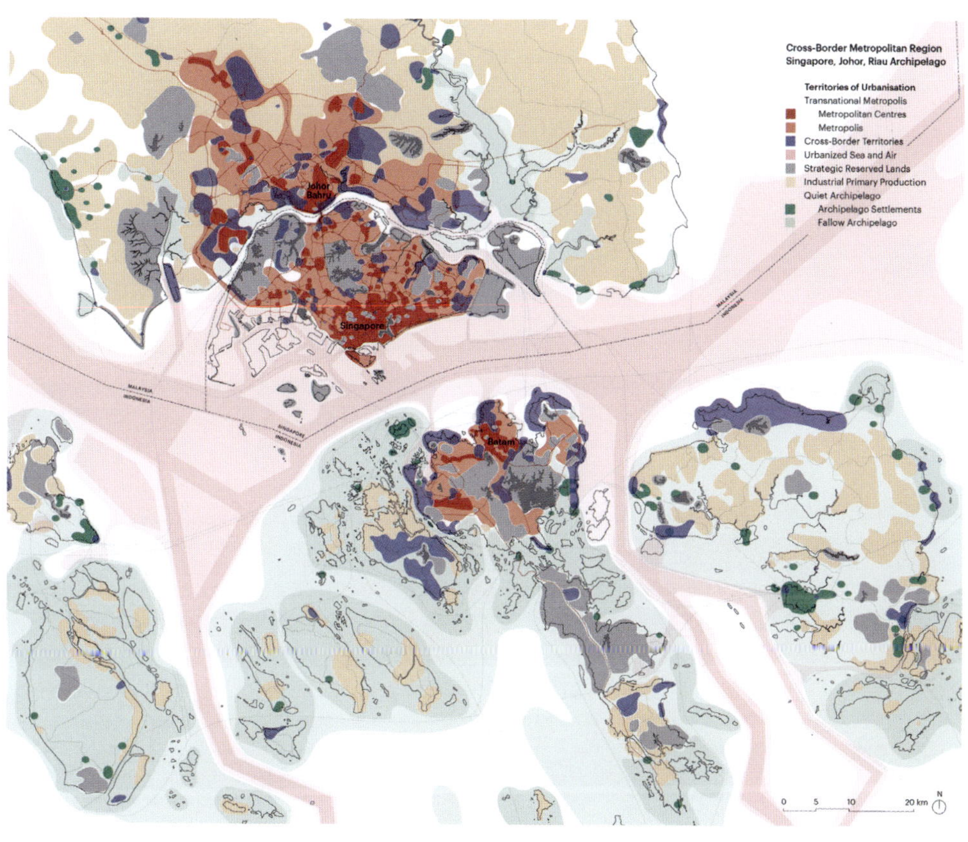

02

Region Singapore, Johor, Riau Archipelago: Territories of Urbanisation. Work in progress, December 2015. Assistant Professor of Architecture and Territorial Planning, ETH Zurich and ETH Future Cities Laboratory Singapore: Hinterland,, Singapore Beyond the Border. Research: Architecture of Territory 2011-2015. Map research, design and mapping: Karoline Kostka 2015.

Hinterland—
Singapore
Beyond
the Border
Sand
Labour

Photographs by Bas Princen

SELF-BUILDING PROCESSES AS CRITICAL CONSCIENCE

Recetas Urbanas

The architecture office of Recetas Urbanas (Urban Recipes), led by architect Santiago Cirugeda, proposes actions of self-building or auto-construction as a radical alternative to the 'official urbanism' dominated by established economic and political interests. The purpose of these projects or 'recipes' for intervention is to rebuild citizens' capacity to recuperate a critical conscience and respond to spatial injustice.

Strategies of self-building enable architects to answer to the particular needs of the groups with whom they work and the contexts in which they design. It is a model that accommodates the involvement of people and communities in the creation and construction of their spaces.

In the present moment it is essential for radical architects and their communities to be more prepared and act faster, because the agents of 'official urbanism' continue to pursue their own interests every day, without needing to listen to ordinary people or reach a consensus to make a decision. Self-building allows the disenfranchised to take part in shaping their city.

The characteristics of the self-building approach may include: participatory strategies, fast development, appropriation of space, reuse of materials, efficient deployment, creation of networks, development of pedagogical activities and, of course, the low cost of implementation. This construction model, eclipsed by excessive legal regulations that favor established interests, needs to be revived as an option for critical intervention. It can serve as a counter-technique against more conservative, entrenched visions of urban development.

Such radical actions may provoke reactions, such as censorship or legal challenges by the government. Recetas Urbanas has endured such challenges in the course of previous projects in Seville, Spain such as the 'Chicken' House, The Nest, La Carpa Art Space and the Proyectalab. Perhaps the most important goal is to provoke public debate.

The projects presented in the exhibition are licensed to the public domain and may be replicated or adapted by citizens elsewhere, including their strategic design and juridical aspects. Recetas Urbanas recommends that citizens conduct thorough research on the locations and situations in which they may wish to intervene. Citizens will assume any physical or intellectual risks produced by such interventions.

NB: Legislation on self-building does not currently exist in Europe.

01

02

03

01 Institutional Prosthesis, a.k.a. 'the hedgehog'. Recetas Urbanas, Espai d'art contemporani de Castelló (EACC), Castello, Spain, 2005. 02 The Nest, temporary installation by Recetas Urbanas on the rooftop of a former police station that now belongs to the Bòlit contemporary art center, Girona, Spain, 2008. 03 La Carpa, a self-built arts space in Seville, Spain (2010-2014), with Cirugeda's iconic 'spider' structure composed of repurposed containers mounted on steel legs. 04 In Cirugeda's Seville 'Containers' project of 1997, he applied for a license to place temporary dumpsters, then reconfigured them into play equipment, which the neighbourhood was lacking. The project demonstrated his approach of exploiting legal loopholes for the public good. Photos 01, 02 & 03 © Recetas Urbanas. Photo 04 © Santiago Cirugeda.

04

ARSENAL OF EXCLUSION AND INCLUSION: THE BATTLE FOR THE BEACH

Interboro Partners

The New Jersey coast is one of the United States' most iconic places, full of natural beauty and human-made attractions that draw millions of visitors every year. But New Jersey's beaches are not only the site of relaxation, but also the site of struggle: the struggle for beach access.

Access to New Jersey's beaches is protected by the Public Trust Doctrine, which states that 'the sea, and consequently the shores of the sea' are common or public assets, and that 'no one, therefore, is forbidden to approach the seashore'. However, despite the Public Trust Doctrine and the courts' unambiguous rulings affirming it, on a day-to-day level, 'unimpeded beach access' remains something of a phantom. Towns refrain from building paths, parking lots, and bathrooms. They adopt restrictive parking regulations and residential parking permit programs, and only reluctantly penalize private interests from encroaching on the beach. Homeowners, for their part, post phony 'private beach' signs, bark at people to get off 'their' property, and even disguise access points as front yards. And the different beach badges required by all but a handful of New Jersey towns effectively fragment the beach, and undermine visitors' ability to walk up and down it.

Interboro Partners' project for UABB 2015 highlights some of the tools or 'weapons' that have been deployed in the battle for beach access, and presents several site-specific radical proposed interventions to increase public access to the beach. The Battle of the Beach is presented as a single, large-format tableau printed on canvas and hung from the gallery ceiling.

'The Battle for the Beach' is based upon research conducted for Interboro Partners' *The Arsenal of Exclusion & Inclusion* (Actar, 2015), an encyclopedia of 202 tools or 'weapons' used by architects, planners, policy-makers, developers, real estate brokers, activists, and other urban actors in the United States to restrict or increase access to urban space.

01 Detail from the 'Battle for the Beach' tableau, which highlights tools that have been deployed – or could be deployed – in the ongonig battle for beach access along the New Jersey coast.

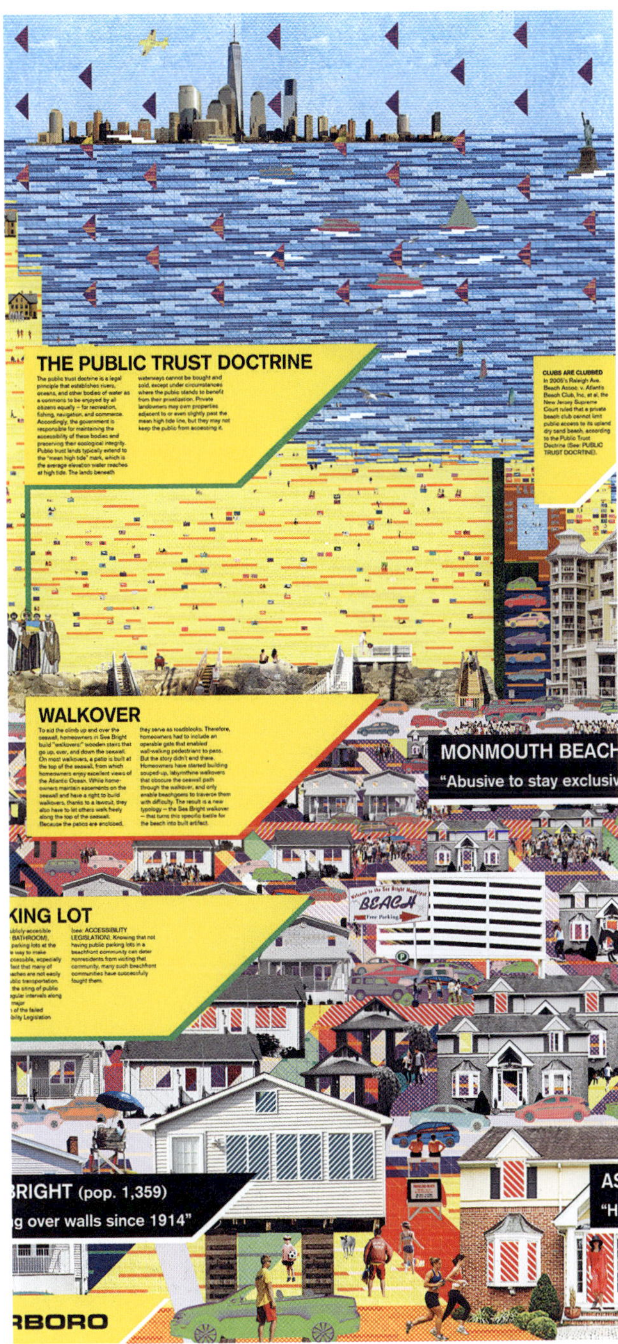
THE PUBLIC TRUST DOCTRINE
The public trust doctrine is a legal principle that establishes rivers, oceans, and other bodies of water as a commons to be enjoyed by all citizens equally – for recreation, fishing, navigation, and commerce. Accordingly, the government is responsible for maintaining the accessibility of these bodies and preserving their ecological integrity. Public trust lands typically extend to the "mean high tide" mark, which is the average elevation water reaches at high tide. The lands beneath waterways cannot be bought and sold, except under circumstances where the public stands to benefit from their privatization. Private landowners may own properties adjacent to or even slightly past the mean high tide line, but they may not keep the public from accessing it.
CLUBS ARE CLUBBED
In 2005's Raleigh Ave. Beach Assoc. v. Atlantis Beach Club, Inc., et al, the New Jersey Supreme Court ruled that a private beach club cannot limit public access to its upland dry sand beach, according to the Public Trust Doctrine (See: PUBLIC TRUST DOCRTINE).
WALKOVER
To aid the climb up and over the seawall, homeowners in Sea Bright build "walkovers:" wooden stairs that go up, over, and down the seawall. On most walkovers, a patio is built at the top of the seawall, from which homeowners enjoy excellent views of the Atlantic Ocean. While homeowners maintain easements on the seawall and have a right to build walkovers, thanks to a lawsuit, they also have to let others walk freely along the top of the seawall. Because the patios are enclosed, they serve as roadblocks. Therefore, homeowners had to include an operable gate that enabled wall-walking pedestrians to pass. But the story didn't end there. Homeowners have started building souped-up, labyrinthine walkovers that obscure the seawall path through the walkover, and only enable beachgoers to traverse them with difficulty. The result is a new typology – the Sea Bright walkover – that turns this specific battle for the beach into built artifact.
MONMOUTH BEACH
"Abusive to stay exclusiv
KING LOT
(see: ACCESSIBILITY LEGISLATION). Knowing that not having public parking lots in a beachfront community can deter nonresidents from visiting that community, many such beachfront communities have successfully fought them.
BEACH
Free Parking
BRIGHT (pop. 1,359)
g over walls since 1914"
RBORO

01

OR THE BEACH
every summer. But New Jersey's coast
is also a site of struggle: The struggle
for beach access.
In theory, everybody has the right to go
to New Jersey's beaches, but in reality
many towns and homeowners along the
coast limit public access with an arsenal
of exclusionary "weapons" such as
phony signs, beach badges, and parking
regulations.
In this mural we show a selection of
battles for the beach that have played
out along the New Jersey Shore over the
past two centuries, highlighting
weapons that have been deployed to
either limit or increase public access.
We also propose an arsenal of newly
MONMOUTH BEACH (pop. 3,290)
"Abusive to stay exclusive"
BATHROOM
BELMAR (pop. 5,738)
"The beautiful sea."
OCEAN GROVE (pop. 4,256)
"Cosmopolis by the sea"
BAYHEAD
SPRING LAKE
ASBURY PARK (pop. 15,855)
"Home of the huddled masses yearning to be free"

RADICAL CAIRO: FROM AGRARIAN LAND TO NEW URBAN FORMS

Marc Angélil and Charlotte Malterre-Barthes, MAS Urban Design – ETH Zurich

With twenty million inhabitants and growing, Greater Cairo mirrors the global phenomenon of unplanned urban growth. Approximately 60 percent of the inhabitants of Cairo – the biggest city on the African continent and seventh largest metropolitan area in the world – are living in so-called informal settlements. The five- to ten-story concrete and brick-infill constructions standing amid fields along Cairo's Ring Road are considered informal because they were built without permits on former agrarian land. The pace of illegal constructions on fertile areas at the capital's fringes has accelerated since the 2011 revolution, and illegal urban sprawl has taken a dramatic turn as it expands onto limited agrarian land.

Yet, the phenomenon of unplanned growth is not new to the Greater Cairo region. In *Understanding Cairo*, David Sims explains that the first developments on agricultural land appeared in the early 1960s, following Nasser's industrialization policies. Marked by incremental construction, settlements have predominantly followed property lines and subdivisions of feddans – the base unit of agricultural fields in Egypt comprising roughly 4,200 square meters of narrow strips of land, 100 to 300 meters long and six to 17 meters wide, framed by irrigation canals.

After the events of January 2011, illegal developments have proliferated faster than ever. Incremental and self-built construction has evolved into a semi-formal scheme offering various housing typologies: from self-built, low-rise structures to semi-professionally built, fifteen-story towers. This unregulated urban growth destroys thousands of hectares of arable land and lacks public services and infrastructure. However, it nonetheless succeeds in providing dense and affordable housing for the popular classes. In Cairo, this mode of urbanisation appears radical because it alters conventional ownership structures and because it implicitly questions the necessity of formal planning.

The ETH Zurich Master of Advanced Studies Program in Urban Design – chaired by Marc Angélil and directed by Charlotte Malterre-Barthes – has investigated informal settlements in Cairo, looking into designs for affordable housing units in the neighbourhood of Ard-el-Liwa. Selected projects for the UABB exhibition show how rearranging existing building components can lead to new urban forms. The exhibition consists of a 1:20 scale model of the studied urban area, showing remains of agrarian land, property lines, and irrigation chan-

01

02

nels that form the base for subsequent urbanisation, as well as the existing streetscape with established housing types of concrete frames and brick infill. Alternative design proposals developed by the MAS Urban Design are positioned on site within the urban fabric.

Credits:
Marc Angélil, Charlotte Malterre-Barthes, and Something Fantastic (Julian Schubert, Elena Schütz, and Leonard Streich) in collaboration with local partners Cluster (Omar Nagati, Beth Stryker). Students from MAS Urban Design 2014-2015: Patrick Abou Khalil, Zoi Alexandropoulou, Bernardo Baillif de Sousa Falcao, Grigorios Dimitriadis, Christine Fisher, Marilena Fotopoulou, Ameya Joshi, Hee Chul Jung, Denise Kouniaki, Maria Kouvari, Tina Lamprou, Alice Merche, Daniel Ostrowski, Elisavet Papadopoulou, Shinji Terada, Francesco Tonnarelli, Faye Vitou, Dimitra Zarri, Kathy Zerlauth.

Students from MAS Urban Design 2015-2016:
Daniel Ariño Espallargas, Aikaterini Christopoulou, Felipe Combeau Oyarzún, Hugo Dos Reis Vieira Pinto, Ekkachan Eiamananwattana, Guido Greco, Georgios Kaldis, Georgios Lavantsiotis, Christina Lazou, Katarzyna Pankowska, Gide Sleiman Haidar, Sofia Symeonidou, Aknaw Taddese, Maria Tsagka, Caterina Viguera Andreu, Olga Vougioukalaki, Yao Wu Ting, Seunghee Yang and Yuki Ueno.

01 Another architecture for Cairo's informal settlements. Model constructed by MAS Urban Design, 2014-2015. 02 Urban Canyon, Ard-el-Lewa, Cairo. 03 'Spontaneous urbanism', View over Ard-el-Lewa, Cairo.

03

RADICAL
CAIRO
From Agrarian Land to
New Urban Forms in Cairo
MAS Urban Design
ETH Zurich

GLOBAL GRIDS: POPULATIONS AT RISK

Center for Spatial Research, Columbia University

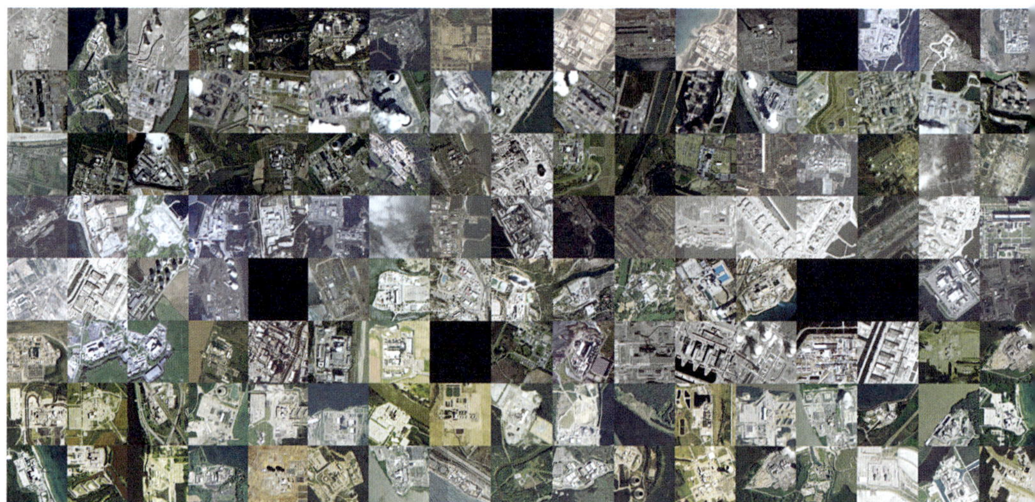

'Global Grids: Populations at Risk' makes visible civilian nuclear power plants in relation to territories of risk. The research team identified and extracted 296 nuclear plants from high-resolution satellite imagery from Digital Globe, through Mapbox, in November 2015, and set these facilities against a dataset called, The Gridded Population of the World.[1] This composite allows us to estimate and display the population vulnerable to potential nuclear accidents based on a radius of 30km, 75km and 175 km from each plant.

Inadvertently, the images captured from Mapbox automatically display another politics embedded within them: a politics of transparency and obfuscation. Notice the blurring, blocking, and even manipulating of the satellite imagery exposed in the grid.

'Global Grids: Populations at Risk' is the first in a series of projects under the title, *Conflict Urbanism* in preparation by Center for Spatial Research, Columbia University.

Credits:

Laura Kurgan (Project Director, Center for Spatial Research), Madeeha Merchant (Project Lead, Research Associate, Center for Spatial Research), Chris Stoafer (Data Scientist, PhD Candidate, Columbia University)

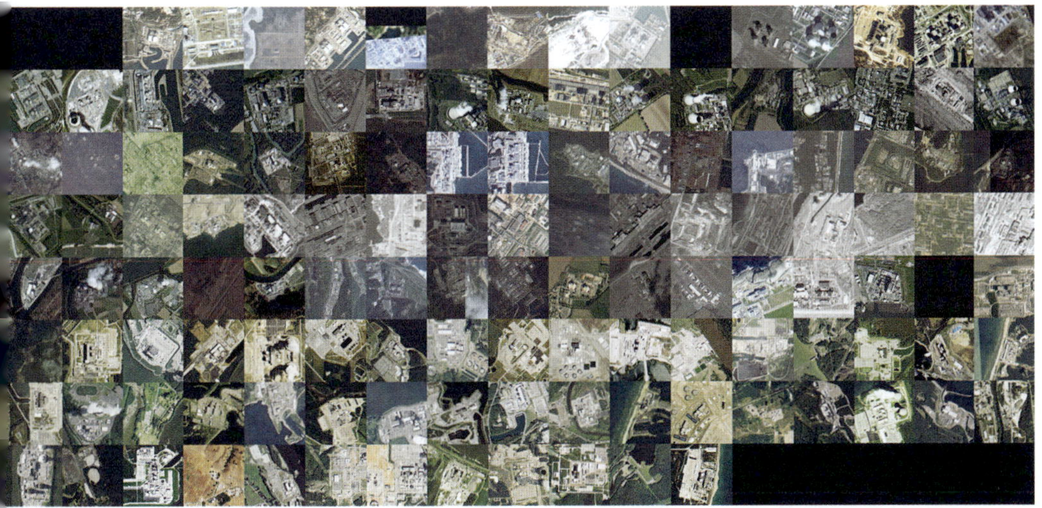

01

01 Gridded Population of the World is a dataset produced by the Center for International Earth Science Information Network (CIESIN) at Columbia University

ARGENTINA: Atucha
Power: 2,054 MWe
Population (30km): 161,784
ARGENTINA: Embalse
Power: 600 MWe
Population (30km): 36,322
ARMENIA: Metsamor
Power: 375 MWe
Population (30km): 647,078
FRANCE: Blayais
Power: 14,560 MWe
Population (30km): 146,710
FRANCE: Brennilis
Power: 0 MWe
Population (30km): 162469
FRANCE: Bugey
Power: 14,320 MWe
Population (30km): 749,673
BRAZIL: Angra
ower: 9,387 MWe
opulation (30km): 175,960
BULGARIA: Belene
Power: 3,812 MWe
Population (30km): 148,180
BULGARIA: Kozloduy
Power: 3,812 MWe
Population (30km): 123,907
FRANCE: Civaux
ower: 5,980 MWe
opulation (30km): 202,234
FRANCE: Creys-Malville
Power: 0 MWe
Population (30km): 86,896
FRANCE: Cruas
Power: 14,640 MWe
Population (30km): 257,627

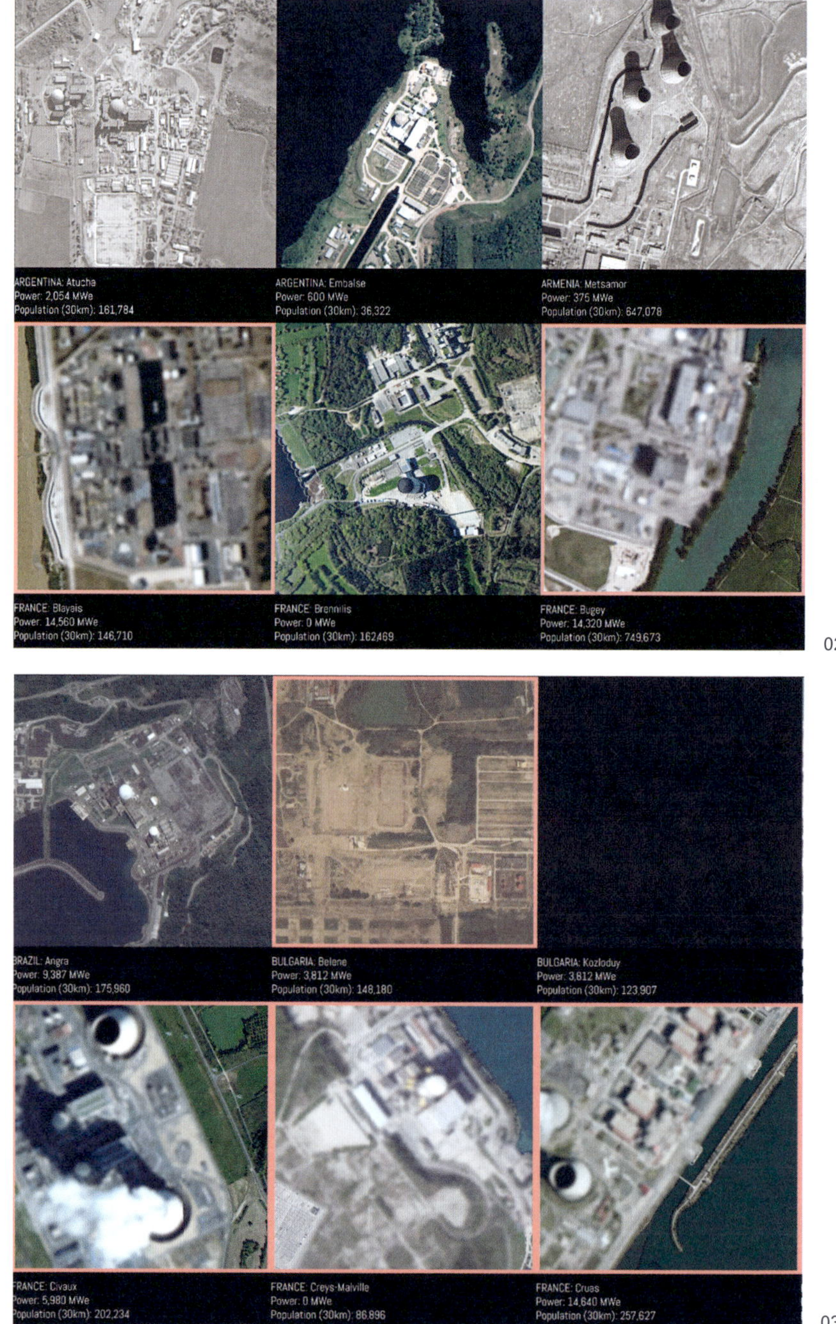

02

03

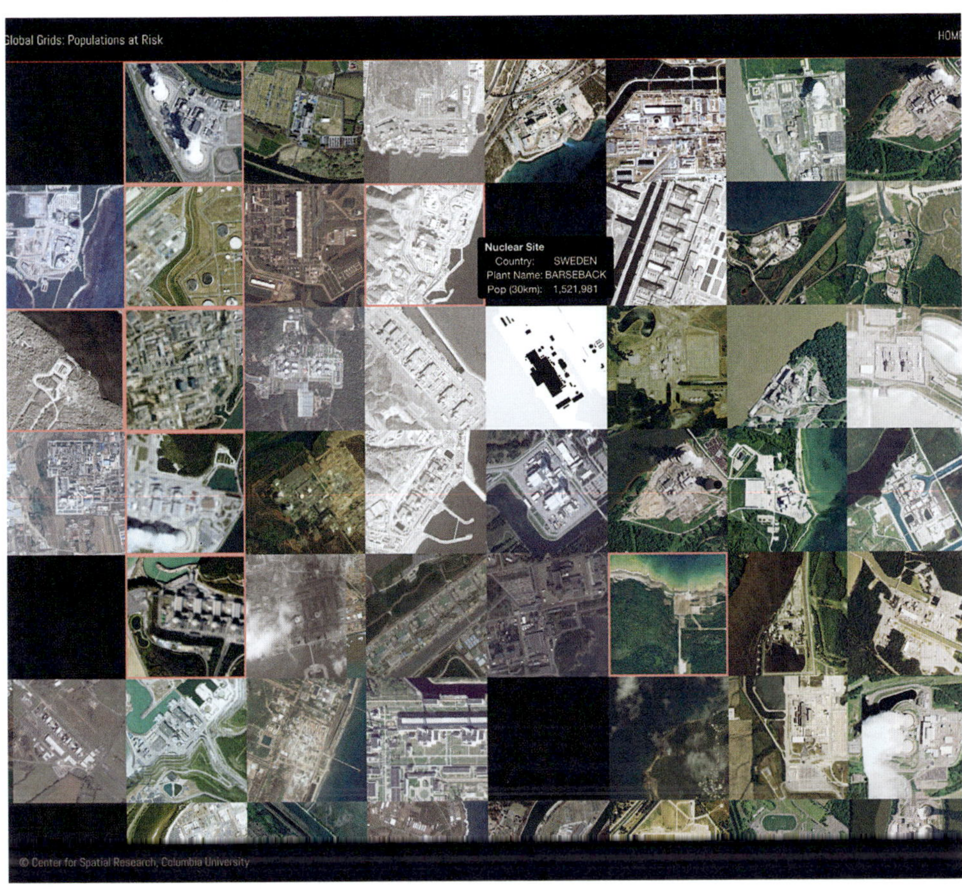

04

01 Center for Spatial Research, Columbia University 2015. 02, 03 The satellite images captured from Mapbox include blurred, blocked,and manipulated views of nuclear sites. Center for Spatial Research, Columbia University, 2015. 04 Screen grab from the web platform of Global Grids. Center for Spatial Research, Columbia University, 2015.

THE MEDELLÍN DIAGRAM: THE VISUALISATION OF THE POLITICAL

Teddy Cruz and Fonna Forman with Matthias Goerlich and Alejandro Echeverri

The Medellín Diagram is a tool to help visualise and manifest the political and civic processes that enabled the celebrated transformation of Medellín, Colombia in recent years. The Diagram is designed as a resource for municipalities and publics elsewhere to learn from Medellín's achievements. Social justice today must focus not only on the redistribution of resources, but also on the redistribution of knowledge.

While Medellín has rightfully captured global attention for the excellence of its public architecture and infrastructure, the city's transformation was initially launched as a political project, as the Medellín Diagram reveals. The movement toward inclusive urbanization began with the reimagining of institutions and cross-sector collaborations to facilitate the exchange of top-down and bottom-up knowledge and resources. It is this reorganization of the political and the civic that enabled Medellin's urban projects to be conceived, designed, funded, built, programmed, and maintained. The key is to understand these processes and their sustainability over time. From the perspective of participatory democracy and social justice, Medellín is a story about how a public restored urban dignity, activated collective agency, and reclaimed the future of its own city. Understanding the complex procedures behind these transformations is important because they offer critical alternatives to the unsustainable and divisive forms of metropolitan growth that are common across the world. The example of Medellín suggests that a radical architecture or urban design project must be accompanied by actions in the political sphere. What we are seeking here is not *political architecture* but the *construction of the political* itself: a radical institutional transformation that prioritizes public as opposed to private interests in the formation of the future city. The story of Medellín exemplifies how a city can confront socio-economic inequality and urban conflict, invest in the most marginalized zones of the city, and reimagine public space and infrastructure as mediating systems for socio-economic inclusion.

The first phase of this research was exhibited at the Medellín Museum of Modern Art in the occasion of the World Urban Forum in April 2013, and the second phase at the Museum of Art in Los Angeles in 2014, as part of the exhibition 'Citizen Culture: Artists and Architects Shape Policy.' Our participation in the UABB 'Radical Urbanism' exhibit

includes the third phase of this urban research project in the shape of a multimedia installation, comprising a series of dynamic process diagrams through video and other visualization tools.

Credits:
Teddy Cruz, Co-director, Cross-Border Initiative, University of California, San Diego. Fonna Forman, Co-director, Cross-Border Initiative, University of California, San Diego. In collaboration with Matthias Goerlich, Graphic Designer, Director, Studio Matthias Goerlich, Frankfurt, Germany and Alejandro Echeverri, Director of URBAM, EAFIT University, Medellín, Colombia

MEDELLIN
CIUDAD MAS VIOLENTA EN EL MUNDO
MODELO DE TRANSFORMACION URBANA - SOCIAL
COMUNA 13
CRISIS
HUGE INEQUALITY
VIOLENCE
ANTIOQUIA: REGION CON MAS DESIGUALDAD DEL PAIS
NARCOTRAFFIC YOUNG POPULATION
ROLE OF STATE CIVIC PARTICIPATION
COLOMBIA EN L. A.
RESPONSE
NOT THRU POLICE REPRESSION BUT AS FACILITATOR OF COMMUNITY PROCESSES
MODELS OF OPPORTUNITY
TRANSFORMATION
(RADICAL LEFT) CORPORACION REGION (REFORMIST LEFT)
DISSOLUTION OF ARMED STRUGGLE INTO SOCIAL REFORM
RADICALIZATION DIVISION (ANTAGONISTIC)
DEBATE
PARTICIPATION (AGONISTIC)
HOW TO CONSTRUCT PEACE?
HOW TO CONSTRUCT A PUBLIC CONSTITUTION
SOCIO-POLITICAL-ECONOMIC DEMOCRACY
CIVIL RIGHTS
90's CONSTITUTION
PRESIDENTIAL COUNCIL FOR MEDELLIN
CONSEJERIA PRESIDENCIAL PARA MEDELLIN
MARIA EMMA MEJIA
CORPORACION REGION
COMUNAL FORUMS
FOROS COMUNALES
SEMINARIO ALTERNATIVAS DEL FUTURO DE MEDELLIN
COMMUNITY
KNOWLEDGE EXCHANGE
INSTITUTION
DIALOGIC PROCESSES - KNOWLEDGE
DIALOGUE
OTHER FORMS OF KNOWLEDGE IN MEDELLIN
COMMUNITY DEBATES
T.V. COMMUNICATION
INTERFACE W/ PUBLIC
PARTICIPATION
DEBATE
COMMUNICATION
CO-EXISTENCE
URBAN POLICY
TRANSPARENCY
CONSTRUCTING TRUST
COLLECTIVE'S IMAGINATION
COMMUNITIES EVERYDAY
POINTS OF ACCESS
ACADEMIA RESEARCH
GOVERNMENT POLICY
TRANSITIONS: FROM COMMUNITY TO INSTITUTION FROM INSTITUTION TO COMMUN
TERRITORIAL MANAGEMENT
(KNOWLEDGE)
DESIGNING RE-DISTRIBUTION
RESOURCES
INDER
CEDEZO
OPERATIVE INTERMEDIARY SPACES
MEDIATE KNOWLEDGE
SOCIO-ECONOMIC RELATIONS
(CAPACITACION) INFRASTRUCTURES TO DECENTRALIZE RESOURCES
UNE
CULTURE
MAP OF PUBLIC MANAGEMENT
BANK OF OPPORTUNITIES
EMPRESAS VARIAS
RESOURCES
TACTICAL ORGANIZATION
NO ICONIC FIGURE W/OUT FACILITATION
NO PROTAGONISTS ONLY PROGRAMS
EXPLORA
MORAVIA
CASA AMARILLA
CRITICAL PROXIMITIES
TRANSFERENCES
BORDERS SITE INTERVENTION
INDEPENDENCE PATH
BOTANICAL GARDEN
OPERATING @ VARIOUS SCALES
OBJECTS - FIELDS
PRODUCING CULTURE
IT IS NOT ENOUGH TO GIVE INFORMATION
PROCESSES TO CONSTRUCT MEANING
BUILDING COMPREHENSION TRUST
LARGE INTEGRATIVE URBAN SCALE (PLAN)
SMALL SCALE INTERVENTION (STAIR)
TO ANTICIPATE ENCOUNTER
CIVIC

01

RE-THINKING RELATIONSHIPS
INSTITUTIONAL TRANSFORMATIONS AND THEIR SPATIAL CONSEQUENCES
FORMAL/PHYSICAL-SOCIAL
SPACES ARE DESIGNED IN TANDEM WITH SYSTEMS OF CULTURAL MANAGEMENT
SPACE - PEOPLE - PROGRAMS
PLUGGING SPACES W/ INTELLIGENT PROGRAMMING
BUILDINGS ARE NOT THE ONLY PROTAGONISTS. THESE PROJECTS ARE MADE OF A COMPLEX, TRANSVERSAL RELATIONSHIP ACROSS INSTITUTIONS
PUI
CIVIC CULTURE
CAJAS DE COMPENSACION
COMFAMA COMFENALCO
EDUCATION + CULTURE AS INSTRUMENTS TO BUILD CITY: CREATIVE ACTS OF CITIZENSHIP
DESIGNING COLLABORATION
EDUCATION
INDER
EDU
UNIVERSITIES
MUNICIPALITY
EPM
CIVIC VOLUNTEERS
CORPORACION REGION
WATERSHED
CUENCA KNOWLEDGE SYSTEM?
METRO
OTHER SPACES THAT EDUCATE
CENTER
EXPLORA
PRO-ANTIOQUIA
BOTANICAL GARDEN
VISIBILIZAR LAS RELACIONES
RECONOCER LA CIUDAD
PERIPHERY
COLEGIO
ACCESS
CABLE
CRITICAL PROXIMITY
PARK ARVI
TERRITORY VISUALIZATION
LUDOTECA
NEIGHBORHOOD MEMORY
ECONOMY
(CAPACITACION)
EDUCATION CULTURE ECONOMY
SPACE - ECONOMIC SUPPORT - ACCESSIBILITY
CEDEZO
INFORMAL ENTREPRENEURSHIP ECONOMIES. SOCIAL
SOCIAL ORGANIZATION = CULTURE
CORPORACION CULTURAL NUESTRA GENTE
HOW TO ENABLE OTHER FORMS OF PROGRAMMING FROM COMMUNITY?
OTHER FORMS OF CREATION
C.C. MORAVIA
COMPLEXITY IN SOCIO-CULTURAL PROGRAMMING
ARTISTS AS INTERLOCUTORS
COMMUNITY COLLABORATION
CASA AMARILLA

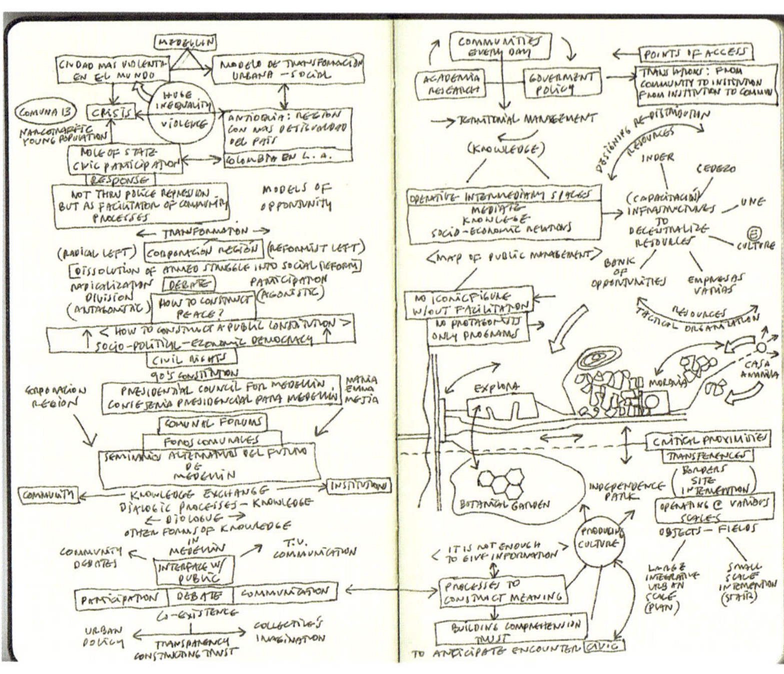

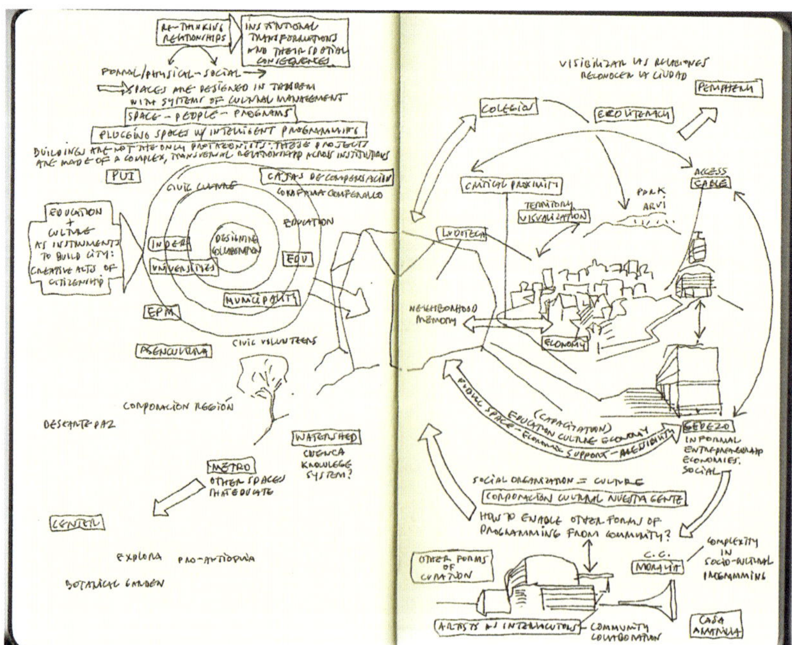

02

top down

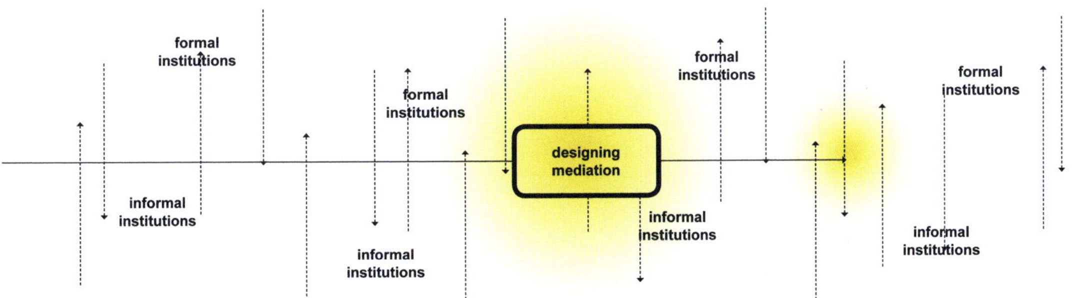

03

bottom up

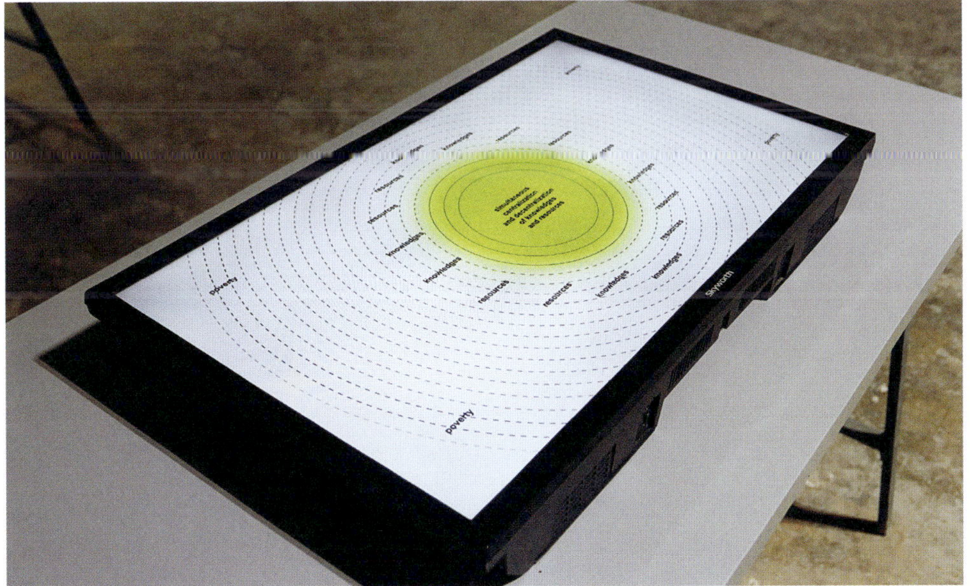

01, 02 Process sketches for the construction of the Medellín Diagram.

03 Still from the video animation of the Medellín Diagram.

RADICAL REUSE

Muck Petzet

To redirect the process of building and citymaking toward a more sustainable future, architect Muck Petzet proposes a radical shift: the priority of reuse over new development. Before inventing something entirely new, we should look to discover and redevelop the potential of existing physical, historic, architectonic, and social resources. In decisions about demolition or reuse, all these opportunities have to be taken into account in a holistic lifecycle assessment.

Within a growing and developing world society, our need for new dwellings and cities is indisputable. However, these buildings should be conceived in a way that both complements and contributes to existing elements. If one looks closely enough, there is always some latent potential for rediscovery.

The tabula rasa is a myth — a false promise artificially constructed by erasing valuable heritage. As the often shrinking postindustrial societies of highly developed countries have already overspent on resources and embodied energy, our second chance is not renewal or replacement but improvement of the existing.

Radical reuse enriches new developments with layers and traces of history, providing identity and authenticity to the otherwise replicable 'new'.

The 'Radical Reuse' pop-up pavilion conceived by Muck Petzet for UABB highlights the potentials of radical reuse and demonstrates its practical implementation and strategies for application in the work of his Munich- and Berlin-based office, Muck Petzet Architekten.

01

02

01, 02 Muck Petzet's 2015 proposal for a high-rise 'plug-in' in the existing historic swimming pool of Hubertusbad in Berlin Lichtenberg, demonstrating radical reuse. © Muck Petzet Architekten. Rendering by PONNIE Images.

URBAN EARTHWORKS

Anna Heringer, Martin Rauch and Mu Jun

Cities consist of materials.

The choice of building material defines who profits from this transaction – and therefore ultimately determines the level of equality within a society.

As architects, we have a responsibility to actively pursue construction that promotes sustainability and empowerment, celebrating collaboration and social capital. Conventional modes of construction in concrete and steel can no longer continue for lack of available resources: sand, gravel and energy from fossil fuels. In contrast, earthen construction is a traditional and local, and therefore sustainable, building method that has rarely been given serious consideration as a building material for urban contexts in contemporary research.

We firmly believe that this aesthetically pleasing, technologically advanced, climatically relevant, and common-sense material could engender a radical reimagining of contemporary cities.

This project imagines a future where earthen cities are produced by their citizens – a perhaps radical, experimental utopia of urban transformation. The installation of 'Urban Earthworks' comprises material samples, images, collaged visions, and a 1:1 scale mock-up of a modern rammed-earth wall. This full-scale prototype shows a minimalistic living room imagined for an urban context. It demonstrates how a scaling-up of current earthen construction technologies is technically feasible in an urban setting through the prefabrication of elements.

The construction allows Biennale visitors to enter an alternative conception of the home and experience the significantly reduced amount of space necessary to feel comfort when the material properties of earth are fully exploited. This project thus explores the potentials of rammed earth as a contemporary building material, showcasing state-of-the-art techniques as well as a vision for widespread adoption on the urban scale.

Credits:
Project Concept: Lindsay Blair Howe
Site Supervisor: Lu Lei
Construction Supervisor: Leonar Stieger
Construction Team: Zhao Yiqian, Li Xin, Liu Zhiwei, Dang Xiaojie
Production Assistance: Clemens Quirin, Emanuel Falk

01 'Prefabricated' walls, or segments of rammed earth mass-produced in a warehouse to be installed on site with cranes. 02 Envisioning a city made of earth rather than concrete. Collage by Lindsay Howe.

01

02

COLLECTIVE CITY

Alexander Eisenschmidt / Visionary Cities Project

This exhibition explores spatial, organisational, and material ingenuities born out of the forces and pressures of the contemporary city, answered by the architectural amateur, and used by everyone. The examples highlighted here are important to the way the world is built, influential in its capacities to mobilize, and mesmerizing in its strangeness, yet outside the architectural radar. The exhibition documents, organises, and projects a catalogue of existing inventions and tactics found across the globe (often outrageous, sometimes humorous, but always embedded in the here and now) with the ambition to establish a dictionary of ideas that can act simultaneously as a reality-check and sourcebook. We are interested in how the dynamics of global urbanisation effectively influence architecture; or to put it more bluntly, how the intelligences of the existing city can be engaged architecturally.

From a street-runway intersection in Gibraltar, via the Osaka baseball stadium-turned-model village, to stilt houses in international waters at Biscayne Bay, the project understands these conditions as saturated with potential for a new kind of architectural urbanism. Together these examples form a new city that is fragmented and yet collective, hence the title of the exhibition, 'Collective City'.

The exhibition has three parts: a catalogue of urban inventions and tactics gathered from around the world, a panorama drawing that collages these inventions into one collective city, and a media platform for visitors to share and contribute their discoveries.

The catalogue is structured according to 26 keywords, from *advertisement* to *camouflage* to *quicksand* and *zoning*. It identifies a series of photographs, clearly describes the tactics pictured therein, and gives the location of each example. For the panorama, these examples of essential ingenuities – seemingly 'primitive' but saturated with intelligences – are woven together into a massive drawing of a city in which the individual fragments find new relationships and juxtapositions, articulating a new kind of urbanity that is collective. The media platform presents all the findings and lets the public upload their own descriptions, photographs, and impressions, which will lead to a growing archive of urban ingenuities.

Credits:
Visionary Cities Project: Alexander Eisenschmidt (Director), and Chicago Team: Matthew Busscher, Daisey Martinez, Paul Mosely, Pedro Medrano, Isabela Rolim, Janina Sanchez, Anton Tonchev, Surama Viera

Acknowledgements:
Frank O. Carlson & Co. and College of Architecture, Design and the Arts at the University of Illinois at Chicago

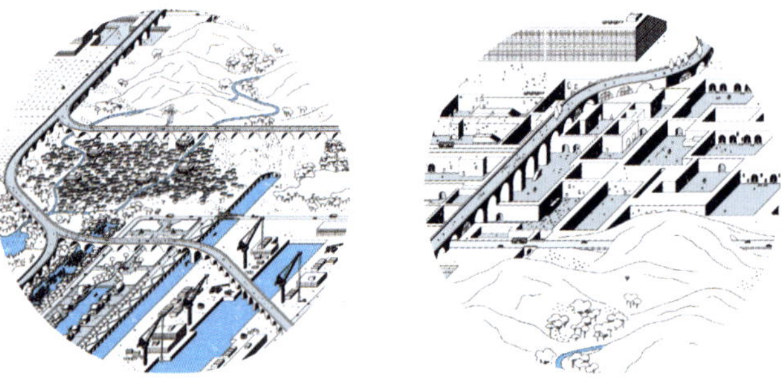

01 Panorama drawing (with enlarged details below) from 'Collective City' by Visionary Cities Project.
02 Catalogue of urban inventions and tactics gathered from around the world, from 'Collective City' by Visionary Cities Project. © Alexander Eisenschmidt.

01

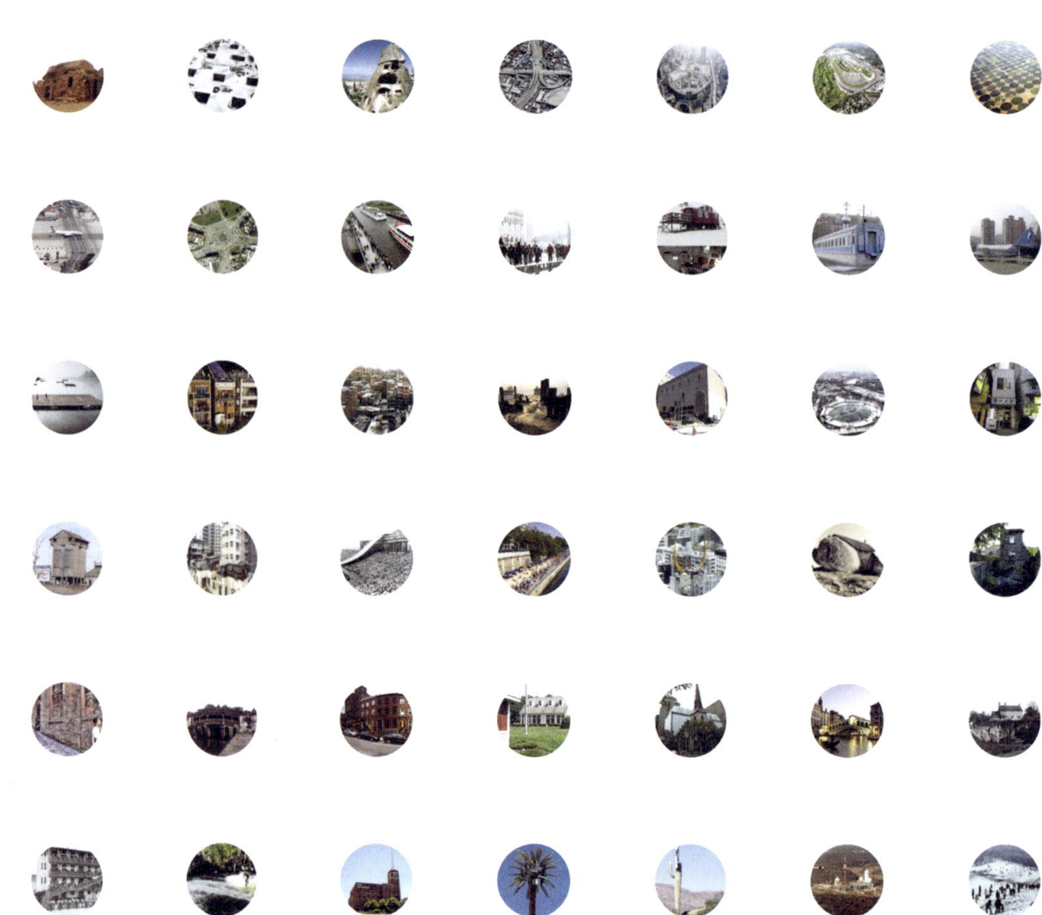

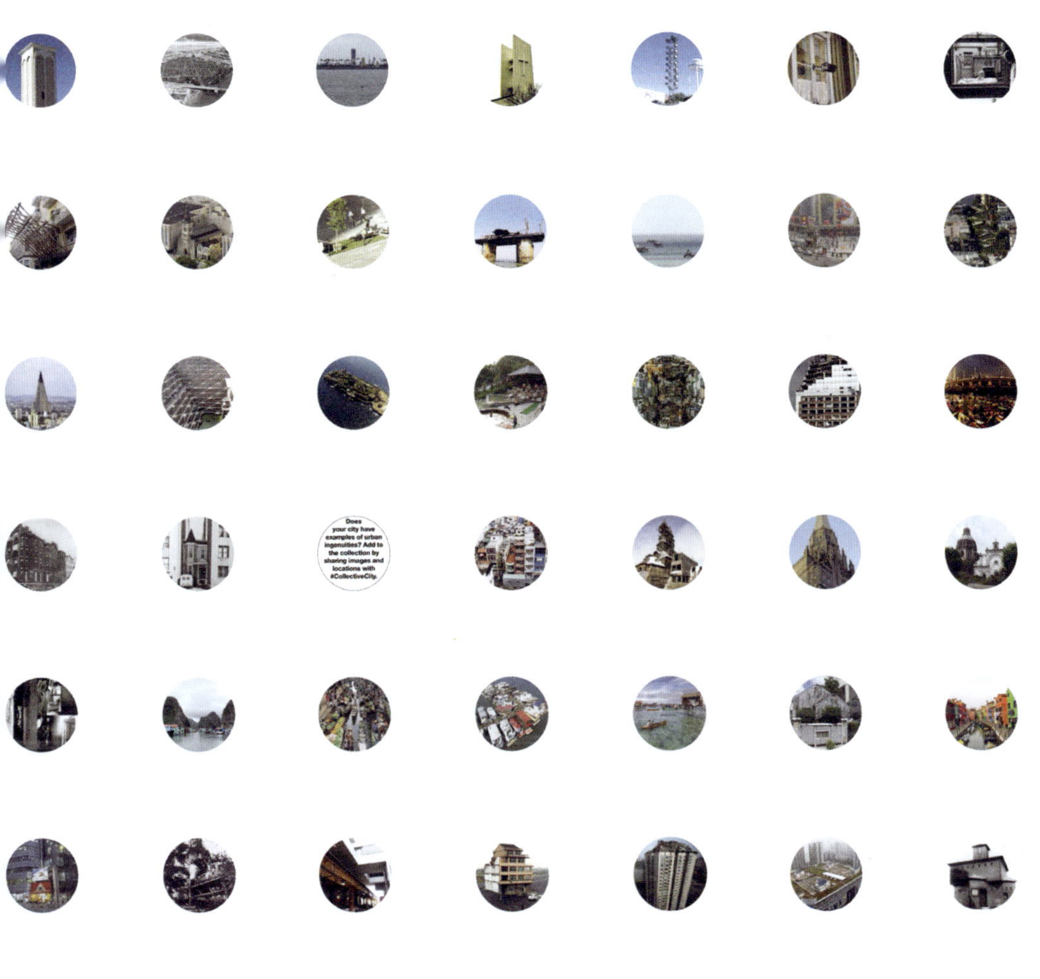
Does
your city have
examples of urban
ingenuities? Add to
the collection by
sharing images and
locations with
#CollectiveCity.

02

OPPORTUNITY AND TRANSFORMATION

Wolff Architects

Architects shape only a small segment of most cities. The rest is shaped by the general populace. Therefore the future of cities depends on the freedom that people have to transform cities to suit their needs. Opportunity supports urban transformation.

This exhibition shows the emergence of a radical domesticity in Du Noon, Cape Town, over the past 15 years. The government-subsidised housing scheme of Du Noon is characterised by extensive service infrastructure, good access to jobs, and rapid densification. In this context, inhabitants have reorganised their dwellings as sites of entrepreneurship. They run all kinds of businesses from their homes, from shops and daycare centres to bars and rooms for sublet. These specialised yet diversified houses create local oppotunities for living, working, and socialising. A specialised domesticity becomes the means of claiming economic freedom. Intense opportunity leads to a radical urbanity.

In the context of limited resources, architects must fundamentally understand what citizens are capable of doing for themselves and what infrastructure can do to support urban opportunity. Architects should see their role as setting up opportunities for people to live, work, and socialise while decreasing societal vulnerability.

The construction of opportunity is as important as the construction of infrastructure.

Credits:
Wolff Architects, Infestation, Afterlife

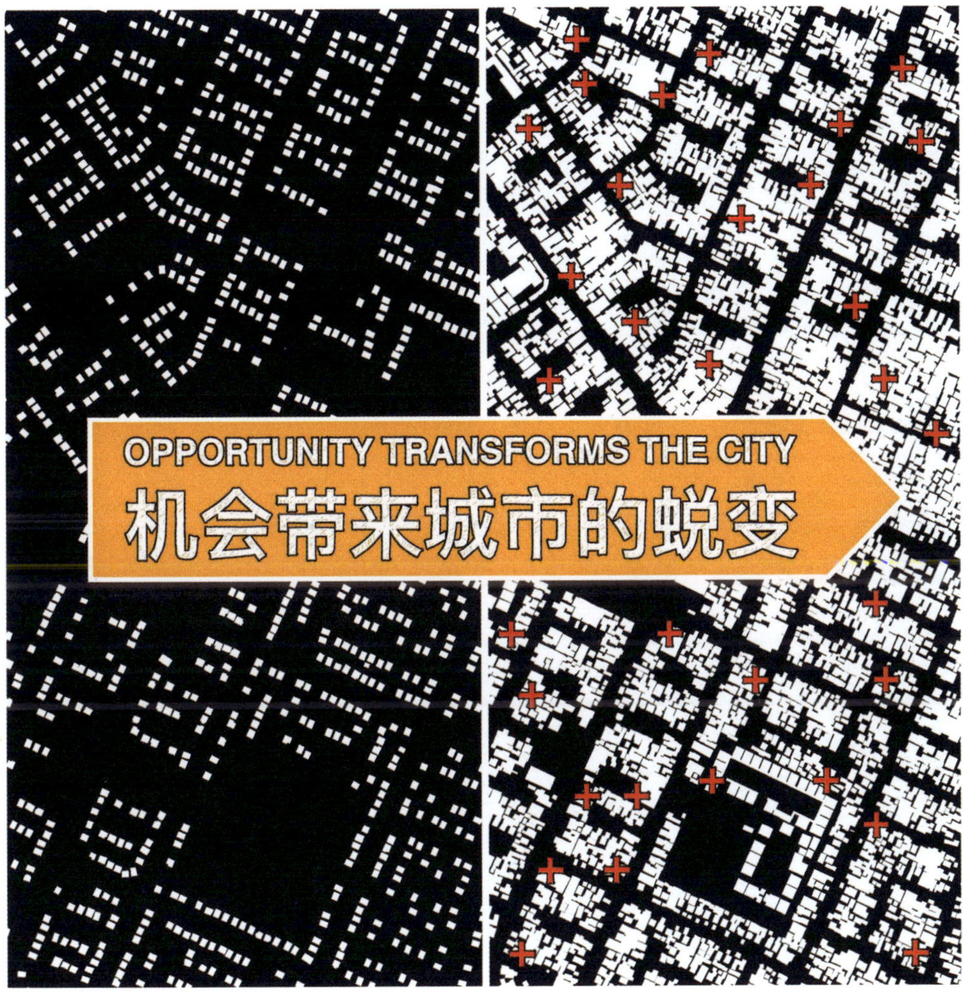

01

01 Manifesto page by Heinrich Wolff.
Installation view by Wolff Architects.

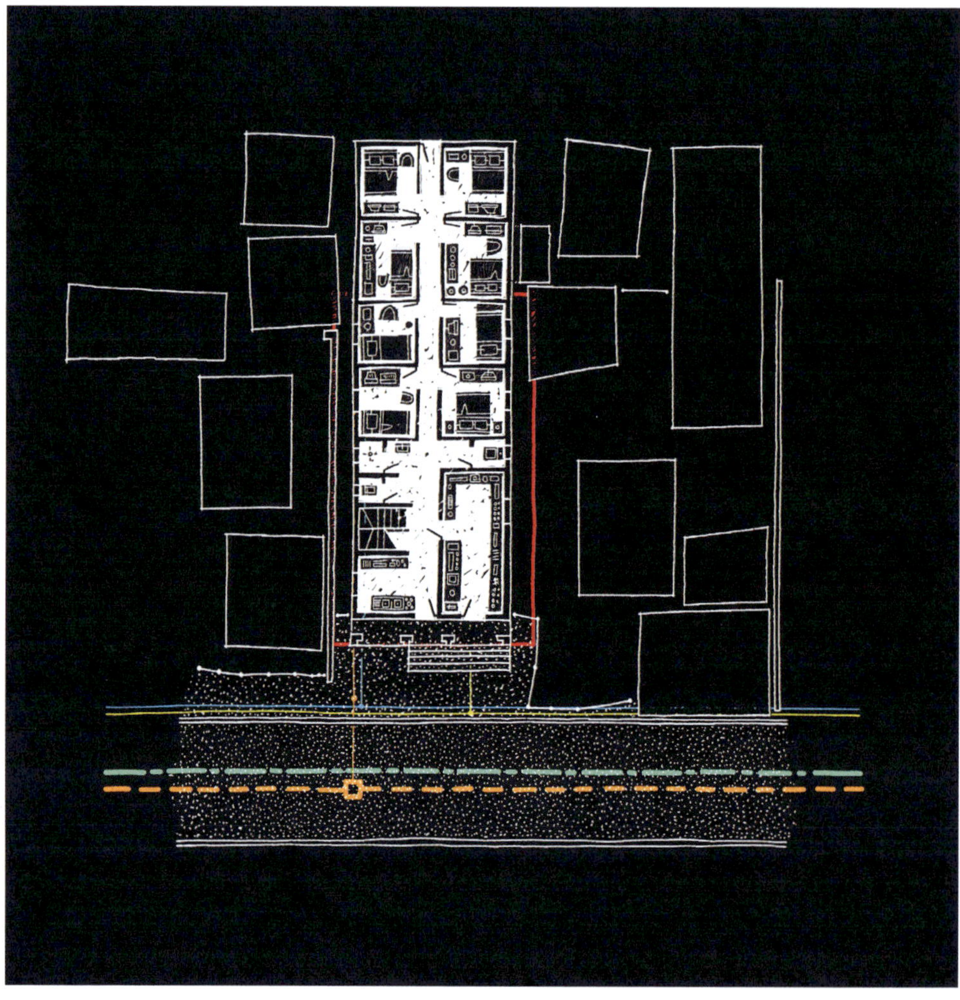

02

02 Project for an apartment house in Capetown by Wolff Architects.

03

03 Project for a day care house in Capetown by Wolff Architects.

REFUGEE CAMPS OF THE WESTERN SAHARA

Manuel Herz Architects

The Western Sahara is a country located at the western edge of the African continent. Formerly a Spanish colonial territory, and since 1975 occupied by Morocco, it has been called the world's last remaining colony. With the beginning of a guerilla war against Morocco, most of the Western Saharan population had to flee across the border into Algeria where it settled in refugee camps, today housing approximately 160,000 Sahrawis.

Even though the Sahrawis do not have control over their territory, they proclaimed independence of the Western Sahara on February 27, 1976. Its sovereignty is recognized today by 34 countries, though its status remains unresolved.

The Sahrawi population, having lived for 40 years in refugee camps in the border zone of south-western Algeria, has developed a unique set of urban and architectural tools and design methodologies to deal with the conditions of transience and liminality. Instead of seeing the camps as a place of limitation, the Sahrawis have used them proactively as a tool of nation building. In fact, the camps have become the sites of architectural invention and can be understood as urban laboratories.

Life in the Sahrawi refugee camps gives rise to specific conditions that test and question some of the underlying tenets of the discipline of planning. For example, landownership does not exist the Sahrawi camps. Therefore, the inhabitants must develop other methods to claim control over land and to develop private homes. These methods include, amongst others, techniques of negotiation and sharing.

The design and construction of the huts and houses in the Sahrawi camps negotiate elements of transience and permanence. Even though the Sahrawis have lived for almost 40 years in the camps, the tent is still a common residential typology. Beyond its cultural significance and certain climatic benefits, the tent expresses to the onlooker that the population has not resigned itself to a life in the camps. The tent is the physical representation of a political demand for a return to the home country of the Western Sahara.

More recently the Sahrawis have started to develop and build architecturally designed houses. These buildings are the expression of the desire to create comfortable and aesthetic spaces for living. On the other hand, they can also be seen as a first step towards accept-

ance of continuous life in the refugee camps. Perhaps the situation teaches us that permanence and temporality are not in fact a pair of opposites, but rather different means of expressing a political dilemma.

This pavilion is based on research from the book, *From Camp to City: Refugee Camps of the Western Sahara*, edited by Manuel Herz (Lars Müller, 2013).

Credits:
Concept and research: Manuel Herz
Assistance: François de Font Reaulx
Manuel Herz is the principal of Manuel Herz Architects, based in Basel, and is the head of research and teaching at ETH Studio Basel: Contemporary City Institute.

Editor's note:
'Refugee Camps of the Western Sahara' was awarded the 'Golden Dragon' prize by an independent jury.

01

1 -
SADR Management/Protocolo SADR 管理/协议

2 -
Ministry of Development and Construction 建设部

3 -
Ministry of Health 卫生部

4 -
Ministry of Justice and Religious Affairs 司法和宗教事务部

5 -
Ministry of Culture 文化部

6 -
Ministry of Youth and Sport 青少年和体育部

7 -
Ministry of Defense 国防部

8 -
Ministry of Information 信息部

9 -
Ministry of International Affairs 国际事务部

10 -
Ministry of Education 教育部

11 -
Parliament 国会

12 -
National Archive 国家档案馆

02

01 Rabouni, established in 1976, was transformed in 1987 from a residential camp into a center of administration for the Sahrawi government in exile. It has become the de-facto capital of the refugee nation. Institutions such as the parliament, ministries, national archive, and the national museum are housed in buildings that shape the urban fabric of Rabouni, reflecting the semi-autonomous status of the Sahrawi refugees. 02 Ministry buildings of Rabouni, Algeria. Map and photos by Manuel Herz Architects.

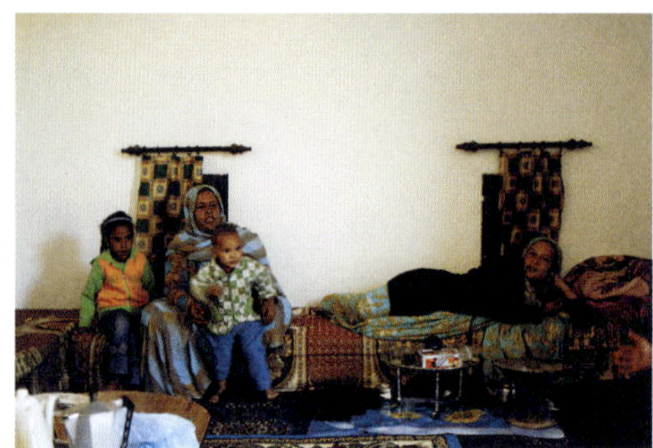

03

03 Scenes of public life in the camps. Clockwise from top left: living, shopping, working, recreation, learning, and mobility. 04 Satellite view of Smara Camp, Algeria, home to 40,000 Saharawi refugees (detail). Courtesy Manuel Herz Architects. Photos by Manuel Herz Architects.

04

DO YOU HEAR THE PEOPLE SING?

Crimson Architectural Historians with Hugo Corbett

In the last decade we have witnessed how the street has ever more frequently been the location and at the same time the topic of riots and sometimes violently suppressed protests: from the anti-globalist manifestations in Seattle and the anti-austerity protests in Athens; via the Arabic Spring uprisings in Tunis, Cairo and Tripoli; and the Gezi Park protests in Istanbul; the anti- FIFA and Olympic Games protests in Rio; to the 'Umbrella Revolution' in Hong Kong.

These protests had one thing in common: they symbolically but also physically politicized public urban space. Public space is the arena where a struggle for the way the country or city is governed unfolds. At the same time public space itself has to be conquered from the police and the order troops for it to function as a place of democracy and freedom of speech.

Sometimes public space is not only the backdrop but has the leading role in this struggle for the emancipation of the people. For example: what gave rise to the immense anti-Erdogan protests in Istanbul were his building plans for the combination of a giant mosque and a shopping mall, in a reconstruction of a long-demolished Ottoman Barracks building in one of the largest secular public spaces in the city, Gezi Park. Another example is how the protesters of the Umbrella Revolution in Hong Kong used the plaza underneath a democratic government building. Despite the plaza's original function as a civic space, the protesters were summoned to leave by the owners of the building. They then turned their umbrellas, painted with pro-democracy slogans, in the direction of the troops, which earned their protests the name, 'Umbrella Revolution'. The protesters accompanied this act with the singing of the anti-oppression song, 'Do You Hear the People Sing?' from the musical, Les Miserables. The umbrellas, the level of organization and discipline of the protest, the smart use of symbolic spaces in the city, combined of course with the protesters' ability to burst into song, offered a powerful glimpse of what real democracy in Hong Kong might look

01

like. In that sense the protests were themselves a radical form of urbanism, holding great promise for this city.

This 'Radical Urbanism' is what many of the extremely diverse protests all over the world have in common. Everywhere the status of the street and the issue of 'ownership' (Who owns the street? The police or the protesters, the shop owners or the mourning parents of youngsters shot by the police?) lies at the centre of the debate. The form of the protests, the ways they are organized, the symbols they deploy to bring their message across, the public spaces they occupy, carry meaning. The protests and riots tell another story about the city, offering images that differ from the official ones. These actions offer temporary alternative ways to organise, govern or even plan the city. From the circles on Tahrir square back to the barricades of the Amsterdam Nieuwmarkt Riots in 1975, protests and riots are the essence of 'Radical Urbanism'.

For UABB 2015, Crimson Architectural Historians evokes this worldwide history in a panoramic drawing, 'Do You Hear the People Sing?' that is composed of scenes of riots and protests, fused with their spatial environments. It presents an allegorical street scene in which architecture, protesters, instruments of authority, slogans and other paraphernalia tell a story of the street as the place where democracy is viscerally shaped and represented.

01 Crimson Architectural Historians' panoramic drawing, 'Do You Hear the People Sing?', composed of scenes of riots and protests, fused with their spatial environments.

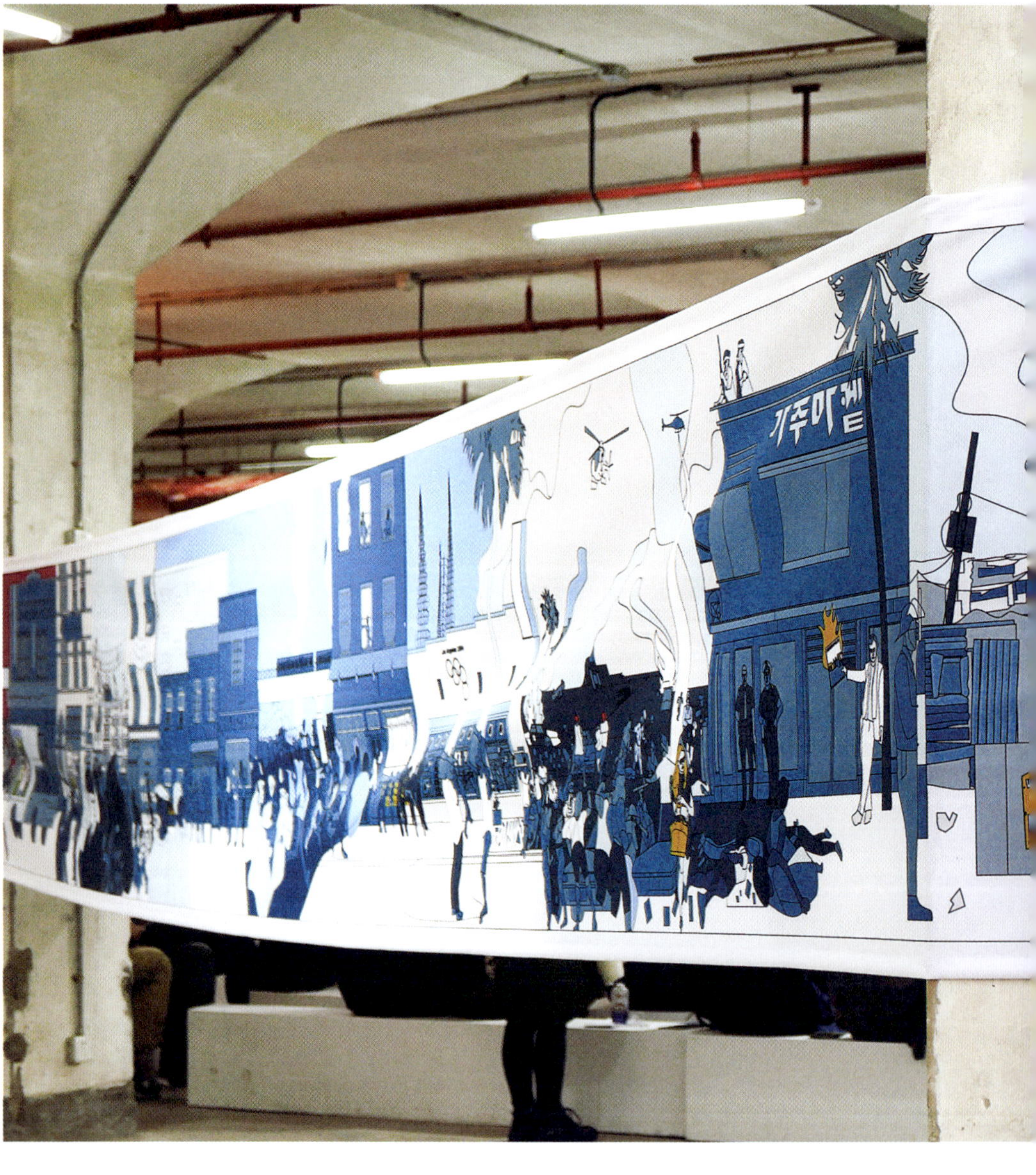

ESINHA
O POVO E
DO U HEAR THE PEOPLE SING?

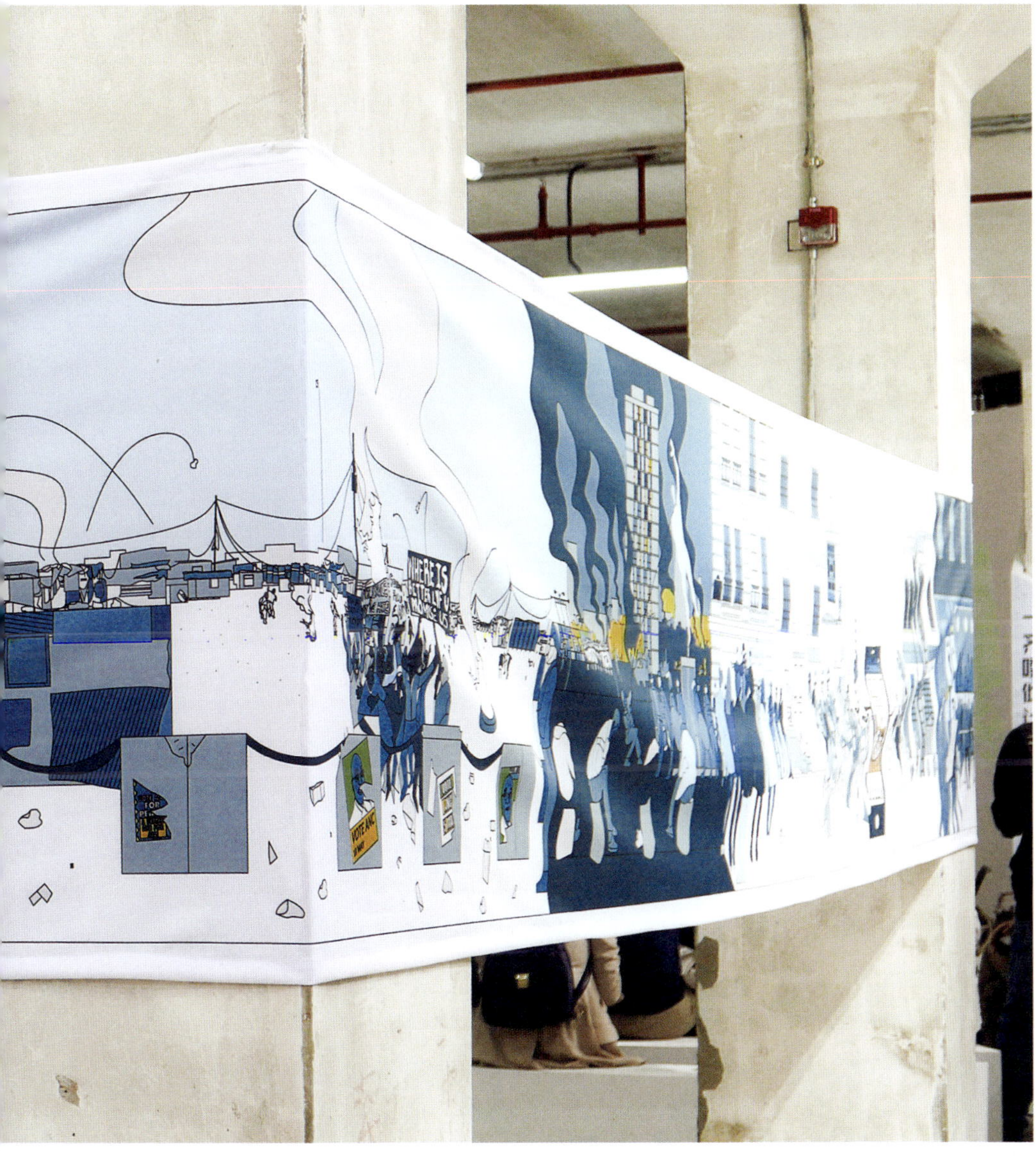

NETWORKED URBANISM

ecosistema urbano

'Networked Urbanism' installation by ecosistema urbano demonstrates a working method and an overall strategic vision that relies on short-term, punctual, and powerful interventions in urban space. Oriented toward specific and emblematic sites, this strategy contrasts with conventional planning strategies that require long-term development and a large investment of resources. By working quickly and economically, ecosistema urbano's projects empower people and engage citizens in the tangible transformation of the places where they live.

The installation displays a selection of pilot projects exploring urban improvement in both a physical and immaterial sense. Taken together, the selected projects form a critical catalogue of diverse urban contexts. Networked Urbanism embraces urban complexity and the new tools developed to address it.

'Networked Urbanism' thus reflects the approach of 'Urban Social Design' developed by ecosistema urbano, a group of architects and urban designers operating within the fields of urbanism, architecture, engineering, and sociology. The group's work is characterised by attention to the urban context, social factors, and design understood as an action, an interaction, and a tool for transformation. Based in Spain, Ecosistema Urbano has completed research and design projects in Norway, Russia, Paraguay, China, Ecuador, Honduras, Bahrain, and Italy. They have also developed digital tools to facilitate collective creative exercises and visualize data, promoting participatory urban design processes.

Credits:
Principals: Jose Luis Vallejo and Belinda Tato
Team: Antonella Milano, Marco Rizzetto, Jorge Toledo, Luisa Zancada, Julia Casado, Alice Clementi, Alessandro Benedetto, Carlos León, Pascual Pérez, Luis Mauricio Franco, Bingyu Guan, Francesca Savio, Clara Medina, Antonio Díaz

01

01 Recycling suburbia with socio-environmental responsive urban prostheses. ecosistema urbano, Vallecas Eco-boulevard, Madrid, 2008.

02

02 Playful urban device. ecosistema urbano, Energy carousel in Dordrecht, the Netherlands, 2012.

03

03 A network design process for collectively reimagining public space. ecosistema urbano, main square of Hamar, Norway, 2013. Photos courtesy of ecosistema urbano, Emilio P. Doiztua and Christoffer H. Nilsen.

NETWORK
DESIGN
网络化设计
DREAM
HAMAR
梦哈马
network
design process
for collectively
reimagining
public space
URBAN
REVITALIZATION
ASU-LAB
historic
centre
of asuncion
SEA
生态再组合

人工树木
SPAIN
socio-
environmental
urban
prostheses
城市公共
环境植入
AIR TREE
EXPO
2010
CHINA
再生郊区

DOMESTIC URBANISM IN OROSHIMACHI, SENDAI

Atelier Hitoshi Abe with Masashige Motoe and wowlab

Public and private space have traditionally defined opposite poles on the spectrum of human habitation, where public space is associated with urbanity and private space with domesticity. The planning of urban, public space has typically involved a top-down arrangement of anticipated activities, while domestic space is organized more informally in response to existing patterns of use.

However, in the current milieu, these seemingly opposite spatial domains have become increasingly intertwined.

Domestic space has expanded beyond the home into surrounding environs, resulting in a domestication of urban space. In response to this phenomenon a much more nimble approach to planning, herein referred to as 'Domestic Urbanism', has started to evolve that is more aligned with the 'rearrangement' of furniture in the domicile than the traditional master plan.

Presented for UABB 2015 is a working case study of 'Domestic Urbanism' that has been evolving in the Oroshimachi region of Sendai, Japan. The redevelopment of Oroshimachi has avoided the typical process of urban regeneration, in which existing cityscapes are razed to make way for new development. Instead, a much more delicate process of community-driven development has taken shape. An independent agency in Oroshimachi, initially formed to support local business, has established a platform within the community to connect creatives and entrepreneurs with local businesses and facilities to form a network of activity. This process has allowed for a more immediate and fine-tuned decision-making based on community feedback, where various elements within the community are restructured internally.

This exhibit attempts, through motion graphics, to visualize the process of redevelopment of Oroshimachi. It includes key data from various companies that have been active in Oroshimachi as well as key events and town planning policies, arranged in chronological order. By turning the jog dial, what becomes evident is how a series of small yet nimble actions, interventions, and events have aligned to significantly transform the region.

Credits:
With special thanks to the Sendai Oroshisho Center

01

01 Aerial view of Oroshimachi. Courtesy of Sendai Oroshisho Center.

RADICAL TEMPORALITIES (THE EPHEMERAL CITY)

Felipe Vera and Rahul Mehrotra in collaboration with Diego Pinochet

Rahul Mehrotra and Felipe Vera have systematically analysed cities and settlements that are built with an explicit expiry date. Rather than understanding urbanisation as a process by which space is permanently transformed into hard agglomeration, their research focuses on reversible structures and architectures made of lightweight elements.

The extraordinary intensification of pilgrimage practices in recent years has translated into the need for larger and more frequently assembled structures for hosting massive gatherings. Among the examples analysed are ephemeral constructions deployed for the Haj as well as a series of temporary settlements constructed to host Indian celebrations such as the Durga Puja, Ganesh Chaturthi, and the Kumbh Mela — the latter being a religious pilgrimage that, according to official figures, supports the congregation of more than 100 million people and the habitation of seven million people in fixed space for the 55-day duration of the festival.

'Radical Temporalities' also considers the natural disasters, induced or exacerbated by climate change, that require the deployment of temporary shelters to house large populations of displaced inhabitants. Recent cases include camps in the Philippines, Haiti, Chile, and several other instances of 'temporary cities' built in the context of disaster. Another source of large-scale displacement is political conflict, which has spurred the creation of enormous refugee camps around the globe. Additionally, non-religious cultural celebrations are increasing in scale as well as frequency. They, too, cause the erection of temporary structures within and outside urban areas. Extensive music festivals like Exit in Serbia, Coachella in California, and Sziget in Budapest motivate the construction of extended ephemeral settlements that for short periods of time congregate incredibly large groups of people.

The index of ephemeral cities also includes mining and oil towns, military bases built in contested territories, transaction-induced pop-up cities, temporary structures that house spectators around sporting events, or even the disruptive constructions inside formal spaces, such as the camps of the Occupy movement. Mehrotra and Vera study these diverse cases in an effort to understand their workings and potentially to extrapolate strategies for urban design and planning in the future.

Credits:
Design and Production: Paulina Leyton, Juan Pablo Corral

01

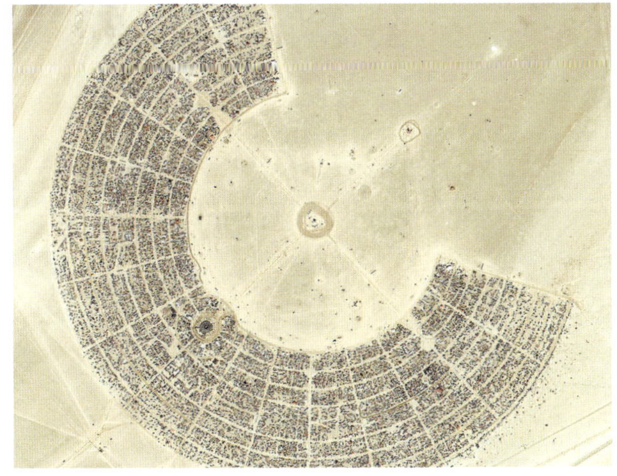
02

01 Kumbh Mela aerial view by Felipe Vera.
02 Burning Man, a temporary city in the Nevada desert. Aerial view from Google Earth.
03 Ephemeral Cities Global Map by Felipe Vera.

E01. Añelo
E02. Salar de Olaroz
E03. Pico Truncado
E04. Chiquicamata
E05. Pabellon del Inca Hotel
E06. Maria Elena
E07. Escondida
E08. El Salvador
E09. Cerrejón
E10. Morococha
E11. Orinoco Belt Oil Fields
E12. Macaé
E13. Cerrado Fields
E14. Tierras Bajas Project
E15. Athabasca Oil Sands
E16. Hull-Rust-Mahoning Mine
E17. Betze-Post Gold Mine
E18. Belridge Oil Fields
E19. Louisiana Offshore Oil Port
E20. Potash Phosphate Mine
E21. Oil Extraction Wells
E22. Chevron Oil Refinery
E23. Greenland
E24. Gartzweiler Surface Mine
E25. Ffos-y-fran
E26. Kiruna City
E27. Creil
E28. Belchatow Coal Mine
E29. Kimberley diamond mine
E30. Chevron Oil Refinery
E31. Grasberg Mine
E32. Duri Oil Fields
E33. Seaweed Farms
E34. Jubail
E35. Nahalal
E36. Ulan Bator
E37. Norilsk
E38. Mirny Mine
E39. Oil Rocks
E40. Ranger Mine
E41. Mount Whaleback
E42. Fish farm, Ma Wan Town
E43. Marine Acquaculture
E44. Arctic oil extraction
C01 AfricaBurn
C02 Bestival
C03 Boom Festival
C04 Burning Man
C05 Byron Bay
C06 Coachella
C07 Creamfields
C08 Download Festival
C09 Electric Daisy Carnival
C10 Electric Picnic
C11 Glastonbury Festival
C12 High Sierra Music Festival
C13 Lightning in a Bottle
C14 Nowhere
C15 Oppikoppi
C16 Pushkar Camel Fair
C17 Westman Island Festival
C18 Wickerman Festival
C19 Beltane Fire Festival
C20 Brooklyn Hip-Hop Festival
C21 Comic-Con International
C22 Concurs de Castells
C23 Cooper's Hill Cheese-Rolling
C24 Hard Music Festival
C25 Il Palio
C26 Festival of the Sahara
C27 Inti Raymi
C28 Jaisalmer Desert Festival
C29 Kazantip Republic
C30 Naghol Land Diving
C31 National Pyrotechnic Festival
C32 Outside Lands
Legend
Refuge
Disaster
Celebration
Transaction
Extraction
Religion

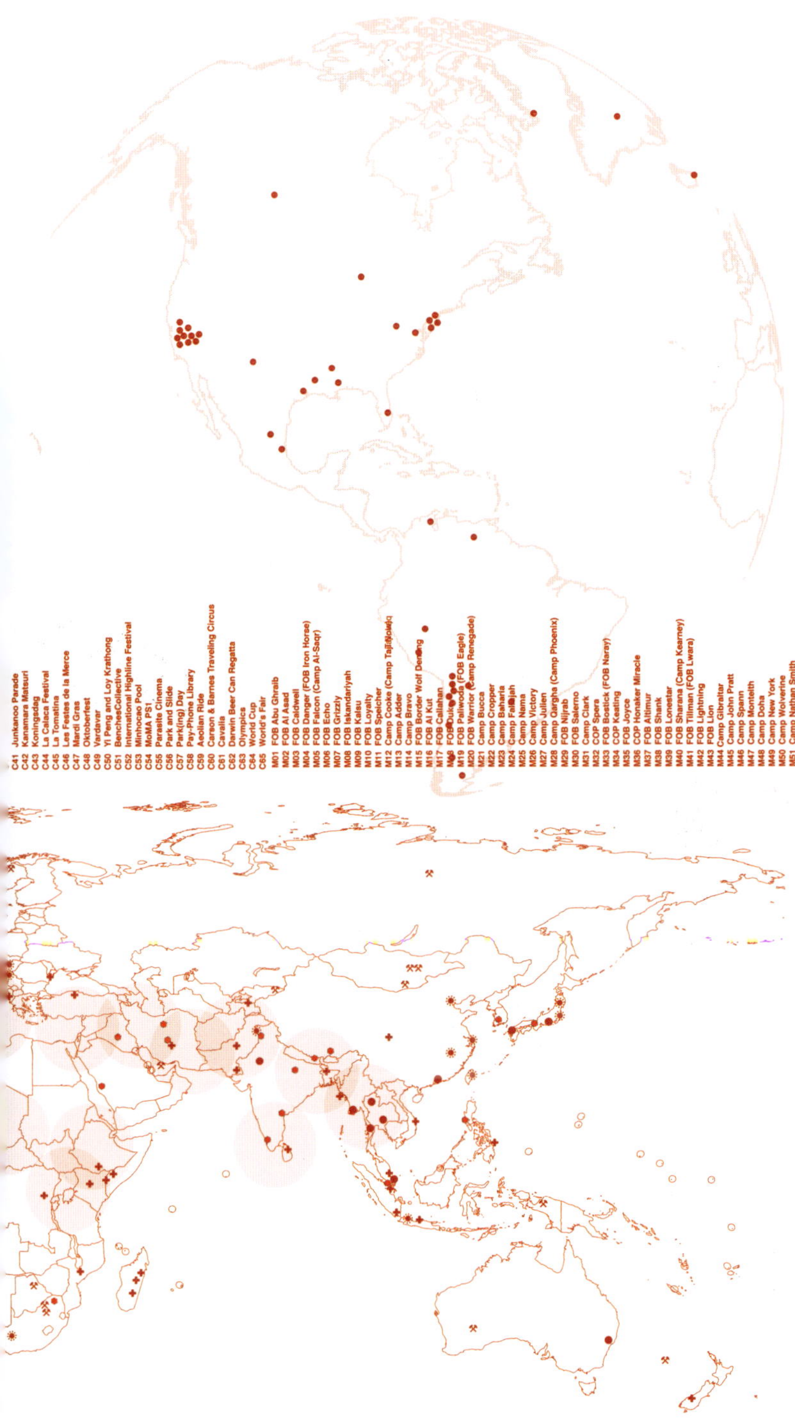
C41 Junkanoo Parade
C42 Kanamara Matsuri
C43 Koningsdag
C44 La Calaca Festival
C45 La Tomatina
C46 Les Festes de la Merce
C47 Mardi Gras
C48 Oktoberfest
C49 Vardavar
C50 Yi Peng and Loy Krathong
C51 BenchesCollective
C52 International Highline Festival
C53 Minhocao Pool
C54 MoMA PS1
C55 Parasite Cinema
C56 Park and Slide
C57 Park(ing) Day
C58 Pay-Phone Library
C59 Aeolian Ride
C60 Carson & Barnes Traveling Circus
C61 Cavalia
C62 Darwin Beer Can Regatta
C63 Olympics
C64 World Cup
C65 World's Fair
M01 FOB Abu Ghraib
M02 FOB Al Asad
M03 FOB Caldwell
M04 FOB Danger (FOB Iron Horse)
M05 FOB Falcon (Camp Al-Saqr)
M06 FOB Echo
M07 FOB Grizzly
M08 FOB Iskandariyah
M09 FOB Kalsu
M10 FOB Loyalty
M11 FOB Speicher
M12 Camp Cooke (Camp Taji
M13 Camp Adder
M14 Camp Bravo
M15 FOB Border Wolf De
M16 FOB Al Kut
M17 FOB Callahan
M18 FOB Duk
M19 FOB Paliwoda (FOB Eagle)
M20 FOB Warrior (Camp Renegade)
M21 Camp Bucca
M22 Camp Cropper
M23 Camp Baharia
M24 Camp Fallujah
M25 Camp Nama
M26 Camp Victory
M27 Camp Julien
M28 Camp Qargha (Camp Phoenix)
M29 FOB Nijrab
M30 FOB Salerno
M31 Camp Clark
M32 COP Spera
M33 FOB Bostick (FOB Naray)
M34 COP Keating
M35 FOB Joyce
M36 COP Honaker Miracle
M37 FOB Altimur
M38 FOB Shank
M39 FOB Lonestar
M40 FOB Sharana (Camp Kearney)
M41 FOB Tillman (FOB Lwara)
M42 FOB Lightning
M43 FOB Lion
M44 Camp Gibraltar
M45 Camp John Pratt
M46 Camp Spann
M47 Camp Monteith
M48 Camp Doha
M49 Camp New York
M50 Camp Wolverine
M51 Camp Nathan Smith

03

网络化都市主义
In contemporary urbanism around the world, it is becoming clear that for cities to be sustainable, they need to resemble and facilitate active fluxes in motion rather than static material configurations.

our gaze from
pace alone to those
ime, allowing more
nuanced readings
ons of the urban.
Ephemeral Urbanism can teach us how to reintroduce temporality to urbanism's imagery inviting us to ponder aspects of material temporality —such as dematerialization and disassembly— as an integral part of the design of buildings and cities.

THE URBAN-DATA COMPLEX

Forensic Architecture

Can architecture provide new tools of political analysis and intervention? This question is central to the work of Forensic Architecture, a research project and consulting agency based at Goldsmiths, University of London. Since 2011, the project has assembled a team of architects, artists, filmmakers, lawyers, activists, and scientists to undertake research that gathers and presents spatial analysis in legal and political forums. The team investigates the sites of contemporary conflicts in order to monitor state violations of human rights and international law.

Forensic Architecture employs architectural methods and new sensing technologies to examine buildings, ruins, cities, satellite imagery, and an increasingly prevalent type of testimony: images and video clips taken by citizens and uploaded online. From the drone warfare in the Pakistani frontier regions, through the forests of Central and South America to the battlefields of Israel-Palestine, violent conflict raises a host of theoretical, historical, and aesthetic questions at the thresholds of vision and law.

At UABB 2015, Forensic Architecture presents two recent investigations that encapsulate the idea of reading and reconstructing violence through the city form. The exhibited work includes:

01

1. Hannibal in Rafah. Undertaken in close partnership with Amnesty International, this investigation focuses on four days of the summer 2014 attack on Gaza by the Israeli military. The controversial 'Hannibal' directive resulted in the heaviest civilian death toll of the entire conflict, and the extensive destruction of Rafah's built environment.

2. Nakba Day Killings. On May 15, 2014, two Palestinian teenagers were shot and killed by Israeli forces in the town of Beitunia after a day of protests marking Nakba Day. At the request of Defence for Children International Palestine (DCI-P), Forensic Architecture undertook an investigation based on multiple media: sound, image, film, and testimonies.

Credits:
Eyal Weizman, Christina Varvia, Nick Axel, Francesco Sebregondi, Camila E. Sotomayor, Vere Van Gool, Shourideh C. Molavi, Gustav A. Toftgaard, Dorette Panagiotopoulou, Jamon Van Den Hoek, Rosario Güiraldes, Hania Halabi, Jacob Burns, Mohammed Abdullah, Kent Klich, Ana Naomi de Souza, Susan Schuppli, Chris Cobb-Smith, Marc Garlasco, Sophie Dyer, Solveig Suess, Steffen Kraemer, Lawrence Abu Hamdan

02

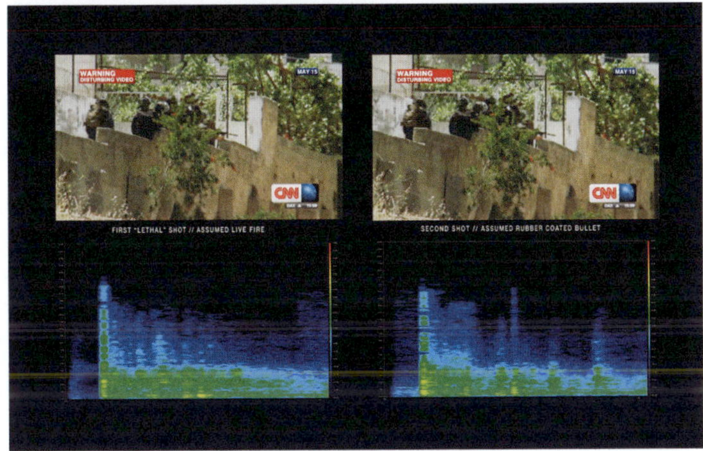

03

01 The image complex was the methodological device for unlocking Hannibal in Rafah. It is a set of time-space relations between hundreds of images and videos that connect through metadata, smoke plume morphologies, testimonies and other clues. 02 The master drawing of the Rafah investigation includes viewpoints and plume measurements from every photograph and video sourced, craters from airdropped bombs and artillery observed on the satellite images, tank paths and armoured vehicles on the move, possible tunnel routes as well as testimony mappings. 03 The investigation of the Nakba Day Killings required the comparison of sound produced by live fire versus rubber-coated bullets. Sonic visualisations allowed Forensic Architecture to determine the lethal shot.

STEREOTYPES: DUMP, CAMP, AND GRAVEYARD

AGENCY

'StereoTypes' projects three near-future urban scenarios that extrapolate from the contemporary fusing of military and domestic space to imagine new potentials and liabilities.

Current military training initiatives focus on the physical form of developing cities, which constitute a collapsing 'securocratic' territory. Simulated favelas, slums, shantytowns, and 'ghetto blocks' appear today in military installations throughout the world. At the same time, humanitarian organisations build simulated informal settlements to prepare for complex emergency and response scenarios. Private companies, tech start-ups, and logistics experts construct empty replica cities as urban laboratories. One such environment, the Center for Innovation, Testing, and Evaluation (CITE), currently being planned in New Mexico, would eclipse its military predecessors. The appetite for urban simulation will only continue to expand.

'StereoTypes' consists of a series of nine large metal prints proposing new futures for nine real-world sites. These sites represent three of the most frequently simulated and contested informal urban typologies: the Dump, the Camp, and the Graveyard. More specifically, inhabited landfills, protracted refugee camps, and squatter-occupied cemeteries represent an evolving frontier of international security interests, increasingly targeted as hotbeds of dissidence and victims of exploitation by violent non-state actors. AGENCY – an interdisciplinary, U.S.-based practice – identified nine 'sister' sites for research and speculative design. Their process was to extract components of each site and transplant them into a new urban scenario, creating models for 'training neighbourhoods' of a super-scale simulation city.

AGENCY imagines new models of 'securocratic timeshares', in which civilian and military actors are mutually responsible for the design and developmental logic of this shared city. Training scenarios are grafted onto public space and building code, fostering a type of counter-code that incentivises security challenges and risks. The relentless order of militaristic organisation is broken by the contingencies of simulation and informal development. Urban form is written as a relational scenario. Islands of experimentation and unpredictability inhabit a field of authority and control. Evacuation and occupation are ingrained in the complicit urban fabric.

Credits:
Ersela Kripa and Stephen Mueller, Principals
Christopher Taurasi, Research and Graphics
Liang Zhihao and Wang Yicheng, Installation
Xin Yu, Installation Coordination

01 StereoType | Camp (Balata). 02 StereoType | Camp (Al Zaatari). 03 StereoType | Graveyard (City of the Dead).

04 StereoType | Dump (Olusosun).

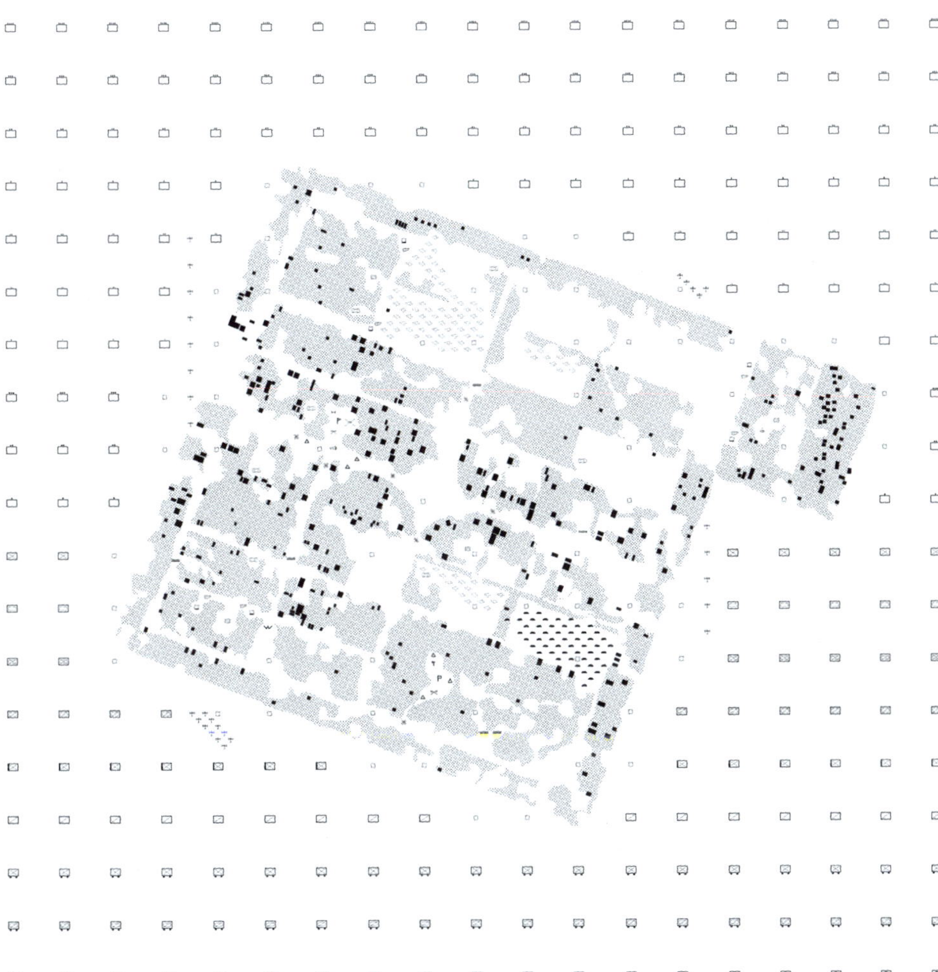

05

05 StereoType | Graveyard (Makati).

MOMENTS IN-BETWEEN

Iwan Baan

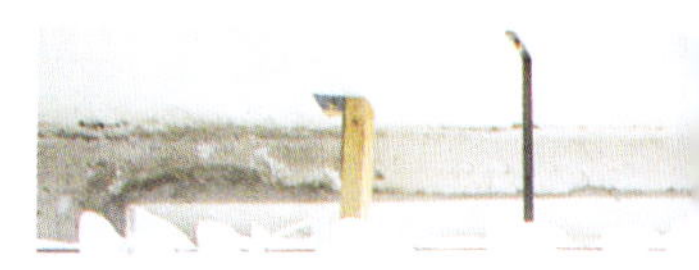

Diane Arbus once said, 'the camera is a kind of license'. My work as a photographer has granted me a license – to travel, to interact, to witness, document, and observe – places and people across the world.

Many of you visiting this exhibition may know my work from photographs in magazines, books, or newspapers. But there is a lot that you can't see in a photograph. The sound of the resident jazz-band. The epic rainstorm that challenges the rammed-earth walls of a centuries-old village in the north of Ghana. Or the story that a toothless farmer recalls about how life is changing in rural china.

I use Instagram to share the sort of secrets that are happening all around me when I am photographing. You'll see here very little 'architecture' as these are moments that occur between the buildings, between the travels, and between the commissions.

01

01 Sunday morning at the beach in Baku, Azerbaijan.

02

02 Desert sand castles in the Uyghur territory of Xinjiang Uyghur Autonomous Region in northwest China.

03

03 Above the never-ending sea of São Paulo.

04

04 Flying over the blanket of dwellings and shops that make up Kibera, an informal community in the centre of Nairobi.

UPROOTING URBAN DESIGN AS WE KNEW IT: THE 'NEW NORMAL' AND THE RETURN OF UTOPIA

Pedro Gadanho

1.

Imagine Los Angeles as a huge slum. Evaded by its rich elites, abandoned by the creative classes that once furnished its allure, the spread-out metropolis is the violent stage for the ancient game of the survival of the fittest. This is the scenario posed by South-African film director Neill Blomkamp in his 2014 feature film, *Elysium*. Taking both the rise of inequality and the idea of gated community to their logical epitomes, this Hollywood production proposes that privileged populations would finally migrate to a super-slick, perfectly landscaped satellite orbiting the Earth. Barely visible in the skies, this ultimate technological achievement of the libertarian mindset would leave the impoverished masses to fend for themselves on the surface of an exhausted, polluted planet.

Elysium illustrates the intellectual high-end of trends in recent popular film entertainment that divide neatly into two main categories: the reenactment of the classic catastrophe movie, and the new teen-oriented dystopian flick franchise. Like slums and gated communities for architecture, these two typologies probably represent the fastest growing genres in the film industry today. Since the middle of the 20th century, the best minds have decoded popular Hollywood productions as a parti-cularly clear manifestation of our collective subconscious, and today we should stop and consider what the advance of these genres means to contemporary society, and indeed to the fields of architecture and citymaking.

In the omnipresent science fiction movies of the 1950s, alien invasions stood for the menace of Communist subjugation. More recently, an unstoppable proliferation of zombie movies has been equated with a social divide in which the working classes are portrayed as 'walking dead'. Catastrophe movies have a long pedigree, but have become particularly vehement since the 1973 oil crisis. They now signal the emergence of a 'new normal' of permanent catastrophe in which climate change, terrorist acts, major technological accidents, and massive refugee crises have become an everyday blight. What may be more interesting to consider here, however, is the sudden and mounting popularity of dystopian fictions. Faced with pervasive depictions of dystopia – and what these express about our most ingrained collective fears at the moment – one may start to understand the reemergence of utopian thinking, its inverse, as a radical political stance.

2.

The 'new normal' of perpetual crisis is reflected in various sectors of current thinking. In economics, it relates to the potential advent of a 'secular stagnation', as former U.S. Secretary of the Treasury Larry Summers has put it. The implication is that constant economic growth is no longer the macro-economic rule. In political terms this has translated – and will continue to translate – into the imperative to inflict austerity as a permanent norm. This imposition, on the other hand, represents nothing but a compulsory anticipation of the need to rethink the use and consumption of resources, soon clearly to be insufficient to sustain a world population that is growing both in absolute numbers and relative affluence. This being said, we won't even address the 'new normal' of the increasing number of scientific reports indicating a steady progression towards the mass-extinction of the human race.

The field of architecture and urban planning has done little to accommodate and reflect such notions. The majority of the field is still clinging to traditional notions of practice, thus blindfolding itself to violent massive change. In its mainstream version, it takes refuge in the lack of responsibility that comes with its willing transformation into an obedient, *a*critical service industry. In its intellectual sectors, it hides behind the bubble of disciplinary autonomy, through both the infantile embrace of parametricism, and the stubborn clasp of a vaguely minimal and conceptual formalism.

The 'new normal', however, demands a radical transformation of practice. And radical practice means the fundamental uprooting of the meaning of architecture as we used to know it, not to mention the faster mutation of the role of design thinking. This is where an utopian drive that was dormant during some decades of post-critical numbness kicks back in.

3.

As seen against a normative proliferation of dystopian scenarios, 'doing the right thing' is now a radical gesture. From the more conservative standpoints of the 'new normal' – characterised by a desperate need to deny the situation itself – the belief in the ability to effect change, the desire to strike a balance between opposites so as to overcome impending disaster, are now the attitudes under attack.

Today, even the suggestion to reposition a given practice towards a greater political and social responsibility may be dismissed as extremist. With respect to urban design, any hint at the need to address the informal sectors of developing urban conglomerations whose populations suffer the effects of poverty will be disregarded as an expression of *slum-porn*. This stratagem has, of course, the goal to ridicule any deviation from the kind of normative practice that inherits the neo-colonialist, rationalist legacy of Western modernism. Above all, however, such petty ploys reveal a notorious incomprehension of the degree of radicalness that the present moment asks for – not unlike the historical moment in which the early modern avant-gardes countered the intensification of industrialisation and the catastrophe of global war with the demand for a new language.

Curiously, it is in the face of a doubly dystopian mindset – i.e. the penchant for disaster and its simultaneous denial – that we can understand an almost inevitable reemergence of radical modes of utopian thinking. Above all utopia was born as an instrument of critique. More's *Utopia* produced a critical assessment of the status quo by devising an alternative, placeless model of the state, as well as the organisation of the polis that commanded it. The 'new normal' desperately calls for this sort of critical assessment. Thus we should be seriously considering – or celebrating – the alternative modes of practice that have emerged in recent years as seismographers of a wide-ranging adjustment to a new context. We should be setting, or at least recognising, the theoretical frameworks that evaluate the nature of the transformations at hand, while radically uprooting obsolete and inadequate disciplinary norms.

4.

But we should know better than to throw out the baby with the bath water. If we want to strike a new radical balance, we cannot dismiss the knowledge, the technologies and the design intelligence that has accumulated in the culture, or disciplinary discourse of architecture. In fact, it is only fair to expect that the radical urban practices that may offer a response to the emergence of the 'new normal' find their seeds and sources in the recent, if unbuilt history of architecture and urban design.

The renewed interest in the so-called radical urban practices of the 1970s offers an opportunity, as I have modestly tried to suggest in the exhibition, 9+1 *Ways of Being Political* (2012), to reinterpret the work of Archigram, Superstudio, Archizoom, and other radical designers, as a source of political inspiration, rather than as a mere iconographic archive from which to extract fashionable forms.

The poignancy of such proposals at utopian references lies precisely in their unrealised status. Had the designs been achieved, their historical potential would probably have been exhausted. On the contrary, their wildly imaginative, unbuilt ideas are now ripe for a technological and conceptual upgrade, as well as for what Brillembourg and Klumpner call 'an unflinching engagement with social reality.'

Ultimately, this was the underlying reasoning in some of the design scenarios created for for the exhibition *Uneven Growth, Tactical Urbanisms for Expanding Megacities* (2014). On one hand, in the work of Hong Kong-based Map Office with the Network Architecture Lab, one could discover a conscious reprise of Superstudio's dystopian urban tales so as to produce a political critique of current totalitarian *dérives* based upon a fierce urban and territorial expansion. On the other hand, in the proposal of Pop Lab MIT with Mumbai-based Urbz, one could identify a continuation of Yona Friedman's ideas as filtered through the logic of self-construction and 'home-grown' communities, as a visionary form of opposition to disruptive gentrification processes.

When it comes to a potential notion of radical urbanism, these positions hint at a new and necessary conjunction of top-down disciplinary resources with tactical, bottom-up impulses. However, they also make clear two variants of radical practice corresponding to the reuse of dystopia as a tool of cultural critique and, on the other side, a desire to revisit utopian blueprints as a source for socially and politically committed visionary design thinking.

5.

What we now call 'traditional' top-down urban planning – that is, the orthodoxy that defined Western modernisation from Haussmann to Le Corbusier – originally appeared as a radical and uprooting force. The full eradication and hygienisation of the historical urban tissue was the only way forward, justified by an ideal vision of the city. In the field of architecture, such ideas have become deeply naturalised. They still represent the discipline's subconscious tenet for the 'new normal'. Curiously, the attempt to overcome such a mentality is what now breathes the potential of revolutionary political radicalism.

Pedro Gadanho is the Director of the Museum of Art, Architecture and Technology (MAAT) in Lisbon, Portugal. He previously served as Curator of Contemporary Architecture at the Museum of Modern Art, New York.

HOW RADICAL IS 'RADICAL URBANISM'?

Justin McGuirk

The last movement to call itself 'radical' left no trace on the city.

Superstudio, Archizoom, and the other members of Radical Design loom large in the history of 1970s Italy, but they traded in ideas and images, not buildings. Since not building was the whole point, they were doomed to success. Their position was articulated by Germano Celant, in an essay of 1972[1], as one of refusal – the refusal to be commercialised, to become a tool of the client. A radical architecture, in Celant's view, 'offers nothing but its ideological and behavioural attitudes'.

This was certainly neither the first nor the last time that architecture had sought refuge in images. But when the avant-garde confines itself to paper it is normally because there is no alternative: during recession, under ideological oppression, or because its visions are unbuildable. What is interesting about Celant's argument is that it is a response to architecture's very success – a response to too much building, too many 'finished objects'. His proposed solution is to opt out of the system and adopt a McLuhanite stance in which architecture is an expanded medium of thought.

This is a luxurious position. Those who argue for the autonomy of architecture are probably not as interested in society as they pretend. This is not to dismiss architects as cultural producers

1 — Germano Celant, 'Radical Architecture,' in *Italy: The New Domestic Landscape: Achievements and Problems of Italian Design*, ed. Emilio Ambasz (New York: The Museum of Modern Art, 1972), 380-387.

– Superstudio's collages were in many ways prophetic, as resonant of our networked present as they were of the gridded midcentury. Indeed, there is a shortage of radical image-making today (who are the Superstudios or the Hans Holleins of the 2010s, wielding the pure, propositional image as a tool to assert that *Alles ist architektur?*). However, should we not liberate the notion of the radical from the avant-garde? Most often the radical has been the preserve of a cultural elite, of 'high' architecture. In the early 20th century, from Constructivism to Corbu, the avant-garde was still coupled to a progressive socialist vision, but that has long since ceased to be the case. Today's self-professed avant-garde of digital form-makers and parametricists could not be more irrelevant to the urban challenges we face. So perhaps we need a new definition. Is it possible to be radical and to effect actual urban and social change?

The only way to begin answering that question is by asking what we mean by 'radical'. We associate it with sudden change, and in particular with a modernist doctrine that wilfully broke with the past. And because mankind is hardwired to fear such change, we read into it a form of extremism – the 'radical Left' or 'radical Islam'. However, returning to the word's Latin origins – root – we might see it not just as root-and-branch change but as root-and-branch *growth*. In other words, a radical city is one that has been built up from the roots, or by what we loosely term the 'grass roots' – by the underprivileged many. There is an opportunity to divorce the radical in architecture from its traditional connotations of cultural elitism.

Given that informal cities represent the prevailing form of urban growth across the Global South, one might argue that radical urbanism is not so much a practice but a context. It is the ability to operate in a self-built urban environment generated with such speed and on such a scale that it has rendered the formal provision of architecture and urban planning impotent. In all of these senses, the favelas, comunas and townships are the radical city. Indeed, this is consistent with Celant's argument that Radical Design was radical because it operated outside the architectural system. The informal city does just that. And it is because of these communities' self-reliance, during decades of disenfranchisement, that they also embody a political radicalism – one thinks of how the barrios of Caracas were a stronghold of Chavez's Bolivarian revolution in Venezuela.

The radical always exists at the margins. But it can be brought closer to the centre, gradually accepted within institutional norms. In *Radical Cities* (2014), I argued that just such a process has been underway in Latin America over the past 20 years. The book studies an archipelago of projects across the region that have attempted to address the extreme urban inequality created by mass migration and political neglect. Taken collectively, what they represent is the acceptance of the informal city and the return of political responsibility for what were once considered outlaw zones. These improvements to infrastructure, housing and transport in self-built communities amount to an attempt to re-institutionalise areas that had long existed outside of institutional responsibility.

This process of gradual slum-upgrading is far more sensitive and pragmatic than the so-called radicalism of Corbusian mass housing systems from the mid-century, which erased the informal to create a tabula rasa. Starting from scratch is so much more radical, in theory, than incremental change. So why call Latin America's recent interventions 'radical'? Again, it is the context more than the practice. Slum builders have far superseded what could ever have been achieved by paternalistic governments when it comes to incorporating millions of people into the city – in that sense alone, the slum, for all its privations, has been the more effective tool.

One could easily argue, and some have, that *Radical Cities* is not radical enough. My contention was that 'activist architects' such as Urban-Think Tank, Alejandro Aravana, and Teddy Cruz were radical not just in operating in the margins but in not waiting for the system to invite them in. By goading politicians into action and self-initiating projects on behalf of the poorest – incidentally, Celant also saw self-initiation as a condition of Radical Design – they were challenging the traditional role of the architect as at the service of a patron. But perhaps, instead of acting as these benign mediators between poverty and power, true radicalism would involve letting the people look after their own interests. Relying so heavily on architects seems to ignore the revolutionary potential of the user-generated community. Perhaps radical urbanism is no urbanism, at least of the professional variety.

Certainly that position has had its moments. In the 1960s, Cedric Price, Reyner Banham, and others published *Non-Plan*, a call to abandon sclerotic regulations and return the city to citizens and their natural self-organising talents. John Turner took a similar position in arguing that the slum-dweller's shack was more empowering than a flat in a peripheral tower block. But neither Price nor Turner quite anticipated the scale of informal settlement in the developing world. And, more importantly, while spontaneous communities are perfectly capable of building themselves homes, they cannot build themselves, say, a piece of transport infrastructure. Or, at least, they should not have to. One notable exception was a community in Cairo, which, in the chaos following the Arab Spring, built itself four access ramps to the elevated highway that had long overshot it. I've heard this phenomenon heralded as the 'wikicity'. But this approach seems far from wise.

Extreme self-reliance and adhocism are not conducive to effective infrastructure projects. Ultimately, supporting participative citymaking does not have to result in *nostalgie de la boue* – it doesn't mean condoning the jerry-rigged city. If the 'activist architect' can achieve anything, it is to connect these popular impulses to the public resources and strategic planning required to deliver them. The radical city requires new systems that support and liberate its citizens, especially those currently disenfranchised by them. That means intervening in the 'dark matter' of legislation and zoning laws but also creating new construction systems.

To return to Cedric Price, his notion of the 'anticipatory architect', one who provides open structures that citizens can inhabit and adapt as they see fit, seems purpose-built for the radical city. Even in Price's day this was not a new idea: Le Corbusier's Dom-ino House of 1914 was just that. In theory, open systems offer both framework and freedom – forms that can accommodate the informal. The challenge of the radical city today is that so much of it is a *fait accompli*, a fact on the ground. How much harder it is to adapt and retrofit dense hillside communities after the fact. Architecture needs to anticipate and facilitate spontaneous urban growth. What was lacking in the late 20th century, apart from political will, was anticipation – and that is precisely what has to change in the 21st century.

Justin McGuirk is the Chief Curator at the Design Museum London and the head of Design Curating & Writing at Design Academy Eindhoven. His book, *Radical Cities: Across Latin America in Search of a New Architecture*, was published in 2014.

AUTONOMY & AUTODIGESTION

Lydia Kallipoliti

The word 'autonomy' has a twisted history in architectural production.

It is most often associated with Peter Eisenman – founder of the Institute for Architecture and Urban Studies in the 1960s and editor of its journal, *Oppositions* – who has consistently argued for an inner logic exclusive to architectural thought; a logic so tightly insular that it cannot migrate to other disciplines or applications. According to Michael Hays, Eisenman developed a posthumanist paradigm founded on the antihumanist theories of Michel Foucault and Claude Levi-Strauss.[1] This intellectual legacy helped Eisenman to conceive of a kind of autonomy in which, in Hays's words, 'authorship can resist the authority of culture, stand against the generality of habit and the particularity of nostalgic memory, and still have a very precise intention'.[2]

While autonomy was interrogated as an ideational vehicle to fortify the boundaries of disciplinary fields, it was also, during the 1970s, used to popularise an ecological and libertarian way of living and acting and to herald 'autonomy' from the grid of urban supplies. In *Architectural Design's* January 1976 issue, entitled

1 — See K. Michael Hays, "The Oppositions of Autonomy and History," in K. Michael Hays (ed.), *Oppositions Reader: Selected Readings from a Journal for Ideas and Criticism in Architecture, 1973-1984* (New York: Princeton Architectural Press, 1998), p.x.

2 — K. Michael Hays, "Critical Architecture: Between Culture and Form," in *Perspecta* Vol. 21 (1984), p.27.

Fig. 1 **Cover of *Architectural Design* (AD), January 1976, on 'Autonomous Houses'.**
The cover was drawn in ink by Clifford Harper, a British underground illustrator who contributed to Undercurrents magazine and Radical Technology.

'Autonomous Houses' and edited by Martin Spring and Haig Beck, 'autonomy' not only harkened back to a grass-roots mentality and a pastoral iconography,[3] but also implied an existential separation of the individual from the urban fabric and ultimately from the social sphere (fig. 1). Following the oil crisis and a decade of environmental debates, the terms 'self-sufficiency', 'self-reliance', 'life-support' and 'living autonomy' became part of a pervasive lexicon describing alternative technologies that continue to preoccupy the British avant-garde. The biological definition of autonomy refers to a system's organic independence and self-governance. Transferred to the domestic realm of architecture, this concept was used to advance the idea of the house as a closed system, un-rooted from an urban context. The self-sufficient, autonomous house was like a restored Garden of Eden and a real-time habitation experiment where architecture, systems theory, and human biology could blend in the hope of radical social reform

These positions represented two entirely different, but parallel threads of autonomy in architecture culture throughout the 1970s. On the one hand, the countercultural environmental movement equated autonomy with organic self-sufficiency and presaged the emancipation of the individual from authoritative state mechanisms. On the other hand, for the Institute for Architecture and Urban Studies, autonomy heralded the emancipation of the discipline itself, by excluding the human from architectural thought and production.

It is precisely in the wake of this ideological battle that an expanded history of architectural autonomy can be written. Autonomy should be seen as a type of operational closure or detachment from context, whether this detachment is defined as the liberation of the individual from authoritative state

3 — See 'Cooperative Autonomies', notes by the editors Martin Spring and Haig Beck, in the contents page of *Architectural Design* Vol. XLVI (Jan. 1976). See also Peter Harper and Godfrey Boyle (eds.), *Radical Technology* (New York: Pantheon Books, A Division of Random House, 1976).

mechanisms, or as the liberation of the discipline from questions of culture, politics, and history.

On the one hand, the title 'Autonomy & Autodigestion' suggests that these two ideals of emancipation reflect a stagnant idea of utopia in reinventing the world from scratch by demarcating the borders of disciplines and territories. If the planet is now becoming one city by means of increasing urbanisation, and if the discipline of architecture is increasingly fused with biology, policy, fabrication, ecology and governance (among other fields), we could rightfully ask: autonomy from what and from whom? As Manfredo Tafuri argued in the 1970s, there are no more utopias in the era of late capitalism.[4] Any idea of utopia ends up eating its own roots, as suggested by the word 'autodigestion'.[5] But on the other hand, it is precisely this investment in the realm of impossibility, of redefining the reality of our built world and our disciplinary territories, which allows architecture and the city to reconstitute themselves.

The next question becomes: is 'Autonomy & Autodigestion' a radical form of urbanism?

This exhibition answers an emphatic 'Yes.' Indeed, 'Autonomy & Autodigestion' might be the last vestige of a radical form of urbanism and of disciplinary production: that is, to take a position and its opposite and examine them exhaustively, reciprocally, until either there is nothing left or something new comes out. The spectre of Western thought, 'all things in moderation,' originating from ancient Greek philosophy (πάν μέτρον άριστον), might no longer be applicable to a world defined by the seeming excess of a singularly urbanised planet. As Joyce Hsiang and Bimal Mendis write, 'No part of the world remains unaffected

4 — Manfredo Tafuri, *Architecture and Utopia: Design and Capitalist Development*, trans. Barbara Luigia La Penta (Cambridge, Mass: MIT Press, 1976).

5 — The word 'auto-digestion', otherwise stated as 'self-digestion' or 'autolysis', describes a process whereby the stomach's pancreatic enzymes destroy its own tissue; in other words, it is a pathological digestive process where the stomach eats its borders by receiving the wrong signals. In John Hopkins Medicine Library online, see http://www.hopkinsmedicine.org/healthlibrary/conditions/endocrinology/pancreatitis_85,P00681/ (accessed November 4, 2015).

Fig. 2 **Sphere of the Unknown—The urban envelope from the depths of the ocean to outer space.** Courtesy Plan B Architecture & Urbanism, Joyce Hsiang and Bimal Mendis. Exhibited in 'City of 7 Billion: A Constructed World'.

by the cumulative impact of human activity. Through complex processes of exploration, habitation, cultivation, transportation, consumption, and surveillance, the world has become completely interconnected'.[6] And it is in this interconnected world that we can invent new worlds as well as create new forms of space and urbanization, which might enable us to effect change (fig. 2).

'Autonomy & Autodigestion' posits citizenship as an active agent to reclaim the city, to address growing inequality created by climbing real estate values, and to use creative ingenuity to mark new territories; in the use of local resources, in seizing, squatting, communizing, and taking ownership of urban space. The bottom-

6 — Joyce Hsiang and Bimal Mendis, curatorial statement for the exhibition, *City of 7 Billion: A Constructed World*, at the Yale School of Architecture (Sept. 3–Nov. 14, 2015).

up nature of the projects and the empowerment of local voices through the formation of federations speak to a quiet and slow upheaval against the masterplan, the urban grid, and the distribution of power through authoritative networks; they speak of a social insurgency against the city plan as an authoritative control mechanism over cities, bodies, ecologies, and atmospheres.

Beyond taking up questions of inequality and social justice, 'Autonomy & Autodigestion' proposes a radical space, and a radical urban formation. It speaks of a city emerging from within the very fabric of the grid, an alternative localised organisation: a seed, a juncture, a focal point, rising from the roots or the *radix* (as the etymology the word 'radical' suggests) of the city's texture, from the inner workings of the city itself. This new formation is neither a central, decentralised, nor networked grid superimposed on the city's form. It is rather a spatial federation, a byproduct of urban processes and daily practices. It questions the structure of our urban fabric and thus our social fabric, as well as the spatial distribution of power in the urban sphere.

As argued by Paul Baran's 1964 paper, 'On Distributed Communications Networks', a distributed communication network – as distinct from a centralised or decentralised network – offers greater flexibility and the possibility of partial operation in cases of shutdowns from the main supply network (fig. 3).[7] Similar principles apply to other types of urban supply networks. Revisiting Baran's paper, Stijn Peeters argues that there is yet another network model to consider: the federated network.[8] The word itself hints at similarities with the political concept of a federation, where users may potentially become members of a coalition and act coherently as a group. An urban block micro-grid, partially powered by resident

7 — Baran, Paul. "On Distributed Communications Networks." *Communications Systems, IEEE Transactions* on 12.1 (1964), pp. 1–9.

8 — Stijn Peeters, "Beyond distributed and decentralised: What is a federated network?" *Unlike Us #3, Social Media: Design or Decline* in http://networkcultures.org/wpmu/unlikeus/resources/articles/what-is-a-federated-network/, accessed April 27, 2014.

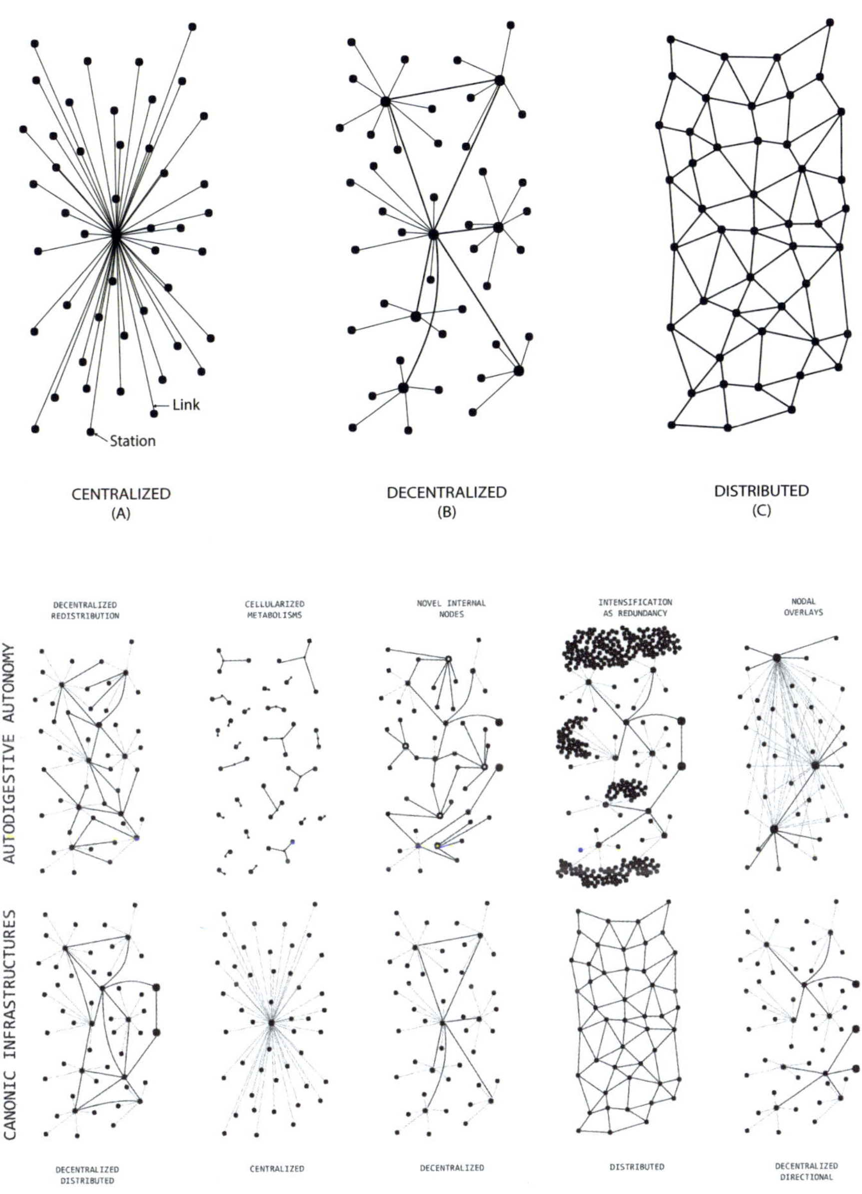

Fig.3 Illustration from Paul Baran, 'On Distributed Communication Networks', 1962.
Fig.4 Diagram for alternative micro-grid urban organisations, Meg Studer, 2015.

activities, constitutes an example of a federated network. A micro-grid displays a collective and a communal initiative to organise the distribution of energy, and thus a measure of civic power, at a local level. It is an attempt to change the city from within, by growing the seeds of alternative organisations and spaces inside it, and by defying and hence redefining the grid of centralised control (fig. 4). Within the premises of a defined urban territory, a radical form or urbanism might be one that enables civic federation, or one that enables residents to become community stakeholders by providing them with tools to act coherently as a group and to develop infra-structural mechanisms.

Therefore, 'Autonomy & Autodigestion' marks the demise of the city, of nature and of citizenship as indeterminate fields of their own, and subsequently proposes their translation in terms of resources and their exploitation in a continuous cycle. It speaks of the formation of new economies and self-sufficient islands in the city, detached from the centralised grid of authority and control. The autonomous worlds in such propositions document a larger disciplinary transformation in the late twentieth century toward self-management, citizen participation in the making of cities, and a new form of a synthetic naturalism that displaces the laws of nature and metabolism from the domain of wilderness to the domain of urban space. Now it is possible for anyone or anything to emerge as a potential builder of urban infrastructure. New cities are growing within cities.

Exhibition and Project Credits:
Lydia Kallipoliti, Meg Studer, Kyong Kim with the assistance of Royd Zhang and Ellen Wong

Lydia Kallipoliti, PhD, is an Assistant Professor of Architecture at Rensselaer Polytechnic Institute. Trained as an architect and engineer, she is Principal of EcoRedux research network and ANAcycle design+writing studio.

AUTONOMY &
AUTODIGESTION
自主性和自我消化
1997
1990
1985
1

AUTONOMY &
AUTODIGESTION
GARBAGE
CITY
MICROBIAL
2004
2004
1976
1972
1970
1969

ISLAND CITY
2007
1990
1971
1950
MANIFESTO #4
宣言#4
DEGROWTH CITY
LIMINAL ISLAND
Grande Hotel Beira: Shelter For Anyone
Kowloon, Walled City: City of Darkness
Street Farmer: Farming clearings in a concrete jungle

SEVEN CITIES

Lydia Kallipoliti
and Meg Studer

GARBAGE CITY MANIFESTO #1

Garbage City is a phantom city; one that we cannot see or do not wish to see. First, *Garbage City* grows out of the metropolis and exists as a secondary invisible layer enmeshed in the urban fabric. Second, *Garbage City* is an unintentional city that sprawls on the cheap land surrounding developing capitals and is informally built up from masses of obsolete materials. *Garbage City*, however, is not a fiction. It is the byproduct of a city that grows without control and beyond our sight. It encroaches through the urban fabric to the blank lands surrounding cities; it invades the water and even the air we breathe.

The term 'garbage housing' was adopted in the late 1960s by the British pioneer of 'garbage architecture' Martin Pawley. Pawley translated the laws of nature and metabolism, in a logistical and operative statistical game, by suggesting the immediate reuse of the leftover materials from global consumption. Perceiving buildings as an interface of global resources, Pawley proposed that consumer byproducts be fed back into the loop of production as new building materials. With his various writings on garbage architecture, Pawley merged two predicaments of the time, the housing crisis and excessive waste flows, hoping to salvage two crises by feeding one into the other. His aspiration

GARBAGE CITY

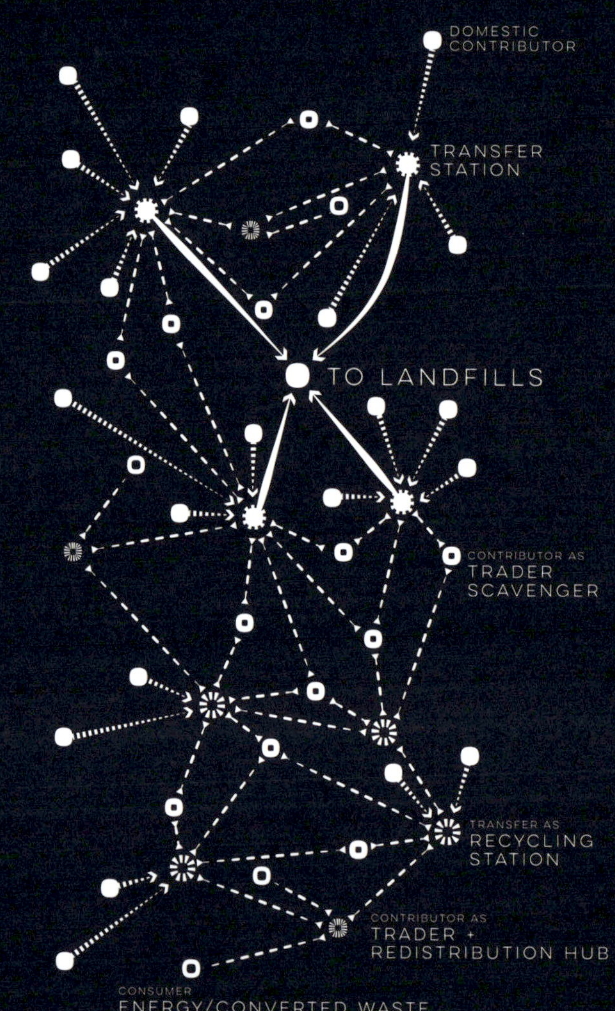

REWORKED, RECYCLED

was that by-products of urban environments might be recycled just as natural systems recycle their wastes. Pawley conceived Garbage Housing to confront a vast and urgent social problem, namely the solid waste crisis, for which the US National Academy of Science called for solutions by 1966.

In recent decades, garbage is no longer an issue that relates solely to quantity. It now also relates to the intricacy of the waste matter and its material composition. Electronic waste, known as e-waste, is the largest growing sector of waste in the world. Electronics recycling has become an excruciating task that requires a new type of intensive manual labour reportedly exported to Asian slums and prison houses. The process of purging indestructible waste has given rise to 'para-economies' on a global scale. Heaps of accumulated obsolete matter are exported out of western metropolises and re-lived by a population charged to convert waste into capital. Recycling waste to money is as much a subject of theoretical analysis as a factual constituent of capitalist production. Waste needs to go away; and this very process of purging, transporting and carrying into oblivion all that is worthless is utterly profitable.

Similarly, the Great Pacific Gyre in the North Pacific Ocean is a by-product of social reality. Wasted fragmented materials coagulate and manifest as islands, cohering from a soup of waste to cell-like locales, places that exist beyond our perception of urban daily life. These emergent *Garbage Cities* now force us to delve deeper into the geochemical affinities between capital and excrement.

MICROBIAL CITY MANIFESTO #2

Most revolutions start from the streets. However, the one called for in Microbial City does not begin in the streets nor in public demonstrations, but from the inner city: the domestic interior of the urban fabric. To battle the highly structured detritus of metropolitan imagination, a radical urban practice can start from the house and the way of inhabiting the land. *Microbial City* suggests that we may effect change in the city as a whole, through tactical changes in small pieces – islands of habitation taken 'off the grid' of energy supply.

In the late 1960s and early 1970s, amidst debates over pollution, the overpopulation of the earth, global catastrophe and the social role of science and technology, tinkering with biology – or managing the living matter of humans, animals and plants – was examined as an alternative and radical model of urbanisation. At the time, political radicals learned how to milk a cow rather than how to fire a gun. The cow's excrement could be used as an engine, in order to produce methane. Essentially the cow was a tool that would enable the city's resident to detach from the grid of energy supplies and the authoritative mechanisms of the state. At the time, biotechnical research brought close two fields that had been considered disjunctive: high technology, in the form of microbial

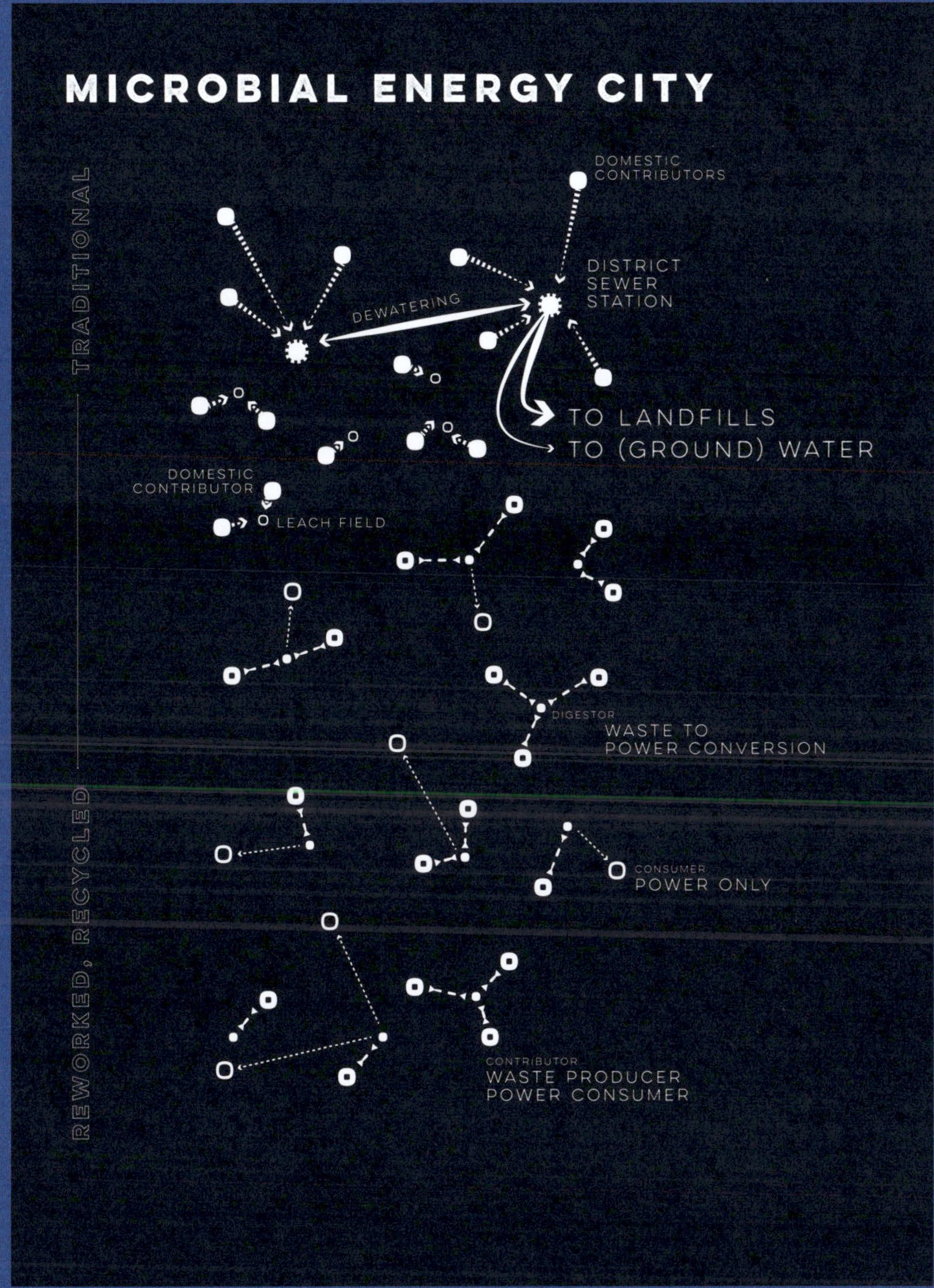
MICROBIAL ENERGY CITY
TRADITIONAL
DOMESTIC CONTRIBUTORS
DISTRICT SEWER STATION
DEWATERING
TO LANDFILLS
TO (GROUND) WATER
DOMESTIC CONTRIBUTOR
LEACH FIELD
REWORKED, RECYCLED
DIGESTOR
WASTE TO POWER CONVERSION
CONSUMER
POWER ONLY
CONTRIBUTOR
WASTE PRODUCER
POWER CONSUMER

management and material conversion; with rural life, in the form of living in proximity with nature.

The Ecological House built by the Street Farmers in 1972 was not only a house, but also a manifesto. Through the recirculation of all resources, it announced a radical urban reconstruction that would proceed by ripple effect from the domestic sphere to all the city's fabric. The process of building a house was in many respects a reactionary social practice that spoke of a new urban vision, reconstructing the city from the inside little by little. Thirty years later, this type of research by group of radical leftist urban provocateurs, has been taken up anew by the Philips Corporation to produce an experimental probe for a domestic ecosystem that challenges conventional design solutions to energy, cleaning, food preservation, lighting and human waste. If our world is at present in a state of disturbed equilibrium, the planning of sustainable cities and environments may in fact dwell in biological processes, which are less energy-consuming and non-polluting.

DEGROWTH CITY MANIFESTO #3

Degrowth City is the physical counterpart of capitalism's decline in the late twentieth century. It is the city's periphery, niche, obsolescence, decay and abandonment; it is the leftover urban space that no longer serves any purpose and lies lifeless like a carcass. As Julia Czerniak has pointed out, *Degrowth City* is 'formerly urban'. It is a city of past glory whose urban character has devolved radically due to economic, demographic and physical change.

Degrowth City is the materialised junkspace of the defunct idea for unstoppable progress and economic growth. It is the sum of urbanisation that we do not know what to do with. When faced with the urgency to revitalise *Degrowth City*, the architect and the urbanist are confronted with anxiety and melancholy. A sense of emptiness follows the realisation that the empire to which we have laid all hope is nothing but a powder of formless ruins and we are only left with fossils of a past that cannot be reassembled.

To deal with such conditions of de-urbanisation and urban wilderness, we might need to consider practices of removal, demolition and destruction. The subtraction of buildings is as important as the making of buildings, yet it is an unexplored and unwanted field of inquiry and practice. In uninhabited rustbelt areas, abandoned buildings often become toxic and harmful; they are literally

DEGROWTH CITY

a source of pollution, even after they cease to consume energy. Could we learn how to destroy them instrumentally little by little? Could we conceive other forms of occupation with non-humans to further the use of these sites and prevent their demise?

In the 1970s, several years before Detroit's urban blight and the emergence of the term 'rustbelt', the Street Farmers suggested planting the streets of London and releasing cows as a practice of radical urbanism against the authoritative mechanisms of the state. Orchestrating destruction was a creative act for the group that explored the aesthetics of erasure and unbuilding. At the same time, the Italian Radicals announced an urbanism of 'counter-design', with Allesandro Mendini's King Kong, defying the city and the city's plan. They proposed a vast unbuilt grid, with pieces of nature, animals and plug-in ports to power-up and create immaterial environments. Today, along these lines, the economic theory of 'degrowth' questions the limits of growth and the idea of linear progress imposed in all aspects of production and daily life through the channels of capitalism. To persevere on a course of growth as we have known it only serves the growth of capital itself, rather than the making of cities of urban environments.

As Ursula Le Guin recently pointed out, the power of capitalism seems inescapable. So did the divine right of kings. Power, nevertheless, can be resisted and changed by humans. Resistance and change often begins with art and imagination, and this is where architecture and urbanism come in.

ISLAND CITY MANIFESTO #4

Island City is an independent enclave growing within the city; it is internally governed and detached from the grid of urban supplies. We can describe this island as a microcosm of the city as a whole, a microcosm, nevertheless, administered on a different set of laws, rules and systems of thought and production. For *Island City*, blockage and seclusion from the surroundings is critical to its identity. The territorial demarcation of boundaries enables material and spatial organisations that would not have been probable in the open field.

William Golding's *Lord of the Flies* (1954), lucidly pictures how a closed system – whether it is a territory, an ecosystem or a social system – produces its own output and regenerates it as input, and starts to behave unpredictably, derailing from the system's original goals. In the novel, a group of young people are cast away on an island, but their situation parallels that of people enclosed in walled cities, like the former City of Kowloon. Walled communities are social experiments as well as spatial experiments; they are new worlds within which elements, materials, people, information and behaviours need to be packed and reorganised in new ways.

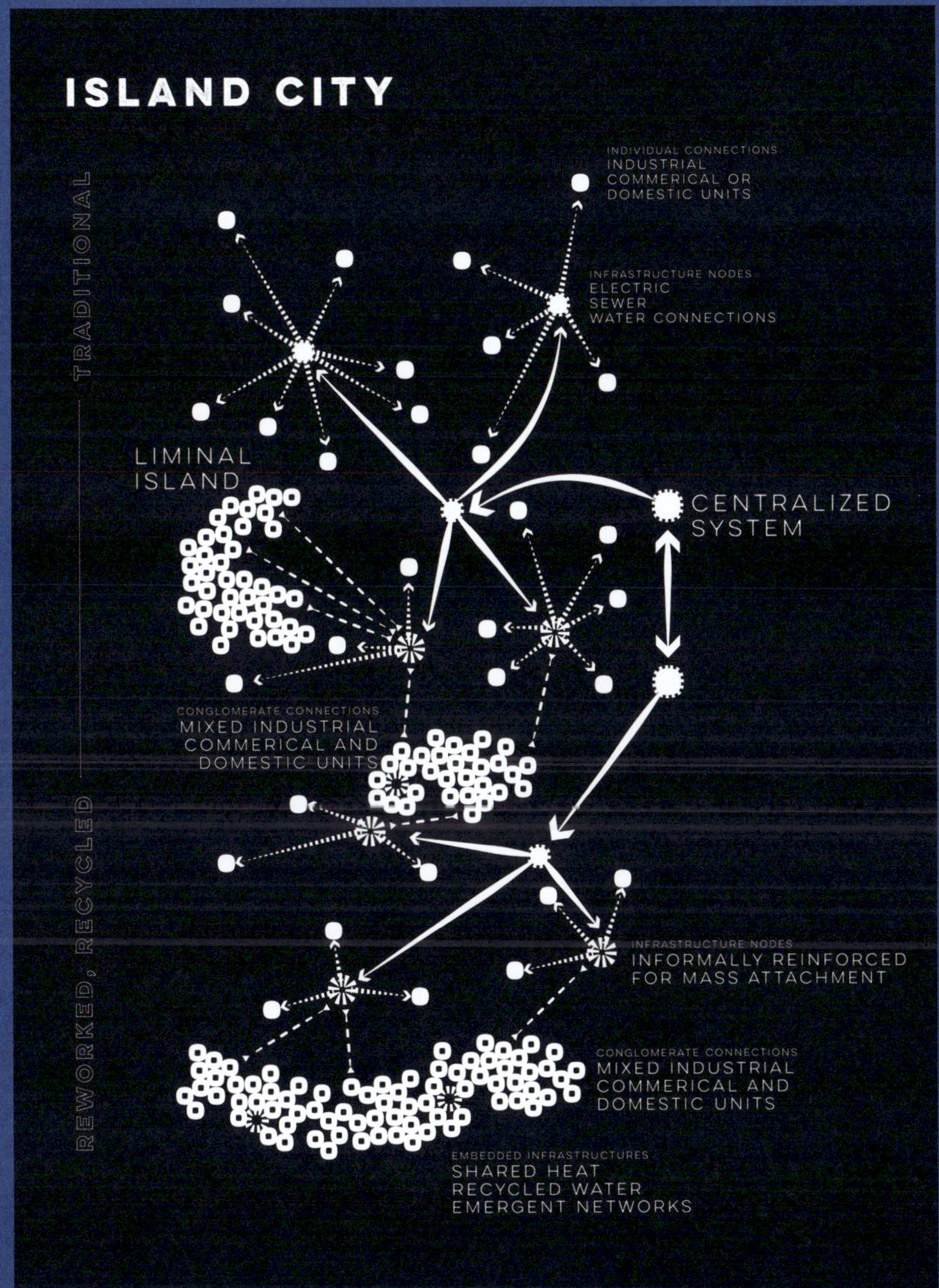
ISLAND CITY
TRADITIONAL
REWORKED, RECYCLED
INDIVIDUAL CONNECTIONS
INDUSTRIAL
COMMERICAL OR
DOMESTIC UNITS
INFRASTRUCTURE NODES
ELECTRIC
SEWER
WATER CONNECTIONS
LIMINAL
ISLAND
CENTRALIZED
SYSTEM
CONGLOMERATE CONNECTIONS
MIXED INDUSTRIAL
COMMERICAL AND
DOMESTIC UNITS
INFRASTRUCTURE NODES
INFORMALLY REINFORCED
FOR MASS ATTACHMENT
CONGLOMERATE CONNECTIONS
MIXED INDUSTRIAL
COMMERICAL AND
DOMESTIC UNITS
EMBEDDED INFRASTRUCTURES
SHARED HEAT
RECYCLED WATER
EMERGENT NETWORKS

Island City is established without permission, without any authorised planning or design process; it is the self-constructed and autonomous space of its dwellers. As such, it is heterogeneous and unique, often associated with chaos, poor infrastructure and crime. *Island City*, however, does not mean disorder. In *Island City*, the condition of blockage enables the production of spaces by using what is available on the spot. Blockage becomes peculiarly productive, as it induces an unforeseen development of material constitutions within the island; the living laboratory.

RESOURCE CITY MANIFESTO #5

Resource City starts with the disclosure of NASA's Earthrise image to the public in 1968, which constituted a profound rupture in human imagination. Previously unknown outside of fictional constructions of cartographic imagination, the reality of the Earth seen from space was captured by the astronauts aboard Apollo 8. It revealed the anatomy of the planet and suggested an external limit to human evolutionary expansion. Earthrise had a profound impact in our understanding of the planet as one body, a unitary interconnected system with finite resources, which needs to be managed. Stewart Brand's *Whole Earth Catalog* (1968-72), published the image of the earth to announce a new mindset: 'access to tools'. The logistics of global resources, information management and classification of goods were no longer just analytical tools, but also propositional tools; logistics and statistics helped to document and therefore reconstruct the world in a different order.

Buckminster Fuller, John McHale, and Ian McHarg played a seminal role in formulating this discourse, explaining ecosystems with parallels between the earth and human processes. A physiological diagnosis of planetary resources was precisely the agenda of Fuller's 'World Design Science Decade' series of the 1960s, which took cognitive analytical form in McHale's *The Ecological Context*

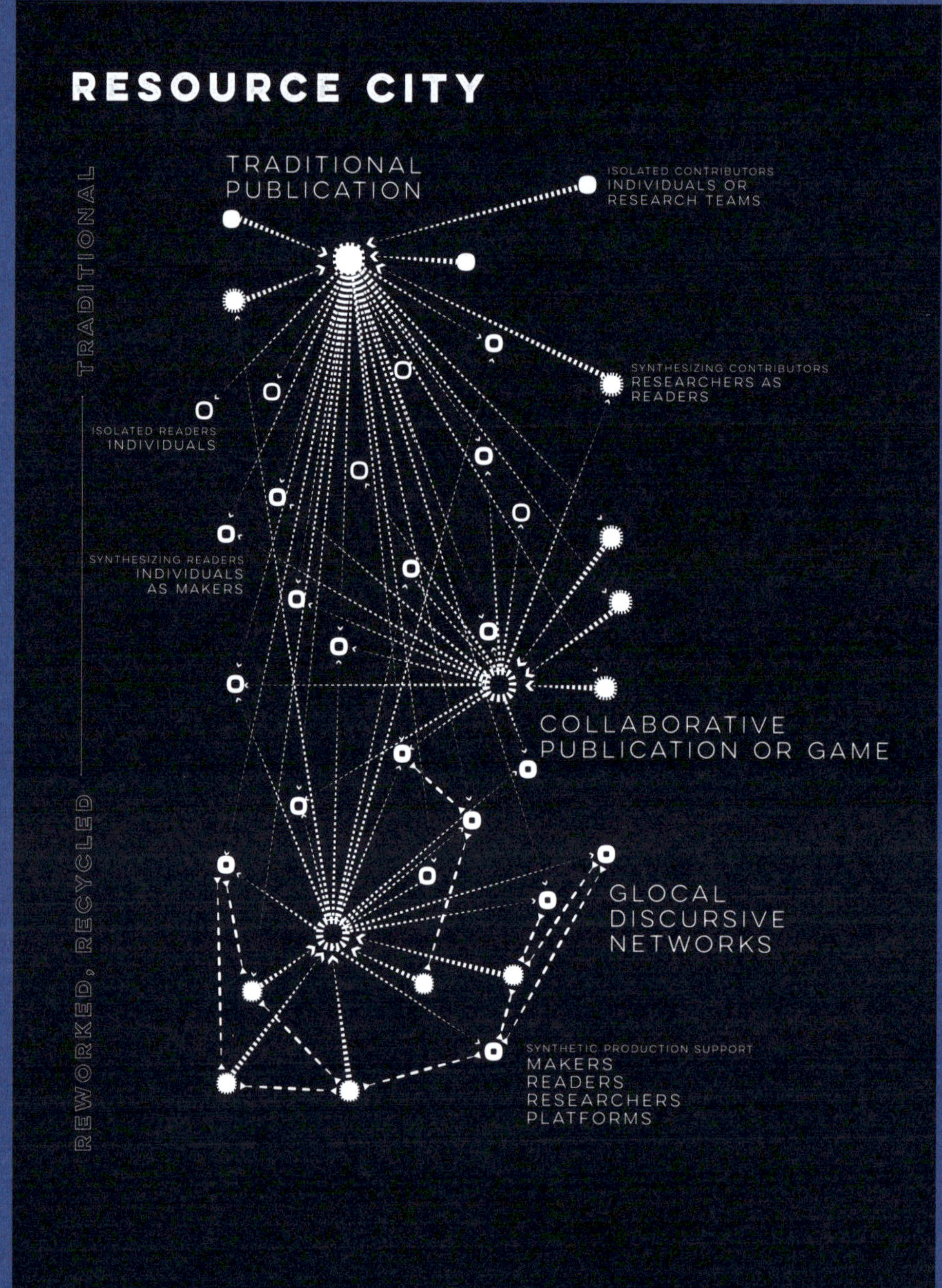
RESOURCE CITY
TRADITIONAL
REWORKED, RECYCLED
TRADITIONAL PUBLICATION
ISOLATED CONTRIBUTORS
INDIVIDUALS OR RESEARCH TEAMS
SYNTHESIZING CONTRIBUTORS
RESEARCHERS AS READERS
ISOLATED READERS
INDIVIDUALS
SYNTHESIZING READERS
INDIVIDUALS AS MAKERS
COLLABORATIVE PUBLICATION OR GAME
GLOCAL DISCURSIVE NETWORKS
SYNTHETIC PRODUCTION SUPPORT
MAKERS
READERS
RESEARCHERS
PLATFORMS

(1970). Through systemic management of resources, the totality of the earth could or should serve as a stage of concerted planning and action, giving rise to a new empire of balanced conservation and consumption.

The projects in *Resource City* point the origins of a common observation today: Our planet is becoming one city by means of increasing urbanisation. Along these lines, architecture and urbanism are fused with biology, policy, ecology and governance. No part of the world remains unaffected by the cumulative impact of human activity. Through complex processes of exploration, habitation, cultivation, transportation, consumption, and surveillance, the world is governed and designed not just by vision, but also by tools.

COMMUNE CITY MANIFESTO #6

Commune City is an experiment in living. It is a flexible, non-urban organism continually changing and evolving, empowered by citizen participation and detachment from the mechanisms of the state, both in terms of power and law. Unlike *Island City, Commune City* is not walled off from the urban fabric by means of a physical barrier, but by means of distance. It is the effort to reinvent civilisation far from the metropolitan centre and to create a self-sufficient living laboratory, an autonomous unit able to sustain itself, cut off from the main urban networks.

Commune City is able to defy urban mainstream production by recycling its waste, producing and distributing its energy and by achieving a new equilibrium as a social and natural system. As a laboratory, *Commune City* needs to produce its own language, by defying law and institutionalisation and by inventing an autonomous system of new policies, as well as an autonomous system of energy.

Featured on the cover of *AD*'s 'Autonomous Houses' issue of 1976, *Commune City* appears under the umbrella of 'autonomy' both to popularise an ecological and libertarian way of living and acting and to herald 'autonomy' from the grid of energy supply as a political statement against consumerism and capitalism. Clif-

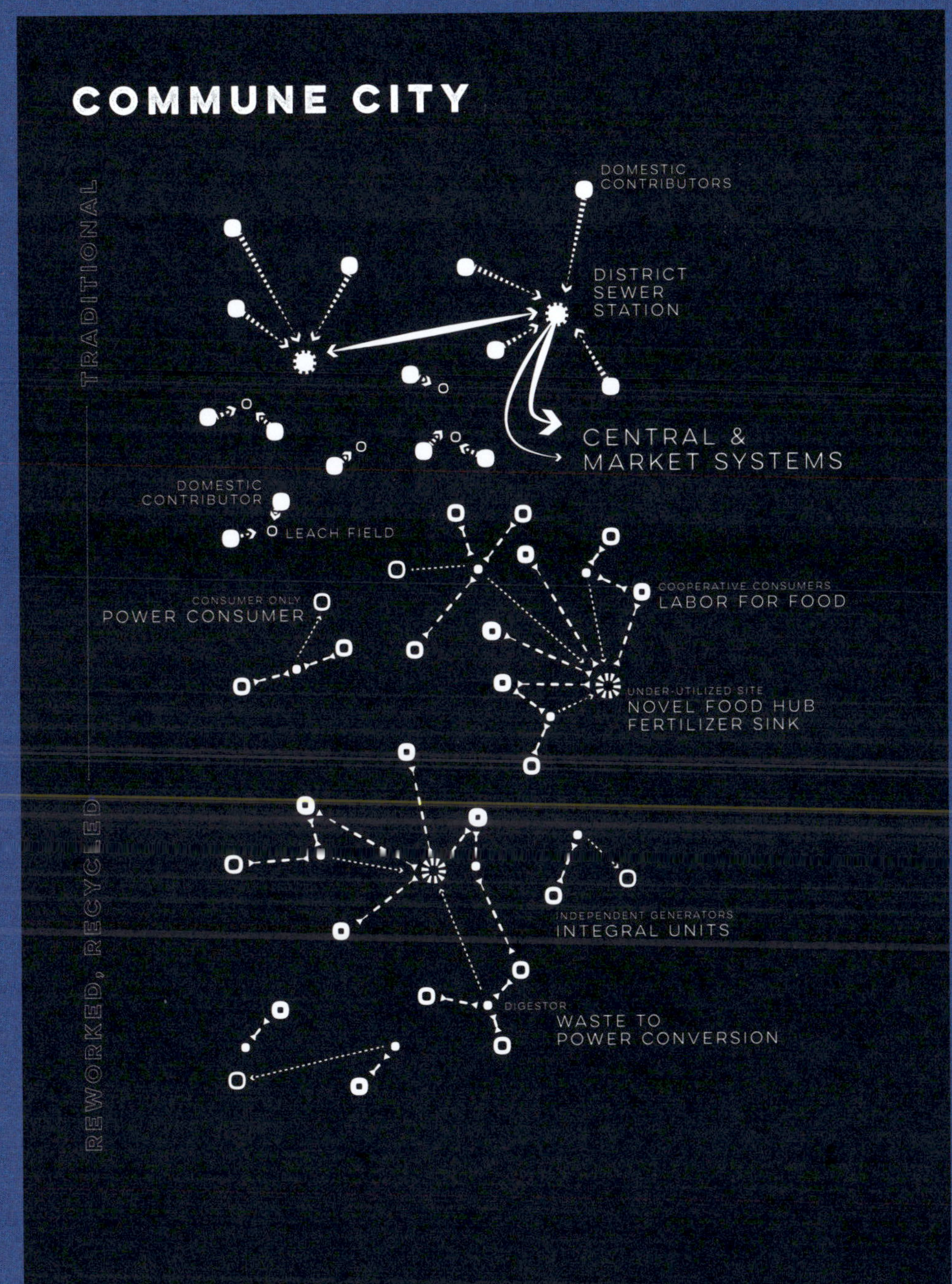
COMMUNE CITY
TRADITIONAL
REWORKED, RECYCLED
DOMESTIC CONTRIBUTORS
DISTRICT SEWER STATION
CENTRAL & MARKET SYSTEMS
DOMESTIC CONTRIBUTOR
LEACH FIELD
COOPERATIVE CONSUMERS
LABOR FOR FOOD
CONSUMER ONLY
POWER CONSUMER
UNDER-UTILIZED SITE
NOVEL FOOD HUB
FERTILIZER SINK
INDEPENDENT GENERATORS
INTEGRAL UNITS
DIGESTOR
WASTE TO POWER CONVERSION

ford Harper's 'Visions' series of drawings of collectivised gardens, community workshops and autonomous terraces gave visual form to environmental autonomy as a tool for political liberation. Harper's drawings were published in the book *Radical Technology* edited by Peter Harper – who later became the Director of the Centre for Alternative Technology in Machynlleth, UK – along with Godfrey Boyle and the editors of *Undercurrents* magazine.

The self-sufficient communities that Harper proposed in the 1970s harkened back to a grass-roots mentality and a pastoral iconography. They offer an intriguing counterpoint to technology-driven notions of self-sufficiency. Today's environmental visionaries need to reconcile previous notions of rural environmentalism, including farming and localism, with the instrumentalised regeneration of resources via technology.

In biology, 'autonomy' refers to a system's organic independence and self-governance, a notion that has been transferred to the urban sphere to advance the idea of a collectivised living space, un-rooted from its urban context. *Commune City* is like a restored Garden of Eden and a real-time habitation experiment where architecture, systems theory and human biology blend together in the hope of radical social reform.

DO–IT–YOURSELF CITY MANIFESTO #7

Do-It Yourself City is the messy and fuzzy imprint of occupation on the urban fabric. It reveals the city as it has been seized, deformed or transformed and lived by its inhabitants. *Do-It Yourself City* does not only call for participation, advocacy and active citizenship in spatial production; it also calls for partially relinquishing control in the design process of cities and environments.

The spontaneity of civic occupation has fostered architects' interest in vernacular and informal settlements at several historical moments. Thus we recall the work of John Habraken in the 1960s, Bernard Rudofsfky's *Architecture Without Architects* (1964), the PREVI project (Proyecto Experimental de Vivienda) in Peru in the early 1970s, and most recently, Elemental's Quinta Monroy project in Chile (2003-05). There is a substantial legacy of 'plug-in' structures, incomplete unfinished frames waiting for individual occupation, or a legacy of 'incrementalism', as described by the Museum of Modern Art at a 2015 symposium in New York. The aspiration in the genealogy of these projects is the defiance of uniformity and the complexity of a non-homogeneous textural grain, emerging from numerous personal choices and living patterns. *Do-It Yourself City* is semi-controlled and semi-organised; it offers a board game on which life unfolds and diversifies, yet still lies upon a defined territory of action.

With vast regions of the urbanised world built in slums, *Do-It Yourself City* obliges us to face and learn from this reality. It reflects the multidimensional nature of urban space and the unpre-

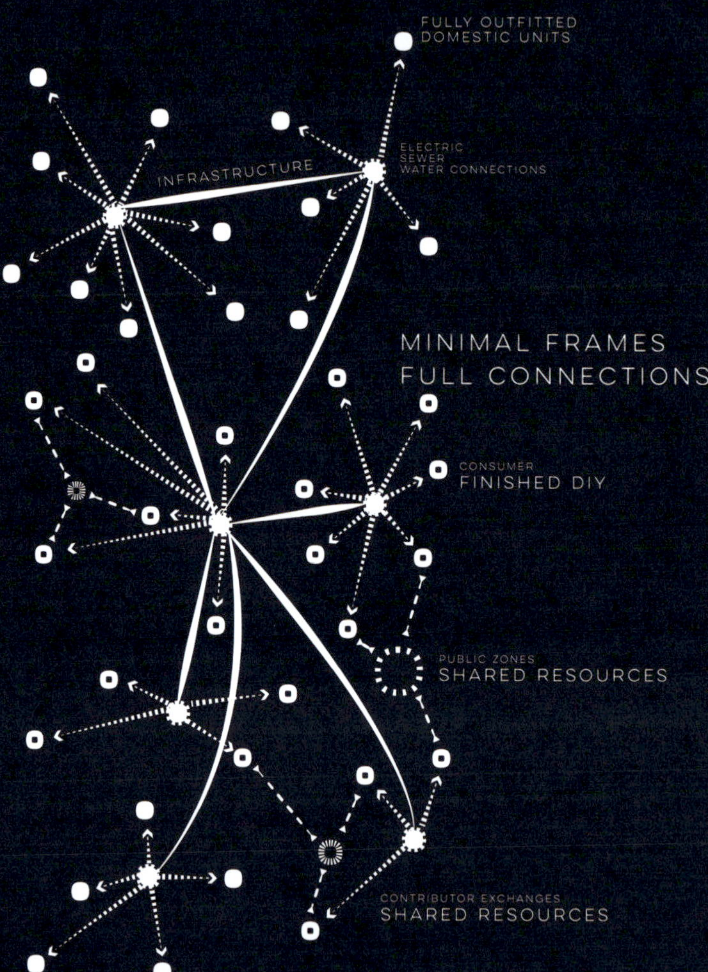
DO-IT-YOURSELF CITY
TRADITIONAL
REWORKED, RECYCLED
FULLY OUTFITTED
DOMESTIC UNITS
INFRASTRUCTURE
ELECTRIC
SEWER
WATER CONNECTIONS
MINIMAL FRAMES
FULL CONNECTIONS
CONSUMER
FINISHED DIY
PUBLIC ZONES
SHARED RESOURCES
CONTRIBUTOR EXCHANGES
SHARED RESOURCES

dictability of life. The architects and planners who have engaged with questions of informality, time, and the right of forming the city, deeply believe that architecture can serve as a framework for social transformation. At the same time, they share a disposition for design processes rather than objects, and they defy determinism in design thinking. They resist the romance of the 'architect's hand' and the modernist ethos of the master plan. Behind the curtains of Torre David, they ask us to witness the reinvention of the architect's identity and to expand our perception of design authorship. In these new conditions of incremental urbanisation, the architect can only be an editor, a thinker, a tinkerer and a critic of physical resources and ideas.

813
COLLAGE

Woven textile banner designed by Thonik suspended at exhibition entrance.

TOWARDS COLLAGE ARCHITECTURE

Aaron Betsky

Collage is making a comeback. Architects are turning back to techniques first pioneered in the art world more than a century ago.

They are looking for ways to avoid the traps of building for the powerful in a manner that fixes their clients' values and value in place and imposes it on the 'other 99 percent'. They are looking at architecture not as the imposition of an abstract order the architect has conceived in her or his head, but as the thoughtful gathering together of what already exists so as to make urban patterns (rather than forms) that open themselves up to different interpretations and uses over time.

In part, this renewed interest in collage stems from the imperative of reusing what we already have. In an era in which, on the one hand, we threaten to drown and suffocate ourselves in waste and, on the other hand, we deplete non-renewable resources while polluting our planet and changing our climate, the directive to architects that they should first reuse existing buildings and materials would seem an obvious one.

The integration of computer and communication technologies into the discipline makes this kind of reuse easier: architects can find and harvest what exists with greater ease. Many architects also realize that the making of things is not the creation of form on a blank sheet of paper or screen, but rather the manipulation of data in order to allow for new possibilities to emerge. In addition to this 'emergent architecture',[1] there is also the prevalence of Photoshop architecture: the gathering of images to create collages that are both new and seem to be no more than a deformation of an existing landscape.[2]

This drive toward reuse and reorganization over supposed invention is allied with tactical urbanism, which is to say, the notion that top-down planning has turned out to be a failure. Not only do people always behave differently than what planners (or any sort of pseudo-scientific futurologists) predict, but planning has often failed to impose order on existing conditions.[3] By the 1980s, planners moved away from *tabula rasa* schemes whose components were componentized and ideally mass-produced objects aggregated into abstract towers. They first attempted to mimic existing neighbourhoods and forms and even to recall more 'organic' communities from previous eras.[4] When that approach failed to create true diversity or even answers to our society's diverse needs, they turned to collage as a way of creating a more fluid order. This started in the Netherlands in the late 1980s with the work of landscape architects who saw their projects as weaving new forms and infrastructure into existing patterns,[5] but really picked up steam during the late 1990s in South

1 — Emergent architecture is the name the L.A.-based architect Tom Wiscomb has given to this sort of work. See his *Emergent: Structural Ecologies* (Los Angeles: Aacdu, 2009). The architect Patrik Schumacher has termed it 'parametricism' and argues that it is the only manner in which we should be building. See Schumacher, *The Autopoiesis of Architecture: A New Framework for Architecture* (London: Wiley & Sons, 2011). The first definitions of this new form were given by Greg Lynn in *Animate Form* (New York: Princeton Architectural Press, 1999), while the arguments for its 'organic' character were best formulated by Lars Spuybroek in *NOX: Machining Architecture* (London: Thames & Hudson, 2004).

2 — Winy Maas, who has espoused this mode of architecture most consistently, has taught it at the Technical University of Delft (http://thewhyfactory.com/output/copy-paste/), but has not articulated the theory in written form. Most of the discussion on the topic (cf. http://www.archdaily.com/tag/photoshop) remains concentrated on the use of Adobe Photoshop to alter presentations.

3 — For the best survey of tactical urbanism, at least in South America, see: Justin McGuirk, *Radical Cities: Across Latin America in Search of New Architecture* (London: Verso Books, 2015). See also Mike Lydon and Anthony Garcia, *Tactical Urbanism: Short Term Action for Long-term Change* (Washington: Island Press, 2015, and Pedro Gadanho, ed., *Uneven Growth: Tactical Urbanisms for Expanding Megacities* (New York: The Museum of Modern Art, 2014).

America. These more socially critical designers see their work as consisting of the tactical appropriation of existing structures. Rooted in community design-build projects of the 1970s, as well as in the squatters' movement of the same period, this is a form of urbanism that regains the discipline's function as critique and enabler of social revolutions.

Denial of the Object

These developments away from pre-established orders are predicated on a series of denials, above all else the denial of the object:

> ...it is here proposed that, rather than hoping and waiting for the withering away of the object (while, simultaneously manufacturing versions of it in profusion unparalleled), it might be judicious, in most cases, to allow and encourage the object to become digested in a prevalent texture or matrix. It is further suggested that neither object nor space fixation are, in themselves, any longer representative of valuable attitudes... Cross-breeding, assimilation, distortion, challenge, response, imposition, superimposition, conciliation: these might be given any number of names and, surely, neither can nor should be too closely specified... Ultimately, and in terms of figure-ground, the debate which is here postulated between solid and void is a debate between two models and, succinctly, these may be typified as acropolis and forum.[6]

Thus in 1978 the English architectural historian Colin Rowe and his collaborator Fred Koetter summed up a movement that had been brewing in

4 — By this I mean the movement for 'new urbanism', which is in reality a nostalgic recreation of early 20th century neighborhoods. It has since developed into something much more sinister, 'form-based codes', which seek to subject cities to such nostalgia by building it into building and zoning regulations.

5 — Of particular note is the work of Riek Bakker in Rotterdam and Leidsche Rijn, of the firm Palmbout in various locations, and of West 8, also in Leidsche Rijn. See Riek Bakker, *Ruimte voor de Verbeelding* (Rotterdam, 010 Publishers, 1994); Frits Palmboom, *Drawing the Ground Landscape Urbanism Today: The Work of Palmbout Urban Landscapes* (Basel: Birkhauser Verlag, 2010). See also my *False Flat: Why Dutch Design Is so Good* (London: Phaidon Publishers, 2005).

6 — Colin Rowe and Fred Koetter, *Collage City* (Cambridge, Mass.: The MIT Press, 1978), 83.

architecture for more than a decade. Against the certainties of a modernism that relied on abstraction and consistency to establish an order it wished to impose on existing conditions in order to cleanse and obliterate them, erecting on that empty plane objects that were at once monumental and transparent, Rowe, Koetter, and others proposed a modernism that would reweave the urban fabric so that there would be no break in either time or space, but rather a continuous reorganization of what was. No more utopia, no more object; no more break with the past and building for the future; no more alignment between architecture and power; architecture would be a subversive, critical, or, as they put it, ironic force that would put 'people' back in the heart of the modern project.

Collage and assemblage have their roots at the beginning of the 20th century, when artists began picking up scraps from their studio — and later the street — to create objects that both represented things out of these scraps, and were present as collections of objects. They tore and shredded what they found, layered the shreds together, and made their paintings and sculptures into moments of intensity where these objects came together, rather than into finished objects in and of themselves. They enjoyed the marks of time and use on the objects they found, and also the fact that they were often disused, as this formed an implicit critique of the endless cycle of production and consumption central to capitalism. Collages were also arguments for the beauty of art in itself, as they did not refer to outside orders or signify something external, but rather found value embodied in the collection the artist had made.[7]

Rowe and Koetter's counter-proposal, though rooted in this art movement (to which they referred in their volume), went back to the period after the Second World War, exactly when canonical modernism became allied with both corporate and governmental bureaucracies.[8] The erection of whole neighbourhoods and even cities laid out according to the principles condensed by the International Congress of Modern Architecture (CIAM) almost immediately led to a reaction calling for preservation of diversity, the human scale, and even the very neighbourhoods once condemned as blighted.[9] The desire to integrate and reuse existing urban form because of its history and human scale, which would vouchsafe the city's humanity, became the mainstay of the preservation movement, which divided architects.[10]

The convulsions of this period produced new attempts to save the object in architecture: Sigfried Giedion, Fernand Léger and Jose Luis Sert called for a 'new monumentality' in 1943[11]; while the architecture of the 'New Brutalism' movement, so named by the critic Reyner Banham in 1955, exaggerated the object while dissolving its edges into colonnades and ramps, so that the object intermingled with (often dark) spaces.[12] The call for learning from pre-modern cultures in order to preserve CIAM's tenets while giving up the solace of discrete forms — which was articulated by those writing the program for the tenth CIAM meeting, who then split off as Team X — remained on the

7 — For surveys of the field, see: John Enderfield, *Essays on Assemblage* (New York: The Museum of Modern Art, 1992); Diane Waldman, *Collage, Assemblage, and the Found Object* (New York: Harry S. Abrams, 1992).

8 — For a critical overview of this process, see Reinhold Martin, *The Organizational Complex: Architecture, Media, and the Corporate Space* (Cambridge, Mass.: The MIT Press, 2005). 'Canonical modernism' as defined by the 1932 International Style exhibition at MoMA and the accompanying publication, Henry-Russell Hitchcock and Philip Johnson, The International Style (New York: The Museum of Modern Art, 1933).

9 — See Eric Mumford, T*he CIAM Discourse on Urbanism, 1928-1960* (Cambridge, MA: The MIT Press, 2000).

10 — A new generation of architects professed renewed interest in the humanistic tradition and in works such as Geoffrey Scott's *The Architecture of Humanism: A Study in the History of Taste* (New York: Houghton Mifflin, 1914) and T.S. Eliot's *The Use of Poetry and the Use of Criticism: Studies in the Relation of Criticism to Poetry in England* (London: Faber, 1933).

11 — Jose Luis Sert, Fernand Léger, and Sigfried Giedion, 'Nine Points on Monumentality', position paper, 1943.

12 — Reyner Banham coined the phrase in an article, 'The New Brutalism', *Architectural Review* (Dec. 1955), and subsequently elaborated it in his book, *The New Brutalism: Ethic or Aesthetic* (New York: Reinhold Publishing, 1966).

whole a theoretical enterprise.[13] Only a few structures, most notably Georges Candilis and Shadrach Woods' 1963-1970 Berlin Free University 'mat' building, managed to realize even some of their principles.[14]

The impulse to question the tenets of mainstream modernism with more force (or, as the case might be, more weakness) came from outside of architecture. In fact, the hugely influential exhibition *Architecture without Architects*, which the Museum of Modern Art in New York mounted in 1964,[15] served as a clarion call for the counter-movement. It was, as the title indicated it should be, ignored by most architects, but picked up by counter-cultural builders whose bible was not a text of architecture, but rather The Whole Earth Catalog — appropriately enough an assembly of techniques, examples, and components rather than a reasoned manifesto.[16]

Similarly, both economic forces and the taste culture turned towards renovation and restoration, with the rehabilitation of both buildings and inner-city neighbourhoods, along with the nascent 'loft movement', proving to be much more popular in terms of public acceptance than whatever convoluted forms architects were producing. It was no wonder that critics such as Manfredo Tafuri added architecture to the list of things, from God to the monolithic corporation, which were now dead. The more complex were the orders that architects tried to devise, and the more pure and total the signs, the more they said and did nothing, while all around them the urban environment

13 — Cf. Max Risselada, Dirk van der Heuvel, eds., *Team 10: In Search of a Utopia of the Present 1953-1981* (Rotterdam: NAI Publishers, 2006).

14 — The building has not received a full stand-alone treatment, but see Gabriel Field, *Berlin Free University* (London: AA Publications, 2004).

15 — Bernard Rudofsky, *Architecture Without Architects: A Short Introduction to Non-Pedigreed Architecture* (New York: Doubleday Publishers, 1964).

16 — Stewart Brand, *The Last Whole Earth Catalog: Access to Tools* (New York: Random House Publishers, 1971). The first edition was published in 1999, but it was only the 'last' one that received wide distribution.

continued to reinvent itself in ways architects could not seem to understand.[17]

Early Visions of Collage Architecture

Out of the ruins of modernist architecture and exactly as ruins, theoreticians began to reconstruct new forms that were fragmentary, elementary, and contingent on the conditions in which they would appear. Joseph Rykwert examined the possibility of *Adam's House in Paradise* (the title of his 1962 book)[18] being a hut made by gathering together materials, as Gottfried Semper had suggested a century before in *The Four Elements of Architecture* (1851), contrary to Laugier's more rationalist interpretation of the archetypal structure in his *Essay on Architecture* (1755). Charles Moore delighted in the shapes and objects of everyday life and began producing forms that reused the 'vernacular',[19] and architects in Italy turned towards restoration as an activity that they understood to be at the core of their discipline.

Two texts summarized these developments and bookend the emergence of this first call for collage in architecture: Robert Venturi's *Complexity and Contradiction in Architecture*, published in 1966, and Rowe's and Koetter's text twelve years later. The latter came out almost simultaneously with *Delirious New York* (1978), a semi-fictional evocation, or 'retroactive manifesto' of 'Manhattanism' with which the architect Rem Koolhaas first made his name in 1978.[20]

Venturi's book consisted of a rambling excursus through classical architecture in which

17 — Manfredo Tafuri, *Architecture and Utopia: Design and Capitalist Development*, trans. Barbara Luigia La Penta (Cambridge, Mass.: The MIT Press, 1976 (1973)), 150-169.

18 — Joseph Rykwert, *On Adam's House in Paradise: The Idea of the Primitive Hut in Architectural History* (New York: The Museum of Modern Art, 1962).

19 — Charles Moore, Donlyn Lyndon, Patrick Quinn, Sim van der Ryn, 'Toward Making Places', in Kevin Keim, ed., *You Have to Pay for the Public Life: Selected Essays of Charles W. Moore* (Cambridge, Mass.: The MIT Press, 2001), 88-109.

20 — Rem Koolhaas, *Delirious New York: A Retroactive Manifesto for Manhattan* (New York: Monacelli Press, 1994 (1978)).

he ignored the cannon (the acropolis, *pace* Rowe and Koetter) and concentrated on lesser known architects and buildings. It was the ways in which objects constructed in the cannon adjusted themselves to the context, were open to multiple interpretations, reused existing structures or even materials (the *spolia* from Roman ruins), and dissolved space into fragments that interested the author. In these buildings he saw the justification of architecture that was not 'either/or' but 'both/and':

> I like elements which are hybrid rather than "pure," compromising rather than "clean," distorted rather than "straightforward," ambiguous rather than "articulated," perverse as well as impersonal, boring as well as "interesting," conventional rather than "designed," accommodating rather than excluding, redundant rather than simple, vestigial as well as innovating, inconsistent and equivocal rather than direct and clear. I am for messy vitality over obvious unity. I include the non sequitur and proclaim the duality."[21]

In the second half of *Complexity and Contradiction*, Venturi sought to demonstrate the vitality of such an approach with his own work. Yet, on the whole, the work remained object-oriented, even if the structures' coherence was sometimes in doubt and their monumentality was undermined by irony and wit. Venturi, after all, proclaimed the 'difficult whole'[22] and saw himself as a traditional architect. Similarly, his follow-up volume, written with his wife and partner, Denise Scott-Brown, and Steven Izenour, *Learning from Las Vegas* (1972) was, for all its marveling at the

21 — Robert Venturi, *Complexity and Contradiction in Architecture* (New York: The Museum of Modern Art, 1966), 16.

22 — *Ibid*, 14.

beauty of signs, still a call for the making of buildings that could appropriate the sign's power, not the abandonment of architecture to the realm of semiotics.[23] They stopped short of exploring the notion of an 'electronic expressionism'. In the end, they sought order: 'Chaos is very near; its nearness, but its avoidance, gives...force', they quoted August Heckscher as saying.[24] They still believed that complexity and contradiction could be assimilated into the object of architecture.

Rowe, as we have seen, called for a move beyond the object, and Koolhaas offered concrete examples of how that might be possible. *Delirious New York* was neither a survey of architecture's cannon nor a call for making architecture in a particular manner, but rather an evocation and intimation. Koolhaas called up images of a possible Manhattan, grounded in the research he had done while at the Institute for Architecture and Urbanism, whose qualities where magical as much as they were concrete. He saw the order on which the city was founded —the grid — not as a constraint, but as an enabler. Within each block, a whole universe could flourish:

From now on each metropolitan lot accommodates—in theory at least—an unforeseeable and unstable combination of simultaneous activities, which makes architecture less an act of foresight than before and planning an act of only limited prediction. It has become impossible to "plot" culture...from now on each new building of the mutant kind strives to be "a City within a City." This truculent ambition makes the Metropolis a

23 — Robert Venturi, Denise Scott-Brown, Steven Izenour, *Learning from Las Vegas* (Cambridge, MA: The MIT Press, 1972).

24 — *Ibid.*, 53.

collection of city-states, all potentially at war with each other."[25]

What the block made possible was an implosion of life that gave rise to the fantastical. Modern technology had indeed liberated people: not, as the believers in machined forms and abstractions had believed, to live in a more efficient and equal manner, but rather to explore their desires and fears. Koolhaas liberated modernism's unconscious and, like all dream worlds, it consisted of memories whirling around each other, continually constructing, dissolving, and reconstructing momentary realities. The city of memory, which for Koolhaas was also a model for the future (and his own architecture), was a collage.

Rowe and Koetter made the latent notion of collage explicit in *Collage City*, even while thinkers such as Aldo Rossi tried to repress its implications back into abstraction. They based their book explicitly on the desire to get away from 'politics' and towards the 'people'; on a kind of populism, in other words, that avoided Le Corbusier's choice between architecture or revolution. They also based it on a study of the people, which is to say anthropology, and specifically on the work of Claude Levi-Strauss.[26]

Levi-Strauss, in his seminal (but by now somewhat discredited, at least in terms of its forensic research, let alone its terminology) book *The Savage Mind* (1966), argued that 'primitive' cultures were unable to think in abstractions and static order.[27] They worked with concrete objects at hand, refusing to imagine other worlds. They had

25 — Rowe and Koetter directly cite Levi-Strauss on pp. 102-105.

26 — Rowe and Koetter directly cite Levi-Strauss on pp. 102-105.

27 — Claude Levi-Strauss, *The Savage Mind* (Chicago: The University of Chicago Press, 1966 (1962)), 1-33.

no grander project, no sense of making something that did not yet exist, but were instead content to recreate something from the past. There was no *telos* and no grand plan. To create momentary orders that came out of and were contained within the relations between those things was the purpose of their activity. Their order was time-based and evanescent, Levi-Strauss wrote:

The characteristic feature of mythical thought is that it expresses itself by means of a heterogeneous repertoire which, even if extensive, is nevertheless limited. It has to use this repertoire, however, whatever the task in hand because it has nothing else at its disposal... The 'bricoleur' is adept at performing a large number of diverse tasks; but, unlike the engineer, he does not subordinate each of them to the availability of raw materials and tools conceived and procured for the purpose of the project. His universe of instruments... is also always heterogeneous because what it contains bears no relation to the current project, or indeed to any particular project, but is the contingent result of all the occasions there have been to renew or enrich the stock or to maintain it with the remains of previous constructions or destructions.[28]

This world of 'magic' was to Levi-Strauss the basis of art (and thus, though he did not articulate it, architecture). Art was, in fact, the symbiosis of science and magic, of craft and abstraction, and of the impermanent and the enduring. He did not, however, call for art to become like a collage, finding in Western art rather a sublimation of this

28 — *Ibid.*, 17.

technique.[29] This is especially odd because, by the time he was writing, there was a long tradition of collage in art making. The work of Kurt Schwitters, Hans Arp, Hannah Hoch and Max Ernst — as well as the work of Picasso and Braque before they smoothed their cubism into the flat, pre-planned picture plane (although Picasso continued to use cast-off materials to create three-dimensional collages into his late life) — found continual resonance among artists around the world, offering a narrative within modernist art that stood in contrast to the attempts to create ever more precise orders and abstractions. Seven years before the publication of *The Savage Mind*, Robert Rauschenberg had created his first 'combine' (*Bed*, 1955), while Alberto Burri and Antonio Tapies were engaged in similar efforts in Europe.

Postmodern Scaffolds, Façades, and Pastiches

There was, however, no such legacy of collage in architecture. What Rowe and Koetter were calling for was what Venturi had found in the idiosyncrasies of monuments and Koolhaas discovered in the reality of urbanity. It was what drove the constructions created by self-educated amateur architects and 'hippies' who used the *Whole Earth Catalog*. It was what the authors saw, as the quote above indicates, in the Roman Forum. Their model — as they could not find one within the discipline of architecture itself — was the museum. This collection of artefacts brought memories into one place in concrete forms. Yet they rejected the

29 — *Ibid.*, 22-29.

closed and (by implication) elitist nature of such institutions, calling instead for a '"city as scaffold for exhibition presentation'."[30] It would be a construct in which objects and events would be in continual flux, suggesting:

A two-way commerce between the fabric of the museum and its contents, a commerce in which both components retain their identity enriched by intercourse, in which their respective roles are continuously transposed, in which the focus of illusion is in constant fluctation [sic] with the axis of reality.[31]

Rowe and Koetter had an immense influence during the 1970s and 1980s, both in the work of established practitioners such as James Stirling, whose work seemed to want to prove, at least in plan, the possibility of a collage city; and among young architects in the United States, such as Michael Graves and Peter Eisenman. It is also without a doubt that the early work of Bernard Tschumi, in particular his design for the Parc de la Villette in Paris, which won an international competition in 1982, is an attempt to realize Rowe's and Koetter's vision.[32] Koolhaas as well tried to make architecture of scaffolding in projects such as the Kunsthal Rotterdam (1992), though his totalizing vision usually won out over his interest in coherent fragments.[33] What these architects — and certainly their less talented colleagues — produced, though, wound up being more pastiche than collage. Unable to let go of the plan as an ordering device and stuck in a profession that demanded that they design in a way that produce

30 — Rowe and Koetter, 136.

31 — *Ibid.*, 137.

32 — Tschumi became perhaps the foremost theoretician of collage-based architecture and urbanism (or, as he would call it later on, "event architecture," before he even built Parc de La Villette. For a concise recapitulation of his arguments, see "Six Concepts," a lecture he gave at Columbia University in 1991, in Bernard Tschumi, *Architecture and Disjunction* (Cambridge, Mass.: The MIT Press, 1994), 228-259; see also his *Event Cities*, published that same year by the same publisher.

33 — The work of Koolhaas and his firm, OMA, came out of the Architectural Association, where both Tschumi and the original OMA partners studied and taught, and seemed, at first, heavily dependent on collage. As they began to build, however, the work became more and more cohesive, with the Kunsthal having the most collage aspects of all their early work.

predictable and affordable results, architects were left with only one place where they could play out the notion of a scaffolding for memories and associations: the façade.

Postmodernism, as the varied reactions to the modernism of the International Style and CIAM came to be called, mostly comprised images and pictures. It found its justification in the semiotic focus of Charles Jencks' *The Language of Postmodern Architecture* (1977) and the post-structuralism adopted by Eisenman and others. The apotheosis of this development was the 1980 appearance of the *Strada Novissima*, a collection of façades running the length of a medieval rope factory in Venice, which served as the coming-out of a generation of practitioners whose varied and often colourful images floated over generic forms and structures, their plans only somewhat modified by either geometric overlays or the depth of 'poche planning'.[34] Perhaps only Frank Gehry's work of the period, which sought to combine 'normal' materials such as chain-link fence, plywood, and exposed wood members, came close to creating three-dimensional collages one could inhabit. But even in Gehry's case, the plans and overall order he gave his structures were remarkably conventional and predictable.

34 — The installation was documented in fragments in various articles at the time. See http://www.domusweb.it/en/from-the-archive/2012/08/25/-em-la-strada-novissima-em--the-1980-venice-biennale.html. For the theoretical background, see Paolo Portoghesi, *The Presence of the Past* (London: Academy Editions, 1980).

Millennial Experiments

Thus the call for collage in architecture went unanswered for several decades, before changes in technology and the desire to resist the continual appropriation of architecture's experimentation led to a revival. This active re-appreciation appeared first in a notional form, in the continually mutating (or 'morphing') forms of architects such as Asymptote (Hani Rashid an Lise Anne Couture), whose early work brought together images of cars, household objects, shoes, people, and cities into time-based collages that one could only see as projections. Similarly, the artist-architects (at that time) Elizabeth Diller and Ricardo Scofidio created site-specific installations and performances as collages that questioned social relations.

The computer seemed to offer a variety of possibilities for making collages because it does not accept the restrictions of linear geometry or fixed form. The unlimited combinatory possibilities inherent in the medium have more often led, however, to propositions for forms that are tortured, rather than questioned. Distended shapes hint at the fluidity of the object, but, in the end, the work tends to gel at the point where the architect presses the print (or 'execute') button. The early work of Jesse Reiser, in which he proposed warping 'found objects' such as Philip Johnson's Glass House, offered a promising direction that the architect himself abandoned.[35] Similarly, Mark Foster Gage has moved from a radical questioning of form to the making of beautiful, but skin-deep proposals for skyscrapers.

The Dutch group MVRDV has picked up on these early explorations of new media. After creating a number of three-dimensional worlds out of data during the 1990s and early 2000s, they have recently moved into what they call 'Photo-

35 — For Reiser's argument on collage, see his *Atlas of Novel Tectonics* (New York: Princeton Architectural Press, 200), 69-75.

shop Architecture', in which they collage together found imagery to create all-over coverings for thin structure. They do not let collage penetrate into the process of design and construction, however, nor do they break down the dominant order of the plan. Rather, they argue for the irrelevance of these controlling devices in an era in which we live completely through images. If our cellular phones become thin enough, we will be left with just the images floating on their screens, they argue, and architecture should emaciate itself in a similar manner.[36] The photographer Filip Dujardin has, along with some of his colleagues, taken this proposition further, imagining buildings consisting of existing structures he bleeds into each other.

Other architects are choosing the route of collage in a more radical manner, proposing to make buildings out of found materials. Nowhere has this happened with more zest than in the Netherlands where, in the early 1990s, the design collective Droog showed how materials could be reused to form, for instance, furniture made out of scrap wood or vases which were half plastic and half traditional porcelain, tied together with tape. Some of the designers affiliated with Droog, such as Richard Hutten and Piet Hein Eek, started applying these principles to the making of interiors and buildings, and soon architects picked up on the idea. The most notable example of this sort of practice is Superuse Studios, formerly 2012 Architecten, who have devised Harvest Maps, computer programs that let users and designers, as well as sellers, enter in resources out of which buildings can be

36 — Winy Maas, conversations with the author, Rotterdam, June, 2014.

constructed. Superuse has made buildings out of truck tires, washing machines, and kitchen sinks.[37]

Other notable examples of such radical reuse (as opposed to the much more standard integration of recycled materials into buildings) include Rural Studio, an Auburn University, Alabama-based program in which students and faculty collect car windows, excess lumber, sandbags, and whatever is at hand to create both homes and civic structures in Hale County, the poorest in the United States. In China, Amateur Architecture Studio makes buildings out of recycled bricks and roof tiles, while the versatile artist Ai Wei Wei has shown how doors, windows, and other elements from temples can be repurposed into new structures. Another artist, Theaster Gates — continuing a methodology developed by David Ireland in his Capp Street House in the 1980s and picked up (whether consciously or not) by Lacaton and Vassal in their 2001 renovation of the Palais de Tokyo in Paris — has shown how this technique can lead to the construction of interiors evocative of the building's history.

In almost all cases, however, these architects discipline their reuse with a focus on the integration of the pieces into coherent form. Few, if any, of the structures have the exuberance and ad-hoc quality some of the hippie structures had in the 1960s-70s. The house Clayton Lewis built for himself on Tamales Bay serves as a good, but unheeded, example of such an approach.[38]

On the other side of the spectrum, some architects have tried to push collage through the

37 — The principal, Jan Jongert, and several collaborators have documented their method on an open-source website, harvestmap.org, and in Ed van Hinte, Cesare Peeren, Jan Jongert, *Superuse: Constructing a New Architecture by Shortcutting Material Flows* (Rotterdam: NAI010 Publishers, 2013).

38 — For a survey that puts this work in context, see Aurora Fernandez Per, Javier Mozas, Javier Arpa, *Reclaim Remediate Reuse Recylce* (Madrid a + t Publishers, 2012).

reuse of imagery, creating something closer to a three-dimensional collage, though one that does not actually reuse, in most cases, found materials. Jimenez Lai and his studio, Bureau Spectacular, draw their inspiration directly from Postmodernism, looking back to the pastiches of the Memphis group in Italy and Michael Graves and Stanley Tigerman in the United States, but adopt them to a culture of eBay and Amazon. His collections of found objects are just part of his collections, which include plans and even whole building elements. They are not always the products of 'high' architecture; like his models, Lai also draws from vernacular house forms to create his mash-ups.[39]

Lai learns from the work of Jeff Koons and others, but his designs also seem to parallel the collages that are common practice in popular culture. Whether in fashion or in music, we have become used to fragments or samples that designers and artists take from existing sources and blend or sew together into forms that are both new and strangely familiar. It remains perplexing that few architects have picked up on what is commonplace in our daily lives and translated that vitality of forms and images into the medium of buildings, however much lip service the firms of OMA, BIG, or REX might give to that culture. Perhaps it will take another generation for the prejudices against his sort of appropriation to dissolve.

39 — Lai did such projects for the Venice Architecture Biennale Taiwan Pavilion in 2014 (http://bureau-spectacular.net/township-of-domestic-parts), for the exhibition *Chatter: Architecture Talks Back in 2015* (catalog, edited by Karen Kice, published by the Art Institute of Chicago, 2015), and for *Shelter: Rethinking How We Live in Los Angeles*, at the A + D Museum, Los Angeles, that same year (http://aplusd.org/portfolio/shelter/).

Resisting the Plan

What has gained more traction than the reuse of finished objects or images is the reuse of disused or unused buildings. The best example of this is the Torre David project by Urban-Think Tank.[40] The Tower is an unfinished skyscraper in the centre of Caracas' financial district that a group of slum dwellers, led by a charismatic priest, took over in 2011 and turned into a vertical squat. Urban-Think Tank's work consisted not of proposing ways in which they could build on what the squatters had already made for themselves, but first and foremost of documenting the inhabitants' lives in collaboration with the photographer Iwan Baan. The power of Baan's images is the perspective they provide, both literally and figuratively, on those lives, showing them in relationship to the existing orders, ranging from the building itself to the city around the structure. Urban-Think Tank provided their knowledge and expertise to the inhabitants, but did not design anything. They became participants and enablers rather than technicians who created forms in which to place the inhabitants.

The bureau of Urban-Think Tank has continued applying this technique in sites all around the world: for example, helping citizens in South African townships to figure out how they can find and use existing materials to extend and improve their self-built dwellings. They have proposed ways in which the abandoned buildings and sites of Athens could become scaffolding for social activity. And yet design always creeps

40 — Alfredo Brillembourg and Hubert Klumpner, *Torre David: Informal Vertical Communities* (Zurich: Lars Muller Publishers, 2012).

in as Urban-ThinkTank explores structures that would allow a multiplicity of activities to grown in them, but that are still, when all is said and done, three-dimensional grids.

What architects have not been able to face is that collage forms a radical critique of the manner in which their discipline is currently structured. Collage proposes that the architect does not solve problems and does not have the inherent ability to improve upon existing situations. Rather, an architect working in a collage mode would be a hunter and gatherer who would collect materials; a magician who would evoke our dreams, memories, and expectations, but leave them as elusive images and forms; and a technician who would provide particular expertise and case studies without pretending that this knowledge would solve any particular problem. The architect, in other words, would have to stop designing buildings according to a preset plan.

Collage is against finished form, proposing instead that formlessness has more force, as it cannot be immediately appropriated by existing elites and constricting structures. By creating forms that are fragmentary and happenstance, collage makers refuse the respite of aesthetics tied to completion, order, and a hierarchy of either materials or shapes.

Collage is against utopia, or any form of either eschatological or teleological justification of current appearances. Collage makers do not see their work as the making of building blocks for a more perfect future, nor do they see their work as the translation of an original perfection into today's contingencies and imperfect situations. Instead, they think of their work as time-based and time-catalyzing. They evoke memories and dreams and give them shapes that are, like our fears, hopes, and recollections, fleeting in nature.

Collage is a moment in time, not monumental.

Collage is the opposite or order and abstraction. It does not base itself on preconceived ideas, nor do its makers pretend that there is a blank slate in which and on which they operate. Collage is wholly contingent and fragmentary. You cannot conceive it before it appears, and it does not lead to another, more perfect order. As such, collage is also a critique of politics and the abstraction of human relations into laws, regulations, and other forms of control.

Collage has no interest in the sacred cow of modern architecture, space. It does not accept such an abstract notion that we can only experience in the negative through its con-stitution in materials. Rather, collages unfold and open up, enclose and draw us through spatial relationships that we can never define.

If collage is such a radical proposition, can it ever be built? What we have today are fragments and sallies beyond the monumental practice of architecture. Time will tell whether collage might allow architecture to unbuild itself.

COLLAGE CITY 3D FLOORPLAN

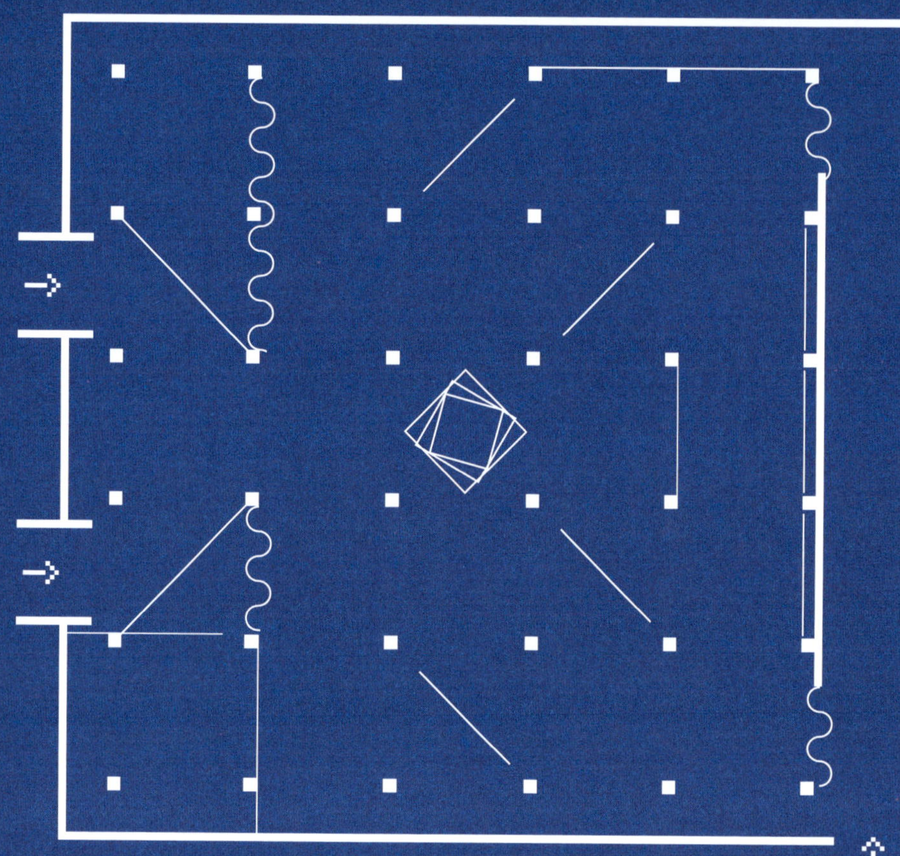

1
Symbiotic Village
Hood Design and Valeche Studio

2
Embodied Pelt
Langarita Navarro Arquitectos

3
Hole in the (Window of the) World House
Dennis Maher

4
Lost & Found
Bureau Spectacular / Jimenez Lai

5
Cacophony Collage
TOPOTEK1 with Rebecca Saunders

6
Check-In Program
Feng Feng + Fei Architect

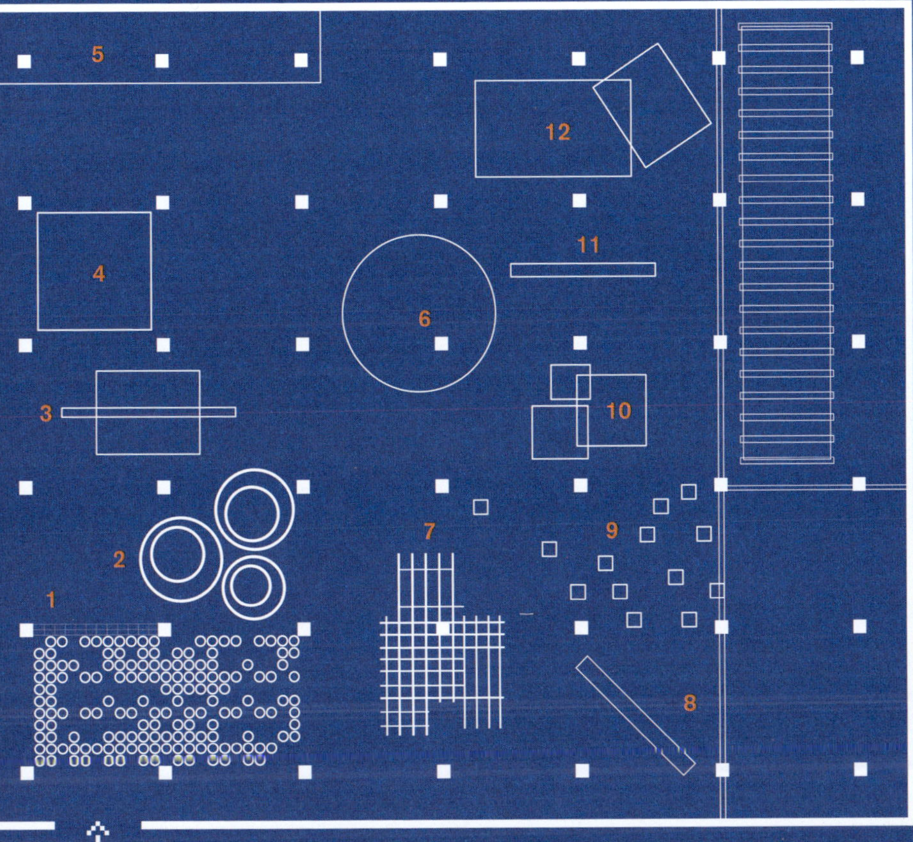

7
WorkScape Theatre
Studio Makkink & Bey

8
RE-
Francesco Delogu and Maria Cristina Finucci

9
Trash to Treasure Lab
Superuse Studios

10
Shenzhen Entropy
Rob Voerman

11
Ecstasies of Influences: Studiolo Wall
Lukas Feireiss and Thomas Tsang

12
Power to the People
Heidelberg Project

COLLAGE CITY 3D
EXHIBITS

SYMBIOTIC VILLAGE

Hood Design and Valeche Studio

'Symbiotic Village' gestures towards the urban typology of the water villages that formerly occupied Shenzhen and the Pearl River Delta. The installation reveals and questions the mundane and ever-changing relationships between people and water. Since the 1980s, planning policies have encouraged an influx of factories and urbanisation in the region, causing ecology to become subservient to the city. The former water villages – built within a network of canals, where farmers husbanded closed loop ecologies that reprocessed waste and produced crops including fish and silk – have largely disappeared. Acknowledgment of this transformation inspires us to question our contemporary condition and to ask, "How can we live *with* water"?

Dozens of spherical aquariums, home to live carp, hang in mesh cocoons (reminiscent of silk) through bamboo scaffolding. A wall of mulberry plants, lit with grow lights; and chains of actual silk cocoons, sewn by installation attendees at a small table; recall the formerly widespread cultivation of the silk worm and processing of silk.

The scaffold cube acknowledges the context of the Dacheng Flour Factory in Shekou. The 'Village' proffered by the installation is a gesture towards the possibility of living symbiotically with water. It considers the connections between an urbanised Shenzhen, defined by both cultural and built boundaries, and the larger shifting landscape and ecologies of the Pearl River Delta. Through an exploration of tactile and linguistic connections, 'Symbiotic Village' offers a new lens for viewing the landscape.

Credits

HOOD DESIGN: *Walter Hood, Creative Director*
Hester Tittmann, Evan Rimoldi, Lan Ly
Hood Design, based in Oakland, Calif., is a cultural and design practice embracing art, architecture, and landscape architecture.

VALECHE STUDIO:
Natalia Echeverri, Ivan Valin, Xiao Han
Valeche Studio is a Hong Kong-based design and research consultancy in landscape architecture, environmental planning and urban design.

EMBODIED PELT

Langarita Navarro Arquitectos

Usually we relate architecture – with its inorganic and inert manifestations – with all that is hard and does not change. However, we propose an alternative view that reveals an organic and soft side: one that breaks down and leaves no trace when it disappears. One that is easy to handle and requires actions from its inhabitants to activate. One that cannot be preserved without affections. To that architecture and to the world it builds we give the name, *pelt.*

Maintenance policies and an overzealous culture of efficiency have been eroding the pelt's trace in the places we inhabit. This trend towards eradication and banishment of soft, ephemeral and personal has been especially intense in offices and workspaces. In these spaces, only a handful of strange remnants of the pelt remain, always present, and at the same time always foreign. They are ghosts of a faraway world that reveal the gap between the sanitised space that we occupy and the alternative realm that we cannot and will not resign. We propose reclaiming their presence and reasserting their powers.

Changing the way we design and build workspaces proceeds from re-examining our collective imaginaries. The ambition of the project is not about creating an imaginary from scratch, as much as amplifying and pursuing the trail of the pelt in current offices, thereby constructing new mythologies. We propose, as a first step, inverting the hierarchies that normally govern the physical transformation of spaces. Against the conventional procedure of keeping what is stable and removing the pelt, we herewith propose the opposite: to identify, isolate and display what changes and mutates to make clear its powers.
To celebrate what is connected with the cycles of life both inside and outside buildings and to evidence the passage of time. The aim is to make visible the ways in which the pelt is materialized – rethinking how the management and transformation of the physical world could expand our practice to include a kind of architectural taxidermy.

The installation design is inspired by a series of photographs of numerous office spaces in Shenzhen and surroundings areas. We have traced the manifestations of the pelt through these images. Vegetation and lighting are emphasized for their ability to negotiate the relationships between the body and the constructed. The project departs from the usual forms of architectural representation and seeks to create a new constellation of imaginaries. It builds its own mythology to revisit the spaces they come from. Both the documentary dimension of research and the physical installation trace an alternative atlas with which to design again with embodied pelts.

Credits:
Architects: María Langarita and Víctor Navarro
Collaborators: Guillermo Diego, Angela Juarranz, Víctor Nouman

Photos by Wang Gen

HOLE IN THE (WINDOW OF THE) WORLD HOUSE

Dennis Maher

Gazing through the window of the 'urban village' toward the urban centre, signs of development and progress will appear as holes in the ground and obstructions in the sky. Very soon, such holes and obstructions will be filled with some other city's collective memories. The city's inhabitants will step outside to discover places that they have never known.

The term *anamnesis* refers to a form of knowledge imbued with the residue of the past. Anamnesis summons those faint recollections which lie buried beneath our faculties for conscious self-reflection. When the gazes of the city's inhabitants no longer invite this form of knowing, the city will cease to be 'theirs'. If there is any corporeal analogue to the megacity's unbounded growth, it is this: in the quest to remember places we once knew, we must free ourselves from the limits of our bodies and connect our innermost thoughts to the movements of matter that surround us. Within any environment of accelerated change, such as that of the Pearl River Delta, the challenge of genuine architectural discovery is to find and retain this space of connection between the intimate and the impersonal. This is the space that will transmit our dreams to the synapses of the world. The 'Hole in the (Window of the) World House' draws an imaginary conduit between two distant sites of architectural fantasy. It proposes a spatial and temporal bridge through the earth, connecting the Window of the World replica park in Shen-

zhen to my own house in Buffalo, New York (the Fargo House) — the place where I live, work, and dream. The Window of the World contains replicas of 130 of the world's most famous monuments, including the Eiffel tower, the Pyramids of Giza, and the Palace at Versailles, all reproduced in miniature within a 118-acre park-like setting. The Fargo House is also a fantastic collection of miniature environments that, with each successive night of dreaming, move me closer and closer to a world of impossible realities and allow me to see myself both larger and smaller than the monuments among which I dwell.

When I walk through my house and pick up a miniature building in my hand, I sometimes regard it as a model, toy, statue, souvenir, or symbol. Other times, I imagine it as an uprooted structure of brick, stone or steel that I have scooped off the ground. I struggle to uplift it with a smile of wonderment, playfulness, and delight. Every so often, I open my house's window and project the weight of that object outward — in this case, towards Shenzhen — and I am certain that when it lands, it will fall upon a day-dreamer's desk in an assemblage of shifting reveries.

Credits:
Project assistants: Yumeng Chen, Meiyan Jin, Hongkai Li, Lesley Loo, Feng Zhu

01

02

01 Dennis Maher, Fargo House. City-Wallscape, 2014. Within Maher's Fargo House in Buffalo, New York, patterns of daily living contend with the instability of matter. Photo by Biff Henrich.

02 Dennis Maher. Fargo House. Library Globe Room, 2014. Operations of making and unmaking, doing and re-doing, erode the house's solidity, exposing a world that is always on the brink of becoming. The house reflects the indeterminate, albeit coordinated exchanges of the surrounding city. Photo by Biff Henrich.

Photo by Dennis Maher

Photo by Dennis Maher

LOST & FOUND

Bureau Spectacular / Jimenez Lai

In our recent shopping sprees, we felt compelled to ask some of our purchased objects a noteworthy question: *why are you here?*

On the occasion of UABB 2015, we will bring home an urbanism full of lost souls, paraded neatly with cordial gaps between them like a team of misfit school friends. We particularly looked for objects that are either made in the Pearl River Delta, or passed through it at one point in time.

Through a rigorous set of rules we carefully drafted, we established a shopping guide to help us acquire objects with particular architectural and urban qualities. In particularly, we were keen on identifying objects with the potentials of communicating cute, friendly, yet dark and mysterious atmospheres. By juxtaposing several personalities next to one another, we were able to choreograph a network of possible relationships. The non-linear shapes against an orthogonal grid produces gaps that contract and expand, evoking many possible activities at the urban scale. Perhaps the mixture of many types of gaps between the many personalities is exactly the type of collage that makes city and culture dynamic. Looking once again at Archizoom's No-Stop City (1969), we were very much taken by the idea of camping in an office space. Not because sleeping in the office is fun, but because the misuse of prescribed architectural program is an interesting soft violation of social etiquette. The high-contrast world of the brightly coloured objects against a blank backdrop is the white tectonic of collage without the glue.

Credits
Jimenez Lai, Steve Martinez

THE 12 POINTS OF SHOPPING

1. Color: find light-hearted and upbeat colours that will work well in a lightbox, producing a cute and optimistic feeling. In other cases, find objects with black linework and white background.

2. Defamiliarize Readability: the vast mix of objects should cause most to become not clearly readable.

3. Architectural and Urban Qualities: look for objects with elements that may contain 'columns', 'ramps', 'canopy', and so forth. As well, look for objects with an abundance of both soft and hard corners – the more we are able to zig-zag, the better we can compress and expand the gaps between objects in plan and in section.

4. Math of Shapes: when in doubt, select objects with clear 'geometric' properties: spheres, cubes, cylinders, pyramids, etc. They can be 'near-spheres' or 'near-cubes', but so long as we can make an argument that they belong to certain categories of geometry. Also, find objects with compositional principles such as a tripartite stack.

5. Size: impose a range of sizes for the objects. Pre-emptively chart the zones against an applied grid, and the distribution of number of objects per zone. This will help us consider the range of sizes of objects we need to acquire.

6. Ease of Relaying Your Shopping Stories: can the punchline be delivered in three to seven words, and would anyone between the ages of eight and 88 chuckle at it?

7. Genre of 'Funny': when generating the comedic moments, consider the use of deadpan. Please avoid slapstick – it is a kind of take-away that becomes a giveaway. Also, avoid sarcasm, as it is too dark too quickly and not mysterious enough. Absurd juxtaposition is a good technique, too.

8. Potential for Dismemberment and Aggregation: find objects that can be taken apart and reassembled to depart from their original meanings

9. Texture: look for a mixture of glossy, furry, matte, and metal. Almost recalling the compulsive behaviour of a serial murderer, sort the similar textures and shapes neatly before we start composing. Make sure there's a premeditated distribution of texture percentages.

10. Genealogy and Relationships Between Objects: can some of the objects be 'cousins'? Are there apparent similarities or contrasts to link and differentiate different families or groups?

11. Orientation: can some of the pieces be re-oriented and become richer architecturally, and more difficult to read as normal objects?

12. Stories of Shapes: be funny about the objects. Not only are we asking 'why are you here', but also we will be imagining silly things we can do in them. A Laurel Broughton toaster is funny because the gaps are meant to be occupiable. An Andrew Kovacs environment is silly because things look slumpy or sloppy on purpose. This demands that we imagine the implied stories of when the objects can be occupied.

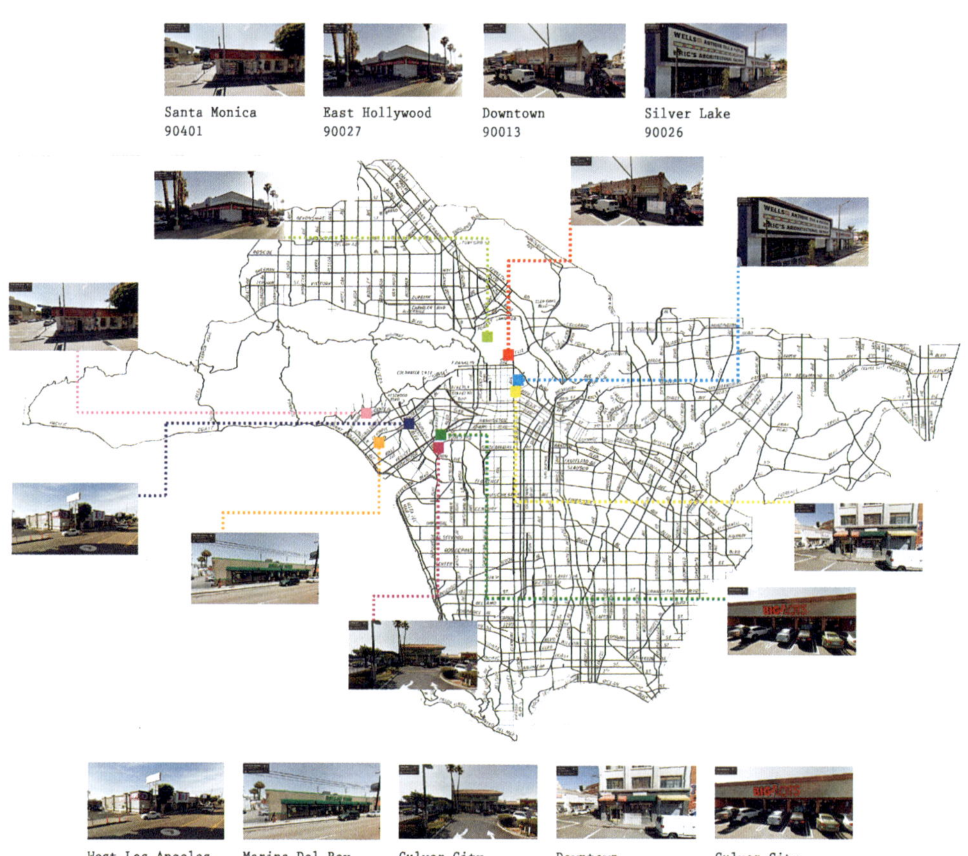

01

01 Map showing the locations of objects recovered in the Los Angeles area. 02 Plan of the Lost & Found objects on a 7x7 grid. The contrast of the brightly coloured objects against a blank backdrop is the white tectonic of collage without the glue.

03 Figure-Ground diagram of the Found Objects, emphasizing their architectural silhouettes.
By Jimenez Lai (Bureau Spectacular)

02

03

CACOPHONY COLLAGE

TOPOTEK 1 in collaboration with Rebecca Saunders

Home to one of the largest migrant populations in global history, Shenzhen and the Pearl River Delta region represent an urban cultural collage of unprecedented scale. But Shenzhen's vast cultural diversity is not reflected in its physical urban landscape. Homogeneous, repetitive, and banal modern structures paradoxically house a massively dynamic and heterogeneous society. Similarly, the various manufacturing industries of the region generate products of mass-produced sameness.

However, the urban soundscape has the power to transcend the visual monotony of the generic infrastructural scaffolding. A keen linguistic observer in Shenzhen would be able to identify diversity through the cacophony of mixed dialects, accents, and colloquialisms from regions that span the vastness of China. As such, where architecture can give the illusion of sameness and finality, soundscapes tend to be less tamed, more fluid and citizen-determined.

Composed of 2,464 identical music box mechanisms, TOPOTEK 1's 'Cacophony Collage', although masked in manufactured uniformity, is a sonic representation of this paradoxical heterogeneity. Produced in China, the components are outwardly indistinguishable. By turning the music box key, however, the visitor reveals an array of inner auditory diversity: each one plays one of 54 different tunes, encompassing a broad spectrum of copyright-free (public domain) melodies.

The melody list, arranged in six musical genres and 14 subgenres, began with the top 20 music box tunes sold in China and expanded to include 14 different nationalities spanning almost 500 years from the 15th century to the 20th century. Chosen and arranged by collaborating composer Rebecca Saunders, the distinctly recognisable melodies exude an innate sense of familiarity and childhood intimacy. Collectively, however, the tunes accumulate in a polyphonic composition, projecting layers of sound into the acoustic space. Heard en masse, the music boxes create a startling sonic image, reflecting a tension between the unit and the ensemble, or the individual and the collective.

'Cacophony Collage' is activated purely by the interactive collaboration of visitors, who compose a unique sonic image and a collective melody – generating a continually evolving and diversified cacophony. As such, a visitor on any given day experiences an entirely unique acoustic landscape, at once deeply personal yet global. The acoustic milieu and assemblage closely responds to the interaction and migration of people through space and time, reflecting the realities and social dynamics of the city of Shenzhen and the Pearl River Delta region.

Credits:
Chiara Feliz Di Palma, Yiwen Chen, Moustafa Hamdi

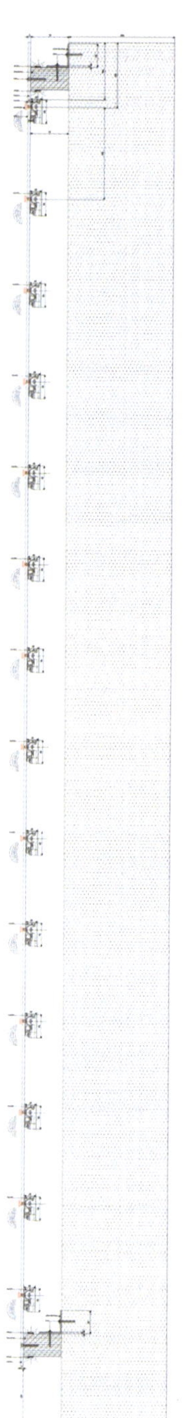

01

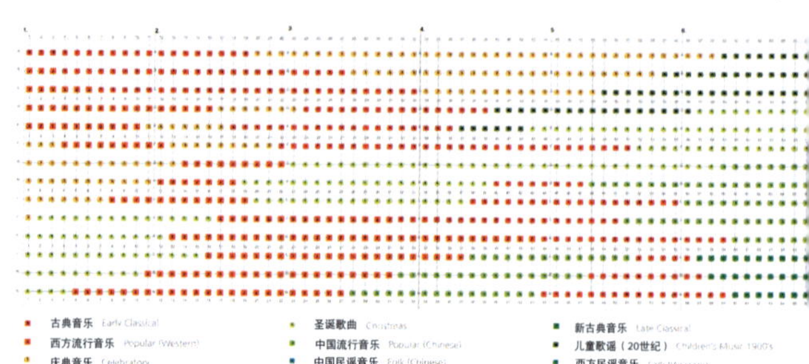

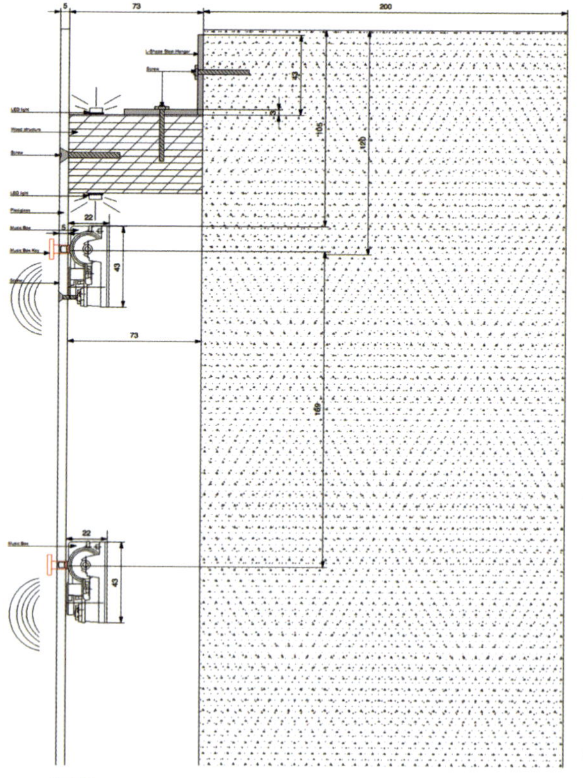

Detail 1

02

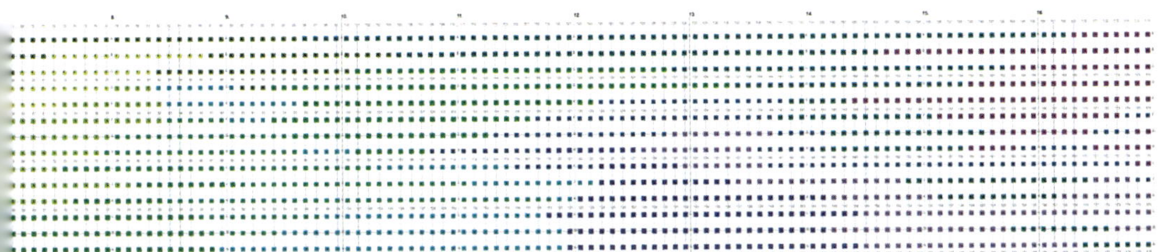

03

04

01 Transverse section of the installation. The 2,464 identical music box mechanisms contain an array of auditory diversity: 54 different tunes, six genres and 14 subgenres, mirroring the heterogeneity and mixed dialects of Shenzhen's population.

02 Transverse section (construction detail) of the wall. Only the hand-operated keys stick out from behind the acrylic panels, inviting visitors to freely activate the sonic collage.

03 Music Box Installation Guide. This chart was designed by TOPOTEK1 to guide construction workers in installing the music boxes in the correct sections.

04 View of the music box mechanisms from behind the acrylic panels. Each music box required 3 screws, adding up to 7,392 screws in total.

曲风流派 MUSIC BY GENERE

1. 2. 3. 4. 5. 6. 7. 8.

- □ 古典音乐 Classical
- ▪ 流行音乐 Popular
- ▦ 庆典音乐 Celebratory
- 民谣音乐 Folk
- 儿童歌谣 Children's music
- 民歌 National

曲风流派细分 MUSIC BY SUB-GENERE

1. 2. 3. 4. 5. 6. 7. 8.

- 古典音乐 Early Classical
- 西方流行音乐 Popular (Western)
- 庆典音乐 Celebratory
- 圣诞歌曲 Christmas
- 中国流行音乐 Popular (Chinese)
- 中国民谣音乐 Folk (Chinese)
- 新古典音乐 Late Classical
- 儿童歌谣（20世纪） Children's Music 1900's
- 西方民谣音乐 Folk (Western)
- 儿童歌谣（19世纪） Children's Music 1800's
- 浪漫主义音乐 Romantic
- 儿童歌谣（18世纪） Children's Music 1700's

曲目 SONG LIST

卡农 Canon in D
约翰·帕赫贝尔 / Johann Pachelbel

朱皮特交响曲 Jupiter Symphony
莫扎特 / Wolfgang Amadeus Mozart

小步舞曲F大调 Minuet in F Major
莫扎特 / Wolfgang Amadeus Mozart

卡农变奏曲 Variations on the theme from Canon
约翰·巴赫贝尔 / Johann Pachelbel

春江花月夜 Moonlit River in Spring
鞠士林 / Ju Shilin

黑眼睛 Dark Eyes
费拉里斯 / Adalgiso Ferraris

雪绒花 Edelweiss
理查德·罗杰斯 / Richard Rodgers

格拉纳达 Granada
奥古斯丁·拉拉 / Agustín Lara

爱尔兰的眼睛在微笑
When Irish Eyes are Smiling
昌西·奥尔科特/乔治·格拉夫
Chauncey Olcott /George Graff

友谊地久天长 Auld Lange Syne
罗伯特·彭斯 / Robert Burns

生日快乐 Happy Birthday to You
米尔德丽德·J·希尔 / Mildred J. Hill

犹太民歌 Hava Nagila
未知 /Anon

欢乐吧,先生们 God Rest Ye Merry, Gentlemen

铃儿响叮当 Jingle Bells
詹姆斯·皮尔彭特 / James Lord Pierpont

圣诞树 O Tannenbaum
恩斯特·安施茨 / Ernst Anschütz

哦!小城伯利恒 Oh Little Town of Bethlehem
拉尔夫·沃恩·威廉姆斯 / Ralph Vaughan Williams

平安夜 Silent Night
/ Franz Xaver Gruber

东方红 The East is Red
未知 /Anon

四季歌 Four Seasons Song
贺绿汀 /He Luting

康定情歌 The Love Song
未知 /Anon

玫瑰玫瑰我爱你 Rose, Rose, I Love

掀起你的盖头来 Lift Your Veil
王洛宾 / Wang Luobin

步步高 Bu Bu Gao
未知 /Anon

茉莉花 The Jasmine Flower
未知 /Anon

勃兰登堡协奏曲 Concerto No. 5
/ Ludwig van Beethoven

钢琴协奏曲 - 皇帝 Emperor Concerto
贝多芬 / Ludwig van Beethoven

儿童圆舞曲 Kinder Symphonie
舒曼 / Robert Schumann

婚礼进行曲 Mendelssohn Wedding March
门德尔松 / Felix Mendelssohn

离别练习曲 Tristesse
肖邦 / Frédéric Chopin

月光 Un Clair de Lune
德彪西 / Claude Debussy

摇篮曲 Too-Ra-Loo-Ra-Loo-Ral
香农 / James Royce Shannon

巴士上的轮子 Wheels on the Bus

快乐地工作 Whistle While You Work
/ Frank Churchill/Larry Morey

10. 11. 12. 13. 14. 15. 16.

10. 11. 12. 13. 14. 15. 16.

05

儿童歌谣（中世纪） Children's Music Middle Ages

民歌 National

绿袖 Greensleeves
未知 /Anon

蟑螂草 La Cucaracha
未知 /Anon

爱之罗曼史 Romance de Lamour
未知 /Anon

漂亮的云雀 Alouette Gentille
未知 /Anon

噗!黄鼠狼逃啦 Pop! Goes the Weasel
未知 /Anon

桑树灌木 The Mulberry Bush
未知 /Anon

蓝色多瑙河 Blue Danube Waltz
小约翰斯特劳斯 / Johann Strauss II

勃拉姆斯华尔兹 Brahms Waltz
勃拉姆斯 / Johannes Brahms

糖果仙子之舞 Dance of the Sugar Plum
柴可夫斯基 / Pyotr Ilyich Tchaikovsky

璇宫艳舞 The Emperor Waltz
约翰斯特劳斯/Johann Strauss II

缆车 Funiculi Funicula
路易兹 · 邓察 / Luigi Denza

梦幻曲 Reverie
克劳德 · 德彪西 / Claude Debussy

安静,小宝贝 Hush Little Baby
未知 /Anon

六便士之歌 Sing a Song of Six Pence
未知 /Anon

一闪一闪小星星 Twinkle Twinkle Little Star
未知 /Anon

伦敦桥 London Bridge
未知 /Anon

在艾维尼奥桥上 Sur de Pont Davignon
未知 /Anon

三只瞎老鼠 Three Blind Mice
拉文斯科夫 / Thomas Ravenscroft

骊歌 Aloha Oe
莉里widely卡拉尼 / Lili'uokalani

奇妙恩典 Amazing Grace
约翰纽顿 / John Newton

阿里郎 Arirang
未知 /Anon

05 The Melody Map, displayed in the exhibition hall, provided visitors with a key to the genres, sub genres and song list of 54 different tunes.

CHECK-IN PROGRAM

Feng Feng + Fei Architect

We enclosed a living space on the first floor of the exhibition hall. It is a stage and a temporary hotel room that opens when the exhibition starts and closes when the exhibition ends. During the three-month Biennial period, you may book your overnight stay in the hotel on the Internet and make it your own territory all day long. No other visitors are allowed to enter that space during your stay.

If we can renovate a former flour factory into an exhibition hall, why can't we make the exhibition hall a hotel concurrently? Your check-in will add a new dimension to the exhibition content. You can make your own plan for that day: sleeping alone, chatting with friends, birthday party, karaoke, anything you might possibly like to do. We have approximately 100 days available for guests to shape and inhabit the space. As for the rest of the exhibition hall, it will be all yours after visitors leave in the evening.

The exhibition venue reuses and re-envisions the old plant, while the hotel reuses and re-envisions the exhibition venue. Our team attempts to achieve a creative symbiosis between exhibition hall and hotel room. Each day of the three-month exhibition will be accompanied by a new and wonderful story. What's the story about? Nobody knows until the end of the day. Together, we will make a 100-day romantic drama series, full of surprises.

Come, with your travelling bag!

创客联盟
NICE
I LOVE CITY
HSBC
海豚村
Je vais Dubai.

ArchiName
PASSION
무한도전

加多寶

加多寶
TUJIA.COM
恭喜发财
优酷

WORKSCAPE THEATRE

Studio Makkink & Bey

In recent decades, we have witnessed the booming trend of interdisciplinary approaches, not only in academia, but also in the domains of architecture and design. Designers and architects find their field expanded beyond the traditional studio or workshop environment, and their concept of creation is liberated from traditional professional boundaries.

The project of 'WorkScape Theatre' explores the possibility of a future working landscape in a theatrical setting through collage. In this installation, Studio Makkink & Bey, a multidisciplinary design studio founded by Rianne Makkink and Jurgen Bey in Rotterdam, the Netherlands, has adapted traditional bamboo scaffolding techniques to create a temporary stage with three workspaces. There is an electronics workshop, a drawing workshop, and a theatre workshop. Each one is made of a specific local material — framed construction safety nets modules, inflated insulation foil panels, and styrofoam planks. Furthermore, these workshops represent domestic architectural languages and archetypes.

Masters-level alumni of Design Academy Eindhoven were invited to gather and play with local materials, collaborate with local producers, and reconstruct a theatrical working scene on the temporary stage. With their interdisciplinary expertise, these designers generated a 'lively working play' for the occasion of the Biennale:

Dan Adlešič (SLOVENIA), a graduate of the department of Contextual Design, explores the aesthetics of interface components such as buttons, plugs, and cables. His works include a range of playful apparatuses that create an environment between reality and fiction.

Echo Yang (TAIWAN), a graduate of the department of Information Design, applies the approach of generative design to an analogue world. She uses obsolete machines such as hand-powered alarm clocks, portable cassette players, and mechanical toys to make drawings, as a way to reveal the internal algorithms of these existent objects.

Fiona du Mesnildot (FRANCE), a graduate of the department of Social Design, compares society to a theatre structure, and develops a design methodology on the basis of theatrical elements. She questions our social norms, and her works re-script, re-stage, and re-act the spectacle of our everyday life in a disruptive way.

Architect **Xian Zheng** (CHINA) and Designer **Hsiang-Ching Chuang** (TAIWAN) captured and reinterpreted the dynamic happenings in this space through drawing.

Credits:
Project Leaders: Rianne Makkink & Jurgen Bey
Project Manager: Hsiang-Ching Chuang 庄翔晴
Guest Designers: Dan Adlešič, Echo Yang 杨维纶, Fiona du Mesnildot, Xian Zheng 郑娴
Photographer: 卓良
Special Thanks: Nine, Corine, Anja

01

Bamboo Scaffolding
Echo Yang
Drawing Workshop
Fiona du Mesnildot
Theatre Workshop
Dan Adlešič
Electronics Workshop
Space for co-installation

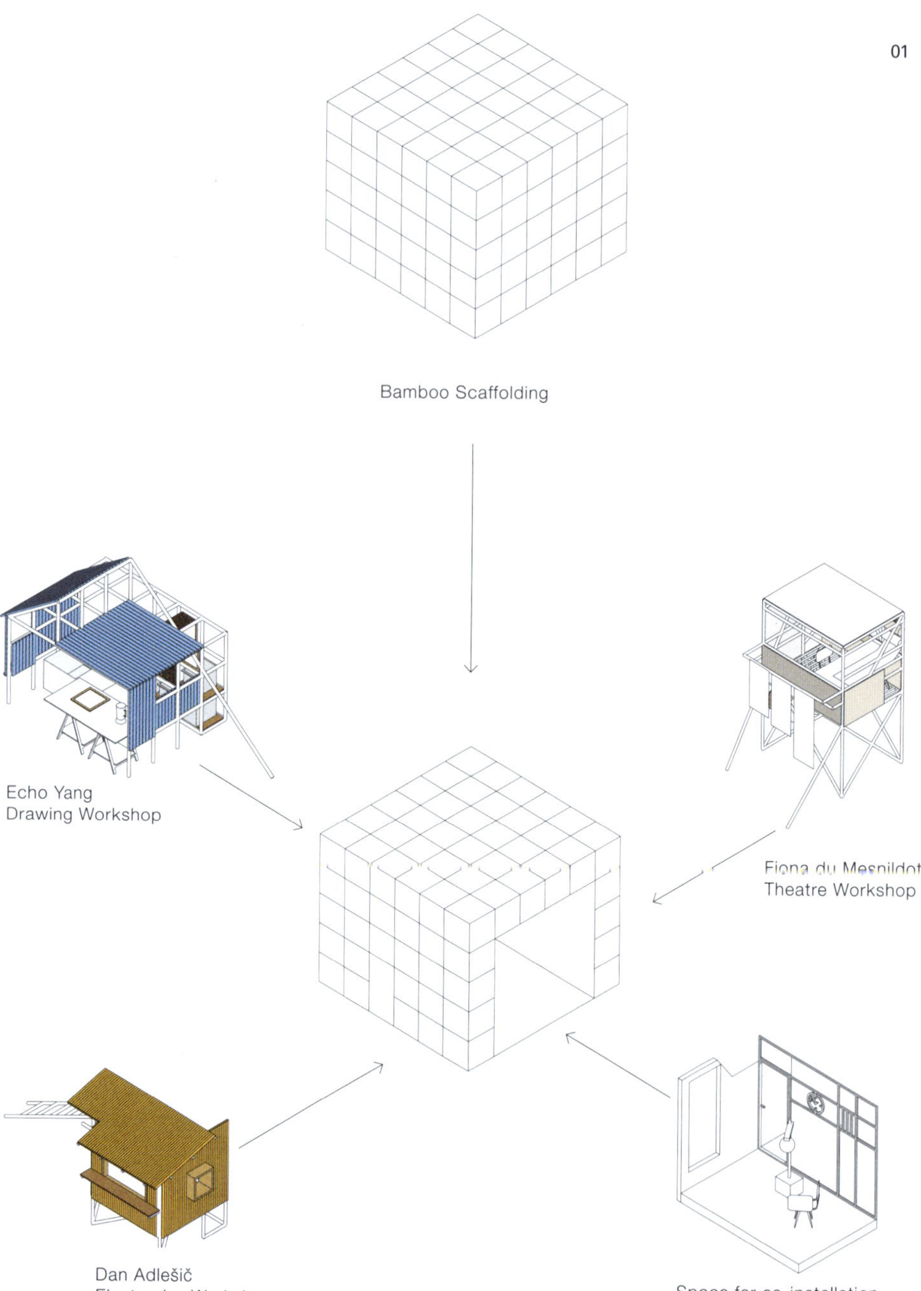

02

01 The installation brings together an electronics workshop, a drawing workshop, and a theatre workshop within a bamboo scaffolding. Each workshop space is defined by different local materials, and evokes domestic archetypes. © Studio Makkink & Bey

02 Collage concept elevation study for WorkScape Theatre. © Studio Makkink & Bey

WOAH!

Theatre

Photos by Maurice Boyer

RE-

Francesco Delogu and Maria Cristina Finucci

We tried to imagine a new archetype, an exemplary primary form that transcends any cultural difference and from which more complex forms can be generated and used, in the architecture of the future, to face the emergency of saving our planet.

Our archetype is made of the solid matter of countless objects that were salvaged from landfills or recycled, then packed into ordinary black plastic boxes that serve as construction modules. We are no longer talking of metric modules or golden ratios: what we are inaugurating here is a new relationship based on the ideal measures provided by the resulting material. Rather than referring to unchanging, ontological structures, this new architectural paradigm is determined by contingency.

The city discards its detritus while at the same time being reborn in a process of self-reproduction. The very same necessity to reinvent the world 'within the limits of our inherited reality' forces us to give a second or third life to buildings or objects, as we used to do in the past.

The image of the building, with its windows shining in the darkness, is multiplied in the mirror walls that surround it, changing our perception of scale and suggesting the idea of a city. In a play of opposites, visitors are then invited to follow a path that takes them from that urban, public environment into the private, intimate space of the building's interior.

Once inside, visitors discover the exuberant polychromy of the discarded objects that constitute the very building blocks of the construction. Everyday objects, so familiar and easily recognizable, still radiate the emotional charge that they used to have when they were being used, and which no transformation or recycling can ever disperse. Their value is not only material, but also poetic. This room of ancestral experiences place proves that we can and must create a *space for well-being* from our very own garbage.

We dedicate this project to the memory of our collaborator Giovanni Vimercati, who left us much too young.

Credits:
Lead artists: Francesco Delogu, Maria Cristina Finucci
Collaborators: Davis Tantimonaco, Giovanni Vimercati

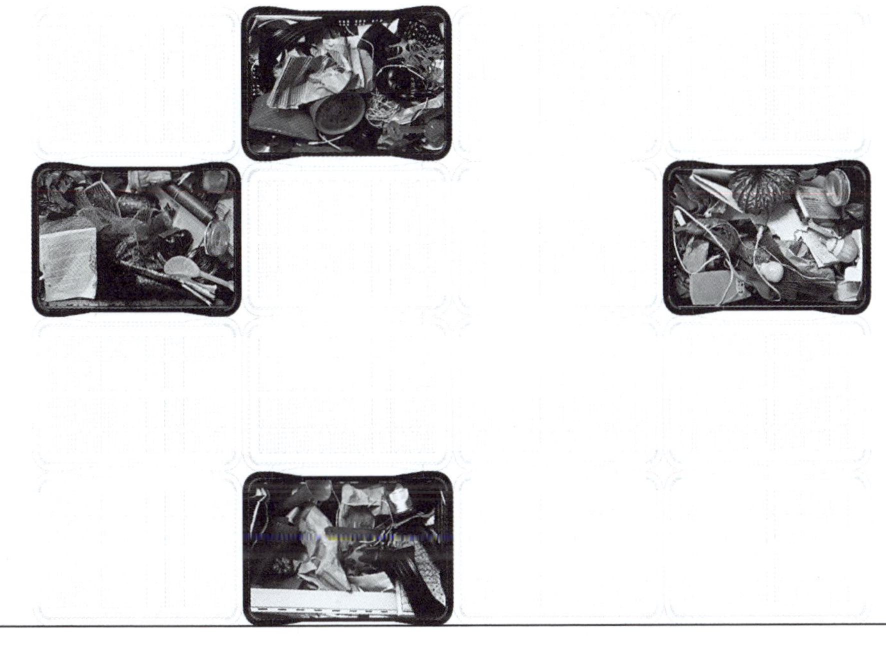

01

01 Concept drawing by Francesco Delogu and Maria Cristina Finucci

消防管

TRASH TO TREASURE LAB

Superuse Studios

'Trash to Treasure Lab' shows the potential of repurposing waste for design and architecture. It includes stacks of materials salvaged from the flows of trash in the region of Shenzhen. These discarded materials pose a collective challenge: how to creatively reuse and repurpose the material for new spatial configurations? Perhaps trash can be filled with new potential to become a kind of secondhand 'treasure'.

The installation design consists of vertical 'columns' of salvaged material suspended inside individual scaffolds of bamboo and construction netting. By implication, these virtual columns suggest a new architectural future for the waste materials.

Adjacent to this experimental Lab, are inspiring examples of design with waste materials by Superuse studios, along with several tools to help suggest ways in which other designers might apply these materials in future projects. The material on display represents only a tiny fraction of the vast volumes that industry produces, and which currently generates little or negative value. The series of designs by Superuse Studios prove that there is a huge creative field to be explored and the potential for new value creation in terms of economic, social and environmental benefits. Our trash service desk offers help to those who seek advice for turning their trash into 'treasure' by seeking more valuable applications of their waste material. 'Trash to Treasure Lab' invites everyone to start designing the circular economy.

The 'Trash to Treasure Lab' is the first project by Superuse Studios' new agency in China.

Credits:
Jan Jongert, cofounder of Superuse Studios, Rotterdam; tutor at the Royal Academy of Art in The Hague and TU Delft.
Junyuan Chen, Superuse Studios China, interior architect and tutor at Central Academy of Fine Art, Beijing.
Kind support by Elsebeth te Kiefte for space layout and graphic design, Tzu Chi Foundation for material research and the Shenzhen Polytechnic for onsite execution.

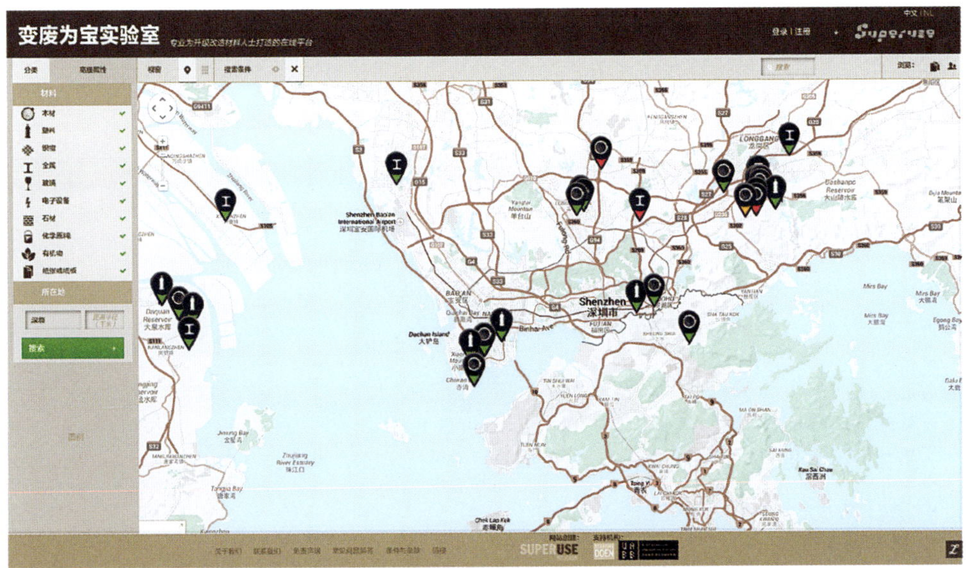

01

02

01 A recent screen grab of the PRD Harvestmap. Harvestmap.com (Oogstkaart.nl) is an online platform and marketplace for designers, architects, and others to access materials and knowledge about reuse, 'superuse' or 'upcycling'. Founded in the Netherlands, the platform now includes user groups in Shenzhen as well as Warsaw, Vienna, Paris and Christchurch.

02 Wikado Playground in the Netherlands, an example of the Harvest Map in action, designed by 2012Architekten (now Superuse Studios). Five discarded wind turbine rotor blades were repurposed as a series of four towers, a maze-like space and central courtyard for the Kinderparadijs Meidoorn Foundation.

掘废料的潜力吧

SHENZHEN ENTROPY

Rob Voerman

In this installation, Dutch artist Rob Voerman shines a light on the lives of some of the millions of migrant workers in the Shenzhen region. Voerman teamed up with poet Guo Jinniu, who lives in Shenzhen and who was a migrant worker himself for 20 years. With this work, Voerman explores and questions how the workers might feel at home in what to them is an alien city, and what we can learn from the way they make themselves at home here. The project creates a platform for these workers to tell about their own life through poetry, performances, and presentations.

Voerman's installation consists of two connected pavilions. One is a cardboard structure with wooden frame. Its stained glass and dark acrylic windows filter coloured light into the dark interior. Furnished with simple furniture, it has a humble, melancholic atmosphere recalling the journey of the migrants who come from small villages.

The other pavilion, accessible from inside the first one, consists of an open space equipped with a stage and two worktables. Poetry and painting are displayed within, and musicians perform on stage every Sunday. In this space, the line between private and public, between work and life, becomes indistinct.

'Shenzhen Entropy' also pleads for a changed mentality in urban planning that comes close to the ideas and thoughts Colin Rowe and Fred Koetter espoused in their 1978 book, *Collage City*. The installation poses the question of whether city planning perhaps can learn something from the intimacy and slowness of village life.

Photo by Rob Voerman

Memories of Luozu Village (No.3)

Guo Jinniu

Xia Dynasty. A carpenter indulged in classicalism, ran his hands through a piece of wood
and made it thrumming like a guitar
Ming Dynasty. The things that the runners of county Yamen ever touched
started to ring like pieces of ironware, and cracked like bones
It sounded like strangers trying to force open a bud

He strolled
from Dong Chang to Xi Chang[1], taking advantage of others' wives,
acting more unscrupulously than Palace-guard Gao[2]
and extorted money from people.

Yuan Dynasty. A man called Timur
A casual laborer on the construction site, who had Mongolian blood
showed others tattoos covering his body from chest to wrist, which described
his dreams of a future Mongol Empire

Hold on, you fearless warrior

Let's lie in ambush in the D major melody
of an old guitar, fiddling around
inside concrete
and steel

Ming closely followed Yuan, when he was hunted after
everywhere. No, he was no spy of the former dynasty
He was
my proletarian comrade

Translated by Eglantine YIN 殷晓媛

1 – Dong Chang and Xi Chang: both were national organization for espionage and secret investigations, under the management of a senior eunuch.
2 – Palace-guard Gao: a notorious Don Juan and bully in the novel 'The Outlaws of Marsh'.

罗租村往事（之三）

文/ 郭金牛

夏。古典的小木匠，他摸过的木头是吉它的美声
明。六扇门的捕快，他摸过的事物
有铁器，碎骨的声音
有陌生人，强行打开花朵的声音

他
从东厂巡到西厂，比高衙内还狠，动别人的女人
收保护费。
元，铁木儿。

一个工地上的小工，蒙古人的后代
纹身，大汗的梦，从胸部扩大到手腕
且慢啊，好汉。
且与和我一起藏匿在

一把旧吉它的D调中，鬼混
于钢筋
和水泥
元。被

明反复追捕。他，不是前朝的奸细
他，是我无产阶级
兄弟。

GUO Jinniu migrated to Guangdong Province (PRD) from his home in Hubei in search of work in 1993. His anthology of poems, *Going Home on Paper,* received the 2013 Artsbeijing.com International Chinese Poetry Prize.

Photo by Rob Voerman

Photo by Rob Voerman

10

Photo by Rob Voerman

ECSTASIES OF INFLUENCES: STUDIOLO WALL

Lukas Feireiss and Thomas Tsang

'Ecstasies of Influences: Studiolo Wall' is a curatorial infrastructure dedicated to the cognitive surplus of the architectural metaphor and the eclectic exploration of how ideas and images, forms, and materials influence and reshape one another over time.

At the heart of this approach is the Biennale curators' idea of collage as 'the assembly of previously made materials, often in a fragmentary or worn state, and repurposing them within a new, but unstable framework'. The 'Studiolo Wall' is conceived as an example of such an 'unstable framework' that draws its inspiration from multiple sources.

Walls are the fundamental element of all architecture and its most powerful instrument. Walls are ubiquitous and their arrangement sets out the spatial matrices within which our lives are defined. They demarcate a before and a behind. Literally and metaphorically, however, walls have two sides to them. Nowhere is bi-faceted condition more apparent than in the built-in cabinetry of an Italian Renaissance *studiolo,* a little room furnished with books, scientific instruments and works of art and nature, devoted to the scholar's study and retreat.

The 'Studiolo Wall' installation in the former Dacheng Flour Factory, Shenzhen, reinterprets the typology of the studiolo for a more public, but still introspective, use. While the external effect of the principal wall suggests a plain surface, its interior accommodates a complex inner life of miniature spaces, cupboards, and alcoves that create transitions between the two sides of the wall. Painted in chalkboard black, the 'Studiolo Wall' invites visitors to pick up a piece of chalk and openly share their personal thoughts and influences, and revisit what others have inscribed on the wall.

As a discursive exhibit suspended within the main exhibition, the 'Studiolo Wall' operates as an interface for social and epistemological action. It argues for an understanding of architecture beyond its functional denotation as a performative metaphor and apprehensive model in revealing diverse degrees of meaning.

Credits:
Lukas Feireiss and Thomas Tsang with Kenneth Chow, Sebastian So, Adeline Chen, Giulia Vallese

01

01 Antonello da Messina, St. Jerome in his Study,
Oil on Canvas, 1475

ECSTASIES OF INFLUENCES

POWER TO THE PEOPLE

Heidelberg Project

The philosophy behind 'Power to the People' is to explore the idea of empowering citizens to think creatively about what is possible for themselves and consequently their immediate environment. Guyton seeks to use art as a catalyst to raise the level of consciousness and recharge the human spirit.

'Power to the People' consists of a house-frame, constructed out of wood, measuring approximately 20 feet by 15 feet. The roof of the frame is turned asymmetrically so as to give the structure an off-balance perspective. The surface behind the frame is covered with a shoe-designed wallpaper, visible from the exterior. The outside of the house thus appears to have been painted with colorful shoes, yet the frame is still visible. While the custom-designed wallpaper faces outward, the interior of the frame features white walls that have been hand-embellished with colorful designs, words, and other symbols including words written in Chinese. The messages featured inside the framed house are intended to provoke thought and offer messages of hope and inspiration.

'Power to the People' helps us to reflect on what's going on inside our own house. The installation refers not only to physical dwellings, but also in a larger sense to the conditions of human existence. The shoes are symbolic of the human soul, left as traces in the environment. The words and symbols written inside of the structure symbolize the inner life of thought and spirit.

The Heidelberg Project, founded in 1986, is a non-profit community arts organization in Detroit. Its mission is to use art and creativity to change lives and communities. Located in one of Detroit's most challenged communities, the Heidelberg Project anchors work in: renewing the human spirit through art, reinvention and revitalization of urban spaces, urban education, politics of creativity, urban ecology, and environmental justice through public art.

Credits:
Tyree Guyton and Jenenne Whitfield

You
TIME
NOW
5
Y.H.W.H
come in
Knowledge
NO
The All in All
HELL
和平

THE ART OF ARCHITECTURAL MONTAGE: BETWEEN GIVE-AWAYS & TAKE-AWAYS

Jimenez Lai

Architectural montage produces effects on the inside and the outside of architecture; it is both sensorial experience and visual communication.

It is a technique that mixes parts together to construct new wholes. The techniques of montage have simmered and matured over the last century. Freshly off of the Russian Revolution of 1917, the new Soviet powers need a weaponized format of mass-communication to sculpt the minds of their new citizens. Motion picture, an invention as new as the ideology they are trying to install, is the perfectly fertile medium for propaganda. This is the birthplace of the Soviet school of montage, and the context of a testing ground for great filmmakers such as Sergei Eisenstein.

Perhaps for the first time in the realm of composition, the consumption of visual effect is no longer static and no longer quite flat. Unlike paintings, film makes it possible to tell a story against the element of time. Not dissimilar to music, film includes a new conceptual instrument to work with: the production of context through sequential juxtaposition. It affords new powers to the art of insinuation. Beyond just rhythm and repetition, juxtaposition can create new meanings out of seemingly unrelated matters.

For example, the early Soviet masters developed Intellectual Montage as one of the techniques in continuity editing. One of the important milestones was the Kuleshov Experiment.

In these short sequences of clips, what remained constant was a still shot of a pensive looking man. The three juxtapositions applied to this framed man were: a dead baby, a bowl of soup, and a seductive woman. The act of stitching together seemingly unrelated matters produced three distinct meanings: sadness, hunger, and lust.

In his book *Delirious New York* (1978), Koolhaas used the Downtown Athletic Club as an architectural example of how juxtaposition can create new meanings: for example, a changing room abuts an oyster bar on one side and a boxing ring on the other. If the filmstrip provides an opportunity to consider a long and serial, dialectical, part-to-part relationship, one can regard the contents within each frame as a parallel to architectural program. This idea of juxtaposition is taken further in Bernard Tschumi's Parc de La Villette proposal (1982-83) — the contrasting parts of the filmstrip no longer are isolated moments of A or B, but rather a mathematical set of A and B. Tschumi eloquently expounded the idea that the montage of filmstrips are as programmatic as actions in the drawings of his *Manhattan Transcripts* (1976-81). Out of the borderless seriality of frames between episodes, new environments are constructed by mixing isolated fragments into the clusters of parts, in acts of architectural montage. This approach of montage affects how program is composed on the inside of architecture, in other words the organization of architectural guts.

The expression of architectural montage as attachments of program is exemplified by two Dutch firms at the turn of the twenty-first century. The Netherlands Pavilion by MVRDV at the 2000 World Expo in Hanover is a three-dimensional collage that expresses the part-to-part relationship between programmatic differences explicitly. On the other hand, the shrink-wrapped volumes of the proposed Bruges Concert Hall (1999) by Neutelings Riedijk Architects implicitly communicate residues of architectural program, rather than explicitly reveal the contents as in the

Fig. 1 Still from *Man with a Movie Camera* (1929) directed by Dziga Vertov.
Fig. 2 Detail of the north facade of the Kukje Gallery (K3) in Seoul, draped in stainless steel mesh, designed by SO – IL. Photo by Iwan Baan.

case of the MVRDV pavilion. The half-hidden bulges of program, in even more contemporary terms, can be seen in the Kukje Gallery's K3 building (2012) by SO – IL in Seoul, where extrusions become protrusions. Circulation and utilities are pushed outside of the simple cubic volume. The function of the stainless steel veil wrapping the building is to ensure that the take-away will not be a dead give-away. It introduces a prolonged sense of tension, a flirtation with no resolution, and a mystery as artfully suspenseful as *Waiting for Godot*.

Another example of ambiguous montage can be found in the melancholic scribbles of John Hejduk. Unlike a Venturi/Scott-Brown 'duck' where the communication of program lies in the exactness of the visual reception, the architecture of Hejduk has an elusive character that may or may not contain exact meanings or expected contents. It is an architecture with qualities of readable communication, but in an indirect and suggestive way that supports multiple readings. Montage offers to architecture the art of insinuation.

Jimenez Lai is the founder and leader of Bureau Spectacular, and a faculty member of University of California, Los Angeles (UCLA). A winner of the Architectural League Prize for Young Architects in 2012, he designed and curated the Taiwan Pavilion at the 2014 Venice Architectural Biennale.

Fig. 3 A House Apart, 2015, by Bureau Spectacular – Jimenez Lai. Proposal for a residence composed of a collection of architectural objects, where every enclosure contains one single architectural program, and the gaps between allow for contractions and expansions of spaces.

COLLAGE SOURCES AND RESOURCES

Gideon Fink Shapiro

We need to better manage our resources, everyone knows, but what about sources?

Architects speak of 'sourcing' this or that component, as if tracing it to its origins. The so-called source might be a fabricator, a region, or perhaps even a specific site of extraction, such as a quarry. Such information is enough to convey the idea that the component came from somewhere, but it goes no further than one or two degrees. It describes not a true origin, but rather a recent stage in a longer journey has no real beginning or end. Even 'raw' materials have a history that reaches back into eons of geology and hydrology. And long after a building comes apart, its ingredients will survive as particles and gases, perhaps recycled in a new building, or more likely mixed into the ground, air, or water. The physical 'source' of a building component, therefore, is nothing more than an abstraction devised for the sake of convenience. It stands in for a recursive series of events and sites stretching from modern factories back to primeval creation. Each source is repeatedly re-sourced. And that is one good reason for speaking not of sources, but of resources.

But resources are not enough to meet our needs — whether in architecture or in broader culture. The problem is not just that resources are finite or even scarce, depending on how we define and identify them. Resources are socially constructed entities, understood as a means to some end. They too, are abstractions. Often they can be quantified as commodities on a balance sheet. Their existence is circumscribed by assumptions about their forthcoming use. 'To define something as a resource is to suspend it between a past "source" and a future "product"', the anthropologists Elizabeth Ferry and Mandana Limbert observe.[1]

The concept of 'source', on the other hand, suggests 'dynamism', 'continuous generation', and 'the potential for creating something else'.[2] Its generative potential leads people to bestow upon it an excess of significance and even a sacred aura. A sculptural *omphalos*, or navel, in the ancient sanctuary of Apollo at Delphi, Greece, signified the spot where the gods were thought to have created the world, while the nearby tholos of Athena's sanctuary, with its circular cella, evokes the navel of the earth in spatial terms.[3] The mountain of Ngaoundéré, in Cameroon, is similarly associated with the navel of the world. The 'sacred spring' that feeds the Roman baths at Bath, England, appears to have been a site of ancient Celtic worship; the Romans then built a temple at the same time as they constructed the bath complex. Many ordinary public fountains across the world are framed and decorated in such as way as to imbue their mundane function with a surplus value: that of social and perhaps sacred meaning. The generative power of the source is missing from the resource. Resources are mundane, expendable, and utterly devoid of enchantment. To have resources without sources is as unsatisfying as to have buildings without architecture.

We need sources after all, even as we renounce the casual use of the term to signify a point of origin. We need to allow places and things to be enchanted, to come alive with meaning and values, to be portals into other times and places and bodies.

1 — Elizabeth Emma Ferry and Mandana E. Limbert, Introduction to *Timely Assets: The Politics of Resources and Their Temporalities* (Santa Fe: School for Advanced Research Press, 2008), 6.

2 — *Ibid.*, 5.

3 — See Vincent Scully, *The Earth, the Temple, and the Gods: Greek Sacred Architecture, Revised Edition* (New Haven, Conn.: Yale University Press, 1979), 111.

Fig. 1 Eugène Cuvelier, Carrière aux Sables de Macherin, 1863. Metropolitan Museum of Art.
'The granite quarries at the edge of Fontainebleau Forest... provided cobblestones for the new boulevards of Paris in the 1850s and 1860s. Here, the piles of freshly cut stone look more like the ruins of a past civilization in a barren landscape beneath a foreboding sky than the building blocks of an emerging imperial capital. At the edge of the this road, quarrymen have built a shelter of rejected blocks.' – www.metmuseum.org

The hunt for open sources

Collage works both ways: it mobilises resources and finds a path back to sources. It speaks the language of the second-hand, but circumvents the one-way chain of expenditure of resources into products. Collage lays bare its sources — identifying new potential in a seeming point of origin — and actualises that potential through incremental acts of transposition, juxtaposition, framing, and naming. In its humble origins as a term for cutting and pasting (the French *coller* means to glue or paste), collage consists precisely in re-sourcing an outworn fragment or perhaps a still-vital one. Everything in a collage is understood to have been found somewhere else, or added at a different time, perhaps just borrowed for a moment.

In the distance between the original context and the artist's selection of a fragment for redeployment lies the difference between source and resource. The resource is the portable, usable thing. And certainly the collage constitutes a kind of product that represents the service of that resource. But unlike economic models of commodity extraction or classical composition, this product is never quite finished. It never quite coheres into a complete whole. A collage remains visibly provisional, suspended between processes of disintegration and reintegration. It hedges between proposing a new formulation and questioning the authority of that formulation by emphasizing its own provisionality.

Collage thus rips a hole in the linear flow of source resource product. This opening allows new tangents to leak in and out, tracing shortcuts to and from other possible sources and other possible products and meanings. The gleaner-artist, hunting resourcefully along the margins of mainstream production, imagines reanimation where others see only empty scraps and dead-ends. The resulting work stays open to reinvention, so long as it continues to articulate or at least acknowledge a sense of its own incompleteness. Collage can turn products back into resources, and find hidden sources within them. These sources are 'open' sources that others can continue to build upon or take in an unforeseen direction.

Ancient Greek architecture is misunderstood by those who would prioritize the coherence of abstract space planning concepts. Instead, Vincent Scully argued, each building along the Sacred Way at Delphi 'acts as a separate unit and makes its own solid presence felt… the movement is like that of free persons in a crowd… Each of the little buildings is therefore an active participant in the life of the site'.[4] The result is a kind of collage of disparate bits that resolutely do not cohere. The violent topography of the site, with its heaving cliffs and thundering clouds, reminded visitors of 'the

4 — *Ibid.*, 112.

precarious footing of human existence in nature', in other words the provisional quality of imposed arrangements.[5] But most poignantly, in Scully's words, Greek temples created a whole environment around them and 'peopled it with their presences' to embody states of being and action.[6]

This ancient legacy offers some precedents for collage in architecture, but the neo-classical movement that developed in the eighteenth century went in another direction. It overlooked a great deal of the dynamic, incremental, and site-responsive qualities of ancient Greek architecture, and instead obsessed over formulations of eternal beauty and compositional coherence. Some of the more adventurous architects of the eighteenth and nineteenth centuries, nonetheless, experimented with collage-esque reformulations of classical tradition.

Piranesi's etched views of Rome from the mid-1700s depict ancient ruins combined with speculative elements of the artist's own making. Originally of Venetian extraction, Piranesi asserted the superiority of Rome's architectural heritage (over that of Greece), and was appalled at the evident lack of stewardship of its former splendour. He did not hesitate to show ancient monuments in a state of ruin — many long since plundered and despoiled — but he showed them in such a way as to inspire a sense of their future as well as their past. Piranesi's imagined view of the Via Appia contains a dense agglomeration of mausoleums, busts, and sculpture, which overflows the boundaries of both space and signification. These riches are transformed into resources and back into open sources for a new architecture. It was perhaps the irregularities and lacunae in the urban fabric of eighteenth-century Rome, as opposed to the planned regularity that the ancient Romans exported around the world, that inspired Piranesi's collage vision. The search for open sources also inspired nineteenth-century eclecticists such as Frank Furness of Philadelphia, who repur-

5 — *Ibid.*
6 — *Ibid.*, 1.

Fig. 2 Giovanni Battista Piranesi, Via Appia, from *Le antichità Romane*, 1756.

posed various Classical and Gothic elements while questioning their conventional use. He experimentally combined inherited fragments with modern technology, and made them both visible. Twentieth-century avant-gardes subsequently took up the quest for open sources, but they focused on a stripped-down vocabulary of primary or 'elemental' forms derived partly from industrial production and partly from geometric abstraction. The architects in these modernist circles, such as Ludwig Mies van der Rohe, embraced collage not as an architectural design technique but as a representational and conceptual device for inserting starkly modern buildings amidst older masonry buildings and arcadian landscapes. The contrast between building and setting could be compared with a collage, but Mies's architecture itself was anything but collage-like, for it was carefully reasoned to bespeak uniformity, regularity, and the logic of construction (despite well-known quirks and meticulous detailing).

Collage may be economical, but it does not make any claims to efficiency or inner logic. It is painstakingly irregular and polyvocal. To practise it is to be a 'hunter and gatherer', as Aaron Betsky puts it.[7]

Collage vision

Such openness is difficult to maintain and control at the scale of architecture and the city. At some level, collage is opposed to design. If the former derives from the French word for pasting, the latter derives from the French word for drawing, *dessin*. The act of putting pencil to paper — traditionally the preferred method of architects and planners — is quite different from gluing bits and pieces onto a board. In a design, the play of resources disappears into the reasoned whole. But drawing and digital modelling can learn from the gathering process of collage.

Moreover, collage is widely visible in the built environment in the form of accidental accruals and separate contributions over time. The collage maker begins by *seeing* the provisionally pasted condition of everything we encounter or make. One day maybe we will be able to put a geolocation tag on something as small as an atom of hydrogen, and trace it around the planet and across the galaxy as it enters and exits different bodies, fields, and voids.

Everything is glued to other things, but only temporarily. The city is a social collage machine with its overlapping cultures and codes; and its ragged junctions of scale, speed, noise, and form. The best cities allow for unexpected juxtapositions of program. Streams of live data and ephemeral media increasingly overlay the experience of place. People, the glue of the city as we know it, are layered, contradictory creatures who carry bits and pieces of other people and places. It is not that everything floats

7 — Aaron Betsky, 'Towards Collage Architecture' in the present volume, 24.

Fig. 3 View through window of the former Dacheng Flour Factory, Shenzhen. Constructive processes of extracting, gathering, fabricating, mixing, and fitting together belie the seeming wholeness of a building as an object, and instead suggest a collage-like trafficking of matter. Photo by author.

freely and interchangeably: collage exploits the fact that objects and images are not neutral, and do not fit seamlessly together. And not all juxtapositions are artful or felicitous, such as the existence of extreme poverty next to bastions of wealth. Indeed, the recognition of contingency leads not only to aesthetic possibilities, but also to ethical and political questions of distribution and access.

The provisional quality of our world generally recedes behind a cloak of ordered stability. Or as Bruce Mau memorably put it, 'For most of us, design is invisible. Until it fails'.[8] Collage vision is always ready to challenge the status quo and test for alternative arrangements. It is one thing to recognise accidents of collage all around, and quite another to cultivate collage as a technique. Lebbeus Woods built an entire practice based on revealing and revelling in architecture's underlying instability. His intricately scarred-over assemblages combined the seeming chaos of the aftermath of a disaster (earthquakes, war, floods) with a series of incremental additions and subtractions, suggesting a collective re-assertion of human intention without denying either the violent forces of change or the freedom of every person.

Less ominously, collage has become widespread in contemporary popular media practices such as music videos, mashups, and social photo-sharing apps. Film has its own rich history of montage, of course, but montage (understood as the sequencing of different frames) does not encompass the juxtapositions occurring within a single frame. The director Stéphane Sednaoui and Björk enacted a collage of city and body for the 1993 music video of Björk's 'Big Time Sensuality', filmed on the back of a flatbed truck in traffic — just one of many examples of using collage vision to re-conceptualize the way space bends around us.

8 — Bruce Mau and the Institute Without Boundaries, *Massive Change* (New York: Phaidon, 2004), 1.

To build is to mix up the order of things

Buildings would seem to have little in common with collage — until one either looks closely at their agglomeration of constructive elements or discovers quirks and contingencies in their design and use. Construction triggers a typically far-flung process of extracting, fabricating, gathering, mixing, and fitting together to make a new whole, which belies the seeming wholeness of a building as an object. It would be interesting to be able to touch a piece of a building and instantly see a map and timeline of where its ingredients came from, how they came together in stages of manufacturing and construction, and the people who put their labour into it along the way.

This feverish trafficking of substance is what the Constructivists celebrated almost a century ago with projects that flouted both classical harmonies and the static force of gravity. They showed, through two-dimensional representations and full-scale installations and buildings, that to build was to mix up the existing order of things. That did not mean that the results of their efforts looked 'mixed-up' in the sense of an arbitrary arrangement. Far from it; their work was carefully composed. But the rhetorical power of their constructions derived partly from the implicit labour of transposition and transformation, the tearing and melding of things from one state of being to another.

Builders have sometimes cannibalized other buildings in collage-like manner. Evidence of this practice from ancient times can be found in the *spoilia* displayed triumphantly by victors or incorporated casually into later buildings discovered by archaeologists. The white Tura limestone casing stones that originally clad the Pyramids of Giza have been reappropriated into mosques and houses, except for some remaining panels at the pinnacle of the Khafre pyramid and a few near the ground. Even the great Pyramids are not the inviolable wholes that architects like to see in them. They are part of an economy of forms, rituals, and materials

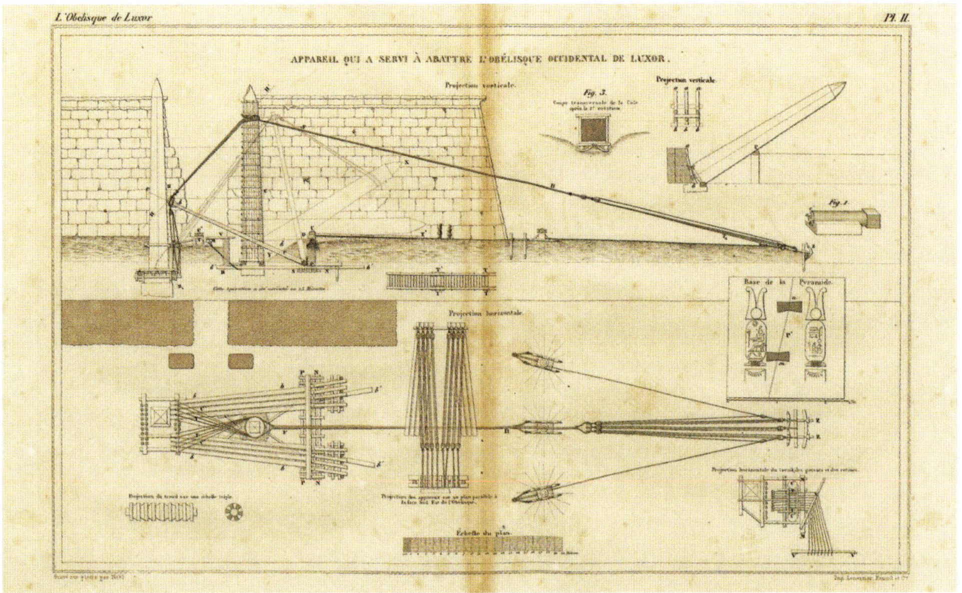

Fig. 4 Jean-Baptiste Apollinaire Le Bas, Elevation and plan of the machines for taking down the obelisk of Luxor and and re-erecting it in Paris, 1831. Heidelberg University Library

moving through time and space. Collage does not give license to plunder. In fact, artists have used their skills (and sometimes, collage techniques) to build public support for endangered architecture, as Piranesi did by selling prints to tourists.

In addition to individual *spolia* that end up in other buildings, one can find whole monuments carted away to foreign settings. The red granite obelisk in the centre of the Place de la Concorde, Paris, evokes an almost incredible series of actions: the removal, in 1831, of one of the two the 23-meter, 250-tonne monolith from its original site at the entrance to the ancient temple of Luxor on the Nile, where its twin remains in situ; the demolition of 'half of a poor village' to create an inclined plane leading down to the Nile[9]; the loading of the monolith into a custom-built ship with

9 — Justin-Pascal Angelin, Expédition du Louxor, ou Relation de la campagne faite dans la Thébaïde pour en rapporter l'obélisque occidental de Thèbes (Paris: Thomine, 1833), 64.

a removable bow; the towing of the sailboat by a primitive steamship across the Mediterranean; the building of custom machinery to hoist the obelisk onto a podium in the Place de la Concorde in 1836, observed by hundreds of thousands of people and accompanied by fusillades of artillery and a live orchestra; and the hieroglyphic inscriptions added to the new base to describe how French engineers pulled off the feat.

The obelisk was ostensibly a gift to France from the ruler of Egypt, though colonial power dynamics complicate the legitimacy of such a gift. Well before the obelisk was physically cut and pasted, so to speak, from the Luxor ensemble to an open plaza, French artists had already isolated it as a stand-alone object or fragment in the graphic space of drawings.[10] The obelisk makes a fine civic monument based on its formal qualities alone, but its presence is much more fascinating — and complicated, even troubling — if one knows how it got there and where it came from. It reflects the discovery of a portable architectural resource in an ancient source. Knowledge of this provenance triggers a strange friction between different times, places, and meanings. Where will the obelisk be in another 200 or 3000 years from now, if it has survived at all? On the one hand it exposes the malleable and oddly contingent nature of the world we inhabit and remake day by day. On the other had it can be seen as a mere representation of its former self, an attempted appropriation of Pharaonic legacy to the self-aggrandisement of another regime. Although the hieroglyphics proclaim the obelisk's modern journey, its disposition as a 'permanent' monument in the heart of Paris gives a sense of inevitability that undercuts its potentially collage-like qualities.

10 — See, for example, detailed studies of both the east and west obelisks of Luxor by Michel-Ange Lancret, Edme-François Jomard, Jean-Baptiste-Prosper Jollois, and Édouard de Villiers du Terrage, published between 1798 and 1812, which show the obelisk against a blank background, isolated from its context. Collection of the Bibliothèque nationale de France, département Estampes et photographie. Other views, such as the 1800 watercolour by François-Charles Cécile, 'Façade du temple de Louxor', in the collection of the Louvre, show the pair of obelisks in relation to the temple architecture.

The artist as remaker

Architects rip ideas off each other all the time, without actually stealing pieces of each other's buildings. They borrow openly or surreptitiously, knowingly or subconsciously. Just as we track the spread of popular videos and articles on social media, we can find new ways to systematically track the spread of architectural ideas or motifs through time and space. Scholars have long pursued this task, but new digital tools will make it possible to sift through larger amounts of drawings, photographs, and even writings to understand historical patterns of reuse and reinterpretation. The results may reveal collage-like patterns of selective recombination. A better understanding of such iterative reconfigurations in architecture would honour inventiveness while giving the lie to the notion of pure originality.

Collage denies the genius of the artist as originator, but celebrates the genius of the artist as a remaker, one who uncovers new possibilities in old things. The imitation of nature and the myth of pure artistic invention give way to the open reconfiguration of things that already exist. Collage announces the 'found' nature of its sources and their plurality. It lays no claim to unity, because its parts do not blend. It makes no pretension to permanence, since it does not appear firmly locked together anyhow. Collage positions itself within a nomadic community of materials and images, which itself constitutes a historical kind of nature, always coming from somewhere and on the way to somewhere else.

Gideon Fink Shapiro earned his Ph.D. in architecture (history and theory) from the University of Pennsylvania School of Design. His research interests span architecture, urbanism, and landscape.

Woven textile banner designed by Thonik, suspended at exhibition entrance.

PEARL RIVER DELTA 2.0: BALANCE IS MORE

Doreen Heng Liu

This is a story about the future of a Chinese city.

1. State of Crisis

This is a story about the future of a Chinese city. It is also a story about the constant conflicts and balance of urban life, spaces, boundaries and mobility in the course of development. It is a new story that is often told, but only in part. What is missing from the narrative is a sense of balance, a concept with deep roots in Chinese culture, which has new relevance today.

Today the world is undergoing diverse and profound changes as well as accelerated urbanisation. Crises such as climate change, population explosion, and shortages of land and energy have become common concerns worldwide. Though China has woken up after a period of stagnation and taken advantage of the last opportunity of accelerated urbanisation, it nevertheless confronts development bottlenecks and the dilemma of whether to continue such acceleration or slow down.

The Pearl River Delta (PRD), a pilot region for China's rapid urbanisation over the past three decades, now stands at the crossroads. Thanks to its importance in global trade networks and immediate proximity to Hong Kong, and booming with a population exceeding 40 million people over a total area of 41,698 square kilometers, this coastal region in Southern China has rapidly grown into the largest megalopolis in the country, and, according to some accounts, the world. Known as 'World Factory', the Pearl River Delta is home to countless factories supported by a massive mobility infrastructure of dense waterway, highway, road, and train systems designed to efficiently transport manufactured goods. However, new demands for industrial transformation, sustainable development, social and spatial changes, and a shift toward information and knowledge as the new 'goods' are forcing the region to reimagine its future.

Driven by the trinity of sweeping globalisation, the powerful top-down rule of the Chinese government, and Western-style modern planning, the region has come to resemble certain Western cities, and to embody the high-efficiency city where capital is put to its highest value. But the region's prosperity is shadowed by numerous crises. The pursuit of fast growth and efficient urbanisation has led to two different consequences: on one side, great wealth matched with glamorous cities, grand infrastructure and the luxury life we have never lived before; on the other side, fragmented urban spaces, divided communities, substandard living conditions, rapid land deterioration, polluted air and water, and an excessive reliance on imported resources.

Yes, we are prospering, but are we living well?

The unhappy juxtaposition of robust economic growth and a deteriorated social and ecological environment, produced during only thirty years' time, is clearly a result of imbalance. The questions raised by Chinese urbanisation have international relevance, as evidenced by broad international concern for Chinese urban affairs. Rapid development has brought miraculous economic success, but at the cost of a more polarised relationship between humanity and nature, and between rich and poor.

2. Collages of Time

As the planning historian Peter Hall has observed, 'Many historical events stubbornly refuse to follow a neat chronological sequence'.[1] He was speaking about urbanisation in Europe and America over the past 150 years, but the same holds true for China, with its overlapping layers of ancient and modern history.

Modernity in China means living and reliving multiple time periods at once. Although China's powerful economy is frequently traced to the 'open door' trade policies introduced by Deng Xiaoping after 1978, there are echoes of earlier periods as well. The early decades of the twentieth century (around the end of the Qing Dynasty) saw heavy trading with the developed West. And centuries earlier, during the Ming Dynasty, Chinese fleets were the largest in the world, connecting Asia and Europe. The 'feudal capitalism' of previous centuries foreshadowed the economic expansion of today, while the modern top-down governing system recalls some aspects of the imperial tradition.

What is modernisation? In its paradigmatic form it is very much a Western discourse coming out of the intellectual culture of the European Enlightenment and the technological growth of the industrial revolution. Its linear notions of time and progress imply a rejection of the past. And indeed, much urban development in China today follows this Western model. China's new cities are large, dense, and centrally planned to an extent that modernist European planners of the last century could only have dreamed about.

It took London 100 years (1800-1900) to grow from a population of around 1 million to 6.5 million; Paris, in the same period, grew from about 500,000 to 3 million; and New York grew from 33,000 to 3.5 million. But it only took Shenzhen only 30 years to expand its population from 10,000 to 10 million.

1 — Peter Hall, *Cities of Tomorrow: An Intellectual History of Urban Planning and Design in the Twentieth Century* 4th Ed. (Oxford: Wiley/Blackwell, 2014), v.

However, real change cannot simply be reduced to a growth curve, like that of rising population or GDP. The dynamics of change and continuity are more complex than typical formulations of modernity and modernisation. Everyday reality departs from the overly simplified, abstract ideal of modernity. China's modernity is a unique and incomplete modernity, coloured by history and culture.[2] The rush toward the future does not eliminate the presence of the past. On the one hand, Chinese culture has shown itself readily adaptable to the shock of the new, and the rapid pace of change. On the other hand, everyday life remains deeply embedded in traditions that endure even amidst new material and spatial forms.

Modernity presents layered collages of time. Multiple phases of development seem to happen at once, or in an unexpected sequence. For example, the growth of industrial manufacturing in the PRD is now paralleled by the rise of digital media and a 'post-industrial' service economy. Rapid migration from the countryside into cities is occurring simultaneously with the urbanisation of the countryside itself. Communism and capitalism coexist, combining the planned economy and market economy. It is as if the trajectory of modernity is flattened, collapsed, and compressed into a single moment in time: the collage of the present.

3. Opportunity PRD: balance and experimentation

The question then arises: for the metropolitan future of PRD, should we repeat the paradigm of Western development, or should we try another way? Already we have seen serious problems in the application of classical Western theories of urbanism

2 — Madeleine Yue Dong and Joshua L Goldstein, *Everyday Modernity in China* (Seattle: University of Washington Press, 2006), 5-6.

to Shenzhen and other Chinese cities. Even seemingly unlimited central planning power does not guarantee a well-functioning, livable city. Top-down processes do not necessarily eliminate uncertainties, but rather introduce new uncertainties born of the disconnect between planners and everyday life.

We have to propose a new approach that accommodates differences and experimentation. Experimentation can take the form of designers working *with* the city instead of *upon* the city. Designers and planners should seek out the opportunities specific to China and the region.

This is PRD 2.0, a vision of a more balanced urbanism. Rather than striving toward an abstract ideal of development, we will move forward by embracing the collages of time that characterise our past, present, and future. The guiding principle of PRD 2.0 is 'balance is more', a play on the old mantra of 'less is more', associated with Mies van der Rohe; and Robert Venturi's rejoinder, 'less is a bore'. Unlike the growth paradigm, which is one-directional, balance supposes multiple elements in relation to each other.

Balance — a concept with deep roots in Chinese culture — is also relevant to contemporary urbanism. Nothing is absolute. Everything stands in context and relation to something else. In Chinese, this is a philosophical proposition known as 命题. Perhaps the ancient idea of 提出, 'nature and human are one', can inform urbanism in the PRD. Shenzhen, already a vast metropolis, needs to balance economic development with social and ecological health.

Even more profound than balance is *flowing balance*. Everything is in motion, ephemeral. Cities, too, thrive when we allow for changes over time. We must adapt to our urban environment, but at the same time the city must adapt to our needs.

In this way we swim in harmony with the current of change. Top-down masterplans alone are too rigid, too static to accommodate flowing balance.

The fullest expression of balance is *multi-dimensional flowing balance.* This means that multiple realities and potentials are considered at once. The people, the land, the spirit, the history, the architecture of the city — all these things and more contribute to PRD 2.0. In place of false certainties, we must embrace ambiguity. The many layers of the past and present create new possibilities for the future.

PRD 2.0 is therefore about re-living the city and readapting urban life for an uncertain future. The paradigm of balance evokes different elements in shifting equilibrium, even as they move and change in relation to each other. The new metropolis is still envisioned as a highly efficient and densely populated city, but also as a city full of possibilities arising from its multiple layers.

Here are 10 urgent and important issues pertaining to land, space, environment, and population explosion in the PRD region, to be considered by urbanists, architects, and all kinds of designers:

1. Urban Regeneration

Transforming, renovating, and consolidating what already exists, including urban villages, factory towns, landscapes, and territories.

2. Instant Urbanism

The design of new towns, integrated infrastructures, public parks, politics of space and territory, free trade zones, and land reclamation projects.

3. Tropical Practice

Regionalism, Lingnan culture and lifestyle, tourism.

4. Infrastructure and Mobility

Integrating urban systems in our built environment.

5. Water
Delta urbanism, floating estates, interfaces between water and land.

6. Resources
Energy, waste and recycling.

7. Informal practices
Making our cities more livable based on research and respect for everyday realities and bottom-up methods.

8. Food and Agriculture
Global food chains and future agriculture in the context of large-scale urbanization, with attention to food security and quality.

9. The virtual dimension
How does information technology change our practice of urbanism and city living?

10. Digital modeling and fabrication
Exploring and applying new parametric techniques to study urban fabric and spatial form.

Doreen Heng Liu

WHAT IS THE FUTURE OF PRD?

Pearl River Delta

Guangzhou, Dongguan, Shenzhen & Hong Kong

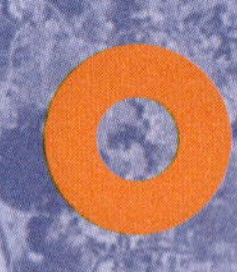

Guangzhou
CULTURAL & ADMINISTRATIVE CENTRE

Foshan
CANTONESE CUISINE & CANTONESE OPERA

The Pearl River Delta (PRD) region in Southeast China includes four dominant cities, as well as numerous smaller cities. Together they make up a vast industrial, economic, administrative, and cultural nexus.

Jiangmen
OVERSEAS CHINESE & KAIPING DIAOLOU

Zhongshan
HISTORICAL & CULTURAL CENTRE

Macau
CASINO & RESORT DESTINATION

Dongguan
FACTORIES & PRODUCTION AREA

Shenzhen
SERVICE INDUSTRIES

Zhuhai
RESORT DESTINATION & GARDEN CITY

Hong Kong
INTERNATIONAL FINANCIAL CENTRE

Floating population
Total population

The floating population of a city includes migrants and temporary workers, and often reflects its speed of economic development and urbanisation.

4648200

12709600

Guangzhou
7287km²

1237700

2463100

Shunde
807km²

3490200

7199100

Foshan
3848km²

7861700

10372000

Shenzhen
1953km²

7037100

8224800

Dongguan

2472km²

212300

7068000

Hong Kong

1108km²

1630900

3122700

Zhongshan

1800km²

1630900

3122700

Zhuhai

1711km²

20000

550000

Macao

29km²

In the traditional mode of urbanisation, rapid economic development and infrastructure comes at the price of quality-of-life measures such as air, water, land, health and community — a paradigm to be questioned.

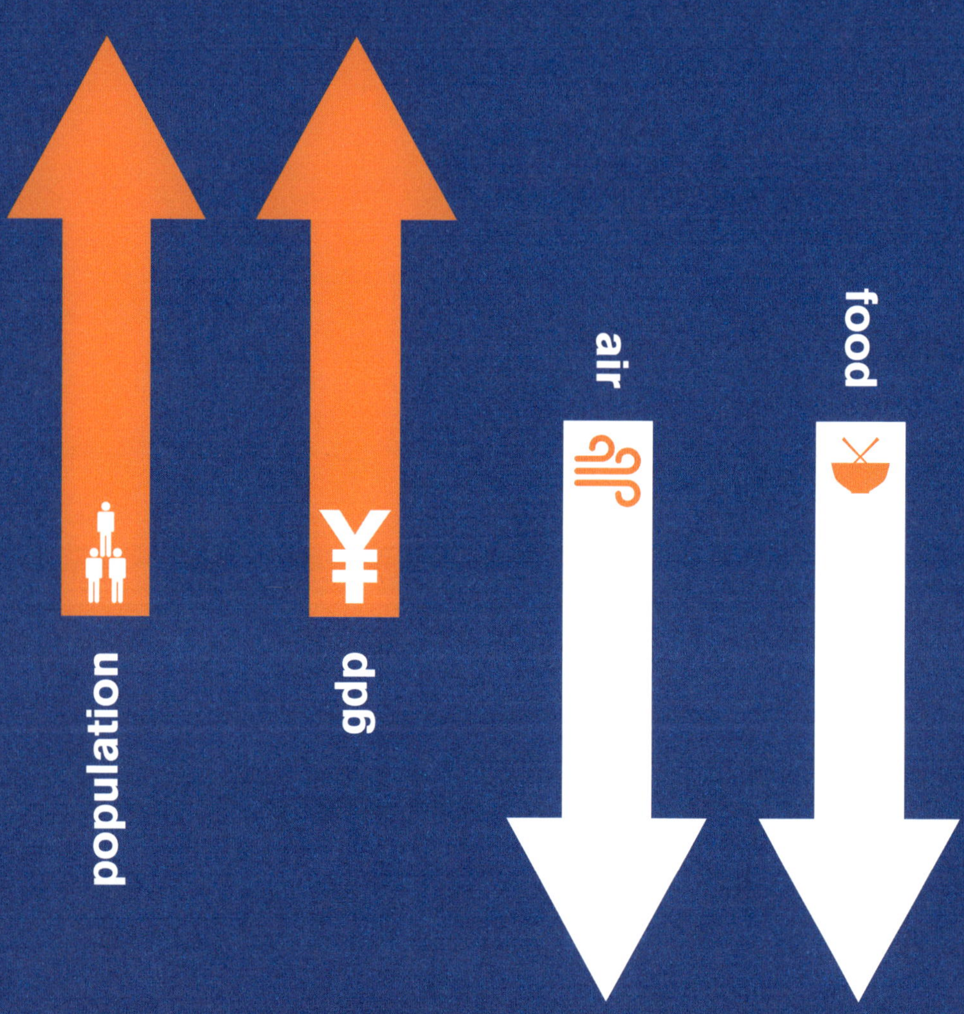

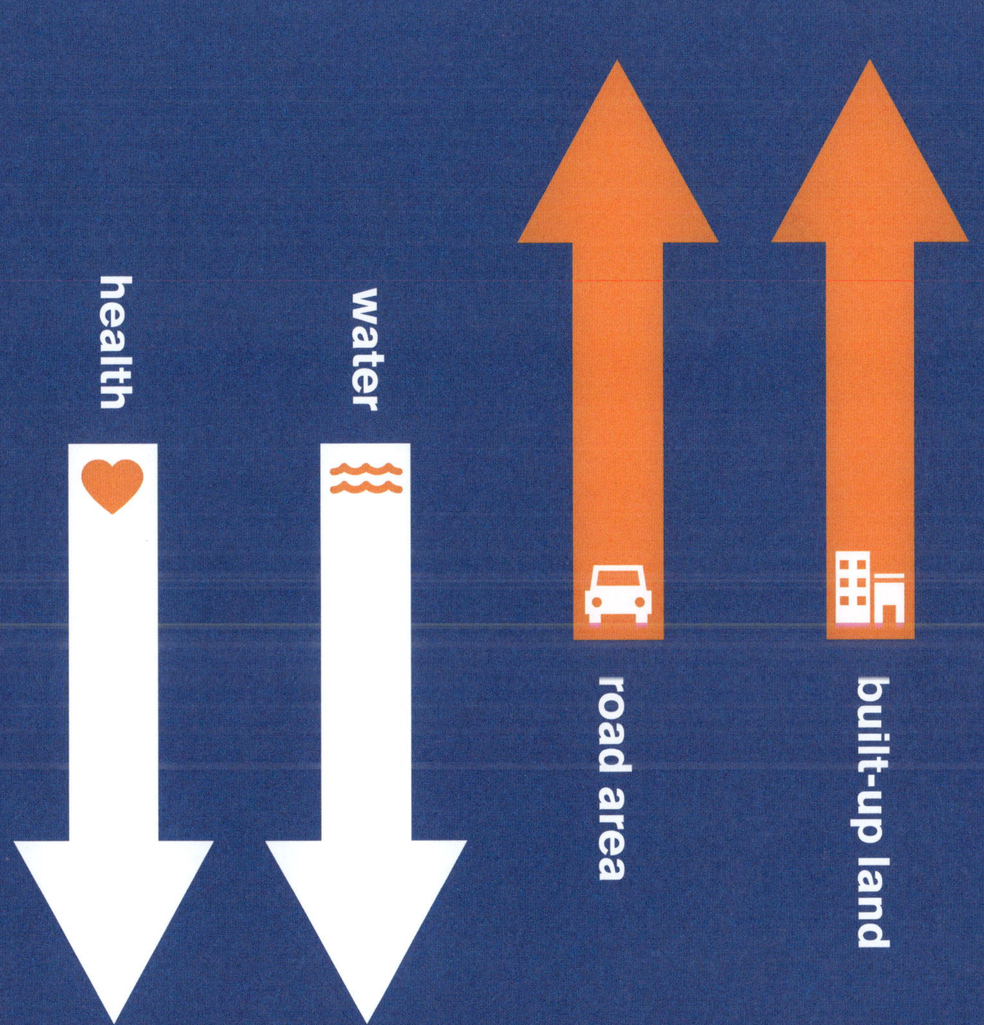
health
water
road area
built-up land

Made in the Pearl River Delta

The Pearl River Delta has grown to become the 'factory of the world' as a result of free trade policies, inexpensive labor, and massive development. However, long-ignored issues have begun to surface in the form of economic slow-downs and social instability.

VIZIO
NOKIA
SONY
cisco

In 1980, Deng Xiao Ping named Shenzhen and Zhuhai two of China's first Special Economic Zones (SEZs), launching a course of exponential growth driven by foreign investment and free trade. More recently, the central government has established four additional SEZs in the PRD region. Looking toward the future, how could such free trade zones be improved to enable not only growth, but also a better quality of life?

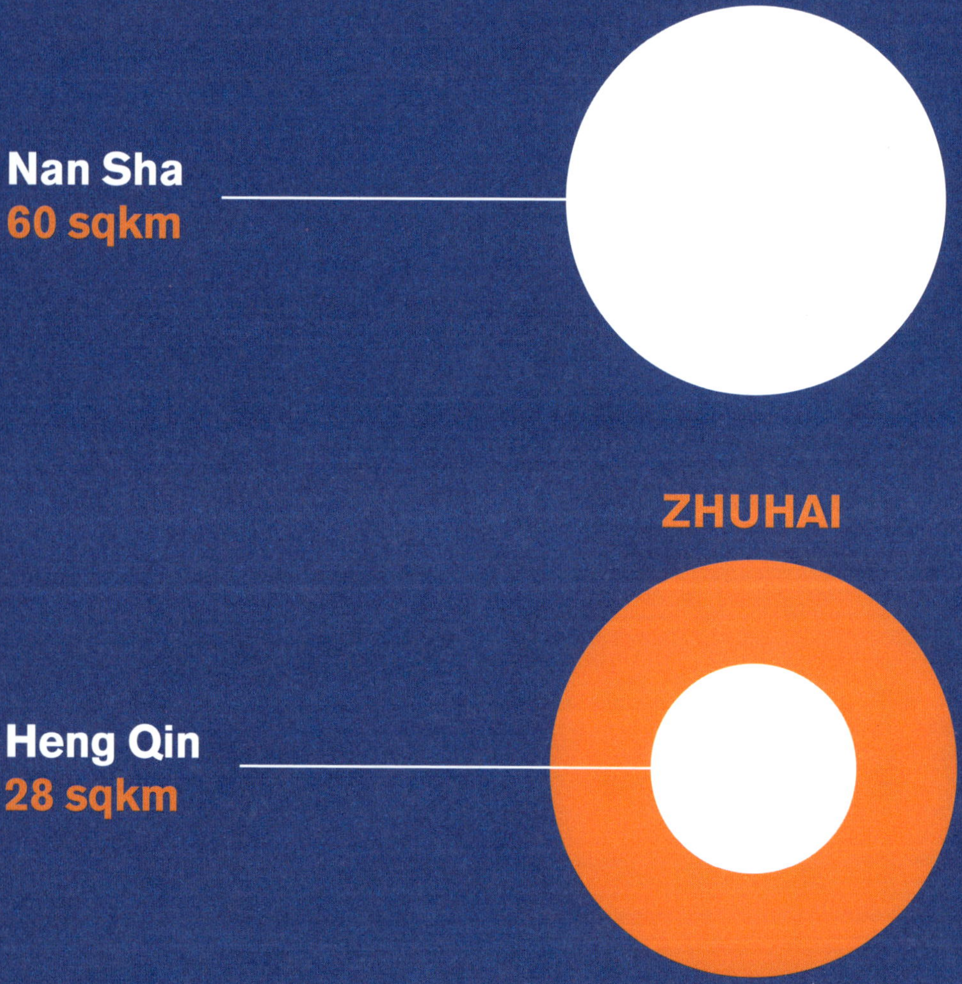

Nan Sha
60 sqkm

ZHUHAI

Heng Qin
28 sqkm

Economic zone

Free trade area

Balanced Infrastructure

Economic, social, and environmental

Balance Is More. The future city should not just repeat the old profit-driven development paradigm, but should incorporate the Chinese concept of *balance*. A more balanced approach to growth would allow us to consider economic development in relation to the quality of everyday life.

Social Networks
Infrastructure
Economy System
Nature Treads

PRD 2.0 FLOORPLAN

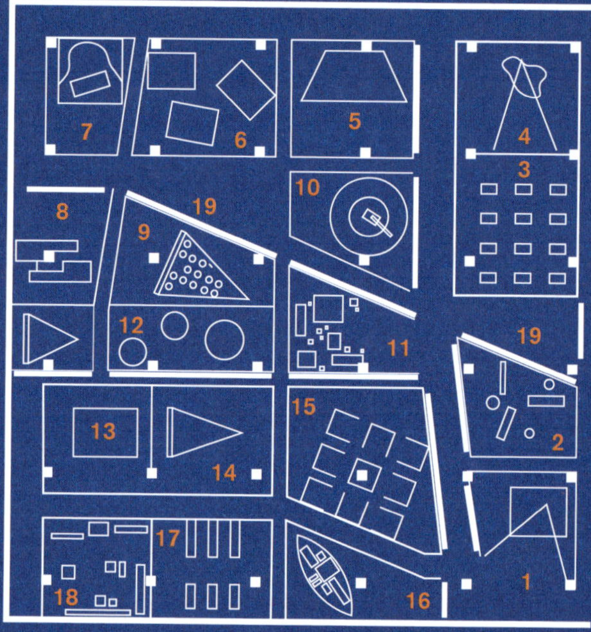

1
Re-Living the Bright City
SIMA Xiao and HUANG Weidong, Urban Planning and Design Institute of Shenzhen (UPDIS)

2
Made in South China (MISC) — Mapping the Cultural Landscape of PRD
Laurent Gutierrez and Valerie Portefaix, MAP Office

3
City of Wind
Philip YUAN, Archi-Union Architects

4
Bay Bar
CAI Zhen and ZHU Rongyuan, China Academy of Urban Planning & Design (CAUPD), Shenzhen

5
Hyper Metropolis – Speculations on Future Hybrid Lifestyle in Shenzhen
MENG Yan and LIU Xiaodu, URBANUS Architecture and Design

6
An Alternative Strategy for PRD Rural Villages
Joshua Bolchover and John Lin, Rural Urban Framework

7
Shenzhen Forest Island
MA Yansong, MAD Office

8
The City that Re-Lives its Memories
Sook Hee Chun, Young Jang, and Ming Yu, WISE Architecture

9
Spatial Economic Network
Ljubo Georgiev, One Architecture Week; Hristo Stankushev, dontDIY; Merve Bedir and Jason Hilgefort, LandCC

10
Wealth Architecture
FENG Yuan, Zhongshan (Sun Yat-sen) University

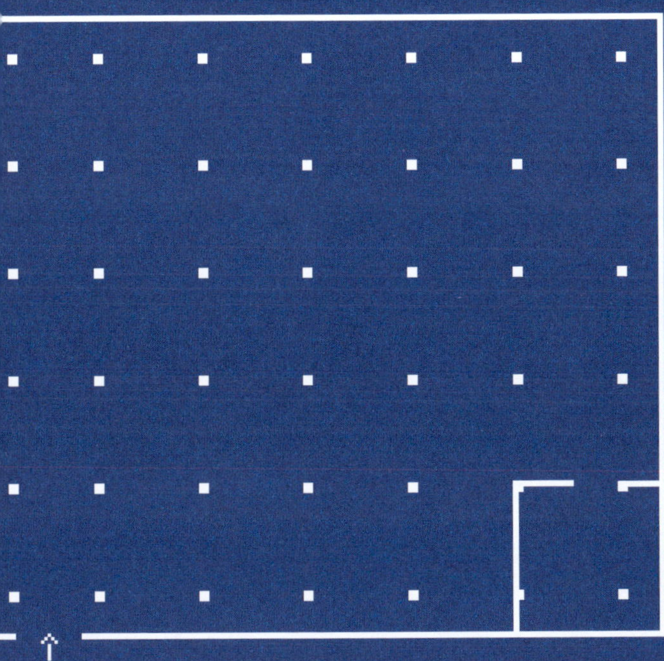

11
Hong Kong Typology
Christoph Gantenbein and Emanuel Christ, ETH Zurich

12
Da Lang Fever 2.0
Linda Vlassenrood, International New Town Institute (INTI)

13
Megablock Urbanisms PRD
Jeffrey Johnson with Stephen Chou and Jiteng Yang, China Megacities Lab, GSAPP, Columbia University

14
Dictionary of Mirrored Gardens
Vitamin Creative Space

15
From Villages to City: The Informal History of Shenzhen
Juan DU, University of Hong Kong

16
n=distortion
Handshake 302

17
Panyu: Rural Becoming Urban?
Margaret Crawford, UC Berkeley; Max Hirsh and Dorothy Tang, University of Hong Kong

18
Material Production — Field Practice of Zini Sugar Refinery, Panyu
Zini Sugar Refinery with TAN Hongyu, Guangzhou Academy of Fine Arts

19
PRD Revisited
Charlie Koolhaas

PRD 2.0
EXHIBITS

RE-LIVING THE BRIGHT CITY

SIMA Xiao and HUANG Weidong, Urban Planning and Design Institute of Shenzhen (UPDIS)

This is not somebody's bright city. This is everyone's bright city.

City is a word with twin shades of meaning. It is more than a container of life. It is life. People generate fortune because of shared production and abundance because of shared consumption. People living in the city create what it exists today, yet fail to plan the future for the city.

The glamour of a city should go beyond a few wise men, encompassing the wisdom of the mass public. In the past, planners took the earth as a canvas, outlining the urban blueprint. In the future, planners should gather public will to forge the city and public wisdom to build dreams. Whether in a building, a road, or a space of any kind, a city will come into being when people come together at a massive scale to live and work. Therefore, the city should care for every one of its inhabitants, and vice versa.

Where there is light, there is also shadow. But the light must come first.

The elements of the exhibit include:

1. Model. A 'bright green ring' is inscribed with the new district of Guangming's dream of being a green city, showing the plan of water, mountains, farmland, and green space that constitutes a good natural base.

2. Solid and Void. An alternating series of 60cm-wide blackboards and mirrors stand vertically to enclose the exhibit space. Light and shadow, void and solid, appear in sharp contrast. The blackboards encourage the public to draw and show their creations, while the mirrors reflect their desire to build a dream green city.

3. Stickers. Colourful magnetic stickers are printed with features including topography, plant species, recreational activities, public services, and infrastructure. The public can choose stickers with the features they like and put them on the green ring in the model. Thus a shared planning dream is born.

黑板和镜子，光与暗，虚与实，
形成强烈对比，
市民共筑绿色城市梦想。
五彩缤纷的小磁贴
寻找
UPDIS共同城市

MADE IN SOUTH CHINA (MISC) – MAPPING THE CULTURAL LANDSCAPE OF PRD

Laurent Gutierrez and Valerie Portefaix, MAP Office

In 2003, a group of emerging artists, architects, filmmakers, curators and writers met to define the contours and specific culture of a booming region – the Pear River Delta (PRD). Coming from different parts of the territory – Guangzhou, Shenzhen, Hong Kong, and Yangjiang, the group gathered in the office of NODE in Nansha, a new town located at the center of the dense urban network. This group is provisionally called, Made in South China (MISC), which also signifies 'miscellaneous'.

MAP Office presents an archive of the PRD through the various works of the MISC group as a foundation of a specific cultural landscape of the region. In the early 2000s, members of the group were preoccupied with questions of rapid urbanization, the place of production, the role of young migrants, public landscapes, and regional infrastructure. Jiang Jung was about to launch the celebrated magazine Urban China. Ou Ning and Cao Fei's documentary film San Yuan Li (2003) portrayed a village overtaken by runaway urbanization. Hu Fang published his first stories about consumerism and theme parks and with Zhang Wei (Vitamin Creative Space), he set up a new kind of art gallery in a market. Xiaodu Liu and Meng Yan (Urbanus) were

01

designing new topologies of public space. Doreen Heng Liu was defining planning strategies of Nansha. Zheng Guogu and the Yangjiang group were starting to use their home and the city as a dynamic laboratory to experiment with architecture and landscape. Chen Shaoxiong was playing with the idea of anti-terrorist tactics with the new towers of Guangzhou. And MAP Office was researching urban conditions with Mapping Hong Kong, HK LAB and the extended territory of the PRD.

Twelve years later, we propose to look back at those early projects and experiments and set up an archive and dialogue about this foundational period. Presenting works that most members of a

02

03

new generation has never seen – including photographs, publications, sculptures, and models condensed into a special installation – we will invite the public to discover the re-making of the cultural landscape of the PRD.

Credits:
CAO Fei, Guangzhou/Beijing
Chen Shaoxiong, Guangzhou/Beijing
JIANG Jun, Guangzhou
Doreen Heng LIU, Nansha/Shenzhen
MAP Office (Laurent Gutierrez and Valerie Portefaix), Hong Kong
OU Ning, Guangzhou/Bishan
Urbanus (MENG Yan, LIU Xiaodu, and WANG Hui), Shenzhen
Vitamin Creative Space, Guangzhou (HU Fang, ZHANG Wei)
ZHENG Guogu, Yangjiang

01, 02, 03 Collage boards by MAP Office, looking back over more than a decade of work by artists and architects working in South China, the foundation of a new era of cultural production.

2
南中国制造
MADE IN SOUTH CHINA

MADE IN SOUTH CHINA
南中国制造

CITY OF WIND

Philip YUAN, Archi-Union Architects

Despite the increasing normalization of human and machine interaction, digital design and fabrication brings greater precision and efficiency to the inherently inaccurate building site.

Robotic building technologies have responded primarily to the legacy of repetitive construction, following the way buildings were made in the past. The promoters of such technologies tout the benefits of reducing time and cost, even if they also have more robust arguments. But aside from these efficiencies, how will digital design and fabrication propel current building culture to establish a novel construction paradigm? How will robots create possibilities for non-standard city formation and redefine the mutual relation between nature, architecture, and infrastructure in contemporary urban systems?

This project takes QianHai, a commercial and industrial cooperation zone on the threshold of Shenzhen and Hong Kong, as a research object to explore the viaability of existing urban railway infrastructure as a driver for contemporary urban development. In this proposal, a series of thermodynamic towers, integrated with a prefabricated roof shading system, are constructed on the site as a primary infrastructure to increase urban vitality. Meanwhile, those towers, also defined as landscape elements, will offer possibilities for creating vertical nature systems in order to liberate the ground space for the development of a high-density urban community. The idea is for railway transportation and robotic construction to allow the habitants to customize the location and formation of their building unit.

Eventually, a bottom-up, self-organising, and highly adaptive urban system driven by air dynamics could be established. This system would accommodate growing demands for social and spatial regeneration within the industrial transformation and sustainable development of the region.

01 City of Wind masterplan by Philip Yuan / Archi-Union Architects

01

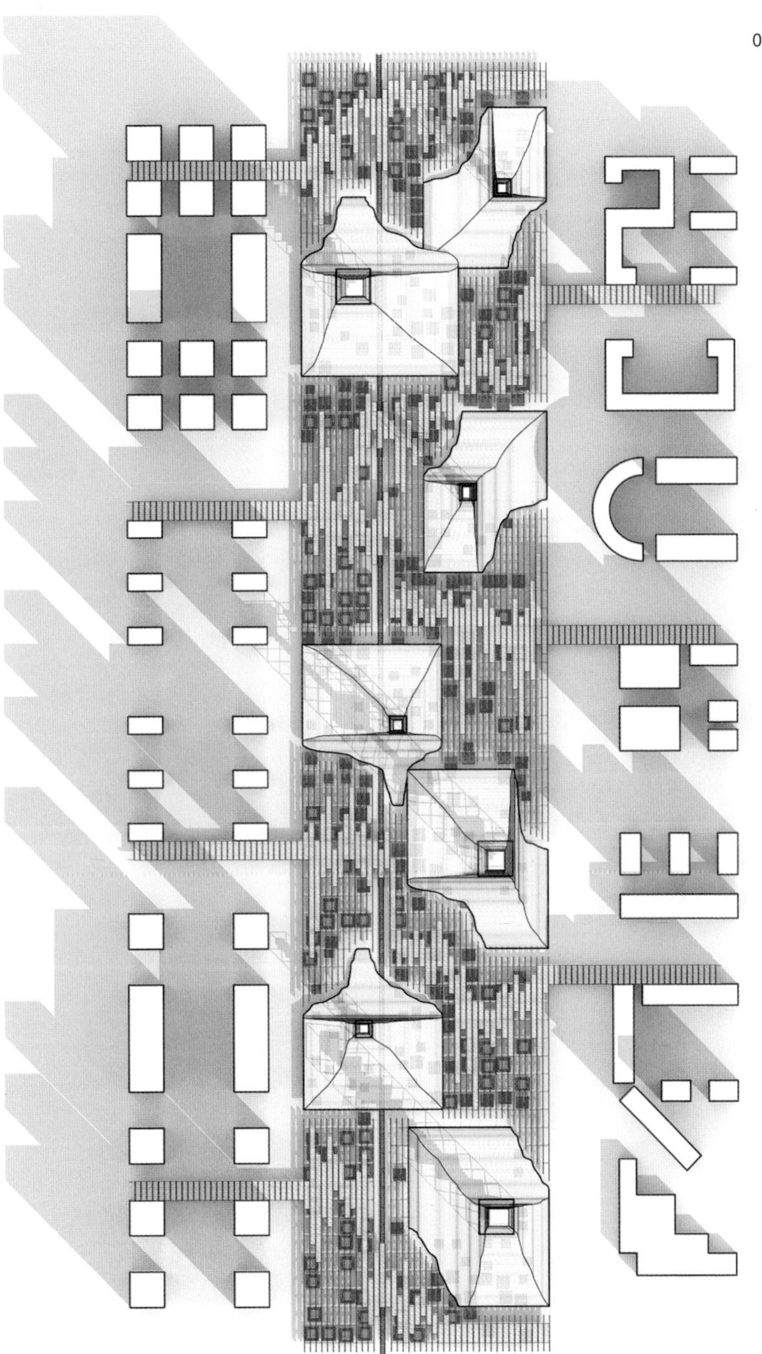

3
METROPOLIS

YPER
塔之城

BAY BAR

CAI Zhen and ZHU Rongyuan, China Academy of Urban Planning and Design (CAUPD), Shenzhen

Using tea and alcoholic drinks as a way to bring people together in public activities, the Bay Bar encourages visitors to explore the history and future of the Pearl River Delta in their own ways. Here they can discover how different people have responded to the multiple demands of urban expansion, and observe some of the tensions and conflicts that have emerged. Visitors are encouraged to think about and identify the potential prospects in re-structuring PRD through various assumptions and scenarios.

Rapid urbanisation in the PRD has given birth to clusters of cities within a short period of time, and these cities vary greatly from one to another. Each person in these cities is affected by various factors, such as the power systems and infrastructures, the 'PRD value' generated jointly by planned economy and market economy, the continuing phenomenon of large-scale migration, and the diversity of cultures that interact and co-exist with each other, contributing to the creation of the 'new Hakkas' culture.

Institute of Remote Sensing, Chinese Academy of Sciences

倾计
一齐嚟倾计 未来乜都有
ECONOMY/ INDUSTRY
倾计
城乡▶规划
URBAN AND RURAL PLANNING
谈
TALK

裂变，
更多城市单元
魔方@城市
Magic Cube @ Cities
点赞 | LIKE
实有值
虚无价
Valuable Materials
Vs
Invaluable Non-materials
PRD1.0的时代，发展的动力是，"物"的聚集、流动、加工与交易。
PRD2.0的时代，发展的动力是，"非物"（信息、文化……）的聚集、流动、加工与交易。
In the era of PRD1.0, the motive force of development is the gathering, circulation, processing and trading of "materials".
In the era of PRD2.0, the motive force of development is the gathering, circulation, processing and trading of "non-materials" (information, culture…).
点赞 | LIKE
总计
gèng
点赞 | LIKE
票数统计

HYPER METROPOLIS – SPECULATIONS ON FUTURE HYBRID LIFESTYLE IN SHENZHEN

URBANUS Architecture and Design, Inc.

In the era of PRD 2.0, Shenzhen will undergo a large social transformation by attracting middle-class and elite populations of migrants to inhabit the city with a new spirit of entrepreneurship. What kinds of new lifestyles and new urban environments will those young entrepreneurs pursue? Will the existing models of urban sprawl and ever-higher towers support the continued upgrade of city development?

In this project, set within the future context of PRD 2.0, Urbanus proposes designs through speculative observations of the transforming social, economic, cultural, and political spheres of Shenzhen. We investigated a series of urban and architectural solutions reflecting the lifestyles of the emerging entrepreneurial class.

The pavilion contains vignettes, collage, models, and an animation evoking a revised urban system with an updated density distribution and new infrastructure. It illustrates a hybrid lifestyle in the 'hyper-metropolis' of the future Shenzhen through major sectional scenes in a 1:50 scaled model.

Credits:
Xiaodu LIU, Yan MENG, Wendy WU, Chang Ho Yeo, Chongyi LI, Yizhe Li, Dillon Wilson. With Enchen RAO, Qiming HU, Fancheng FEI, and Wenzhe YE, Wei ZHOU.

01

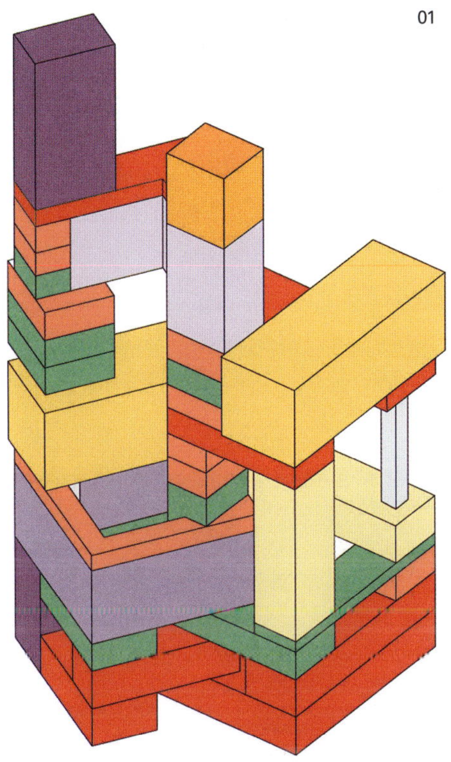

01 URBANUS created a series of speculative studies and designs reflecting the needs of Shenzhen's growing entrepreneurial class, here evoked by the dense layering of various urban programs.

HYPER MET

AN ALTERNATIVE STRATEGY FOR THE PRD'S RURAL VILLAGES

Joshua Bolchover and John Lin, Rural Urban Framework (RUF)

The phenomenal growth and development in the PRD over the past 40 years cannot be considered without understanding the role of villages. From pioneering villages that restructured their economies from agriculture to industry, to urban villages that facilitated migration through dense housing blocks, the village has been the basic building block of the urbanisation process.

After this first wave of industrial urbanisation, what role will the village play in the future of the PRD? As Shenzhen continues to modernise, urban villages are replaced, and factories are succeeded by third-sector service economies. So, what happens to the villages far from the city — the ones where the flood of migrants once came from?

The money sent back home has fuelled the construction of empty villages with many times the original building density, even as people continue to leave. These villages exemplify both op-down and bottom-up processes. They are regulated and prompted by government subsidies, but constrained to the collective boundary of permitted development. This produces urban density in the heart of the countryside. The urban village has migrated back to the rice fields, in form if not in population.

To tackle the potential future of the village, we focus on the modern village house. We consider the current model of housing construction to be prototypical. Villagers have adapted basic concrete frame-and-brick infill to produce a range of urban typologies within the village, from multi-family dwellings to apartment townhouses. Following the lineage of invention from Le Corbusier's Maison Dom-ino to Alejandro Aravena's 'Elemental' housing model, RUF proposed to adapt, modify and design a prototype for a village house. Seen as an evolution of the existing village house prototype found across Chinese villages, the aim is to demonstrate new ways of constructing and growing to accommodate potential shifts in the economy and population as needs change.

Using speculative scenarios, the idea is to test how this prototype could alter the fabric of the village, whilst maintaining the spirit of the collective and the common good.

01

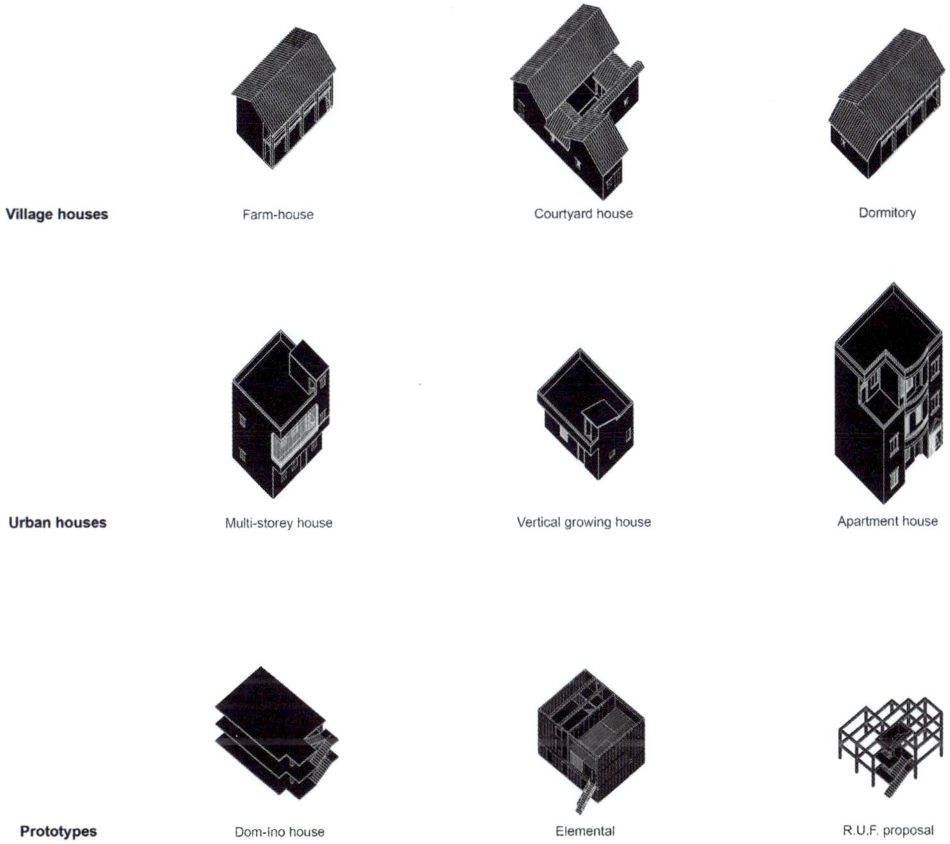

01 Based on studies of typical village houses and urban houses, Rural Urban Framework (RUF) proposed to adapt, modify and design a prototype for a village house.

01

02

01 A view of village houses.
02 A prototypical concrete-frame house surrounded by urban towers.

SHENZHEN FOREST ISLAND

MA Yansong, MAD Architects

Existing Realities

As Lewis Mumford once said, 'The first utopia is the city itself'.

Qianhai of Shenzhen used to be a piece of 'forgotten land'; today, however, it is the effective backbone of the Pearl Delta connecting Hong Kong, Shenzhen, and Guangzhou. Such a privileged geographic location heralds its inescapable fate to be reclaimed and developed. In a postmodern society where high density is exchanged for economic balance, Qianhai becomes another version of Manhattan. The box that represents capital is duplicated endlessly, and overlapped horizontally; the front line of Qianhai is invading the ocean like the expansion of human desires.

Expansion into the ocean is an established method of urban development. Kenzo Tange's Toyko Bay project of 1960 was a utopian attempt to overcome limits such as scarce land, apparent disorder in the city structure, and jammed traffic after World War II. The project sought to accommodate the rapid growth of population and housing demands in Tokyo, and to develop the chaotic city into an orderly, well-organized civilisation on the ocean. Tange considered the ocean as a new type of landform, blending the formerly distinct land and sea through linear architectural structures. A gigantic, continuously intertwined and interlocked loop defined an orderly and open ocean city. Yet, the Tokyo Bay planning perfectly combined idealism with pragmatism in its effort to expand the city through large-scale leveraging of industrial technology.

Practical Ideal

As George Sand observed, truth does not exist in a damaged reality.

Since the 1990s, land reclamation in Shenzhen Bay has led to several problems: pollution and sedimentation as result of reduced tidal flow capacity, weakened hydrodynamics, and a faster natural sedimentation compared to self-cleaning capacity. Based on the

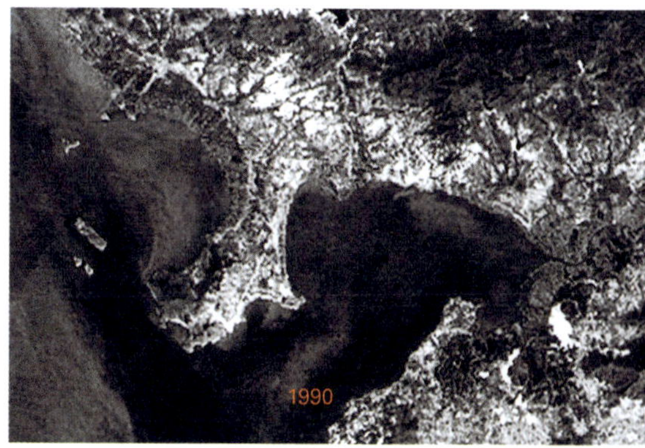

precedent of Shenzhen Bay, the future water circulation in Qianhai is not at all optimistic.

The proposed Forest Island represents MAD's visionary resistance against the impending probability of conventional fill and development. Similar to Central Park in the heart of the New York City, the Forest Island rises from the sea to form a huge contrast with the Qianhai Development Zone on the shore. To ensure the Forest Island remains free from water pollution, water is circulated through the existing reclamation area in the west of Qianhai Bay, making this part of the reclaimed area the only connection and passage with the landside city. Visitors could only access this piece of earth art by giving up motorized transportation and returning to the primitive mobility of walking.

MAD's project for the Shenzhen Forest Island is a public art space connected through pedestrian path networks. It is also a non-city, a non-utopian deviant space that confronts a certain type of easily reproducible reality. It is an imagined escape from modern civilisation. It deals with the wind, rain, sea, and mountains and all other natures to offer a brand-new wonderland apart from the new 'nature' of the human-made world. As a communitarian neighbourhood secluded from economic development, it advocates open and free social rules and creative leisure and entertainment.

The increasing land reclamation in Shenzhen Bay.

MAD's proposed Shenzhen Forest Island is a public art space and idyllic pleasure ground connected to the mainland by pedestrian paths.

THE CITY THAT RE-LIVES ITS MEMORIES

WISE Architecture

If Rome is a palimpsest that retains the traces of its past, Shenzhen feels like a city that is constantly erasing its tracks. For example, urban villages may not be very pretty or the nicest places to live, but is it truly necessary to destroy all of them? They have some redeeming qualities that could be valued in the future. With constant destruction for new development, there will be little left to show of Shenzhen's past.

Therefore, we propose to take a look back and connect with the past. If Shenzhen is a city that erases its memories, our installation is a vision of a city that re-lives its memories.

The installation structure takes the form of the Dacheng flour factory building in which the 2015 Biennale takes place. Basically composed of several levels of concrete slabs supported by a grid of columns, the structure is then filled with ordinary things gathered from the city: brick walls, metal frames, billboards, used furniture, tiles, dishes, old books, plants, bikes, and the like. In a reduced scale, these contents come together as a three-dimensional collage.

Our vision is that in the end, the biennale venue will become like our installation: the factory building will be re-populated by those who bring reusable things, which are used to set up and define new spaces. Instant walls will go up and people will freely outfit their spaces according to their needs. In this way, the city re-lives its memories and regenerates itself by repurposing the ordinary.

Credits:
Sook Hee Chun, Young Jang, and Ming Yu

NO TOUCHING
禁止触摸

SPATIAL ECONOMIC NETWORK

Ljubo Georgiev, Hristo Stankushev, Merve Bedir, Jason Hilgefort

Thirty-five years ago, the Special Economic Zone (SEZ) was conceived and implemented. It subsequently revolutionised the development patterns of the PRD Region and ultimately the world. The metropolitan growth of the PRD was driven by luring Chinese farmers to factories and foreigners interested in the PRD, not just for tax breaks and cheap labor but also for the technologies, skills, and linkages possible in the region. Through producing goods for the international market, the locals provided for their children. The next generation has the potential to become huge consumers, but also to become makers, to form a small-scale society of producers.

The current dominant tool of Chinese urban planning is single-use zoning that rigidly regulates space and allows it to be perceived as a commodity. However, in the PRD there are also several grey zones. Whether in urban villages or even SEZs themselves, there are special spaces that are permitted to operate as exceptions.

Many people in China would probably agree that the SEZ has fulfilled its purpose of spurring economic development. Our proposal seeks to transform the Special Economic Zone into the Spatial Economic Network (SEN). The remnants of SEZs will be built upon to form SENs, to provide new forms of working and living.

The region can invest in its young talent. Instead of providing free trade zones to serve foreign corporations, the SEN will enable individuals and collectives to form their own initiatives and international networks in which to operate and live. Here the emerging productive society would be free not only to make or own products, work across disciplines, and connect to their peers and craft; but also they would be free to make their own rules and spaces within the PRD.

In another 35 years, could Spatial Economic Networks once again transform the development patterns and economic relationships of the PRD, China, and the world, but this time in a different way?

Credits:
Ljubo Georgiev (One Architecture Week, Bulgaria), Hristo Stankushev (dontDIY, Bulgaria), Merve Bedir (LandCC, Turkey), and Jason Hilgefort (LandCC, USA).

Unimaker

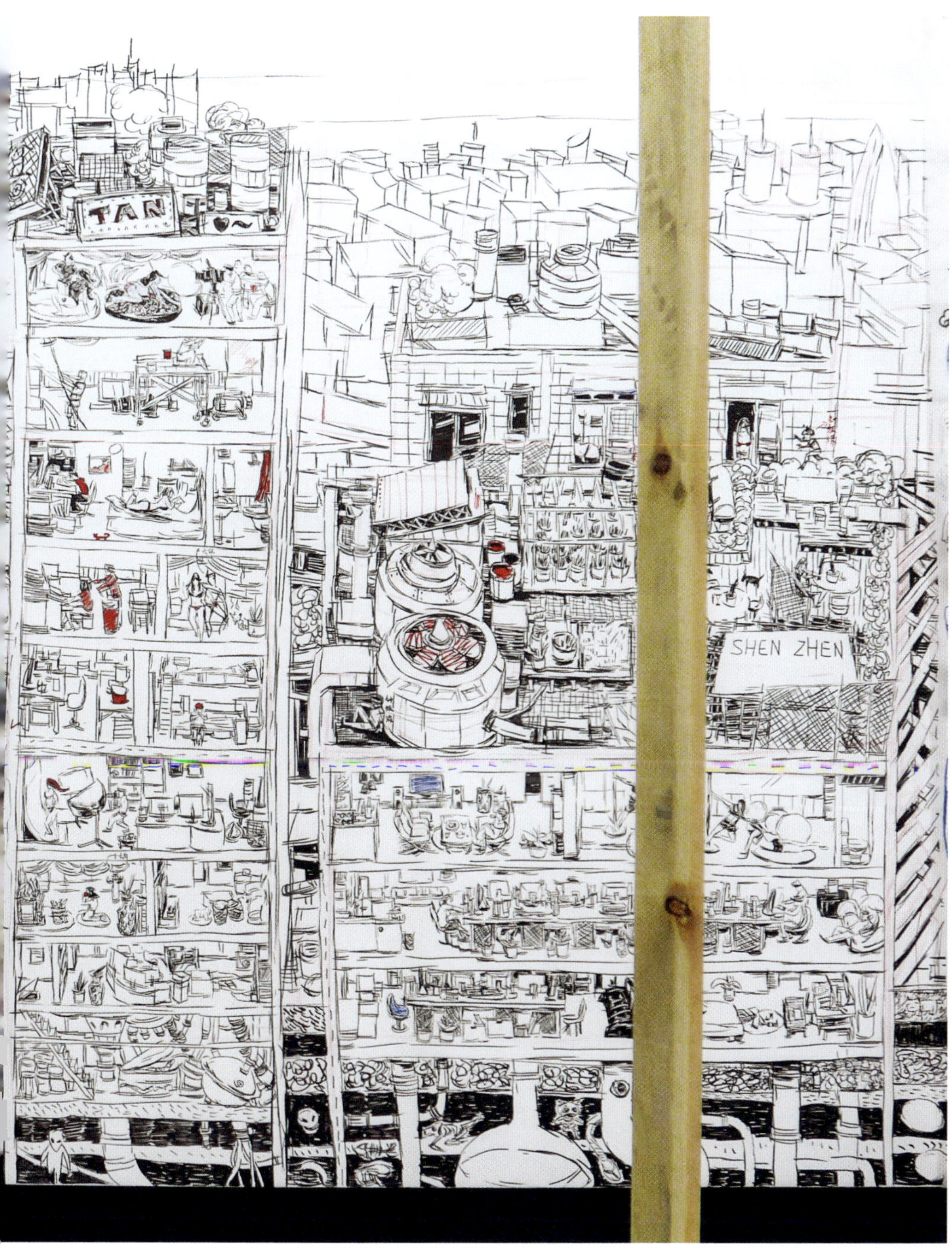
TAN
SHEN ZHEN

WEALTH ARCHITECTURE

FENG Yuan, Zhongshan (Sun Yat-sen) University

'Wealth Architecture', as the name implies, sees buildings as an embodiment of socioeconomic class. Among privately owned buildings, class conforms to wealth accumulation; at the same time, accumulated wealth becomes the catalyst of architectural expression. The strong correspondence between the two can explain the ideographic and symbolic aspects of the appearance of buildings.

The opposite of wealth architecture would be poverty architecture. But since architecture generally requires significant economic resources, 'poverty architecture' is almost an oxymoron. It is at any rate an aberration, notwithstanding efforts by socially minded architects to democratise the nature of architecture. From an historical perspective, private buildings have been developed under systems that allow for the implementation of social hierarchies and wealth accumulation, excepting a handful of particular social systems such as the era of Collectivism in the twentieth century. The fundamental role of wealth architecture is to accentuate the relative prosperity of its patrons vis-à-vis the populace and develop its self-expression through symbols and forms. Wealth architecture not only reflects the order of political economy, but also reinforces cultural hierarchies. Therefore it is important to discuss and analyse the conditions under which the symbols and forms of wealth architecture will continue to evolve and change.

The installation at UABB 2015 consists of a dozen fishbowls containing models of wealth architecture, arranged on a simple table. Here they can be admired and viewed, but also questioned and humoured in their exaggerated self-importance.

Hong Kong Typology

Emanuel Christ and Christoph Gantenbein, Christ & Gantenbein Architects, ETH Zurich

Hong Kong is to some extent the ideal case: nowhere do buildings stand more dramatically in the topography. Nowhere else is such an extreme density so expressively transcribed into built architecture. The overwhelming extensiveness of repetitive structures appears almost surreal. The volumes triumph with their unexpected forms. The proportions of slim towers seem threatening. The sheer size of the buildings is already an architectural feat in itself. Everything is fantastic and simultaneously so evident.

The incisive form of these buildings is the direct consequence of technical or functional constraints. Hong Kong's edifices are not designed to be beautiful. They are built in a pragmatic way. The architecture is the immediate expression of the extreme conditions under which it occurs: the topography, the climate, and the economic circumstances.

As a logical outcome, an extreme architecture of exact and novel building types has arisen: Pencil Tower, Gallery Building, Vertical Factory, Shop-House, Podium and Tower, Double Tube, Slab Composition, and Star Shape Tower.

Hong Kong is the city of sheer typological invention implemented into high performance architecture. Hong Kong is the built manifesto of extreme density. Due to their size and lapidary setting, the buildings develop an uncommonly strong physical presence. They feature basic, clear tectonic structures. Based on an economical use of constructive and formal means, their language swings between an anonymous lack of design and a classical modern expression.

Compared to the orthodox regularity of twentieth-century modern city layouts, Hong Kong refutes the prejudice that no possible urbanity can be built from modern architecture. On the contrary, in certain aspects the city appears to us as an exemplary model for a city of the future: Hong Kong is dense. Hong Kong is urban. Hong Kong is beautiful.

Specific building types have arisen in response to the density and topography of Hong Kong, including the 'Pencil Tower', 'Vertical Factory', 'Double Tube', and 'Star Shape Tower'.

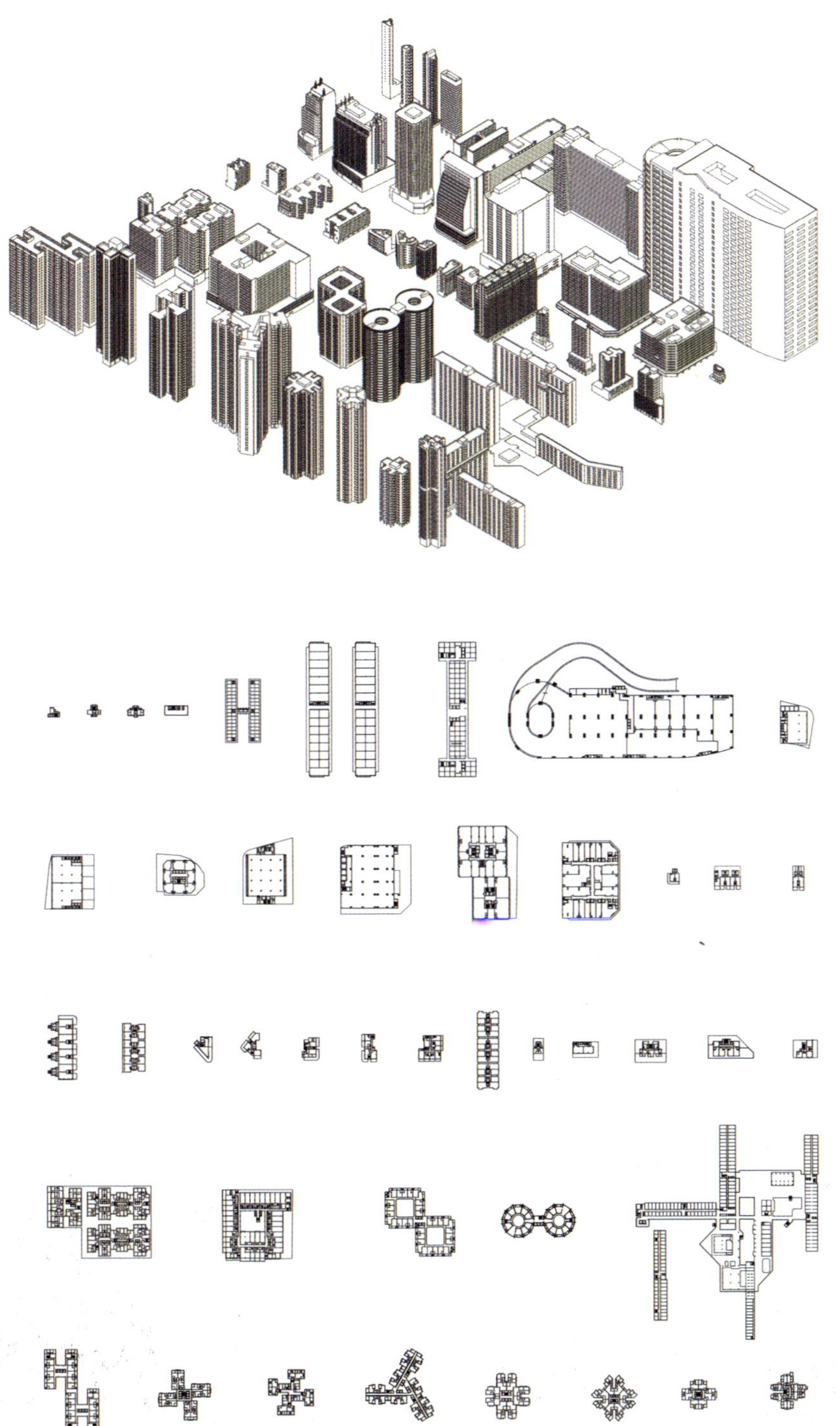

DA LANG FEVER 2.0

Linda Vlassenrood, International New Town Institute (INTI)

To understand Da Lang is to understand Chinese urbanization.

'Da Lang Fever 2.0' is the result of research initiated by Linda Vlassenrood and the International New Town Institute (INTI) as part of its international research programme, 'New New Towns' in Shenzhen. This exhibition is the sequel of the event, 'Da Lang Fever', organised at UABB 2013, which showcased the empowering nature of bottom-up activities for migrant workers in Da Lang Neighbourhood, located to the north of Shenzhen's core in the southeast of Bao'an District. Bao'an district has the largest population of migrant workers of all the districts in Shenzhen, according to the 2010 census. Da Lang covers an area of roughly 38 square kilometers, about 70 percent of which is hilly and mountainous landscape.

INTI now takes its contribution one-step further by inviting Play the City (gaming method developed by Ekim Tan), space&matter (architecture office) and Lard Buurman (photographer) to develop an action plan for real urban interventions in Da Lang Neighbourhood. These participants from the Netherlands have been chosen because of their innovative ways of rethinking twenty-first-century urban planning to include more collaborative, bottom-up efforts. The exhibition, featuring info graphics and documentary photography, will function as a gaming room where 'Play Da Lang' will bring together different stakeholders to collaboratively think about which urban interventions are necessary.

01

01 Industrial Park in Da Lang Fashion Valley
02 Shi Ao Park near Shi Ao Village
03 Hui Yao Canteen in Da Lang Fashion Valley
04 Vacant Hotel in Da Lang Fashion Valley
Photos : Lard Buurman

02

03

04

DA LANG PALA

community space that the public
organize large events.
exercise or just relax together!
self-organized activities
and fun!
我们可以开放一个社区空间，
自主地在这里组织大型活动，
我们可以在这里演出，
或者举行一些集体的休闲活动，
活动不仅简单，有效而且有趣！
火热大浪
DA
LANG
FEVER

MEGABLOCK URBANISMS PRD

Jeffrey Johnson with Stephen Chou and Jiteng Yang, China Megacities Lab, Studio-X Beijing, GSAPP, Columbia University

Megablock Urbanisms

China's default solution for accommodating the influx of millions of new urban inhabitants is large-scale superblock development, a carry-over from the Soviet-era danwei-type urban development planning and the Modernist utilitarian social housing block. Superblocks are spatial instruments with social, cultural, environmental, and economic implications, operating between the scales of architecture and the city. It has been estimated that superblock developments are completed at a rate of over 10 each day,1 housing populations that range from the thousands to hundreds of thousands. These large-scale residential enclaves, which can reach sizes of 40 hectares and larger, are taking over the fabric of Chinese cities. This trend is not only prevalent with new developments at the expanding periphery of cities, but also in existing city centres, at times contrasting starkly with their historical urban context.

Megablock PRD

How has the superblock shaped the urban landscape of the PRD, one of the most rapidly urbanising regions in the world? With its unique history of large-scale urban development, especially during the past three decades, the PRD provides an abundant source of superblock projects for research and analysis. Hong Kong, with its influences rooted in a colonial past and with Great Britain, provided early models of superblock development that were easily adapted in the emerging cities of Shenzhen and Dongguan, and for new growth of historical cities like Guangzhou. As the PRD region has rapidly grown and prospered over the past few decades, the superblock has become the dominant model of urban development. What distinguishes these models from those in other regions in China and elsewhere? How have the superblocks evolved over the past few decades? What kind of urban condition have they created?

What we intend to illuminate through our research are unique and emerg-ing 'Megablock' urbanisms that have the potential to influence the way we conceive of the city in the future, not only in China, but throughout the world. By redefining the superblock—or 'Megablock'—as a laboratory for experimentation and invention, we hope to discover alternative models of urban development.

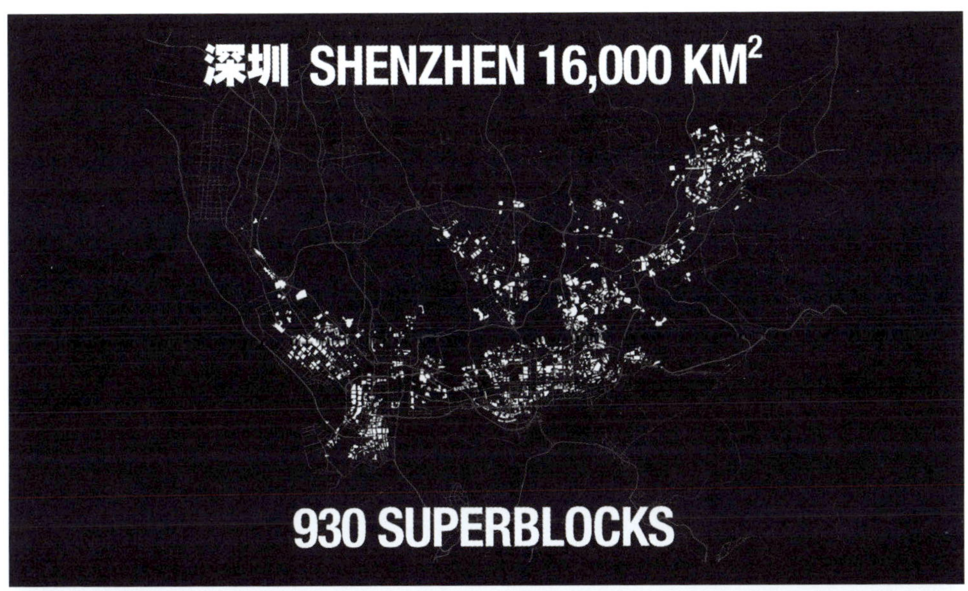

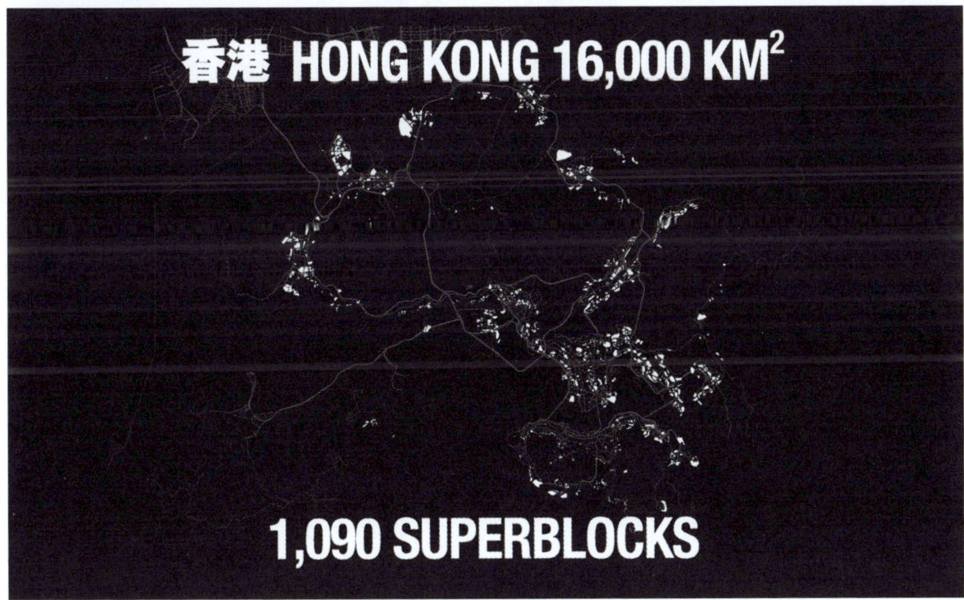

01

01 With its unique history of large- scale urban development, especially during the past three decades, the PRD provides an abundant source of superblock projects for research and analysis.

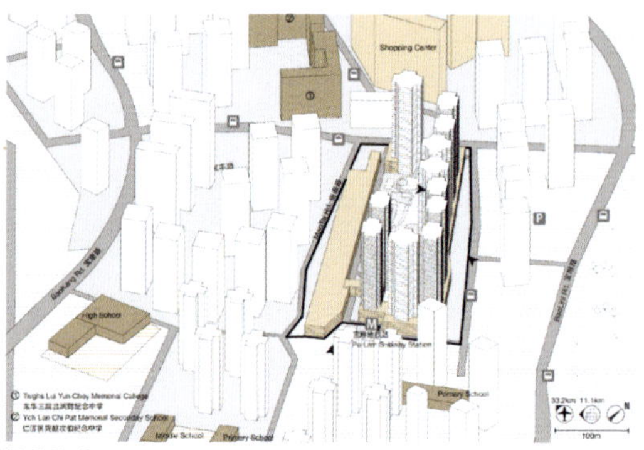

Metro City Phase 2

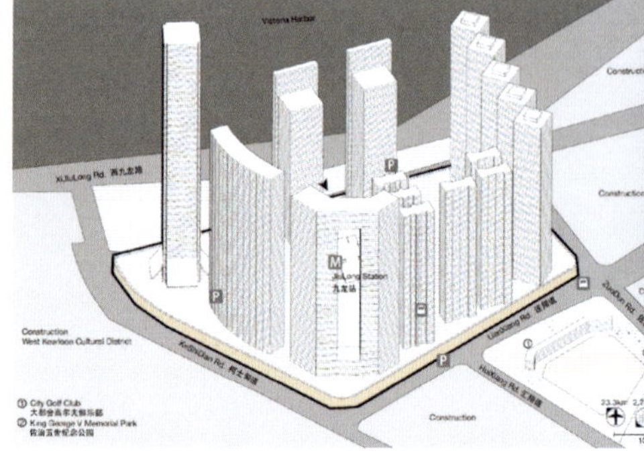

West Kowloon Union Square

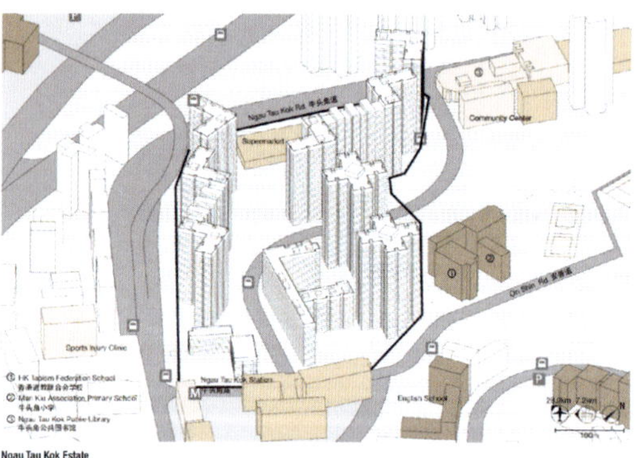

Ngau Tau Kok Estate

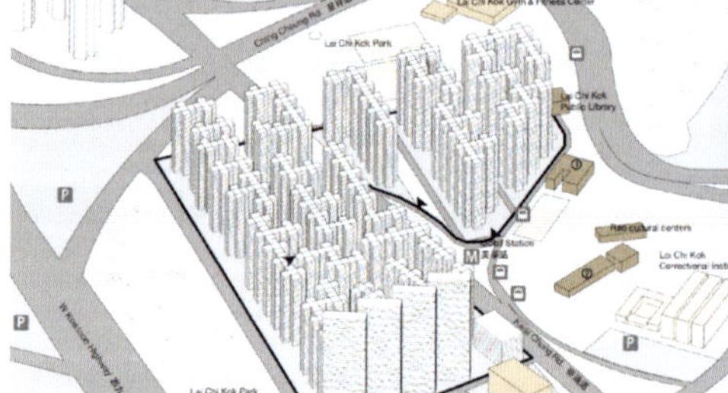

Mei Foo Sun Chuen

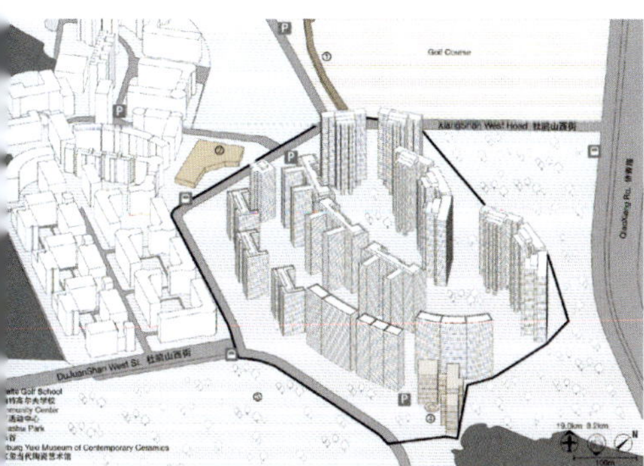

Castle

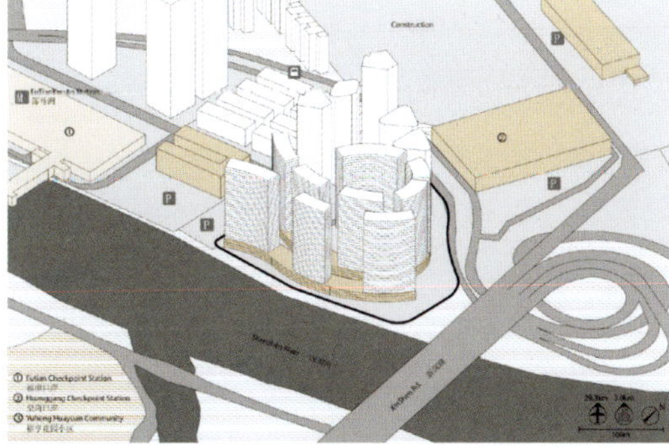

Gemdale Gateway

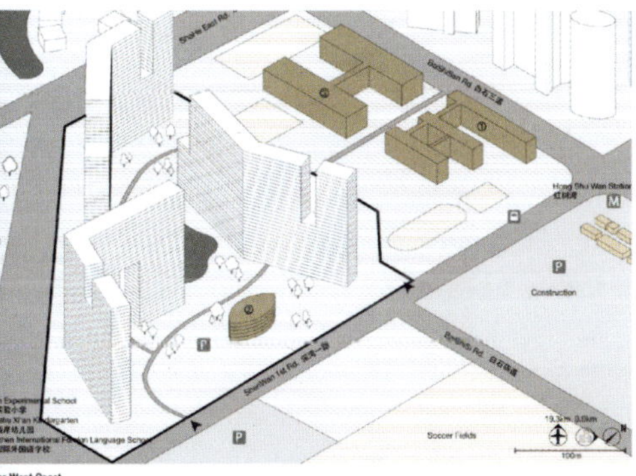

ve West Coast

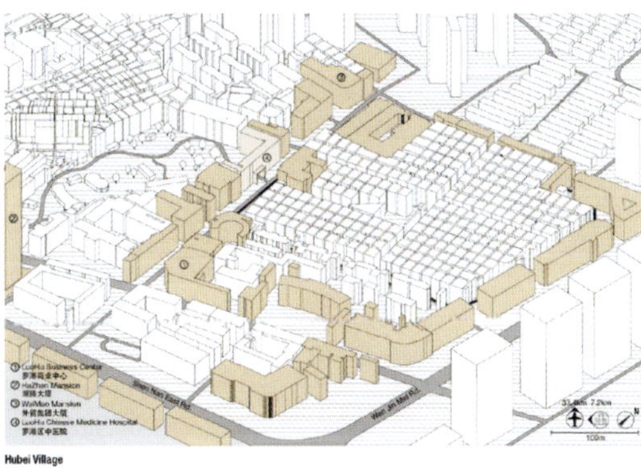

Hubei Village

By redefining the superblock or 'Megablock' as a laboratory for experimentation and invention, the researchers hope to discover alternative models of urban development.

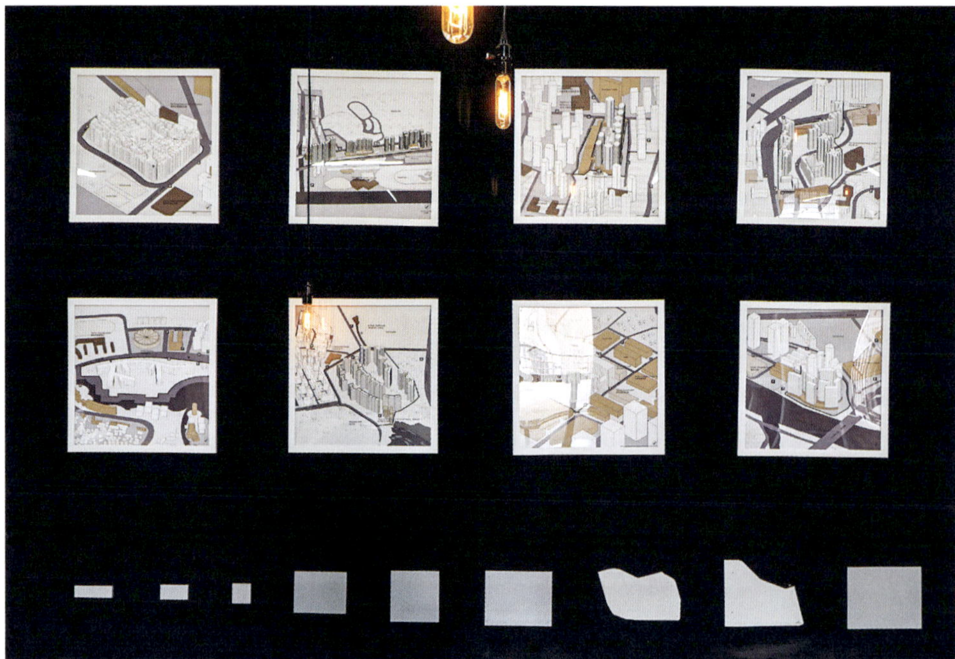

PANYU

DICTIONARY OF MIRRORED GARDENS

Mirrored Gardens Research Team, Vitamin Creative Space

Mirrored Gardens is an experimental space where art meets agriculture. Located on the rural outskirts of Guangzhou, it is conceived not as a confined enclave but as a 'field' that enables the overlap of contemporary art practice, quotidian life, and farming. The architecture of Mirrored Gardens was designed by Sou Fujimoto Architects. After three years (2011-2014) of research, design, and construction, Mirrored Gardens has gradually grown into a kind of returning: the returning to a spatial status that naturally transcends the mundane repetition of human activities. Everyday life at Mirrored Gardens sets off various processes of mutual learning and communication with the environment.

The project 'Dictionary of Mirrored Gardens' observes and reflects upon the processes of daily life of Mirrored Gardens. It comes out of a continuing discussion amongst the Mirrored Gardens Research Team about the role of daily observation, learning, and practices in forming a more organic relation between people and architecture, and also between temporal and spatial dimensions. The premise is that everyday practice can help connect time-based creative activities with spatial forms and the physical environment.

01

02

01, 02 Mirrored Gardens, Guangzhou, 2015
Courtesy Vitamin Archive

FROM VILLAGES TO CITY: THE INFORMAL HISTORY OF SHENZHEN

Juan DU, University of Hong Kong

Established in 1979 as an experimental economic zone for China's eventual sweeping reforms, Shenzhen's transformation from a presumed tabula rasa into a metropolis is held as a miraculous success by local and international observers alike. How did a collection of villages grow into a metropolis of nearly 20 million in just 35 years?

Through drawings, photographs, installation, and other media, this exhibit presents the hidden histories and informal urbanism of the 'Villages in the City' (ViCs)—illegally built informal settlements that house half of the current metropolitan population. From the urban core to suburban regions, there are more than 300 of these enclaves distributed throughout the city, often in the most densely developed and populated areas.

The dense, tightly packed urban villages exhibit radically different social and formal characteristics from the city-proper. While many ViCs are deprived of basic civic infrastructure, they are full of colourful street life, small-scaled public spaces, and eventful pedestrian activities, offering a vibrant urbanity that is rarely found in the standardized blocks that typify modern Shenzhen. Similar to Latin America's favelas or India's slums, Shenzhen's ViCs operate in the grey zones of existing judicial frameworks and represent a unique type of urban informality in Chinese cities. The cultural and spatial history of the former agrarian villages has enabled them to become catalysts for the rapid economic growth and urbanization of the city.

This research and exhibition challenges assumptions about Shenzhen's development history by providing an unorthodox perspective of the villages as the historical foundations upon which the success of the contemporary city grew. The installation is designed to engage visitors to communicate and record their personal experiences and perceptions of the 'Villages' of Shenzhen. Over time, the installation will be transformed and enriched by the stories and textures of visitors' accounts of their own experiences of the city.

01, 02 The exhibition explores the illegally built informal settlements or 'villages' that house about half of the current metropolitan population of Shenzhen.

01

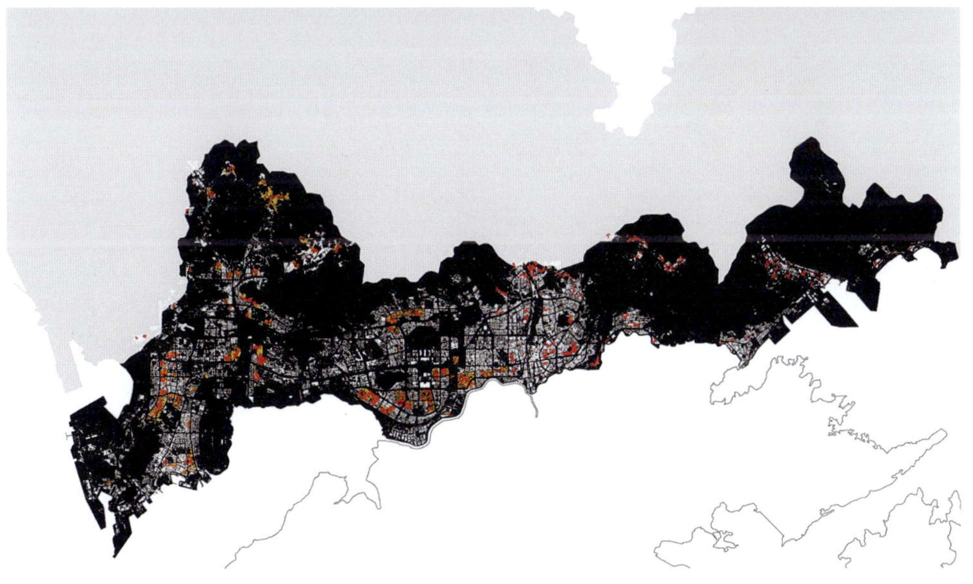

02

MUSIC

MIDDLE-AGE
WORK
BUSINESS

N=DISTORTION

Handshake 302

n=distortion focuses on the social ecology of the PRD mega-cities, conducting an experiment in regional urban planning. In its barest formulation, urban planning involves organising land and population with respect to resources. n=distortion explores the question: how do we need to change our thinking about cities and regions given the fact that cities comprise different areas and populations and have access to different resources? We built this question into our project design, which is simultaneously rigid and open.

The territory is represented by an old wood boat filled with sand and shells. Each 'city' is evoked by a distinctive assemblage or object within the boat. The position of each object corresponds to the city's place in the Pearl River Delta, while the height corresponds to the population of its respective city. To call attention to economic inequality as an ecological factor, funding for the design and construction of each object is distributed based on each city's GDP. In practical terms, this means that while the artists constructing Shenzhen, Guangzhou, Hong Kong, and Macao had cash to purchase supplies; other participants had to construct their objects by scavenging.

The constructed 'mega-cities' are placed together in a salvaged sampan, once the primary source of shipping and livelihood in the delta's economy. The installation simultaneously evokes the tensions between the region's traditional sampan ecology and its contemporary 'container ecology', allowing us to re-imagine the challenges of 'planning' the PRD as a region.

Credits:
Curatorial team: Handshake 302 / Mary Ann O'Donnell
Participating artists and architects include: Xie Shihong, Li Jingfang, Lin Yi, Deng Xianxiong, Lu Yuanliang, Wang Yixin, He Yi, Li Qiqi, Li Yao, Guo Zhenjiang, and Leung Mee-ping.

	City	GDP (billions rmb)	Urban area (km2)	Population (millions)	Project Funding (rmb)	Object base (cm)	Object height (cm)
1	**Zhaoqing**	1.84	14,891	3,92	250	7930.50	90.00
2	**Zhuhai**	1.85	1,724	1.56	252	918.15	35.82
3	**Jiangmen**	2.08	9,443	4.45	282	5092.06	102.17
4	**Zhongshan**	2.82	1,784	3.12	383	950.10	71.63
5	**Huizhou**	3.00	10,922	4.60	407	5816.73	105.61
6	**Dongguan**	5.88	2,465	8.22	797	1312.79	188.72
7	**Foshan**	7.60	3,848	7.19	1030	2049.33	291.58
8	**Macau**	10.85	30	0.54	1471	15.98	12.40
9	**Shenzhen**	16.00	1,992	10.36	2168	1066.88	237.86
10	**Guangzho**	16.70	7,434	12.70	2264	3959.13	291.58
11	**Honk Kong**	24.85	1,104	7.06	3367	587.96	162.09
Total					**12670**	**29630.60**	

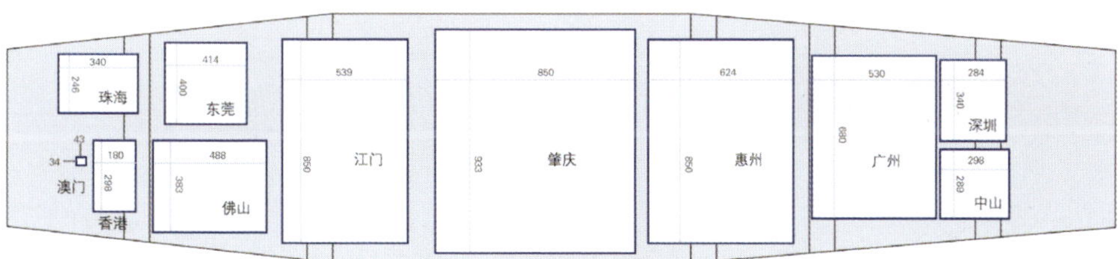

01

作品平面布置图
单位：mm

01 The various cities within the PRD are represented as objects in a salvaged sampan (boat), with each object's placement, size, and budget reflecting that of the corresponding city.

POWER

PANYU: RURAL BECOMING URBAN?

Margaret Crawford, Max Hirsh, and Dorothy Tang

Lying at the heart of the Pearl River Delta, Panyu is neither here nor there: an in-between landscape of industrial estates, villages, farms, superhighways, and ancient canals. It is populated both by villagers who have deep historical roots in the region, and by more recent migrants who have flocked to Panyu's workshops, factories, and office parks. Located on the fringes of larger urban centers such as Guangzhou and Dongguan, Panyu's polycentric landscape is often overlooked, or worse, discounted as a backwater, filled with reminders of Guangdong's rural past that have 'not yet' been modernised and urbanised.

We argue, however, that it is precisely these overlapping 'in-between' valences—between rural and urban, between agriculture and industry, and between villagers and migrants—that make Panyu an excellent lens for interpreting broader changes in the social, aesthetic, and economic landscapes of China's megacity regions. Rather than charting a progressive and irreversible urbanization of the countryside, our study of Panyu demonstrates how the creative juxtaposition of rural, urban, and suburban functions has produced an exceptional heterogeneity of spatial arrangements and village transformation strategies.

In this exhibition, we introduce four archetypal forms of village development. Through the productive combination of visual, archival, and ethnographic research methods, we aim to advance a new understanding of the present conditions and future potentials of China's megacity regions. In so doing, we question prevailing ideas about the future of Chinese cities—which envision an intensification of high-density urban cores and a corresponding decline of outlying regions—by drawing attention to the diversity and dynamism taking place in peri-urban zones such as Panyu. An exploration of four villages thus increases our awareness of social and spatial experiments that are being conducted on the margins of major urban centres, and that open up the possibility of alternative development models that an excessive fixation on high-density urbanization might otherwise foreclose.

Credits:
Margaret Crawford is a Professor of Architecture at the University of California, Berkeley.
Max Hirsh is a Research Assistant Professor at the Hong Kong Institute for the Humanities and Social Sciences, University of Hong Kong.
Dorothy Tang is an Assistant Professor of Landscape Architecture and program director of the undergraduate program at the University of Hong Kong.

01

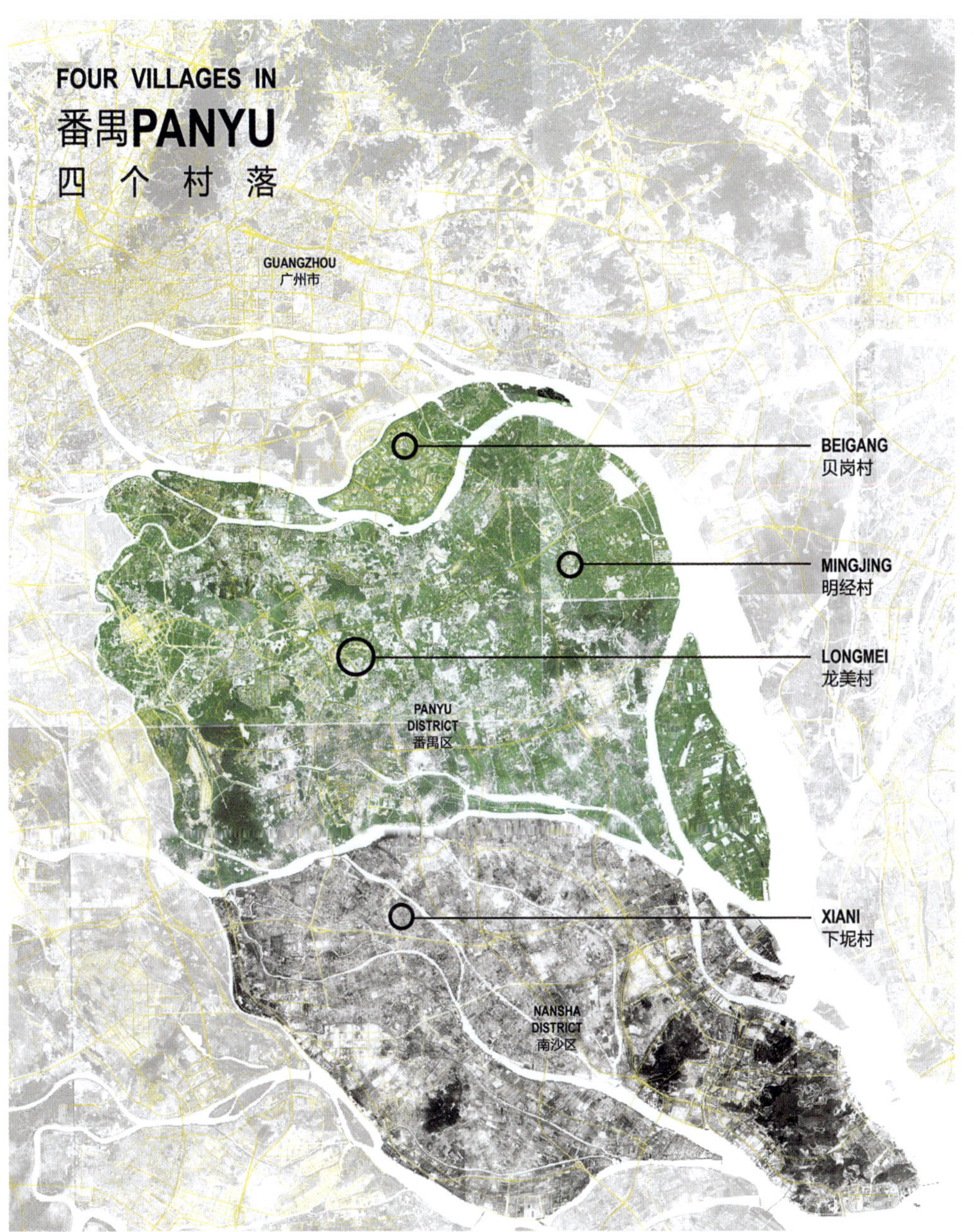

01 Panyu, a peri-urban district of Guangzhou, is often overlooked, but may in fact help reveal broader changes in China's megacity regions.

02

03

02, 03, 04, 05 Views of the four villages chosen for the study, clockwise from upper left: Xiani, Beigang, Mingjing, Longmei.

04

05

BEI GANG VILLAGE
贝岗村

MATERIAL PRODUCTION – FIELD PRACTICE OF ZINI SUGAR REFINERY, PANYU

Zini Sugar Refinery with TAN Hongyu

We are all producers of materials and we all are products of life.

The creative park Zini Hall occupies the former address of Zini Sugar Refinery, which was opened in 1953 at the intersection of Guangzhou, Panyu and Shunde districts along the Pearl River. Today, Zini is a team for art practice, manufacturing, and research. Beyond practicing the crafts of art and building, Zini is a study group focusing on the subject of cultural and environmental sustainability.

Zini Hall has been lucky to survive developers' bulldozers that have demolished old buildings in several rounds of renovation projects and remained in a buffer zone in the rapid urbanisation process. Artisans who were aware of the special opportunities of the site came together with those who shared the similar interests. Together, they bring back to life the spirit of creation in the industrial ruin. Zini Hall has now become a practice space offering beauty and aesthetics in everyday life.

Artisans are here to find ways to pass on and further develop traditional skills; on the other hand, they aim to create a space that is perceptibly integrated into its modern surroundings.

In the coming years, industrialised production methods will further affect artistic and cultural aspects, a process which is too complicated to judge all the pros and cons. Therefore, we have no choice but to engage ourselves in practices. We must contemplate the changing roles of artisans as well as the nature of craftsmanship. Reflecting on our work helps to consolidate our knowledge.

Credits:

Zini Sugar Refinery includes the artist LIU Qingyuan, ceramic art master ZENG Peng, and designers LU Haifeng, ZENG Muchuan, ZENG Zhijun, YAO Wenjun, and GUAN Kangkang. In collaboration with TAN Hongyu, Guangzhou Academy of Fine Arts.

01

02

01, 02 The artists and artisans who work in the former Zini Sugar Refinery include Yi Zhao (left) and Yao Jiang (right).

一切尽在掌握
Ideas
eep Walking

职工俱乐部
73号楼
工具室
水泥仓→
18

PRD REVISITED

Charlie Koolhaas

I lived in Guangzhou between 2005 and 2011, and worked on the Shenzhen Biennale in 2007. During that time, I photographed the PRD area at a moment of intense change, which included the Beijing Olympics, the Asia Games, and a record influx of foreign migration and economic and social development in the area. In 2015 I returned to the area to photograph it in its present state. But today's PRD exists in a radically different world from the one ten years ago: in the grip of an economic slow down, in the midst of myriad violent conflicts, it is a more fearful and uncertain globe.

I found that the euphoria that I had experienced here 10 years ago had turned into something much more cautious and subdued. We are dealing now with PRD 2.0. It stands for a new thoughtfulness and intelligence, visible everywhere, from the built environment to the faces of the children. What had been a flashy architectural style in 2005, stemming from a ferocious desire for experimentation and newness, had evolved into a newly tasteful and progressive style that is sophisticated, subtle, and far from generic, as critics once accused.

On my journey through the PRD, in cities such as Kaiping and Taishan,

I discovered a rich legacy of history, architecture and culture. The people of PRD had invented radically unique aesthetics and ways of living. Historically the area has thrived on its global connections. In the 1920s, the people of Kaiping – returning from America, rich from working on the railways and the goldmines – built glorious mansions in their rural homelands. They invented an entirely original type of architecture that fused Chinese and western styles. Evidence that in China, design and architecture have never solely been the domain of designers and architects. In my view it is this merging of styles and details from both east and west that

defines the look of the PRD. It is characterised by the blurring of multiple DNA's.

In the photographs exhibited here, we can see people living side-by-side with heavy industry. And yet despite its environmental issues, the PRD can teach us much about conservation. We see traditional ways of life applied to new environments. Amidst much waste there remains a fundamental frugality; everything is used and then re-used. People only renew what they need to, as in keyhole surgery.

One of the biggest differences from ten years ago is the pervasive presence of technology in everyday life. In the new PRD, the virtual dimension has merged with public space, inhabited by citizens intently staring at their mobile phones or taking selfies. But despite its technological connectedness, the PRD is a more strictly Chinese place today than 10 years ago. The streets of Guangzhou in 2005 could have been mistaken for any global city, filled with a full spectrum of races and nationalities, a multiculturalism that is all but gone today. There are still traders coming here to do business, but clearly it is harder for them to stay or to live.

Today there is more organisation and structure in the PRD... but I couldn't help missing some of its former heterogeneity and embrace of experimentation.

Photos of the PRD by Charlie Koolhaas in 2015, who returned to document the region after previously living in Guangzhou between 2005 and 2011.

RAILWAY

SOFT INFRASTRUCTURE: DESIGNING THE SOCIETY OF SHENZHEN'S FUTURE

Jacob Dreyer

In the architecture and urbanism communities, the Shenzhen area is practically synonymous with globalized economies of scale and the miracle of manufacturing-driven growth, vast factories and anonymous new districts.

Great Leap Forward, the 2002 book based on fieldwork conducted by seer Rem Koolhaas and his students at the Harvard Graduate School of Design in 1996-1997, solidified an image that quickly became a cliché: the Pearl River Delta was what the West needed to be afraid of, where the mythical jobs lost in Michigan and the Ruhr had gone to, where the world's iPhones were being made. In the years since then, the picture has changed. Evidence of the communities and folkways that this bold new economy created have proliferated, from books like *Factory Girls* to light-hearted comedies like 一路向西 (*Due West: Our Sex Journey*)[1] to the mythologized legends of brotherhood in Dongguan told by artist Li Jinghu. The prosperity and urbanism created by the manufacturing industries have become the seedbed for a new generation of artists, designers, and architects.

1 — A 2012 sex comedy directed by Mark Wu about Hong Kongers visiting Dongguan's Changping district, formerly infamous as a city-sized red light district — an oddly amusing parallel to the manual labor of adjacent Dongguan districts.

The hard infrastructure of the city is there, as are a population once called 'migrant workers' who are now well indigenized: today, Shenzhen is building organic forms of localism, the soft infrastructure of human-scaled neighbourhoods, and seeking to transform the working-class population into educated, socialized middle-class citizens to accompany the new government-approved spaces of culture. What would make up a 'soft infrastructure'—the cultural practices, spaces, and forms of identity that could make a logic of this region, without imposing artificial hierarchies on its inhabitants?

China's economy generally is shifting from 'hard' industries to 'soft'; even as the construction industry lost 15 million jobs nationwide in 2015,[2] the innovation-driven creative economy is booming, optimistically expected to make up about half of future GDP growth. The objective for Shenzhen's decision-makers is not to discard or replace the manufacturing industries, but to build on them with complexity, design, and new ways to add value: from mass manufacturing lawn chairs to cultivating furniture designers. With its unique history, Shenzhen is poised to be a design and innovation hub, a lung of openness without the pretension of Beijing or Shanghai. For Shenzhen to go from primary forms of industrialization to a more bespoke design and manufacturing process, driven by open-source ideas and technology platforms which enable rapid communication, as well as an innovative urban plan that distributes pockets of skills across a greater region of 42 million in an affordable real estate market with a balmy climate, would be to realize an idealized form of the Chinese Dream: a dispersed, high-value adding, low-carbon urbanity.

Local companies like Tencent and the China Merchant's Bank are showing the world what a home-grown Chinese company with deep roots in China's unique, hybrid economy can look like.

2 — Gordon Orr, 'What might happen in China in 2016?' McKinsey & Company, Jan. 2016. http://www.mckinsey.com/insights/strategy/what_might_happen_in_china_in_2016

Interestingly, this panoply of emerging companies—all of which drive their profits by a new vision of a networked society whose collective strivings lead to individual gains in productivity, quality of urban space, and savings rates—see fit to invest in design and aesthetics. This investment is not just a concession to taste, but rather a central part of their business model that dovetails with a new generation of urban development plans.

Fig. 1 Li Jinghu, 'Today's Screening', 2014, video installation, showreel of found film, rhinestone, projection screen, sound, courtesy the artist and Magician Space.

Perhaps the legacy of Shenzhen's development, where collectives of factory workers first faced the global market, can continue to play a role in the identity of new types of creative practice. The tech company Tencent is a global innovator, with a chat platform that is capable of banking, paying utilities, streaming media, and much more; the media space it has created has allowed for the rapid and instantaneous dissemination of all kinds of content, but its affordability and universal reach makes it the media of choice for independent designers and artists. In Shekou, the China Merchants Group is leveraging land ownership and capital to construct a new museum zone of unprecedented size, curated by Ole Bouman. But can authentic culture be grown by directives, whether from shadowy tech CEOs or well-connected bankers? Will the programmers of Tencent and the mid-level managers of CMG take their children to the new design-centric Victoria and Albert museum, and to the innovative exhibitions at the OCT Contemporary Art Terminal (OCAT)?

It is a critical question, though, whether this monolithic mash of state capitalism actually does represent a new social vision, or a mutual admiration society — a hall of mirrors of Chinese men in their 40s convincing themselves that they're all really rich. Simultaneous to the development of this new economy, innovators in architecture, contemporary art, fashion, and design are offering a new depth to Shenzhen's public sphere, or in fact inventing and defining a public sphere through their work.

At the same time, the future-oriented mentality that the region has cultivated may be in danger of getting ahead of itself. The manufacturing economy that Shenzhen was built around is leaving, subject to nostalgia. Li Jinghu's installation Rainbow (2009) displays the simple, utilitarian objects used by ordinary households; they may not be from Ikea, but they constituted a rich folklore and way of life that is in danger of being eliminated along with the factories whose wages bought these items. For some, in China as in Michigan, the notion of creative industries supplanting manufacturing ones can sound like a canard, an excuse for neoliberal urbanism that departs from the social contract of mass employment. When Li asks, 'What is it that gives most ordinary people the ability to endure the arduous and weariness of life day after day?', one wonders whether designed objects can fill this void. Can entrepreneurs and the creative industries that they are supporting replace the vacuum?[3]

3 — Cf. China Merchants Bank's support of the V & A design complex, or OCT 's support of the OCAT museum.

As of 2015, Shenzhen and the PRD region lag in average wages compared to greater Shanghai or Beijing, as well as in percentage of the population that could be considered middle class.[4] Shanghai has 256 Starbucks, Beijing 137; Shenzhen doesn't rank. In an odd way, this is quite indicative: not of degree of Westernization, but of the proportion of the urban population that is middle class. In China, Starbucks is less a place to get coffee than a place to hold meetings under the sign of a socially specific kind of neutrality. Professionals can meet with their colleagues, entrepreneurs gather to plan a rogue launch of a new company; or people simply come to use the Wi-Fi. Shenzhen has factory girls and newly-minted tycoons, but not enough of the middle classes that will be needed for a consumption-driven service economy. Design can serve a critical role in public pedagogy and inspiration for a working class that needs to become an entrepreneurial class overnight, reskilling themselves to match the developments of their city.

Shenzhen famously has a quality of tabula rasa. Without the imperial history of Beijing, or the colonial history of Shanghai (or neighbouring Guangzhou), it is a place without intrinsic traditions or elites; those groups are forming now. The flip side of this is that there are no institutions with deep roots in the nation's history, like Peking University, or traditions that changed the society, such as the political and cultural modernism that emerged in Shanghai during the 1930s. It is easy for elites in the mainland's big two cities to look down on Shenzhen, seeing it as a suburban twin to Hong Kong, the city-state that itself is increasingly an also-ran. The question is whether Shenzhen can lift itself up by its bootstraps once more, transforming Fordist mass-production into a design industry that driven by entrepreneurial zeal and clever technological solutions, applied to products of greater complexity and creativity,

4 — See the Dec. 2015 white paper by the Chinese Academy of Social Sciences (CASS), http://cass.cssn.cn/baokanchuban/xinshukuaidi/201512/t20151225_2800457.html.

while retaining its populist heritage of access for all. It requires an evolution, not a revolution, that will allow the beginnings of local design traditions to form.

Fig. 2 Li Jinghu, 'Rainbow'(detail), 2009, secondhand commodities, dimensions variable, courtesy the artist and Magician Space.

PRD 1.0 took a rural population and brought them through an industrial revolution. Now, the necessary transition is to move towards an information economy. Shenzhen's best contemporary art museum, the OCAT, founded in 2005, symbolizes this transformation: its benefactor, Overseas Chinese Town (OCT) Enterprises Co., was (and is) a real estate and development corporation, which has increasingly built museums of excellent quality around China. Alvin Li, who has curated exhibitions in Shanghai OCAT, actually grew up in a Shenzhen OCT development, and thus personifies the potential crossover from commercial to cultural frameworks. To make this transition in a single lifetime isn't easy, however, and requires a great deal of flexibility.

Perhaps Shenzhen's most iconic innovator is Tencent's CEO Pony Ma, who some have argued invented online social media in China. Shenzhen's white-collar economy will be driven by people like Ma: tech entrepreneurs who have come from dusty backstreets to massively influential disruptor-style companies, ones who don't play by the rules of the old socialist economy, nor by the standards of the Western markets, but invent their own techniques. When we discuss the role of design in Shenzhen's economy, we need to look beyond tangible objects and towards virtual objects. Finance also has a key role to play: whereas most of China's big state-owned banks, pressured into holding toxic loans for political reasons, are based in Beijing, China Merchants Bank in Shenzhen is the largest private bank in China.[5] In stark contrast to cash-poor, state-owned banks, it ranks third among all companies in China in cash liquidity.

Architecture is an important metaphor in China; and although OMA's design for the Beijing CCTV tower gets all of the attention, their second-best building in China is the Shenzhen Stock Exchange. It provides a hint of the anticipation that Shenzhen can pull off the impossible and steal the finance industry from Hong Kong, Singapore, and Shanghai. An economy driven by technology and finance is poised to replace the one driven by manufacturing — suitable, perhaps, for a city whose civic vision is one of technocratically engineered prosperity. In addition to this base of white-collar industries like finance and tech, though, the city needs a more visible creative class to add complexity and beauty to public space. Indeed, the bigger contribution will be to define what the shared social space that we call 'public' even means in this boomtown headed towards adolescence.

5 — China Merchants Bank is 18% owned by a state-owned holding company, but its stock is floated on international exchanges. As such it offers what might be a model for devolution of control of the financial system to markets while realistically acknowledging the continued influence of the state.

In the first stage of China's modern rise, the moment of Shenzhen's inception, the country internationalized, exporting to the whole world. The future will be about successfully articulating the urban periphery, looking inward to the development of the interior; not a great leap forward, but a considered, stylish but stable procession of steps, ones that do not bypass the indigenous culture of the region, nor the aspiring workers who created it.

Jacob Dreyer is a Shanghai-based writer and editor who has contributed to *The Atlantic City Lab, The Architectural Review,* and *Domus.* He authored the book *The Nocturnal Wanderer* and recently edited a special issue of *LEAP* magazine.

Fig. 3 Li Jinghu, 'Waterfall', 2015, android phones, video, electric phone charger, metal, detail, courtesy of the artist and Magician Space.

THE GUANGZHOU OPERA HOUSE: DISSONANCES IN THE ARCHITECTURE OF CULTURAL REFORM

Lori Gibbs

Completed in 2011, the Guangzhou Opera House (GOH) has won acclaim as the largest, most acoustically advanced opera theatre in the world.

Designed by Zaha Hadid Architects (ZHA), with acoustical engineering by Harold Marshall of Sydney Opera House fame, this ambitious project was just one piece of a larger urban development scheme in the Zhujiang New Town District, a new cultural zone of Guangzhou on the banks of the Pearl River.

A curious disconnect is found between the conception, execution, and reception of this grand cultural institution, both within China and abroad. While the local and national government envisioned the opera house as part of a national series of similar venues, architectural critics in the U.K. and the U.S. largely ignored this vision and instead portrayed the opera house as a one-off exercise in avant-garde form-making. Both narratives give the opera house a creative role in realizing contemporary cultural life in the city. This vision of architecture as cultural catalyst, however, is complicated by significant problems with the physical construction of the GOH complex and the desolate character of its public spaces.

Remaking Guangzhou: sites of experimental development

The GOH is a short walking distance from three other recently constructed cultural buildings: The Guangzhou New Library, The

Guangdong Museum, and the Children's Palace. This complex of cultural buildings aligns visually with the Canton Tower, situated on the other side of the river. Each of these buildings has a claim to surpassing international records of size relative to building type.[1]

Fig. 1 The Guangzhou Opera House was planned as just one of several dozen opera houses to open across China, as part of a national cultural reform programme. From *With You At All* (Guangzhou, 2011).

Guangzhou, historically known as a trading port, has experienced unprecedented growth since the beginning of the reform era in 1978. This model of urban and economic change has been

1 — The Guangzhou New Library is advertised as 'the largest open-stack public library' in the world (http://www.nikken.co.jp/en/solutions/GuangzhouLibrary.html); the Canton Tower was the world's tallest tower from 2009 to 2011; the Guangdong Museum reportedly has the 'world's largest overhead steel structure slide work' (http://english.gz.gov.cn/gzgoven/s8974/201105/802739.shtml)

coined the 'Guangdong model of Urbanisation'. Guangdong was the first province in China to 'open-up' economically and experience export-based industrialisation during the reform era.[2] In the Guangdong development model, former rural collectives (set up under Mao Zedong) were transformed into 'corporatized villages' with structures based on shareholding companies.[3] This experimental mode of development has created a new middle class and undergirds a proportion of China's economic success. In this capacity Guangzhou has served as a model of economic reforms and urban development for the nation as a whole.

The nature of architectural projects in the Zhujiang New Town District—with the GOH as a prime example—parallels the strategic vision for economic, urban, and social change. This strategy has led to commissions by foreign architects to envision new settings for cultural life through architectural interventions. Not only does the GOH project represent a concretisation of visions for contemporary life in China, but it is also the largest project ZHA has been able to realise in built form.

However, this period of state-sponsored architectural experimentation may prove short-lived—perhaps it has already passed. President Xi Jinping cast doubt upon the results of such experimental projects as early as 2014, and in early 2016 he called for an end to architecture that is 'oversized, xenocentric, weird' and lacking in cultural tradition.[4] Such declarations will undoubtedly have an impact on the direction that future architectural and urban projects take.

2 — There are multiple development models in China at the provincial level and experimentation in the provinces has been known as part of China's CCP development strategy.

3 — For an in-depth discussion of this model of development see Him Chung and Jonathan Unger. 'The Guangdong Model of Urbanisation: collective village land and making of a new middle class', *China Perspectives* (2013: 3), 33-41.

4 — Cao Li, 'China Moves to Halt 'Weird' Architecture', *The New York Times*, 22 Feb. 2016. http://www.nytimes.com/2016/02/23/world/asia/china-weird-architecture.html.

'With You At All'

An inaugural book titled *With You at All*, published by the Guangzhou Opera House in strategic partnership with the National Centre for the Performing Arts and the Shanghai Grand Theatre in 2011, describes the overarching goal to cultivate arts and culture in contemporary Chinese cities. It envisions dozens of theatres across the nation, similar in function, as illustrated by a map populated with some 31 future theatre locations. The GOH serves as a kind of 'Flagship' for 'Turning Cultural Deserts to Cultural Focus'.[5] The People's Daily of China Overseas Addition adds, 'This design of wonder embodies the concept of open-mindedness of the city'.[6] Evidently the Chinese Communist Party (CCP) invested in the GOH complex as a microcosm of cultural 'openness' realised through economic growth and support by the patronage of a new economic middle-class with disposable income.

The national programme of theatre management was spearheaded by a reformed branch of China's Ministry of Culture run by China Arts and Entertainment Group (CAEG). This large, state-level arts and entertainment association commissioned and planned a national cultural institute predicated on the goals of cultural and institutional reform. Within this institutional context, the opera theatre in Guangzhou was commissioned by Guangzhou's Municipal People's Government as the first building in a nation-wide program to: uphold the spirits of China Central reform of cultural institutions, develop more models for the progress of Chinese style theatres, offer spiritual culture services for citizens in Guangzhou and Pearl River Delta, contribute for building a powerful province and a national centre in culture, strengthen soft power of the country and conduct new explorations and contributions.[7]

5 — *With You At All: Guangzhou Opera House* (Guangzhou: Guangzhou Opera House Strategic Partnership, 2011), 36.

6 — Ibid., 23.

7 — Ibid., 14.

The use of the term 'soft power' in the statement above is intriguing, especially considering some of China's most powerful political leaders are photographed at the GOH in the very first pages of *With You At All*. Such individuals include Wang Qishan (CPC Central Committee and Vice Prime Minister), Li Changchun (former top propaganda and media relations for the CCP from 2002-2012), Cai Wu (Chinese Minister of Culture), and Wan Yang (Guangdong Party Secretary). Zhang Yu, the President of GAEG and Dean of the GOH, describes the cultural management role of the GOH and similar theatres as leveraging 'the cultural resource of different countries, gather[ing] cultural stakeholders and lead[ing] them to achieve greater cultural development'.[8]

The book explains that government officials sought out an architect of 'world-renown' to create a 'Guangzhou Landmark - The City's Living Room'. Quotations from prominent figures aim to show the cultural progress and economic growth symbolised by the GOH's realisation. For example, the president of the Netherlands is quoted as remarking, 'The facilities of GOH [are] rated the best in the world compared with those in America'.[9] The privileging of this comment implies China's competitive stance towards other parts of the world, and reinforces the logic that a building itself can become a vehicle for realising ideas of social and cultural progress, as well as a means of asserting China's rising international significance. The first production at the GOH was Turnadot, also a symbolic selection, as this Puccini opera was censored in China until the 1990s. Indeed, With You at all depicts the GOH as fulfilling a larger national goal of celebrating Chinese culture in artistic dialogue with 'imported culture'. A mosaic of images showcases operas performed by the Opera of the People's Liberation Army, alongside performances by the Russian National Ballet, the Royal Flemish Philharmonic, Sesame Street, and many

8 — Ibid., 44.

9 — Ibid., 14.

other international performers, dancers, musicians, and artists.[10] As portrayed by this viewpoint, the opera house as a cultural institution creates a place for direct Chinese engagement with a spectrum of prestigious international cultural events.

Design vision and realisation

Hadid's design ambitions for the GOH, dating from an international competition in 2002, seem to parallel the official vision of a theatre with the capacity to engender cultural change. Hadid approached the landscape and ground plane of the GOH as a field for architectural manipulation. In other words, the extraordinary form was to be imbued with socially transformative qualities. Here it is worth recalling the influence of Constructivist and Suprematist art and architecture on Hadid's work during her studies at the Architectural Association in the 1970s. Hadid carries forward certain ideas about form and its role in the formation of cultural life from these historical movements, but unlike the Constructivist and Suprematist visionaries, she divorces herself from any political ideology as such. In the absence of an explicit political vision in her work, the client's own political vision conveniently fills the void, as in the case of the GOH.

The plan of the complex reveals multiple layers of open, pedestrianized space, recalling the initial concept of 'sucking ideas of urbanism and landscape into the interior of the project… [producing an] internal density and liquidity'[11] The ground floor of the complex contains an oblique grid of circular concrete columns, an entrance to the 1800-seat auditorium, and the main stage. This level is also home to a Blüthner Piano retail store, immediately visible as one enters or exits the concert hall. Kentucky Fried Chicken is also a popular tenant. The second level

10 — The 'First Lady' of China, Peng Liyaun (Xi Jinping's wife), is president of the People's Liberation Army Art's College, indicating the proximity between arts patronage and political power.

11 — Zaha Hadid, 1983-2004. Madrid: *El Croquis*, 2004.

of the complex is accessible by a spiral ramp and a set of stairs, both of which lead to a large, open-air plaza. This upper levelprovides entry to the smaller, 400-seat multi-use hall for performance art, opera, and concerts in the round; and also to the main auditorium. Practice rooms and a restaurant are tucked away behind the large auditorium on the upper level.

Despite the architect's professed intention to encourage social and cultural interactions within the complex, the cavernous spaces do not effectively foster the vibrancy of an urban 'living room'. The GOH has a heavy material presence and monolithic physical form. Its internal organization leaves vast amounts un-programmed and unpopulated public space on two levels. The lack of outdoor furniture, shade, and intimate spaces distances the realised project from the idealistic visions of both architect and client. Rather than bringing the city inside, the poorly-lit ground floor is overpowered by monotonous surfaces of concrete,

Fig. 2 Bypassing the publicly accessible spaces of the opera house complex, pedestrians head directly to the waterfront.

making the bottom level of the plaza seem more like the inside of a barren parking garage rather than a stimulating public place. By comparison, the nearby library and green belt along the river's edge bustle with pedestrians.

Most problematic of all is the low quality of the GOH's physical execution, which undermines the project's lofty ambitions. As of 2012, spalling concrete on the outer walls of the complex already exposes inner steel reinforcement. This degradation causes rust stains and weakens the impression of the 'fluidity' of the ramping and undulating façade and retaining walls. Granite panels, used as a cladding material, bear some of the worst marks of deterioration. The triangular modules are poorly fitted, and in some cases misaligned with the strict geometrical pattern that characterizes the multi-directional curve of the building's outermost shell. In many places these stone pieces strain to bend around the sinuous curves, apparently unable to meet the vision of the complex as two stones washed up on the Pearl River Bank. Conversations with a project architect, who requested anonymity to speak about a sensitive issue, suggested that the final selection of materials was dictated not by the architect, but rather by the client, to the detriment of the project. The client's heavy-handed role in the project's ultimate manifestation is not unique to China or the GOH project, but their insistence upon stone cladding for the double-curved façade has proven to be one of the most problematic choices in the design process.

In spite of ad-hoc repairs to the cladding, gray residue accumulates on the exterior windows and stone, perhaps caused by the haze enveloping the city – as an ephemeral trace of the hundreds of factories in the surrounding hinterlands of the Pearl River Delta. The GOH won numerous accolades as one of the best buildings of 2011, but it also likely deserved the distinction of having the world's longest punch list.

International reception - narratives abroad

Reviews of the GOH project written by Anglo and American architectural critics praised the building complex largely in terms of its formal and urban qualities. Jonathan Glancey of The Guardian was enchanted by the swooping canyons and grottoes he found while exploring on foot, but noted, 'There's no question, though, that the opera house is best experienced at night'. It is unclear whether this statement is a benign reference to the building's dramatic lighting, or an indirect critique of its construction defects, which are most apparent in daylight. Glancey took a political stance by criticising the city of Cardiff, Wales for failing to realise a similar opera house in the 1990s. 'The world's most spectacular opera house has just opened in China – but it could have been built in Cardiff', Glancey wrote, lamenting the missed opportunity to create 'the most radical and compelling building in Britain'.[12] Glancey's narrative perpetuates the view that an architectural design is a direct outcome of the vision and dedication of a single individual, overlooking key contributions by consultants, staff members, and the client.[13]

In an accompanying video piece, Glancey described the project as, 'A grand avant-garde architecture opera house for everyone... A marriage of high brilliant avant-garde architecture and true populism'.[14] But his reference to the avant-garde fails to recognise its historically transgressive role: a provocative figure or agenda that seeks cultural innovation in opposition to insti-

12 — Jonathan Glancey, 'Move Over, Sydney: Zaha Hadid's Guangzhou Opera House', *The Guardian*, 28 Feb. 2011. http://www.theguardian.com/artanddesign/2011/feb/28/guangzhou-opera-house-zaha-hadid.)

13 — The GOH building's realization is credited to 40 architects within Hadid Architects' office alone, not including the expertise contributed by: the Local Design Institute of Guangzhou, the Facade Engineering Company, Acoustic Consultants, and Theater and Lighting Design Consultants. The logistical apparatus behind such contemporary projects are a far distance from the singular hand of a genius. ZHA is also known for collaborative engagement with engineers such as AKT to successfully realise ambitious forms.

14 — This video was posted on ZHA's website: http://www.zaha-hadid.com/architecture/guangzhou-opera-house/?doing_wp_cron

tutionalized values and settings.[15] It goes far beyond innovative form-making. ZHA's design ultimately supports the official state and institutional visions for the future of culture in the Chinese city.

Fig. 3 Physical imperfections are visible on the southeast corner of the opera house façade. The stone cladding is not well accommodated to the rounded forms of the building, while the glazing and mullion details above appear unresolved and inconsistent.

15 — See Manfredo Tafuri, *The Sphere and Labyrinth: Avant-Gardes and Architecture from Piranesi to the 1970s*, trans. Pellegrino d'Acierno and Robert Connolly (Cambridge, Mass.: The MIT Press, 1987), which emphasizes the transgressive nature of the avant-garde in in various historical and political situations.

Nicolai Ouroussoff, the architecture critic of *The New York Times* at the time of the GOH's opening, noted the project's 'abysmal' quality of construction (which he blamed on unskilled migrant labour). He nonetheless praised it as, 'a magnificent example of how a single building can redeem a moribund urban environment. Its fluid forms — which have been compared to a cluster of rocks in a riverbed, their surfaces eroded by the water's currents — give sudden focus to the energy around it so that you see the whole area with fresh eyes.'[16] Ouroussoff's remarks reiterate the client's marketing language, particularly with respect to the imagery of water and stone. It also reinforces the idea that the building's form possesses a stimulating force, affecting palpable cultural change within the urban context. Both English and Chinese narratives propagate this formalistic vision, but the theatre complex itself has yet to fully realize it. To do so, it would need to offer more habitable public spaces and a higher standard of construction.

Ramifications

The Guangzhou Opera House was supposed to be a regenerative urban intervention. Whether it will ultimately represent either the inaugural building of a sweeping cultural reform programme supported by heads of state, as projected in *With You At All*; or the work of avant-garde architectural genius, as Western architecture critics supposed, remains to be seen. Despite the large government investment in the project, there is no resident opera group. And it seems puzzling that such a high profile project, promoted in China and abroad, could languish in such a degraded physical state so shortly after completion. It is very difficult to find photographs of the building's compromised state through general Internet searches, which instead yield stunning views of

16 — Nicolai Ouroussoff, 'Chinese Gem That Elevates Its Setting', *The New York Times*, 5 July 2011, C1, http://www.nytimes.com/2011/07/06/arts/design/guangzhou-opera-house-designed-by-zaha-hadid-review.html.

awe-inspiring spaces and forms. In a sense, the failures of the project as a built urban space and physical construction remain airbrushed out of the public's perception, for both English and Chinese speaking audiences. But visiting the opera house in person exposes the physical reality and highlights the tenuous relationship between an ideal vision for contemporary cultural life and the practicalities of its construction within the city.

One can only wonder if the ramifications of the GOH were a factor in the recent CCP declaration against 'weird architecture' as a model for envisioning and constructing cultural and public buildings. Might the tensions that emerged between conception, execution, and reception have helped prompt the turn back to 'tradition' as a guide for the future?

Lori Gibbs is a Ph.D. Candidate in Architecture at the University of Pennsylvania School of Design.

Fig. 4 The triangular façade panels, allegedly specified by the client rather than the architect, are most problematic at the double-curved surfaces and irregular window frames.

Woven textile banner designed by Thonik, suspended at exhibition entrance.

SOCIAL CITY FLOORPLAN

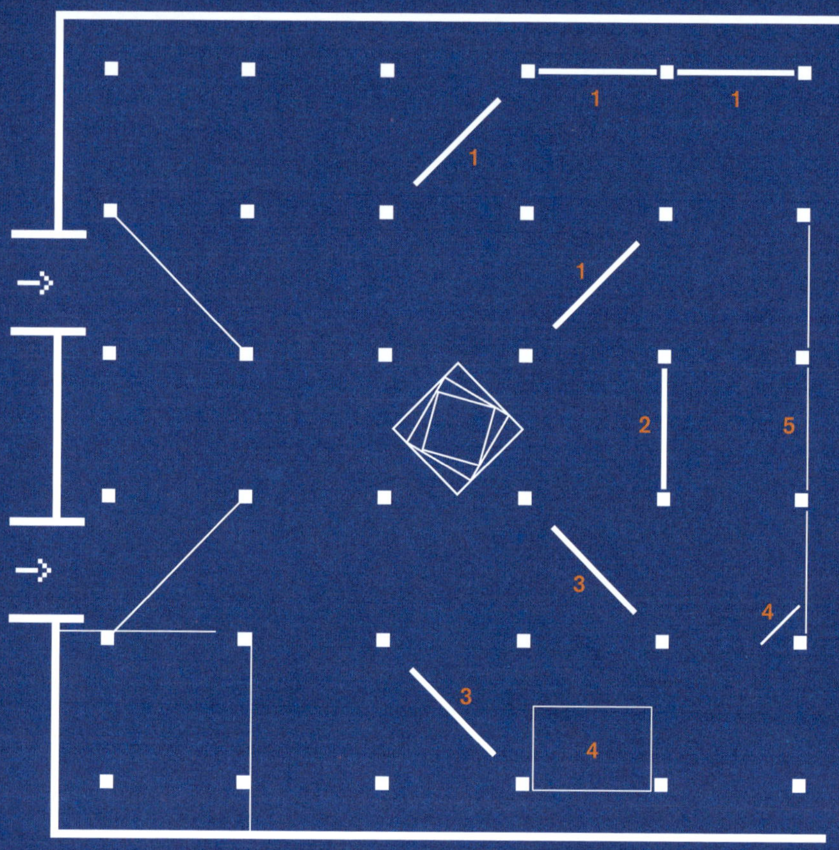

1
Soft Map
Jan Rothuizen

2
Social City
Droog

3
Babel
Mark van der Net

4
Social city TV
Droog

5
Treehousewaterboatappartmenthammocktower
TD (Theo Deutinger, Stefanos Filippas)

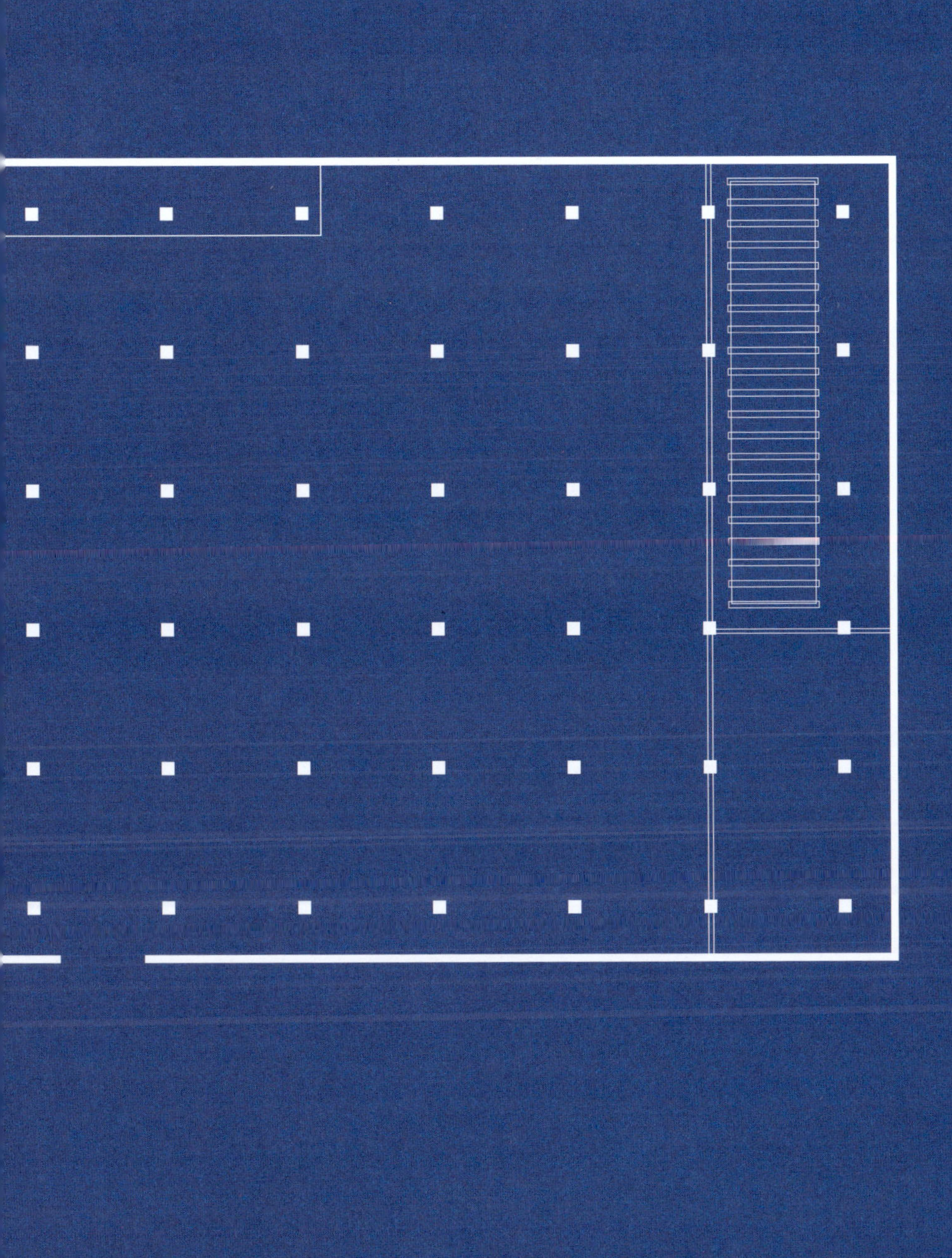

SOCIAL CITY: A PROJECT OF DESIGN+DESIRES

Renny Ramakers

It is time to change the city for the 21st century.

In 2014, in close collaboration with Mark van der Net, I started a city-making program called 'Design+Desires', an extensive research-and-do program with a series of projects in different localities. This program highlights the passions, needs, and dreams of a broad range of individual people. The challenge is to design a city, or a part of a city, based on the diverse and sometimes conflicting desires of citizens.

Today, everything has changed around us, yet the way cities are designed is similar to 50 years ago. Government, urban planners, real estate moguls, and other companies traditionally create cities. But these cities do not adequately cater to our rapidly changing personal, social, and trans-national needs. Nor do these cities entrust true ownership to the citizens. There is a gap between the city that people want to live in and the city that people get to live in, a gap between the way professionals envision the city and the way people in the city organise themselves.

Design+Desires is a new way of city-making. It goes beyond top-down urban planning and takes the richness of the various dreams and desires of citizens as its starting point. The programme has a unique method that combines three techniques: data mapping, active participatory citizens research, and innovative design solutions.

When UABB 2015 invited me to present this new way of city-making, I initiated the Social City project in collaboration with Mark van der Net (OSCity), artist Jan Rothuizen, and architecture office TD. Social City is the first full-scale exercise of our Design+Desires method in Shenzhen and Hong Kong.

Capturing dreams and desires of citizens

We developed the Social City online platform www.socialcities.org with Mark van der Net. This platform was launched during the BDJW 2015 in Beijing. The central feature of this platform is a friendly quiz about urban life. We ask in a very informal and visually playful manner how people want to live in the city (e.g. in what kind of house and neighbourhood, with what kind of mobility and technology, and similar questions). By taking the quiz, participants create their avatar and can see how their desires are implemented in the growing virtual city. The 'virtual' not only means a digital space open to everyone, but also embodies a more hypothetical way to explore how citizens would envision their ideal city life. The data generated from the quiz fuels dialogue and discussion and functions as a guideline in our research-and-do process.

In the quiz, people can choose from among multiple options or they can opt to fill in something original. For example, we ask how you want to earn your money in Social City. People can choose: social welfare, working, gambling, renting out rooms in my house, selling advertisement space on my house, I don't need money, or other. The options might seem a bit unusual or far-fetched, but that is on purpose. Because we deliberately want to offer people new perspectives, which they might not have thought about before, and encourage them to continue in this vein. We want people really to dream. And their dreams give us a richer palette of possibilities and a deeper understanding of their latent desires. When someone opts to live in a tree hut, we envision a person that to a certain extent loves to live alone, in nature, and is adventurous enough to climb up to his or her house.

Fig. 1 An introductory poll asks participants to rate and describe their urban living preferences, habits, identity, and other aspects to generate a growing body of data on Social City.

The quiz allows us to reach out to a broad range of people. The Social Citizens, as we call the people who take the quiz, come from all parts of the world. We do not categorize them by age, gender, education, or profession. Rather, their common ground is that they have all played the quiz and are digitally connected. They reflect the modern city dweller who lives amongst people from different cultural backgrounds, people of different ages, with different professions, people who are all virtually connected with other people. Indeed, with the Social City platform we only reach people who are familiar with the Internet. Yet, we can still observe a vast diversity in their desires. For example, when it comes to the preferred view from their homes, a majority of Social Citizens would like to be able to see the cityscape as well as mountains and

For the Social City project at UABB, Mark van der Net used computing techniques to tap and process the social media output of Hong Kong and Shenzhen. His installation in the biennale reflects a continuously moving pattern of Instagram and Weibo messaging. The Chinese visitors could read a mixture of individual messages, pictures, and desires. The installation, called 'Babel', was loaded with data.

Just as in our Social City project, Design+Desires projects always begin with the tapping of local social media. This technique enables us to see what are people talking about, where they meet each other, what they find irritating, and what their interests are. Communicating and tapping data from Instagram, Twitter, Facebook and other social media platforms is a perfect way to connect with potential participants.

Talking to the people

Next to the digital data mapping, we of course also want to get in touch with people who are not digitally connected. That's why we go out into the streets. Face-to-face interviews not only give us the opportunity to meet a different audience, but it also helps us to have a more profound dialogue with citizens in a given place. We thereby have a better chance to hear what people really want and what the motivations behind their desires are, and what kind of emotions are in play.

For our Social City project at UABB, we invited artist Jan Rothuizen to visualize the way in which a number of Shenzhen citizens live. In order to have a more clear understanding of what they might want, we first needed to look at what they already have. Based on the digital data mined by Mark van der Net, Jan Rothuizen contacted several Shenzhen citizens to meet.

The retired investor Yu Danqing (57), travel office employee Vivien (28), Uber taxi driver Peng Li (38) and factory worker Alan (28) were all eager to partake in the project, and talked freely about their desires and worries. They opened their homes to Rothuizen, who translated their living spaces into richly detailed drawings.

Also during the UABB in Shenzhen, we launched Social City TV. We asked visitors of the biennale how they want to live and what motivates their visions of the ideal city life.

Designing new possibilities

Data mapping and participatory research also guide the design solutions. This part of the Design+Desires program has just started. In the Social City project at UABB we presented our first exercise. Since our Social Citizens expressed very diverse dwelling desires, from living in an apartment block to nomadic living and living in a tree hut, we commissioned TD Architects to design an apartment block in which the whole range of dwelling desires is implemented and combined in one setting. TD's apartment block offers it all: a detached house on the water, space for tents and even tree huts, everything conceived by participants that is technically feasible. Science fiction? Maybe. But we need these kinds of visions to innovate, to look at existing conditions in a different way. The challenge is to bring together the whole range of desires, even if they are conflicting, to unite seemingly incompatible elements and re-generate the city.

Our position amongst other UABB presentations

At the UABB we clearly wanted to make a statement by emphasizing that the first step in city-making is to listen to the dreams and desires of citizens. For me as a curator, the challenge was to bring the various steps, executed by the different collaborating partners, into one coherent exhibition. Therefore we installed a monumental and immersive presentation within the cavernous space of Building 8 as the unifying setting for our Design+Desires program.

We felt that our approach to city-making was seen as something of an oddity compared to the other exhibitions. So far, it seems that the regular audience of architecture biennales has been accustomed to the idea of local bottom-up approaches to city-making, but perhaps has not been fully exposed to the idea that city-making on a global scale can start with small exercises and conversations to elicit the dreams of individual citizens all over the world. For us at Droog, this approach is in our DNA. Because since the founding of Droog, we always took the human touch as pivotal for our design projects. We think this same mentality could also be applied to city-making, because cities do not consist of buildings and infrastructure, but in the first place of people and their dreams and desires.

Design+Desires method applied in Amsterdam

The Design+Desires method can be applied to all aspects of city life. Invited by the city of Amsterdam, we are now working on two local neighbourhood projects. The first is in the 'Dapperbuurt' neighbourhood, which has a high rate of youth unemployment. We will focus on the passions and ambitions of the youth, and the aim is to develop scenarios in which these passions can be transformed into work. The second local project takes place in 'Slotervaart', a neighbourhood which is characterized by post-war social housing—boring building blocks originally intended to solve the housing shortage of Dutch citizens and now a neighbourhood full of immigrants. We will focus on how these residents would envision their house and street, if there were no rules and regulations. With this diverse population we expect a mishmash of styles and identities. We have asked designer Jan Konings and artist Jan Rothuizen to unite these assorted visions in one coherent street view. One of the messages in this project is to reconsider existing rules and regulations and to be more open to imperfection. We will present this re-designed street view during the 'Re-dreaming the Street' symposium with politicians, architects, and residents. The goal is to resolve local issues and create new opportunities in such a way that they can inspire further action beyond the local context.

Research and reflection

In Design+Desires we find research and reflection very important. Every week we update the Social City platform by posting data updates, creating speculative images, and writing articles inspired by the outcome of the user polls. We have reflected on topics such as the possibility of revitalising shrinking cities by welcoming immigrants, the crucial difference between property ownership and participatory ownership of the city, and the idea of flexible citizenship that can be borrowed and swapped between people from different countries.

We aim to push our research data further, for instance to collaborate with the Digital Emotions research group of the University of Amsterdam, of which professor Ellen Rutten is coordinator. Together we are organising the 'Re-dreaming the Street' symposium in which the research group will mainly focus on chaos and imperfection as affectively productive spatial-planning categories in our digitized age. We will then share their insights and data on our platform.

The future of Design+Desires

The Social City project at UABB is a part of the Design+Desires programme, which explores new opportunities for a future city life fuelled by creativity and technology. This project and all the other local Design+Desires projects have a value on their own and at the same time they are building blocks for a larger conceptual city model. We will incorporate the results of what we achieved at UABB in further research and discussion. We continue to collect new data all over the world and go full-speed in the design exercises.

In the brief for the open call for young designers and architects, we have deliberately included seeming contradictions, such as how to incorporate the city into the wilderness, in such a way that citizens can enjoy their urban experience while also enjoying wilderness and nature. Or how to design public spaces in such a way that they protect us against bombs and machine guns, without having armed forces and cameras all over.

Our aim is to focus on all aspects of city life, from work, leisure, and dwelling to mobility and governance. We do this together with universities, companies, and city authorities and aim to open up the city of the 21st century in all its diversity. Without the input of citizens, the city is only a blueprint. Without imagination the future is poor.

Credits:
Curator: Renny Ramakers (Droog /Design+Desires)
Installations Hong Kong and Shenzhen:
Mark van der Net (OSCity), Jan Rothuizen,
TD (Theo Deutinger & Stefanos Filippas)
Social City platform: Created by Renny Ramakers (Droog /Design+Desires) and Mark van der Net (OSCity) in collaboration with Thonik (design)
Implementation technology: Mark van der Net, Eugene Tjoa
Implementation editorial concept: Renny Ramakers, Suki de Boer, Edith Gruson (Pro Arts Design), Judith Lekkerkerker (Ruimtevolk)
Editorial team: Renny, Ramakers, Mark Minkjan, Giulia Cosenza, Yaolan Luo
Social City TV: Suki de Boer
Graphic Design: Thonik
Spatial Design: Edith Gruson (Pro Arts Design), Giulia Cosenza, Yaolan Luo
General Assistance / Project Coordination: Suki de Boer
Production: Haochong Luo (Garden Party Design Studio)

social city
share your desires

social city
share your desires

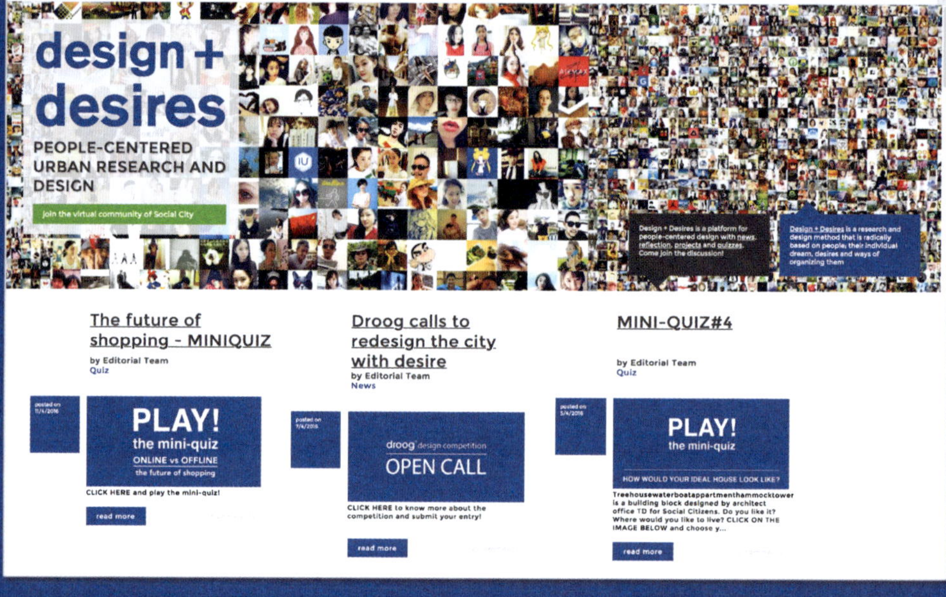

View of the web interface for Social City, offering topical commentary, interactive features, and questionnaires to gather participant data.

View of the ever-growing, virtual 'Social City'

'Radical Urbanism' curator Alfredo Brillembourg is interviewed for Social City TV.

Installation view with data visualisations by Mark van der Net

HONG KONG
24-9-2015 @9h

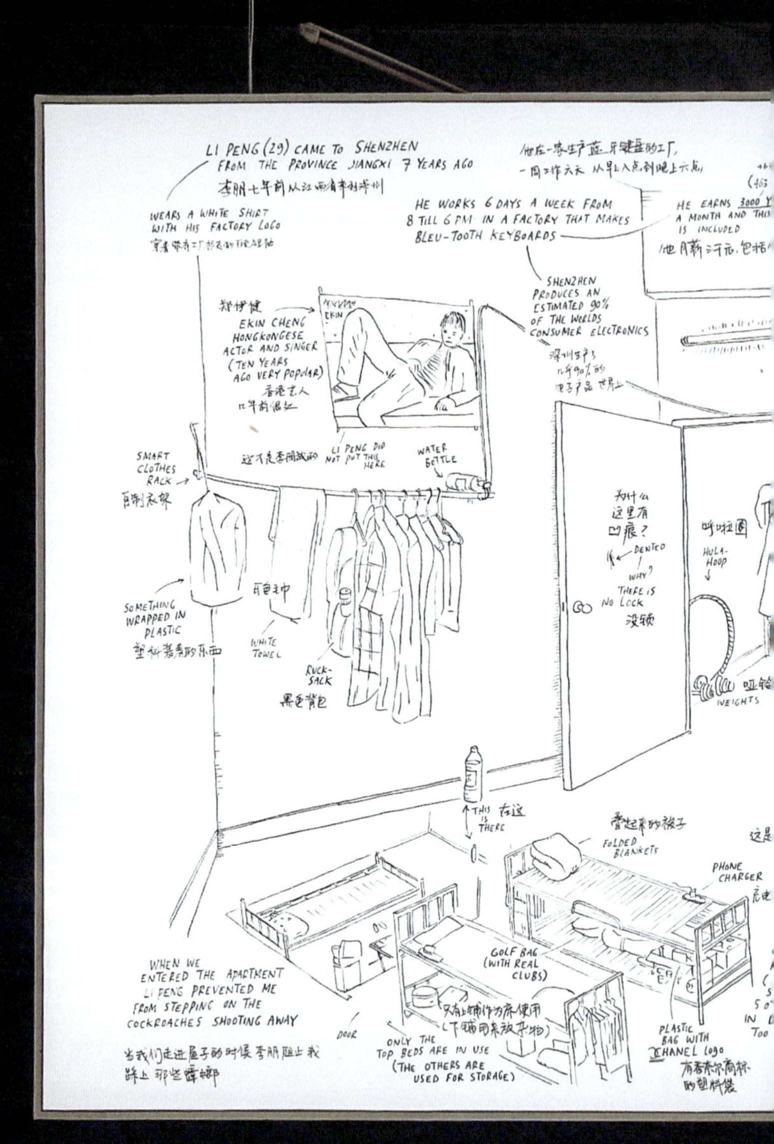

Installation view with ‘soft map’ drawing by Jan Rothuizen

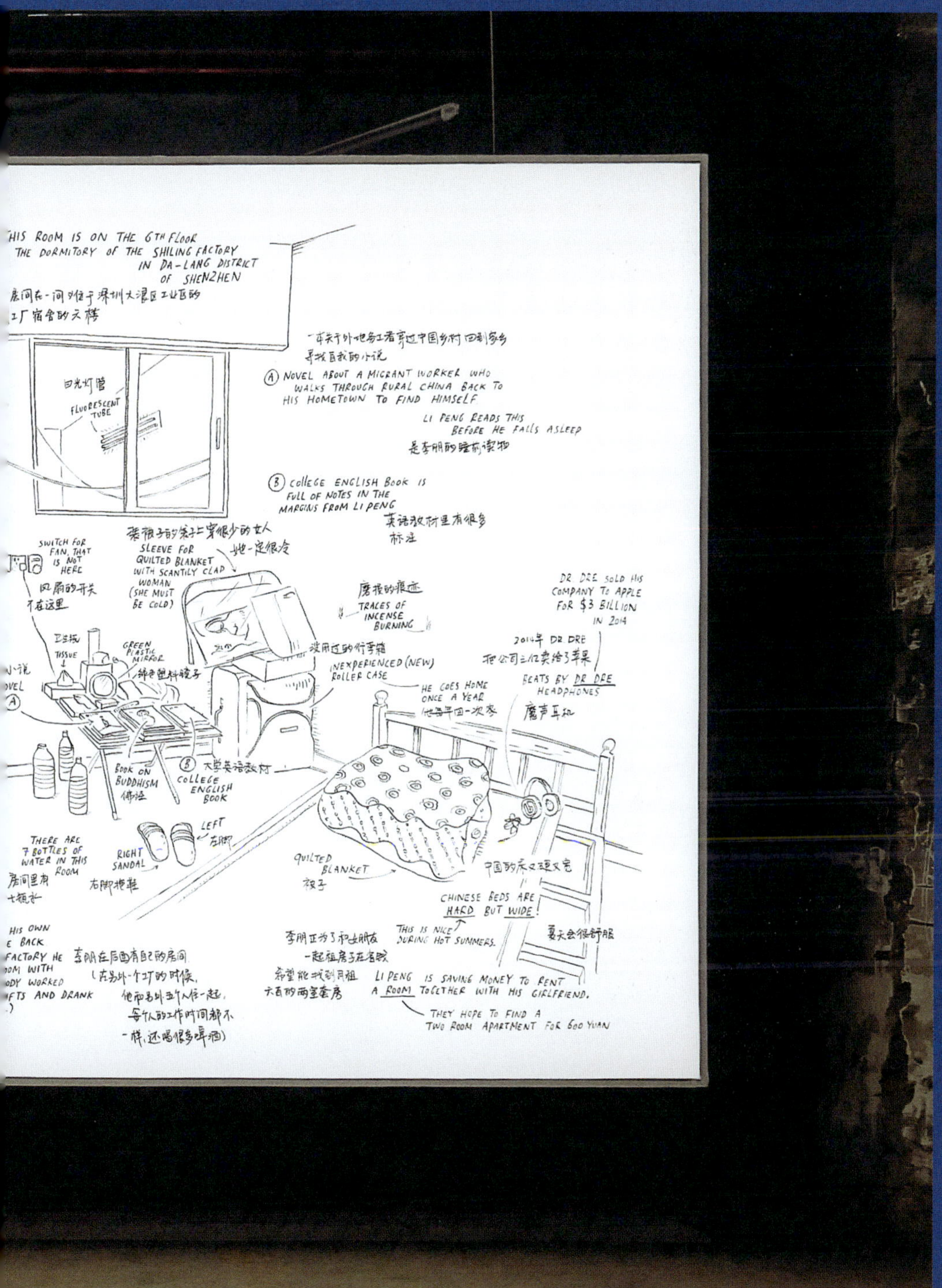
THE DORMITORY OF THE SHILING FACTORY IN DA-LANG DISTRICT OF SHENZHEN
日光灯管
FLUORESCENT TUBE
A NOVEL ABOUT A MIGRANT WORKER WHO WALKS THROUGH RURAL CHINA BACK TO HIS HOMETOWN TO FIND HIMSELF
LI PENG READS THIS BEFORE HE FALLS ASLEEP
是李朋的睡前读物
B COLLEGE ENGLISH BOOK IS FULL OF NOTES IN THE MARGINS FROM LI PENG
英语教材里有很多标注
SWITCH FOR FAN, THAT IS NOT HERE
风扇的开关不在这里
SLEEVE FOR QUILTED BLANKET WITH SCANTILY CLAD WOMAN (SHE MUST BE COLD)
她一定很冷
TRACES OF INCENSE BURNING
DR DRE SOLD HIS COMPANY TO APPLE FOR $3 BILLION IN 2014
2014年 DR DRE
TISSUE
GREEN PLASTIC MIRROR
NOVEL A
INEXPERIENCED (NEW) ROLLER CASE
HE GOES HOME ONCE A YEAR
BEATS BY DR DRE HEADPHONES
BOOK ON BUDDHISM
B 大学英语教材
COLLEGE ENGLISH BOOK
LEFT
THERE ARE 7 BOTTLES OF WATER IN THIS ROOM
RIGHT SANDAL
QUILTED BLANKET
被子
CHINESE BEDS ARE HARD BUT WIDE!
THIS IS NICE DURING HOT SUMMERS.
夏天会很舒服
LI PENG IS SAVING MONEY TO RENT A ROOM TOGETHER WITH HIS GIRLFRIEND.
THEY HOPE TO FIND A TWO ROOM APARTMENT FOR 600 YUAN

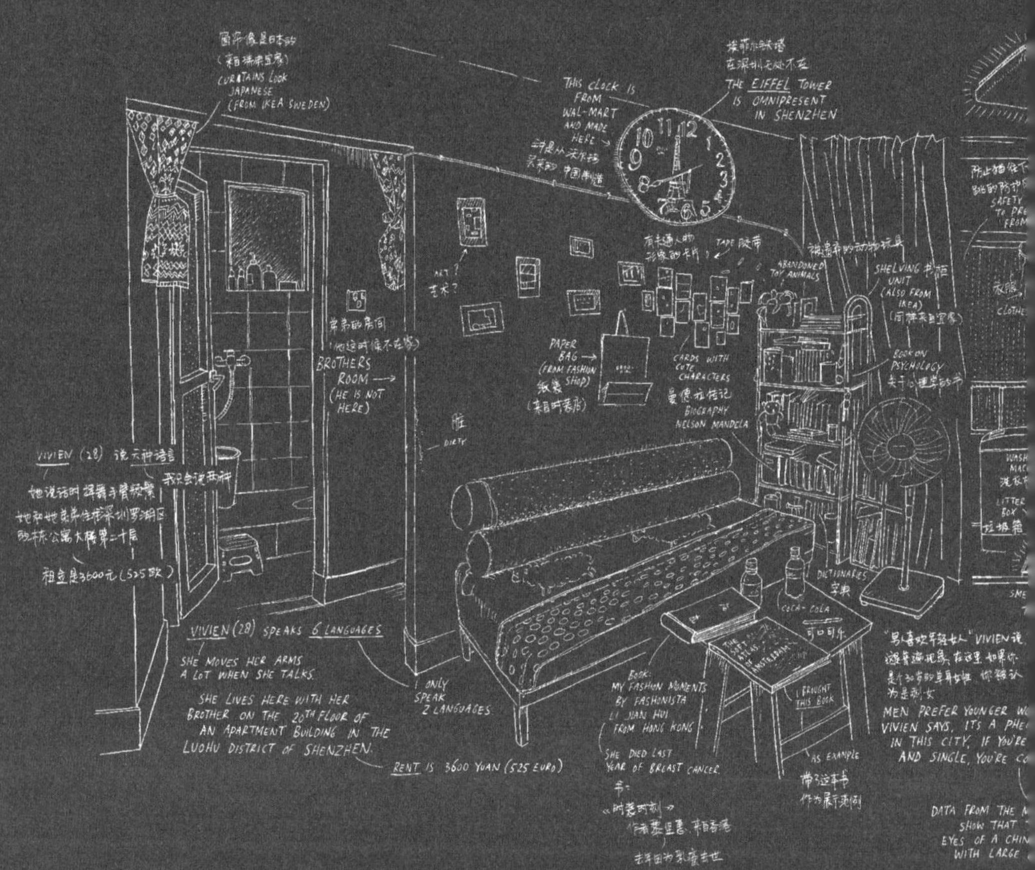

A series of drawings by artist Jan Rothuizen present the homes of four citizens in Shenzhen, and can be read as diagrams, 'soft maps', notes, or even novellas that portray city life at a personal level.

Rothuizen selected and contacted people to meet in real life based on Mark van der Net's digital data mapping of Weibo. Rothuizen says: 'Most of them declined since it was not a business opportunity, but the people I did meet were surprisingly eager

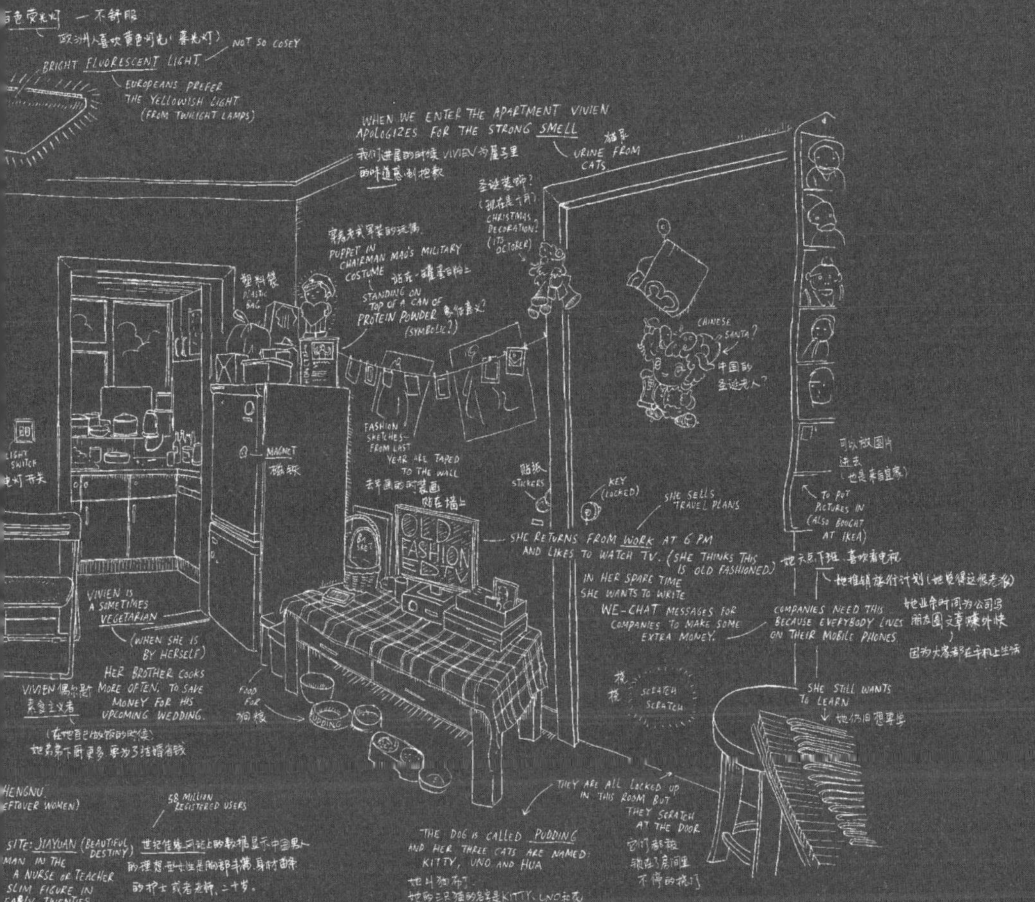

to partake and talked freely about their desires (and worries) and opened their homes to me'.

These include retired investor Yu Danqing (57), travel office employee Vivien (28), Uber taxi driver Peng Li (38) and factory worker Alan (28). Rothuizen's soft maps shed light on individual behaviours and desires, which are crucial elements to understand in urban planning.

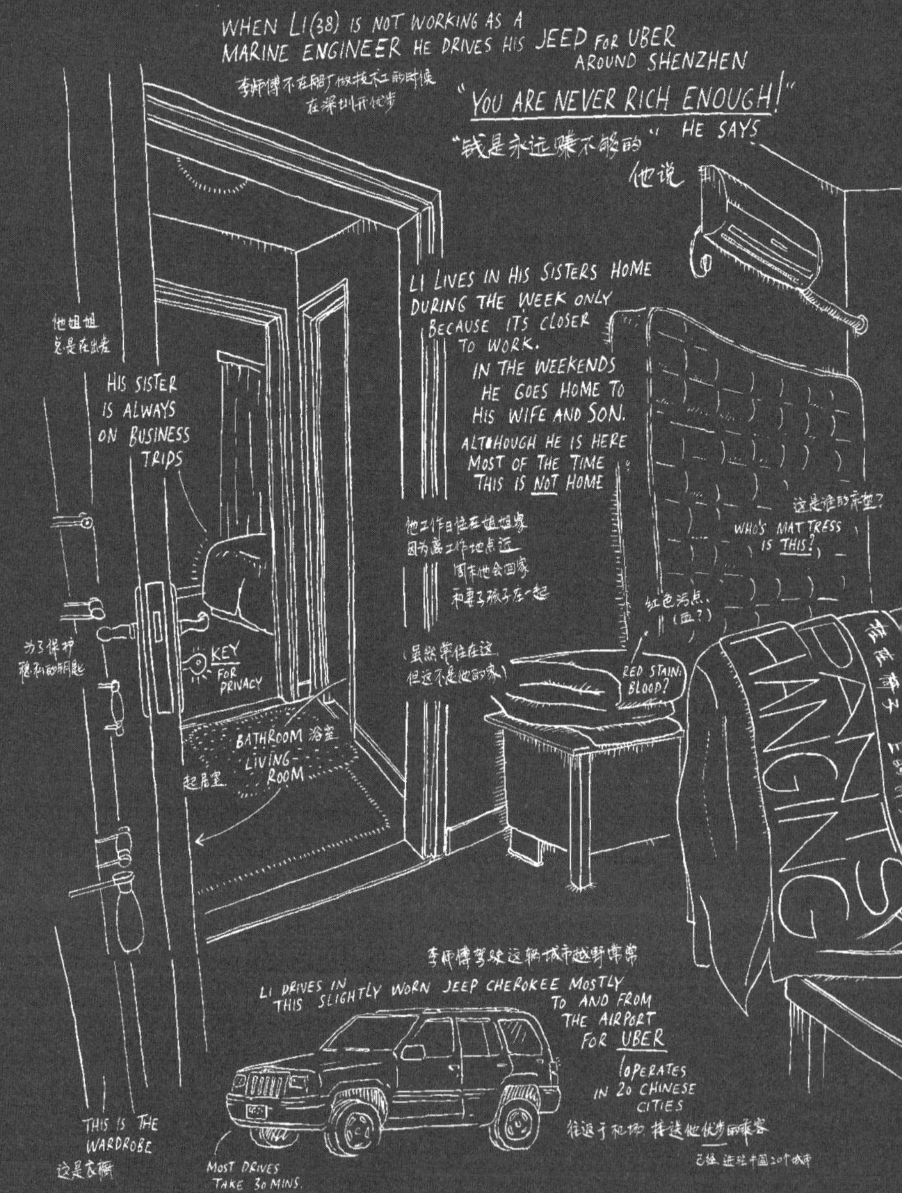
WHEN LI (38) IS NOT WORKING AS A MARINE ENGINEER HE DRIVES HIS JEEP FOR UBER AROUND SHENZHEN
李师傅不在船厂做技术工的时候 在深圳开优步
"YOU ARE NEVER RICH ENOUGH!" HE SAYS
"钱是永远赚不够的" 他说
LI LIVES IN HIS SISTERS HOME DURING THE WEEK ONLY BECAUSE ITS CLOSER TO WORK.
IN THE WEEKENDS HE GOES HOME TO HIS WIFE AND SON.
ALTHOUGH HE IS HERE MOST OF THE TIME THIS IS NOT HOME
他工作日住在姐姐家 因为离工作地点近 周末他会回家 和妻子孩子在一起
(虽然常住在这 但这不是他的家)
他姐姐总是在出差
HIS SISTER IS ALWAYS ON BUSINESS TRIPS
为了保护隐私的钥匙
KEY FOR PRIVACY
BATHROOM 浴室
LIVING-ROOM
起居室
这是谁的床垫?
WHO'S MATTRESS IS THIS?
红色污点 (血?)
RED STAIN: BLOOD?
李师傅驾驶这辆城市越野常常
LI DRIVES IN THIS SLIGHTLY WORN JEEP CHEROKEE MOSTLY TO AND FROM THE AIRPORT FOR UBER
OPERATES IN 20 CHINESE CITIES
往返于机场 接送他优步的乘客
已经进驻中国20个城市
THIS IS THE WARDROBE
这是衣橱
MOST DRIVES TAKE 30 MINS.

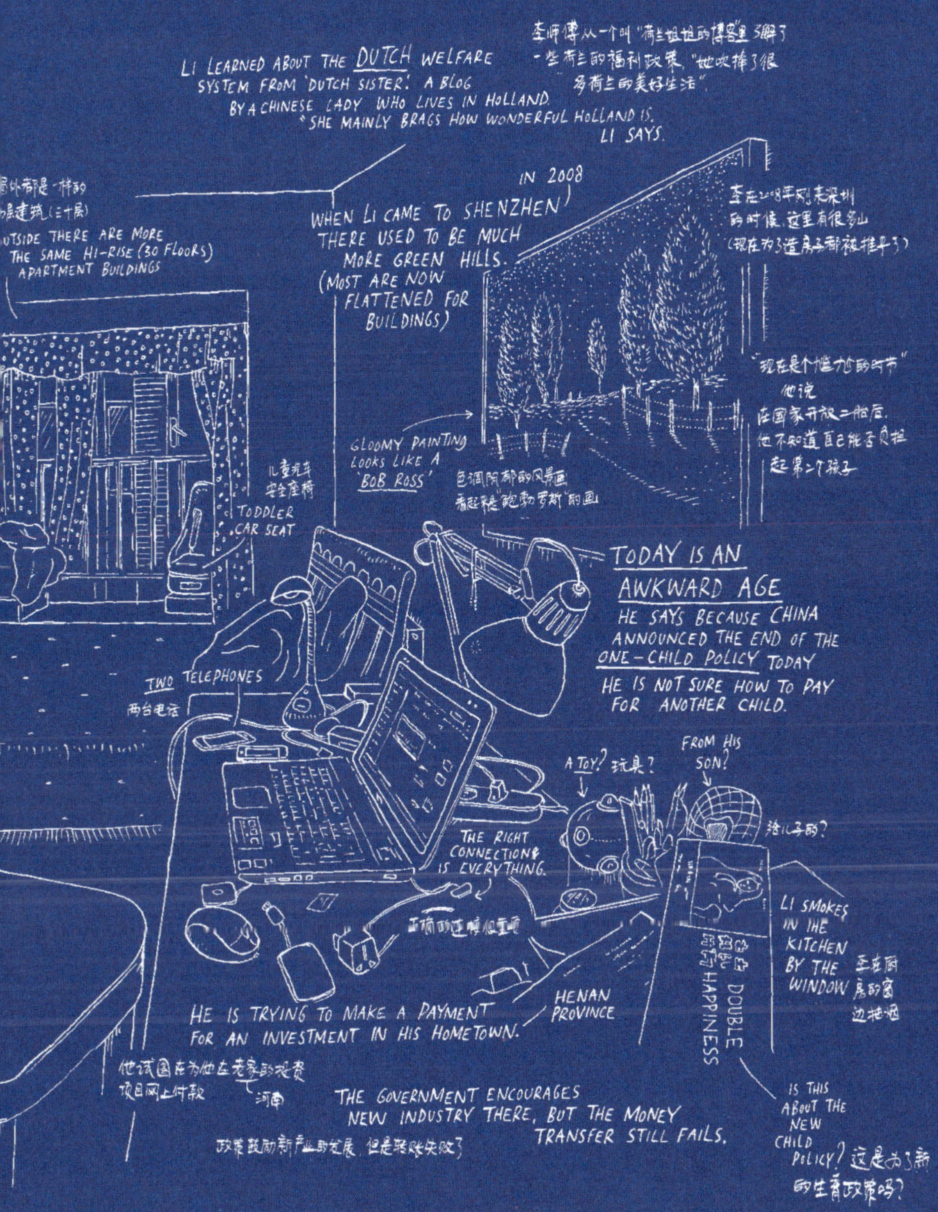

Rothuizen says: 'My drawings show how our ideas of what we want and what we have are two different things. I think that in order to plan what we want, we should start with what we have'.

Square
45.7%

Street
23.3%

Bench
14.2%

World Wide Web
7.3%

My house
5%

I only need private space
4.1%

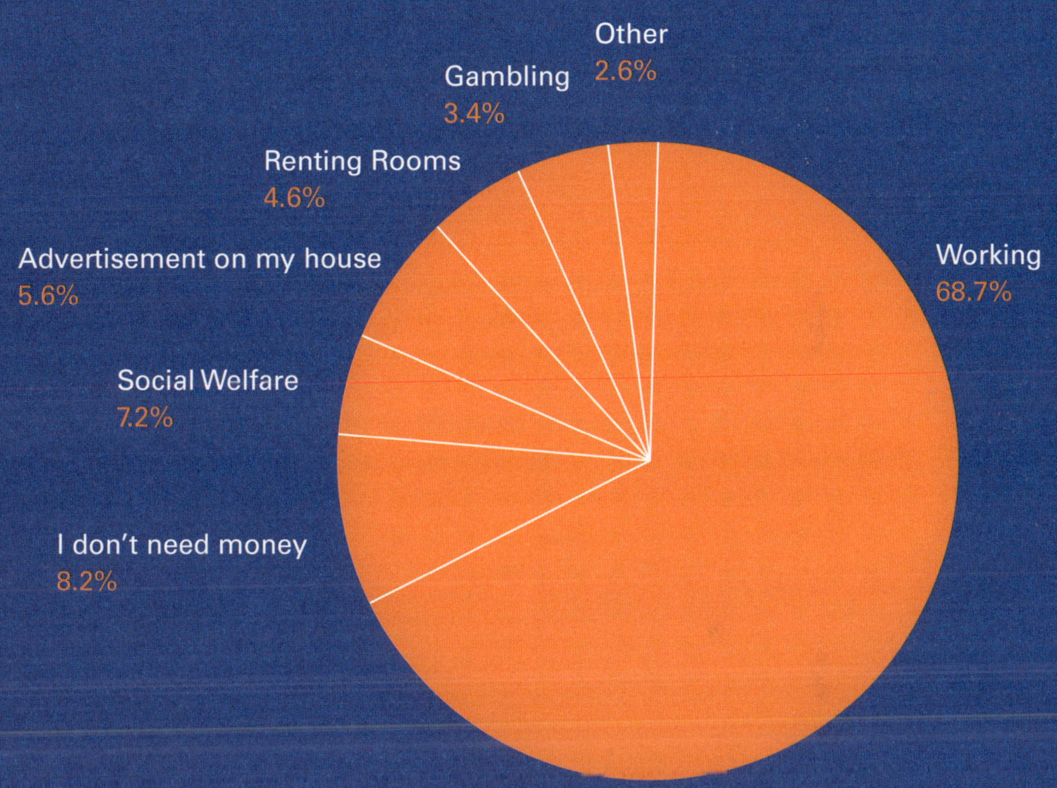

How would people like to make a living in Social City? Most envision 'working' in one form or another, but over 25% propose alternative approaches, such as selling advertisements on their houses, gambling, or going without money altogether.

Results of a poll of Social City inhabitants on the subject of urban mobility.

Cycling
56%

Walking
18.3%

Skateboard
7.4%

Walk
29.5%

Grow vegetables
19.1%

Skate
18%

More than half of the citizens prefer to cycle around the city, while walking is the second most desired means of transport. The skateboard, the scooter or moped, and the bus are next. The automobile is the least-favoured mode of urban mobility. As a follow-up question, Social Citizens were asked what they would do if cars were banned from urban streets. Most respondents simply anticipated the ability to walk around freely, while others cited new possibilities to grow vegetables, hop on their skateboards, hold block parties, jog, or walk their dogs.

Scooter
6.7%

Public transport
6.3%

Car
5.3%

Have parties
12.9%

Run
11.9%

Walk my dog
8.6%

Windmills, solar panels, robots doing the work and the internet-of-everything:

Social City would be well equipped with technology. The abundance of windmills envisioned byt its inhabitants make it the 21st century version of the Dutch landscape from centuries ago. Nine out of 10 Social Citizens also expect solar panels to power up their lives; whether or not to use renewable energy is not even a question.

Solar panels

A LOT
90%

NONE
10%

Windmills

A LOT

74.5%

NONE

25.5%

How do Social Citizens want to feel safe in their Social City neighbourhood?

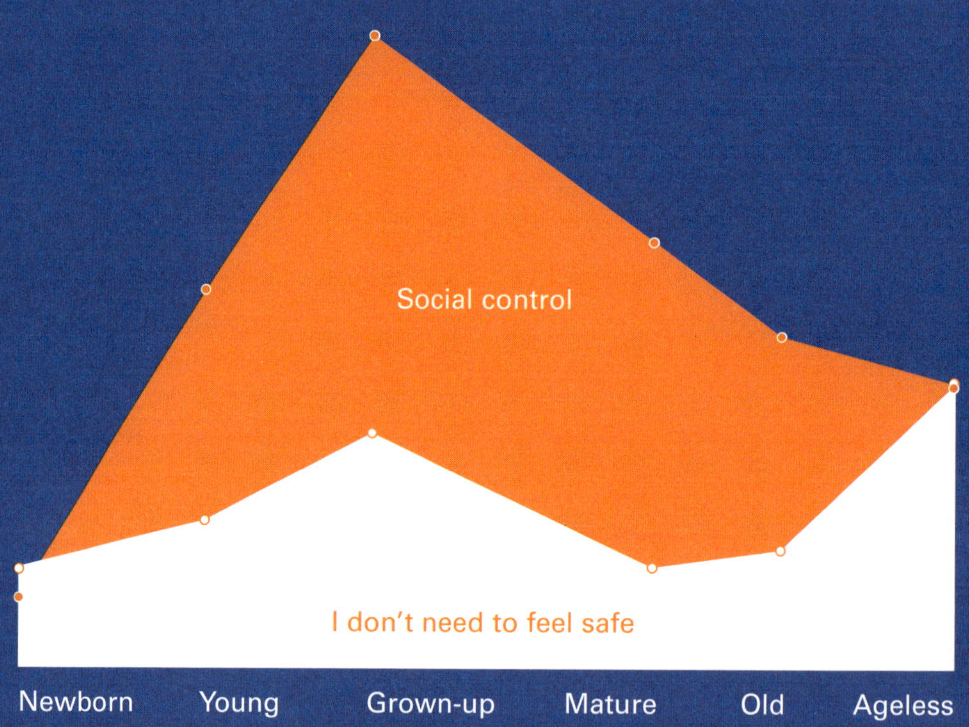

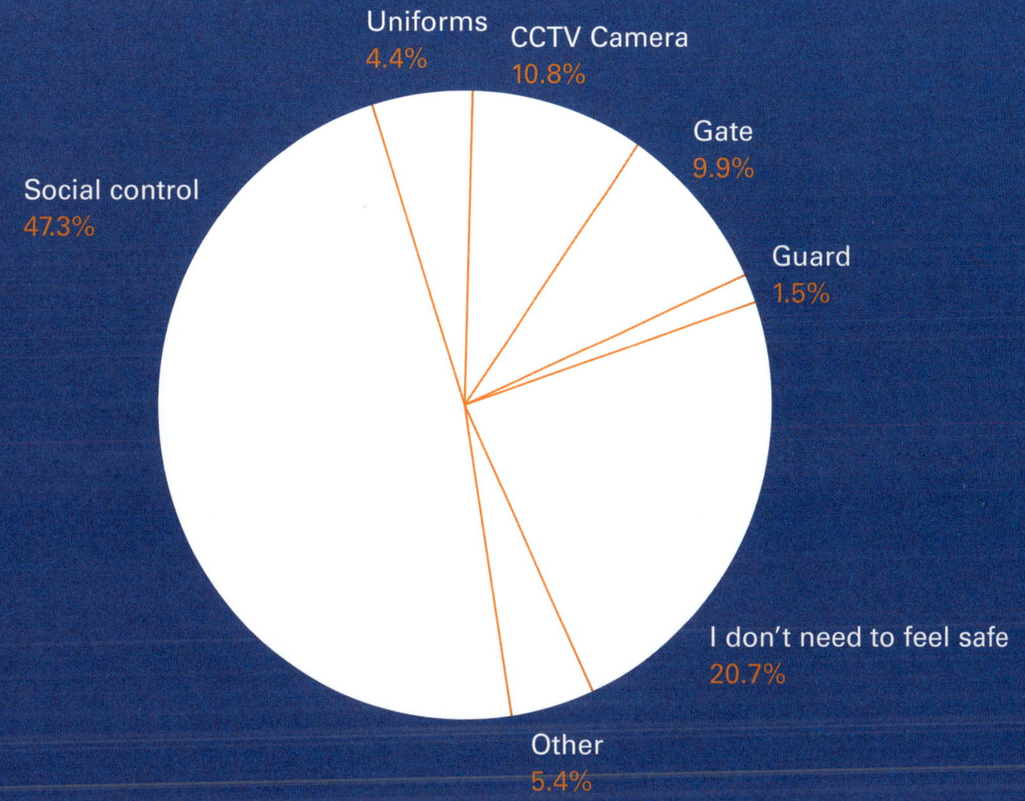

The Social City poll results show social security is favoured over physical safety measures like CCTV, police, and gated communities. One in five even say that they don't need any control.

Ramakers: 'The question is: could we design public spaces that protect us against bombs and machine guns without armed forces and cameras all over? It is not a question. It is a task. Not only a task for urban planners, architects, and designers, but also for our technological forces'.

On the subject of urban governance, citizens of Social City express-ed a desire to exercise direct control, instead of having governmental bodies, companies, computers, or 'nobody' rule their cities, as discussed in this post from 8 January 2016. What would these citizens do if they were in charge? Many say they would tackle specific issues: 'abolish patronizing rules and regulations', 'ban cars, free transportation', and 'opportunities for small entrepreneurship'. Others would reportedly 'establish an animal network' or 'set all robots free'. Several citizens would like to establish a basic income for all. Some just want to have a good sleep, organise parties for everyone, or do not have any ideas yet.

The illustration is inspired by the notion of a self-governing city open to everyone, in which citizens keep refining their system on the top of old one. The rules are open-ended, but the layers of antecedents remain visible as citizens experiment with new modifications.

Citizens
46.7%

City Council
26.8%

Computer
7.6%

Visualisation by Sayme Choi

Nobody
6.9%

National government
6.2%

Multinationals
3.3%

What is the nature of work envisioned in Social City? Among the findings based on participant data, explored in a post on 23rd January 2016: People have more than one job in the future Social City. A job is no longer about labour. Rather, it is about satisfying individual desires.

A plurality of participants (40%) would prefer to work in 'workshops' over offices, homes, shops, factories, or institutions such as a hospital. Only the jobs in which people can express themselves will be occupied by humans, while other services and forms of production will be taken care of by robots.

Workshop
40.5%

Office
26.8%

Home
20.5%

We Are Doing It!

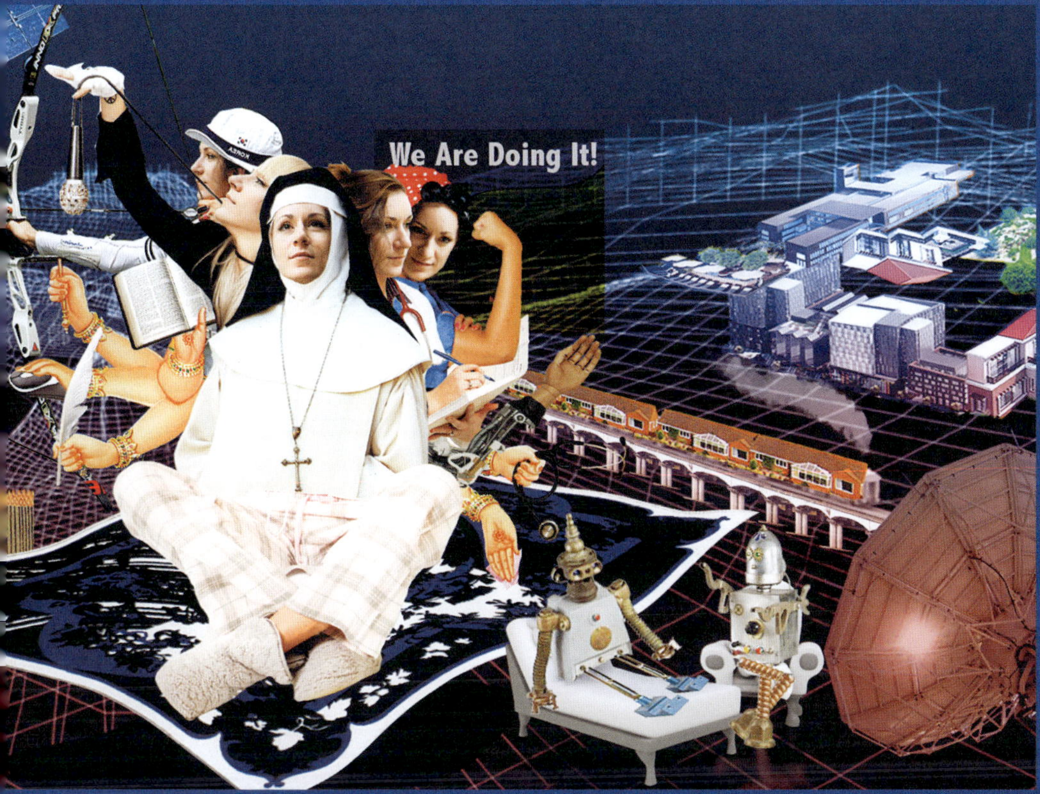

Visualisation by Sayme Choi

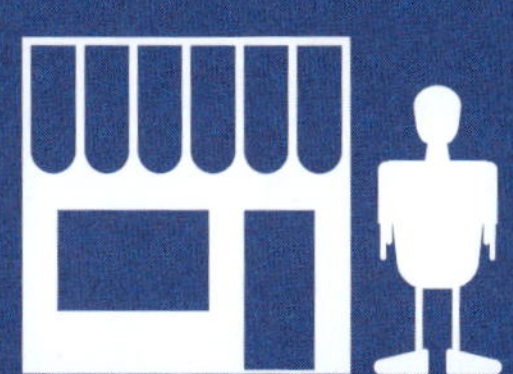

Shop
4.7%
Factory
3.9%
Hospital
3.4%

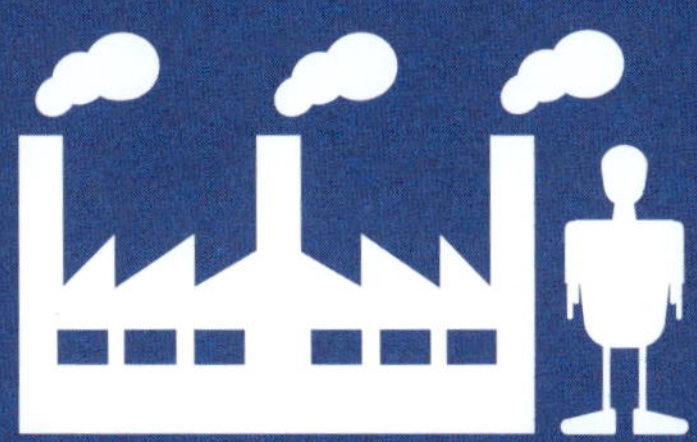

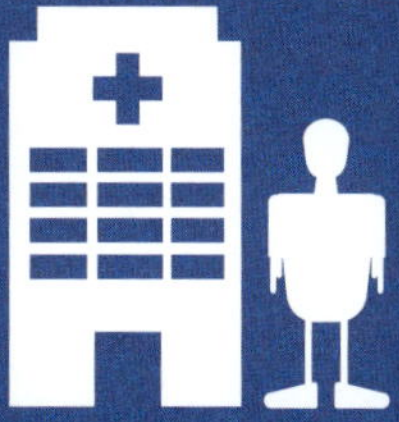

Visualisation by Sayme Choi

Chaosmos: order in disorder. In this vision of Social City, the borders between country, nationality, culture and even religion no longer exist. Everything is acceptable. Social City highlights the diversity, rich contrasts, and uniqueness of individual desires, instead of blurring them together.

Asked what kind of house they would prefer to live in, a plurality of respondents desired a tree hut. The next most desired forms of dwelling were a building block, a detached house, a mobile home, a house boat, or no house at all.

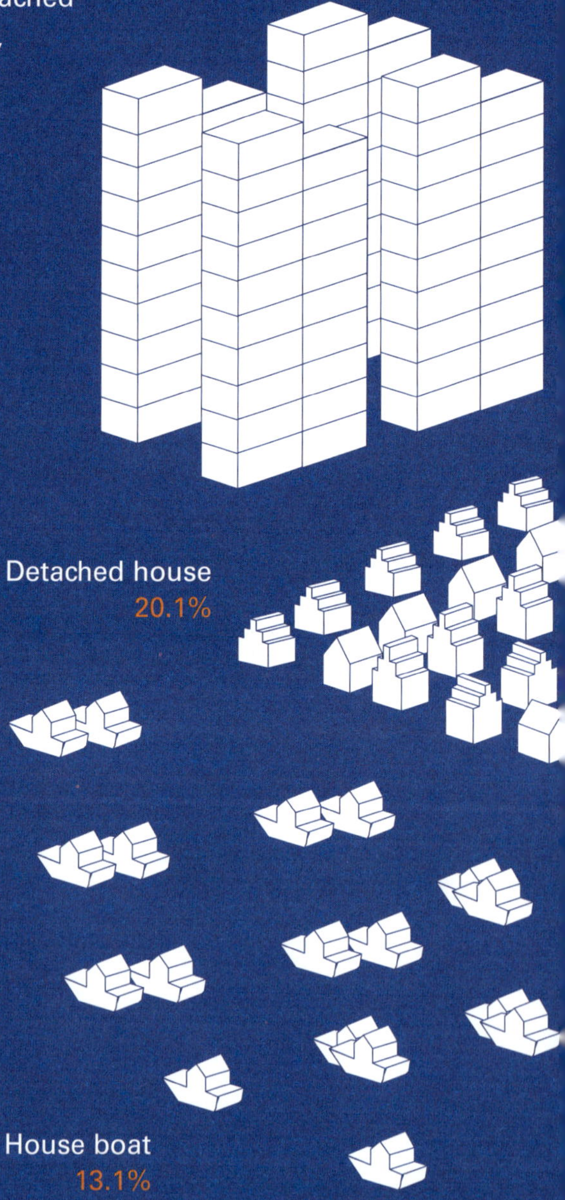

Building Block
21.3%

Detached house
20.1%

House boat
13.1%

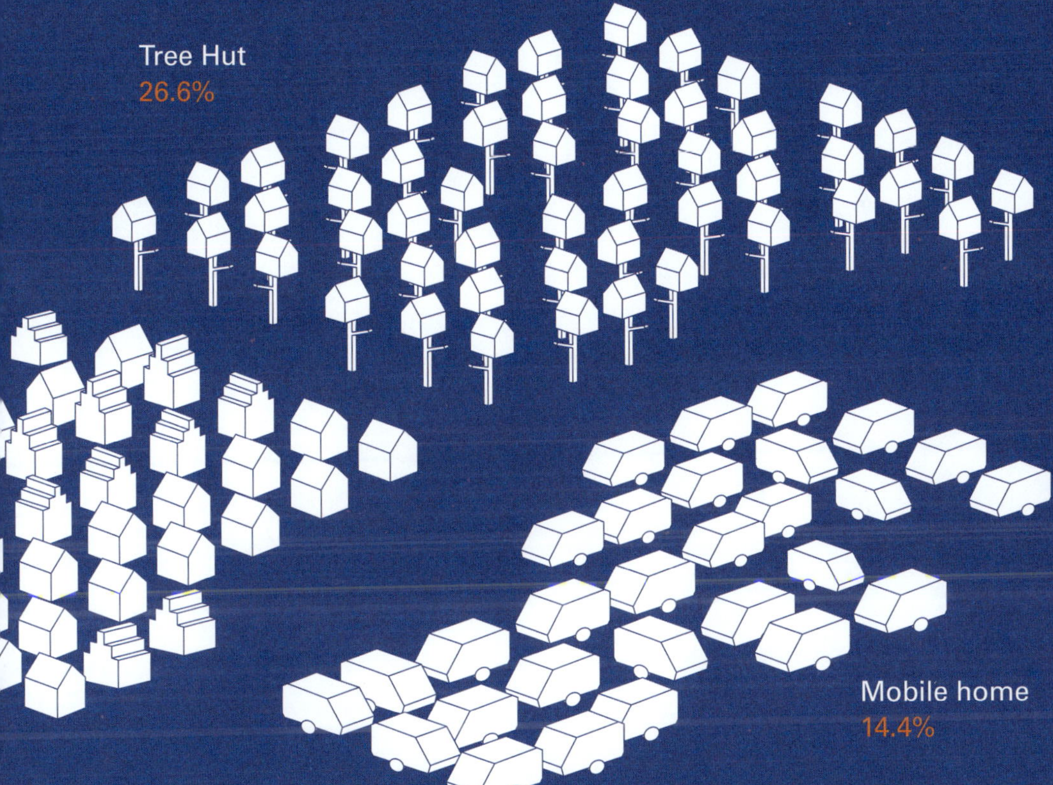

No house
4.3%

Treehousewaterboatappart-menthammocktower

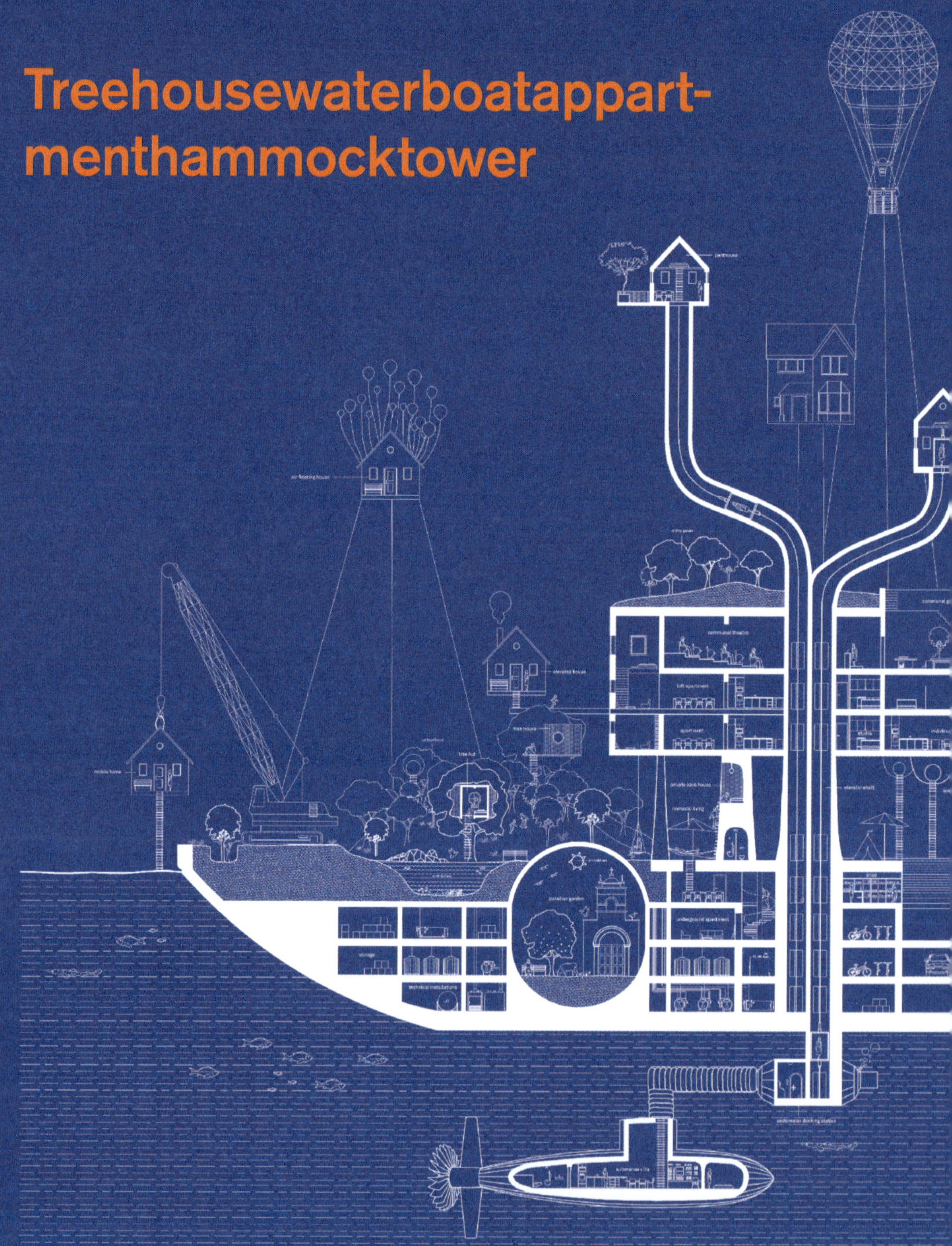

In response, Amsterdam-based architecture office TD (Theo Deutinger and Stefanos Filippas) conceived of the 'Treehousewaterboatappartmenthammocktower', which freely interprets this diversity of desires in a single heterogeneous dwelling.

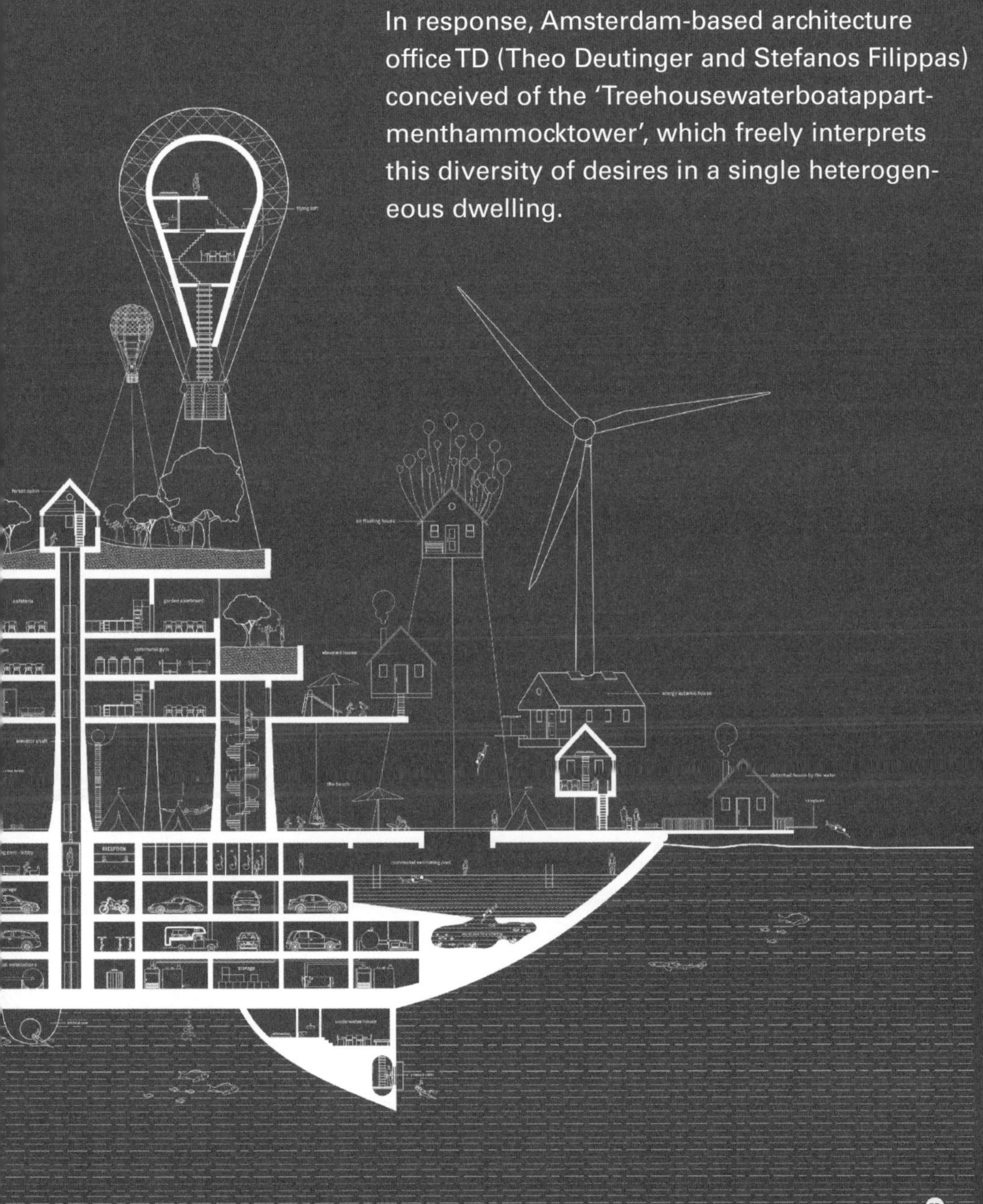

大

Woven textile banner designed by Thonik, suspended at exhibition entrance

A NEW MASS CRAFT

Benjamin Ward

The tools of mass production that in the past signaled alienated labor are folding in on themselves and enabling a global-scale cottage industry.

'Maker Maker' highlights and explores this trend in the contemporary economic—and by extension, cultural—sphere. It brings together designers, artists, and scientists investigating the implicit promise of digital tools to democratise the prototyping, production, and management of object-making.

Objects and objecthood have been fundamentally transformed by technological access. Since the 1950s there has been a global shift in manufacturing paradigms from mass production to mass customisation to mass individualisation to now: a new mass craft where traditional methods are meeting the scalar capabilities of digital fabrication techniques. The resulting objects are unbundling the responsibilities of cities and buildings, in turn moving survival and inspiration into the palm of humanity.

With ever growing accessibility to design software, digital fabrication tools, and proto-marketing tools on the Internet, everyone now has the ability to produce, manage, and deliver almost anything. However, users are demanding more than just another digitally produced thing. They want to connect with the individual maker and with a growing, global material culture.

Those behind this burgeoning new object-based economy position their work between wants and needs. One side is producing objects of desire, while the other side is making objects of utility. Simultaneously these new makers are creating industry, jobs, and new opportunities. These are new city builders who are nimbly addressing the wants and needs of a new millennium armed with an increased democratisation of design, production, and communication.

The 'Maker Maker' exhibition at UABB 2015 aims to bring together the best experiments in making that combine digital and hand-crafting techniques. The participating makers have been selected based on their abilities to put the object first, and build potential economies around it. Some of them depend primarily on human labour, while others are utilising 3D printers, or combining aspects of digital and manual techniques. The important thing they all share is the drive and ability to innovate — and create residual opportunity for future innovation. During the exhibition, some of the makers conducted demonstrations of their techniques and led hands-on workshops.

MAKER MAKER FLOORPLAN

1
Bringing Fungus to China
Philip Ross (U.S.)

2
Shwisty
Ifeanyi Oganwu (U.K.)

3
e-white
Marina Fomenko (Russia)

4
Machinist Sculptor
Chris Bathgate (U.S.)

5
Surface II Surface
Eskayel (U.S.)

6
Resistor V1
Nick Puckett (U.S.)

7
MOBI
Sung Jang laboratory (U.S.)

8
Parlay
Curtis Anthony Parlaitin (U.S.)

9
Hot Networks
Brandon Kruysman and Jonathan Proto (U.S.)

10
Here, There, Everywhere
Thing Thing (U.S.)

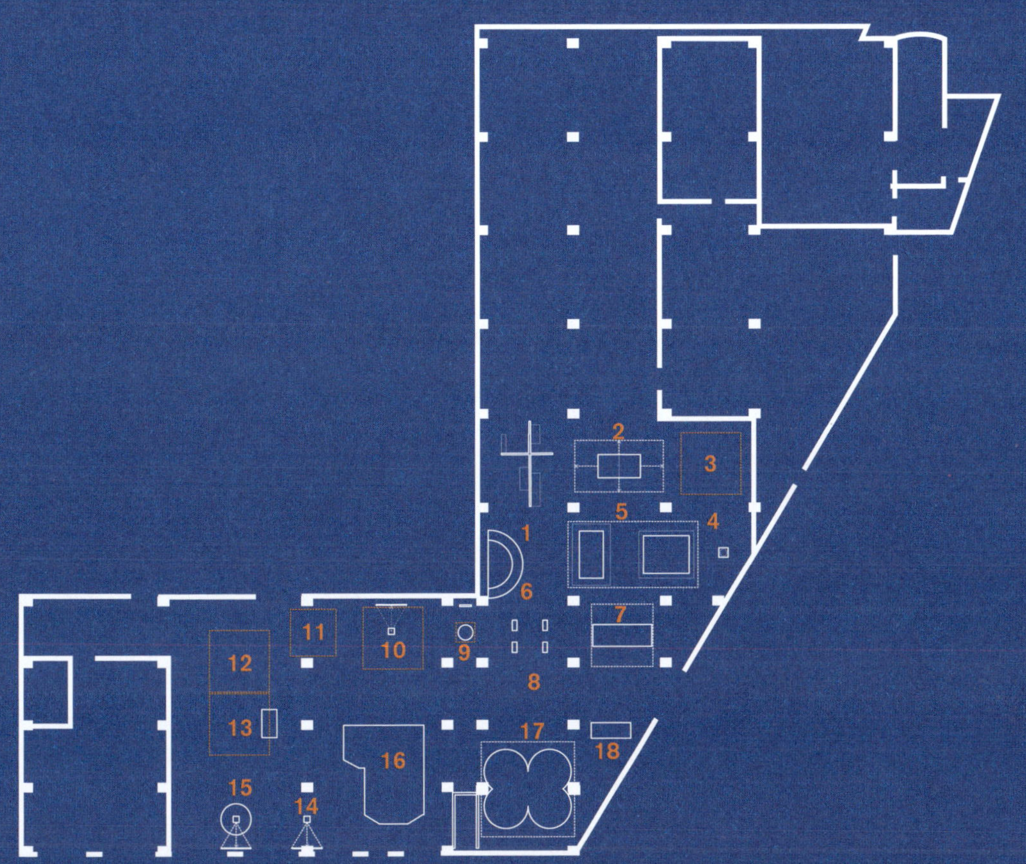

11
FABO (Fablab O)
Jeff Ding and Shenzhen Fab Lab International (China)

12
Smile of Iron
Yoshihito Mizuuchi (Japan)

13
Revolving Light
Chaihuo Maker Space (China)

14
Urban Assemblages: Imminence and Immanence
Olalekan Jeyifous, Vigilism (U.S.)

15
Archipelago
Ben Chang, Young Suk Lee, Silvia Ruzanka (U.S., Peru)

16
Apartment E
Sutton Beres Culler (U.S.)

17
Prototypes for Dissolvable Villages
The Bittertang Farm (U.S.)

18
Brick Maker
Stephen Burks Man Made (U.S.)

MAKER MAKER EXHIBITS

SHWISTY

Ifeanyi Oganwu

Shwisty is an interactive surface that is deployable in both public and private areas. It is designed for work, play, and relaxation, depending on the density of use at any given time.

The work is formed and composed of folded steel plates, which create dichromatic supports and playing surfaces. The construction incorporates manufacturing technologies and processes available in Shenzhen with a long-term view of deploying the work within other urban contexts and using
local fabrication expertise.

For the 'Maker Maker' exhibition at UABB 2015, Shwisty creates an active surface that invites play activities together with the viewing of works of art and design in the gallery.

Dimensions: (H) 76 x (W) 152.5x(D) 274 cm
Material: Mild Steel

E-WHITE

Marina Fomenko

The site-specific installation 'e-white' is created on site from local materials, specifically from electronic waste or e-waste. Artist Marina Fomenko has developed an on-going body of work on the theme of transforming garbage into art objects. Shenzhen is one of the largest industrial centres of China, in which a huge amount of electronic devices are made and used.

For the installation 'e-white', the artist gathered e-waste materials from Shenzhen rubbish dumps and painted them white. In remaking the city's e-waste, the artist creates her own city of miniature houses, monuments, theatres, and warehouse. Thus, that which has become unnecessary for the city finds one more life. The main building materials include computer monitors, mobile phones, electronic boards, and wires.

MACHINIST SCULPTOR

Chris Bathgate

As a sculptor, self-taught machinist, and CNC machine builder, the tools of my craft have become the conceptual foundation for my visual ideas. My sculpture works are not conceived in a top-down fashion. Instead, I begin each work with only a loose concept or visual goal, and then allow elements of my craft, as well as the technical constraints of my process and equipment, to guide the work to its final form. This 'logistics first' approach allows the fabrication process to have a major influence on my creative output, rather than being a means to an end.

I often play on industrial design motifs and experiment with ideas around our relationship to engineered objects. The internal logic of each sculpture suggests intentional design, which in turn implies utility; however, the work is static and ambiguous. As an art object, it refuses to fully transform the medium, making each sculpture feel like an irre-

solvable paradox, full of implied yet undefined purpose.

Machine work is a discipline that requires constant innovation to realize one's creative goals. It is this innovation that fuels future creative insights. For me, it has become a self-sustaining exploration of a craft that, given its ubiquity in modern life, is enormously underrepresented as an art form.

SURFACE II SURFACE

Eskayel

Eskayel is a surface design studio that creates energetically positive, eco-friendly furnishings and accessories for residential and commercial environments. Our strong commitment to environmental consciousness was the key factor leading to our main manufacturing model, which utilizes digital print technologies for both fabric and wall coverings, allowing printing with water based inks on natural and sustainable substrates.

For 'Maker Maker', we exhibit three items that illustrate our various production methods including hand painting, digital printing, hand weaving, and the process through which the creation of these items combines a mixture of modern and ancient technologies.

Indigo Ikat Fabric. 304 X 158 cm. Hand woven, 100% natural indigo-dyed Ikat, 100% Cotton. Made In Sumba, Indonesia.

Traditional weavers on the island of Sumba, Indonesia have woven traditional-style Ikat cloths using non-traditional motifs. In order to make the translation from digital to analogue, we distilled a selection of our signature patterns down to their fundamental elements so they could be woven into the Warp Ikat cloths know as Hinggi—large, hand-dyed textiles historically used as the ceremonial clothing of male nobility. Made in collaboration with Threads of Life Gallery Bali, these heirloom-quality textiles are hand crafted to an exquisite standard.

Recycled Sari Silk Rug – Cocos Thicket. 244 x 305 cm. Hand woven, 100% recycled sari silk, 100 knot count. Made In India.

Our recycled sari silk rugs are hand knotted in India with 100% recycled fibres. The use of sari silk came from desire to up-cycle a product that would otherwise have been discarded, and the fact that the process of re-dying sari silk creates an almost tie dyed kaleidoscopic effect on the fibres.

Grasscloth – Cocos Midnight. 244 x 305 cm. Hand woven, digitally printed, paper-backed. Printed In The USA, woven In China.

Our sisal grasscloth wall coverings are hand-woven in an entirely eco-friendly process. Sustainable and renewable fibres are sun-dried and backed with chemical-free paper making the substrate breathable, VOC-free, and biodegradable. The pattern is printed digitally with water-based inks.

RESISTOR V1

Nick Puckett

Resistor is a series of interactive experiments that present new ways to highlight the dynamic, physical and digital forces that shape the built environment.

'Resistor V1' at UABB presents the shifting landscape of the exhibition as a field of vibrating antennae. A custom Lidar laser scanner is used to continually digitise the surrounding crowds, exhibits, and architecture to create a dynamic map of the space. With each scanning pass, these digital maps are translated into the movement of 250 robotic antennae, which vibrate in response to the current and historic activity in the space. Over time, each antenna builds up an inertia that multiplies or resists the current activity within the exhibition based on patterns of occupation. This process operates continuously during the exhibition, providing visitors with a visualisation of the current state of the exhibition space in relationship to its history.

Credits:
Nick Puckett, Principal Designer
Hector Centeno, Software Development
Izzie Colpitts-Campbell, Hardware/Interface Development

MOBI

Sung Jang Laboratory

The 'MOBI' project was initiated to explore the construct of positive human perception we typically call 'beauty' in abstract form. Two major patterns are identified herein: one, the notion of elegance, founded on the basis of efficiency; and two, the contrasting idea of extravagance, an element of expression and expense. These two components mix in dynamic ways to compose what we perceive as beautiful in form.

'MOBI' attempts to manifest this theory-in-progress into physical work. Its primary goal is to achieve a balanced combination of elegance and extravagance in a formable entity. A modular system is employed at its foundation to allow efficient expansion and flexibility. Developing a structurally stable, yet lightweight system was crucial. Some installations would be self-supporting while resting on the ground, while others could be suspended.

Each unit displays relatively minimal formal complexity on its own—here is the spare elegance of simplicity—but the complexity of the whole assemblage multiplies exponentially with the multiplication of the units, creating the effect of extravagance. The versatile capabilities of 'MOBI' suggest that it can find further practical applications for rapid construction at various scales, from objects to architecture.

For UABB, Sung Jang Laboratory presents 'MOBI' for the first time in the Pearl River Delta, with an interactive architectural build made with tens of thousands of units.

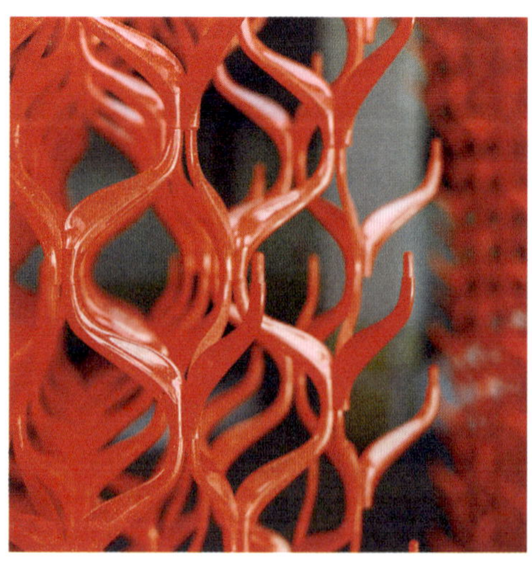

PARLAY

Curtis Anthony Parlaitin

Growing up in the late 1980s and early `90s, you couldn't help but be inspired by how important sneakers were becoming in popular culture. We are all influenced by something or someone and in those days—why not a pair of sneakers? Sneakers that could make you jump higher, or just a pair that made you cool, or ones that not many people could obtain. Each brand marketed their own niche through athletes, musical artists, and designers. Whatever your story is, there is a sneaker for you. Each sneaker represents something special about the individual who wears them, by the name and look they give.

In the past century, sneakers have been highly influential and prized commodities. Resale values of certain models range in the hundreds to thousands of dollars, causing certain sneakers to become almost impossible to obtain. My installation presents 1990s sneaker culture, this important moment in cultural history, preserving it in a form that may remind someone, somewhere of the moment it spoke to them years ago.

My work is made by laboriously weaving different wire gauges together to create the final form. Each sculpture utilizes armatures that seldom share the same characteristics from one to another. The arrays of colours represent diversity. The malleability of each strand can be a struggle and quite repetitive, but the end result works with that malleability. Techniques and processes are devised according to the specific properties of the manufactured material to be translated. Lastly, the wire medium provides agility and freedom to highlight particular details, as it responds to the imagination and hand that guides it.

HOT NETWORKS

Brandon Kruysman & Jonathan Proto

Hot Networks' is an ongoing experiment in repetitive unpredictability. It aims to capture the transient transformation of a material in motion, and uses the randomness and wildness inherent in materials as opportunities for design.

By applying the precision and accuracy of robots with the reaction of prolonged exposure to heat, the objects express themselves in multiple ways: highly iterative and regular on one hand, and completely wild and irregular on the other. While typical manufacturing scenarios are obsessed with the production of large quantities of near-exact objects, the duality of 'Hot Networks' produces a tension in each piece made, where no one object is ever the same and variation in material reactions is encouraged.

HERE, THERE, EVERYWHERE

Thing Thing

So you're looking for a new lamp. While the lamp aisle certainly offers many options, instead of going to the store, try this:

First, make a small fire. Then find a large piece of aluminium foil and fold it in half. Fill the foil with bits of plastic you find lying around your house. You may cut the plastic into bits, or throw the pieces in whole. Roll up the edges of the foil to make a pillow and use a bicycle pump to inflate it. Find a long metal stick and attach the mold. Now turn the pillow slowly over the fire like you are cooking a chicken. Careful! After about an hour, take the pillow out of the flames. Keep spinning while it cools. Unwrap the pillow and voila, a lampshade! Now, all you need to find is a light.

'Here, There, and Everywhere' takes the industrial process of rotational moulding and distils it into a raw performance of movement, metal, plastic, and fire. Every piece is made by hand in unique aluminium foil moulds. The materials are strange blends of plastic: old sand castle forms, buckets, milk crates, powder, straws, shopping bags—and the result is a new and exciting aesthetic. Made in Detroit, USA by experimental designers THING THING, 'Here, There, and Everywhere' proposes a new world of plastic objects made by hand.

FABO (FABLAB O)

Shenzhen Fab Lab International and Jeff Ding

This installation includes a series of workshops to introduce the public to the latest Maker works in Fablab O.

Single quantified dry-cleaning machine

This rapid, wall-mounted dry-cleaning machine is designed to work without water and detergent. It will achieve a quick wash through hot steam and ultrasonic waves and dries clothes with hot air. Simply hang in your coat inside, wait eight minutes, and then retrieve your clean, disinfected, and dry coat. The process is not harmful to your clothing.

Somatosensory axis helicopter

While conventional unmanned aerial vehicles (UAVs) or drones are controlled by remote control, the complexity of the remote control may be a barrier to new users. That is why we envision the use of somatosensory technology to control UAVs based purely on gestures. Our program is based on open-source hardwares rather than the expensive Kinect or other proprietary platforms. We plan to catch the gestures from users by using acceleration sensors, angular transducers, and geomagnetic sensors.

Cube upset machine

Enabling programmers to perfect apps, Android programs and open-source software, this device achieves a two-stage algorithm solution with a minimum number of steps. Using three to six servos, it offers an intuitive, cost-effective solution integrating the programming platform Scratch. Its independent and efficient 'automatic recognition engine Cube' completes effective automated speed reduction with Cube recognition engine.

Wearable warning device for sanitation workers in the road

Intended to protect the safety of sanitation workers, this 24GHz wearable radar device connects with a radar module inside the vehicle. The device embedded in the worker's uniform computes a wave signal through the Doppler effect. Upon receiving the signal via Bluetooth transmission, an alarm of LED lights and buzzer is activated to warn the sanitation workers to avoid the oncoming vehicle. Controlling at a distance of 100 meters, the early warning would come in advance of two seconds.

Light-painting shooting props

This combination of art and technology provides a connection between lighting design and sports.

SMILE OF IRON

Yoshihito Mizuuchi

Mizuuchi combines fragments from various sources and media to create his collage-like installations. His intention is to make works that subvert existing meanings and free viewers' perceptions, allowing multiple different perspectives and unpredicted interpretations. In ideal form, the work opens a continuum — a loop that has no end — between the viewer, artist, and physical installation.

'Smile of Iron' comprises a scale model of the 'Maker Maker' exhibition venue — a wedge-shaped, single-story structure of reinforced concrete, part of the former Dacheng Flour Factory complex — dotted with unexpected elements. The artist found all of the 'holes' in the building and labeled them in the mini-scale model. As visitors pass through some of these locations throughout the building, such as the toilets, light bulbs flash in the corresponding locations of the scale model. The provisional quality of the model reflects the provisional nature of the building's conversion for the Biennale and its probable demolition afterward. The most jarring element is the giant measuring tape, which creates a mash-up of different scales: while the building model is in miniature, the tape is gigantic, causing the viewer to reconsider the scale of the surrounding architecture and changing cityscape.

REVOLVING LIGHT

Chaihuo Maker Space

The Revolving Light is a fascinating device that allows you to change the colour of the light simply by rotating the external frame. Each light comes with a magnetic sucker so you can attach it to walls or tables through a magnetic base of light, and also remove them easily. Due to this simplicity, you only need to rearrange the base of the lights to achieve different styles of light setups in a room. For example, try to put the lights between two mirrors to get a dreamlike effect. The Revolving Light will be exhibiting in the new venue of Chaihuo Maker Space in Shenzhen.

URBAN ASSEMBLAGES: IMMINENCE AND IMMANENCE

Olalekan Jeyifous

This installation consists of a series of digital images of ad-hoc assemblages or urban 'super-structures'. These super-structures, whether towering or sprawling, combine attributes of improvised settlements with the scale of imposing high-end commercial developments in an attempt to amplify some of the inherently sustainable aspects of many 'impoverished' communities throughout the world. The images focus on the organic expansion of these self-organised spaces into privileged real estate, while considering how these ramshackle infrastructures might reconcile environmental and socio-economic issues.

Photos from a selection of rapidly developing megacities serve as the site for my images, which explore how these cities assimilate or exclude their marginalised communities and how such communities, often suffering from a lack of appropriate sanitation, electricity, medical services, and modern communications, can be re-imagined along the lines of greater sustainability. The premise for improvement is the inventive and adaptive extrapolation of their construction methodologies. In burgeoning megacities such as Lagos, Nigeria and others throughout Southeast Asia and South America, communities with economic problems find that the challenges they face are multiplied and magnified by rapid commercial development that disregards their needs.

The 'super structures' in featured in the exhibition seek to illuminate these issues and suggest an alternative to the repressive aspects of economic deprivation and political marginalization. As an accompaniment to the series of images, I am developing one of the imagined super-structures and its environs within the gaming software Unreal Engine 4, in order to create an interactive, free-range user experience.

ARCHIPELAGO

Ben Chang, Young Suk Lee, and Silvia Ruzanka

Our work explores themes of transformation, self-organisation, decay, and regeneration between the built and natural environment. We create interactive objects and situations that make people think about our everyday consumption of throwaway materials, bringing out hidden ways in which we impact our surroundings. The relationships between the human viewer and the landscape are captured within everyday objects: a table, a bowl, a table lamp, and a virtual city, all of which are mutilated, transformed, turned parasitic, and given animistic behaviours and personality traits.

The installation contains three elements: interactive kinetic sculpture, textiles created from plastic bag waste, and video projection of abstracted, continuously evolving urban structures. Together they form a physical and virtual landscape containing the human, animal, urban, natural, and digital worlds, connected through a cycle of commodity waste.

The projected virtual environment constructs imaginary cities from the viewer's image, creating a kind of city as prosthesis or shell, connected with the body. On the table in front, the textile landscape references ocean waste, fungus, natural systems of decay and regeneration interrupted through human intervention. The central interactive sculpture is a metaphorical creature, choked by plastic waste but simultaneously transformed, and given its own strength and agency to respond.

Our interest is in opening up conceptions among the systems of the urban environment, the natural environment, the animal body, and the human body, examining their relationships and the points where they become fluid and permeable.

2k8

APARTMENT E

Sutton Beres Culler

Bamboo scaffolding has been widely used in construction for centuries. Many famous landmarks, such as the Great Wall of China, were built using bamboo scaffolding. Construction workers in Hong Kong and Shenzhen today still use bamboo poles to build traditional scaffolding structures around twenty-first century buildings. With the installation 'Apartment E', we use these time-honoured building techniques and materials to create an immersive spatial experience that allows visitors to enter and walk around the structure.

PROTOTYPES FOR DISSOLVABLE ARCHITECTURES

The Bittertang Farm

The Bittertang Farm has undertaken various projects where the forces of nature become strong characters within the architecture. Built and compiled of biodegradable materials over the course of time, the structures sprout and support life transforming form, shape, and atmosphere according to weather and climate. Their existence is to decay so that other forms and organisms may live.

These structures are more substantial than a tent and are designed to take on lives of their own. Our prototypes range programmatically from performance structures to children's fortresses and to penthouse villages scattered over urban roofscapes.

'Prototypes for Dissolvable Architectures' embraces the ephemerality of an architecture built of membranes, like the semi-permeable cell walls of organisms. Far from aspiring to solidity or permanence, it enables light and air to pass through it, and signals its own fragility. It represents a counter-intuitive use of reclaimed polymer (plastic) material, not to create a smooth sheathing, but rather to create a scalar surface stretched to form a breathable enclosure.

BRICK MAKER

Stephen Burks Man Made

'Brick Maker' by Stephen Burks Man Made seeks to reconsider the unsustainable role of a single country being factory to the world.

Stephen Burks Man Made imported their own 'labour' to China to produce a series of 3D printed hand-woven bricks to be assembled into a free-standing 'hand factory' over the course of the UABB opening event. Each brick is not only a unique work of art, but also part of a larger micro-architectural statement of the collaborative power of the hand in combination with industry.

Woven textile banner designed by Thonik, suspended at exhibition entrance.

PAVILIONS FLOORPLAN

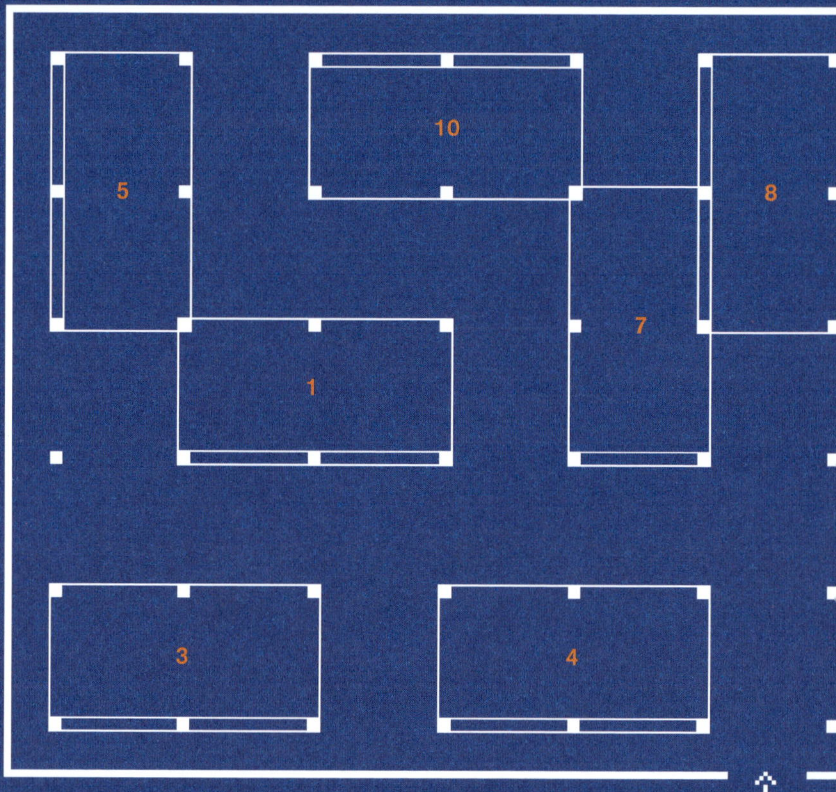

1
Macau Reframed: the City, its People and their Trace
Cultural Affairs Bureau of Macao S.A.R. Government, Architects Association of Macau, Macau Urban Planning Institute, and Center for Architecture and Urbanism (CURB)

2
WAY – seaWAY, railWAY, bikeWAY
Museum of Finnish Architecture, Architecture Information Center Finland, and Helsinki City Planning Department

3
Shan-Zhen: Reconnecting Shenzhen to Shannon
New Horizon_Architecture from Ireland

4
New Industries: Positive Practices of Urban Development
Union of Architects of Russia

5
Hypercity: the Future of Design and Architecture Education
Harbin Institute of Technology, Institute for Advanced Architecture of Catalonia, and Zurich University of the Arts

6
Now, There: Scenes from the Post-Geographic City
Art Center College of Design, Media Design Practices

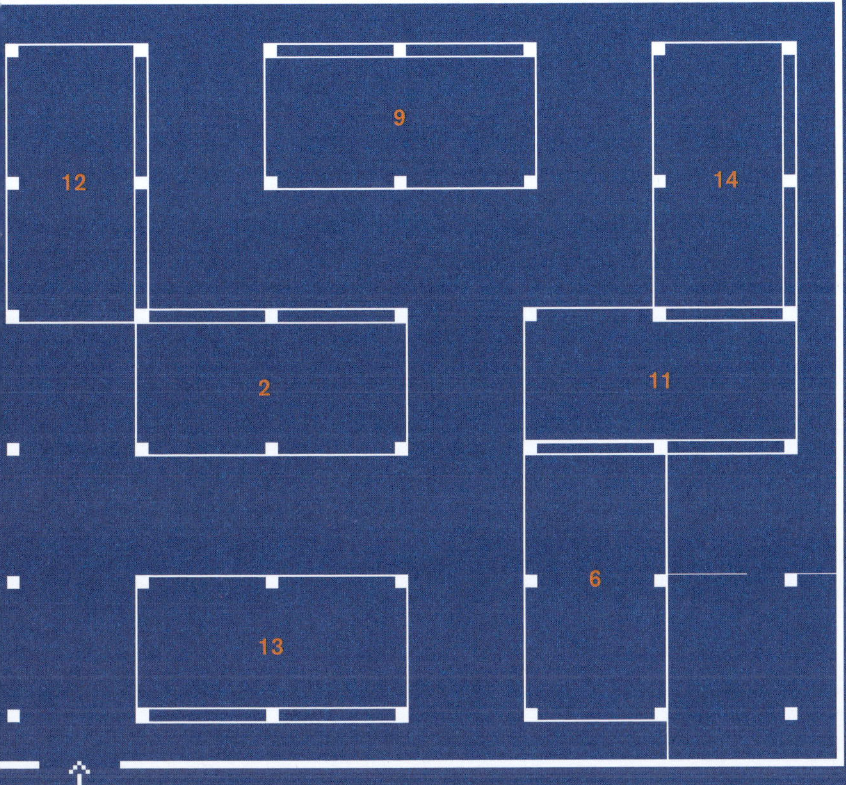

7
Unidentified Acts of Design
Victoria and Albert Museum (V&A)

8
Remake – We Make: Frameworks for Social and Cultural Exchange
Lucy Bullivant with WORKSHOP architecture, Paul McHale, Xin Guo, Yan Gao, and students

9
Household and City
Shenzhen Institute of Interior Design

10
Rethinking Urban Renewal
YIN Yujun, Projective Architecture Office

11
My City
reTUMU Urban Rural Institute

12
Catalonia Pavilion
Miralles Tagliabue and the Enric Miralles Foundation

13
Domestic Affairs
Bureau Europa and the Institute of Relevant Studies

14
Insights of Urbanism and Architecture in Shenzhen: Shenzhen Contemporary Architecture
Urban Planning, Land, and Resources Commission of Shenzhen Municipality; *Time + Architecture*, URBANUS Architecture & Design

PAVILIONS (NATIONAL, REGIONAL AND THEMATIC)

MACAU REFRAMED: THE CITY, ITS PEOPLE AND THEIR TRACE

Cultural Affairs Bureau of Macao S.A.R. Government, Architects Association of Macau, Macau Urban Planning Institute, and Center for Architecture and Urbanism (CURB)

Cities are made by all of us citizens with our small actions and big gestures. Governments, politicians, entrepreneurs, industrialists, real estate developers, bankers, engineers, and architects all take an evident role in shaping the city. But cities are more than a sum of streets, towers, and monuments. There is also the human scale, small buildings, housing units, shop-houses, kiosks, shop fronts, doors, canopies, old neighbourhoods, outdoor furniture, trees, hawkers, and small door shrines. The human side comprises the people, the inhabitants, the local traditions, common materials, vernacular constructions, the craftsmen, and the artefacts they produce to adapt the city to their needs and wishes.

'Macau Reframed: The City, its People and their Trace' embraces the theme of UABB 2015, Re-Living the City, as an opportunity to look to the city we have. It contemplates the needs and skills of its inhabitants, the spaces and small-scale artefacts that populate Macau's urban landscape, and goes a step further to speculate on innovative ways to improve our existing city from

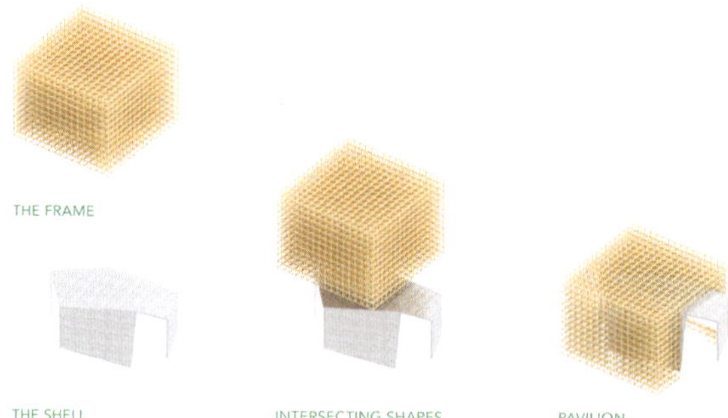

The pavilion design is made of the intersection of two spatial and material entities: the Frame and the Audiovisual Shell. The Frame, constructed in the manner of typical Macau vernacular buildings, is the overall structure supporting the pavilion and creating a permeable exterior boundary. The Shell defines the interior space into three zones, inviting visitors into an immersive, sculptural environment.

01

02

03

the bottom up. The exhibition, coordinated by the non-profit Center for Architecture and Urbanism (CURB), proposes a shift in focus. Instead of concentrating on the exuberance of urban growth, the glitz of new casinos, or large-scale developments, it reframes and re-examines the existing city that citizens keep building everyday.

Both architecture and urbanism are seamlessly integrated in the Macau Pavilion. The architectural aspect is addressed in the pavilion shape, testing an innovative and explorative form, with local construction materials, to create a dynamic spatial experience. The wooden frame, traditionally used in Macau as a hidden structure in vernacular interior constructions or temporary sidings, is uncovered and brought to view, celebrating its aesthetics and tectonics as a highly flexible structure to customise spaces without changing the buildings' structures.

The urban aspect of the exhibition is tackled in the pavilion contents, with videos showing urban space in relation to its inhabitants and the traces of their activities.

The Macau Pavilion thus shows the city under a new frame, as a place built by individuals in a permanently iterative process, addressing the theme of individual daily actions and the possibility of personal intervention in the construction of the city.

Credits:
Main Organizer: Cultural Affairs Bureau of Macao S.A.R. Government
Co-Organizers: Architects Association of Macau and the Macau Urban Planning Institute
Creative Team: Center for Architecture and Urbanism (CURB) with numerous participants including the University of Saint Joseph Faculty of Creative Industries, Macau Design Centre, Ponte 9 Creative Platform, and local creative companies including Urban Practice and Why Design Ltd.

01 Instead of focusing on glitzy casinos and large-scale developments, the Macau pavilion reframes and re-examines the existing city that citizens continue to build and inhabit everyday. Photo by CURB. 02 The human dimension of the city comprises the people, inhabitants, local traditions, common materials, vernacular constructions, craftsmen, and the artefacts they produce to adapt the city to their needs and wishes. Photo by CURB. 03 Smaller buildings, kiosks, shop fronts, doors, canopies, old neighbourhoods, outdoor furniture, trees, hawkers, and small door shrines contribute to the everyday life and reality of the city.

WAY – SEAWAY, RAILWAY, BIKEWAY

Museum of Finnish Architecture, Architecture Information Center Finland, and the Helsinki City Planning Department

The built environment of Helsinki, Finland illustrates a tale of modernism in its local specificity, revealing cultural values and traditions in the larger context of urbanisation, industrialisation, and globalisation. Helsinki was built around a harbor in the 16th century and has more than 120 kilometers of seashore. Since the late 19th century, the shoreline has been gradually altered as islands have been incorporated into the mainland and bays have been filled. As in other coastal cities, the waterfront districts of Helsinki are today undergoing major transformations yet again. The industrial uses that took over in the latter half of the 19th century, leading to the closing off of the waterfront areas, are making way for new public uses today.

The exhibition 'WAY - seaWAY, railWAY, bikeWAY' traces the course of development during the past 200 years along the urban axis leading from Helsinki's West Harbour to the former Töölönlahti rail yard area in the city centre. This axis concretises itself in Baana, a former harbor rail corridor converted into a cross-city pedestrian and biking route. Baana also acts as the focal point of the exhibition concept illustrating three different WAYs, each representing a different historical era with its characteristic way of life, ideologies and organisation of urban space: seaWAY, railWAY and bikeWAY.

Looking at architecture and urban planning as instruments for shaping public space and thereby also for organising life, the exploration of this axis connecting the shore and the city centre sketches the story of the historical transformation of a northern coastal city from the early industrial period through the

01

02

01 Map illustrating the route of the former freight railway tracks, today a bikeway, connecting the former rail yard to the West Harbour. The harbour, formerly dedicated to freight, now serves passenger traffic as a residential district grows around it. Several cultural buildings have opened on the site of the former rail yard. Map design by Tuomo Tammenpää based on orthophotographs from the Helsinki Region Infoshare website. 02 View of the former Töölönlahti rail yard in Helsinki city centre with the Parliament House in the background, 1964. © Helsinki City Museum & O. Karasjoki

03

contemporary moment and into visions for the future. The transformation of the city is both deeply embedded in the local context and also essentially part of a broader global world. The subject is discussed with the help of a visual timeline of a multi-layered installation, depicting both the physical and cultural changes in Helsinki over time. In addition to presenting the three Helsinki WAYs, the exhibition also prompts visitors to bring insight into and give examples of other WAYs out there.

Credits:
Curator: Juulia Kauste, Director of the Museum of Finnish Architecture
Curatorial Advisors: Professor Panu Lehtovuori, Tampere University of Technology; and Architect Jari Huhtaniemi, Helsinki City Planning Department
Exhibition design: Tuomo Tammenpää, Luup Culture
Exhibition realisation: Juho Haavisto, Museum of Finnish Architecture
Production: Museum of Finnish Architecture with the Architecture Information Center Finland and the Helsinki City Planning Department

04

03 The former Helsinki harbour rail freight corridor converted to a pedestrian and biking thoroughfare, 2012. © Veikko Somerpuro & City of Helsinki Building Control Department.

04 The launch of the icebreaker Voima at the still-functioning Hietalahti ship yard adjacent to the Helsinki city centre, 1953. © The Collections of The Maritime Museum of Finland

SHAN-ZHEN: RECONNECTING SHENZHEN TO SHANNON

New Horizon – Architecture from Ireland

Shannon, a rural area in the west of Ireland, became the world's first free trade zone in 1959, designed specifically to engage the USA and the international economy. Located near an international airport, Shannon continued to grow throughout the 1970s, until it was granted town status in 1980 with a population of 7,500.

In 1981 a group of Chinese dignitaries led by Jiang Zemin visited Shannon. They were eager to replicate the principles behind the special economic zone of Shannon in mainland China and a connection to Shenzhen was formed. Following this visit, under the direction of Deng Xiaoping, the Shannon model was used in the formation of Shenzhen, which was, at the time, a collection of towns comparable in scale and size. From the early '80s onwards, a significant number of Chinese leaders have visited Shannon in order to study the model. These include President Jiang Zemin; Premier Zhu Rongji; Premier Wen Jiabao; Vice Premier Huang Ju; Vice Premier Zeng Peiyan and most recently President Xi Jingping.

While Shannon has ultimately grown to just over 9,500 people, in stark contrast, Shenzhen has an estimated population of over 10 million. This model of planning and growth, so successful in Shenzhen, has since been rolled out to over 9,000 other Chinese cities. For the Irish National Pavilion at UABB 2015, two design practices, AP+E and Urban Agency, have collaborated to further develop the historical connection between these two distinct cities and celebrate it by engaging with their local communities in a project they call 'Shan-Zhen'.

'Shan-Zhen' is part of an initiative entitled *New Horizon_architecture from Ireland*; a constituent of Irish Design 2015 (ID2015), a year-long initiative backed by the Irish government exploring, promoting, and celebrating Irish design throughout Ireland and internationally in order to drive job creation, grow exports, and increase competitiveness. Michael D. Higgins, President of Ireland, is Patron of ID2015.

New Horizon_architecture from Ireland presents the work of 10 emerging practices to an international audience,

01 'Shan-Zhen' explores the historical connection between Shenzhen and Shannon, a free trade zone established in Ireland in 1959. Both have been economically successful, but Shenzhen now has approximately 1,000 times more people than its Irish predecessor.

01

selected by curators Raymund Ryan and Nathalie Weadick. These practices were deployed to three high-profile architectural platforms around the world. The London Festival of Architecture (June 2015) produced work by Clancy Moore Architects, Hall McKnight Architects, Steve Larkin Architects, Emmett Scanlon Architects, and TAKA Architects. The Chicago Architecture Biennial (October 2015) included an installation by A2 Architects, GKMP Architects, and Ryan Kennihan Architects. Finally, at UABB in Shenzhen, *New Horizon* presents a site-responsive project designed by AP+E and Urban Agency, two firms doing exemplary work in Ireland and beyond.

Credits:
Curators: Raymund Ryan and Nathalie Weadick
Project design: Urban Agency and AP+E (Architecture Practice + Experimentation)
With support from Irish Design 2015 (ID2015)

NEW INDUSTRIES: POSITIVE PRACTICES OF URBAN DEVELOPMENT

Union of Architects of Russia

Russia has a high proportion of vacant buildings and spaces, which call for reinvention and reintegration. Not only abandoned industrial plants, but also empty churches, historic mansions, and hotels dot the modern Russian landscape, reflecting a changed economic structure. The situation is familiar to many countries in the world, but particularly acute in Russia, which endured multiple social cataclysms in the 20th century.

Post-industrial spaces are commonly seen as havens for creative industries that cannot afford to rent space at commercial rates. However, not all vacant buildings can or should become art studios and museums. The sheer quantity of empty spaces, the variety of typologies and scales, and the unequal artistic merit of the architecture, imply a need for a variety of approaches and tools to return disused objects and spaces into the economic cycle.

Besides serving as art spaces, old buildings can also serve traditional functions such as industrial production, housing, and education. The main obstacle to receiving support from the federal, regional and municipal authorities is the lack of a methodology for comparing and choosing from among the possible scenarios.

In light of these challenges, the Union of Architects of Russia exhibits a selection of projects for the adaptive reuse of former industrial zones and

01

other under-utilised spaces. Embracing a variety of approaches, the exhibition 'New Industries: Positive Practices of Urban Development' highlights projects at different stages of implementation. It shows the potential for rethinking and remaking urban areas.

Russian cities are learning to use their main resources – space and human capacity – and to learn from international experience. The exhibit is thus conceived as a place of reflection and discussion on the past and future of Russian cities.

Credits:
Curators: Jemal Surmanidze, Andrey Asadov, and Nikita Asadov
Collage graphics: Egor Orlov

01 This collage evokes an architectural recombination of elements to generate a new field of meaning and a terrain of everyday life. The infinite diversity and latent potentials of the city are playfully interconnected within a continuity of space. In the tradition of collage and Soviet "paper architecture," seemingly banal and familiar elements become instruments of revitalization. **Illustration by Egor Orlov**

HYPERCITY: THE FUTURE OF DESIGN AND ARCHITECTURE EDUCATION

Harbin Institute of Technology, Institute for Advanced Architecture of Catalonia, and Zurich University of the Arts

How can cities enhance their local identities while being part of a networked HyperCity model? Part of the answer involves design and architecture education.

Organised by three design universities in three different nations, this exhibition investigates the affordances, risks, and opportunities wrapped up in the education of the next generation of designers and architects, who will build and live in globally connected cities, or HyperCities. The presentation revolves around the project of establishing an 'International Graduate School of Design' in Shenzhen. It displays concepts and themes related to inventive educational practice.

The exhibition deals with some urgent questions: what local and the global needs will drive the education of the next generation of architects and designers? How can society, culture, and industry participate in the definition of a new design school? How can rigid, top-down educational models yield to more bottom-up models, oriented toward entrepreneurial discovery and the creative empowerment of the citizenry? How can productive infrastructure, participatory processes, and generative data form a strategic vision for new urban development models?

01

The HyperCity project encompasses an ongoing exhibition and a panel discussion including:

Fragments

An interactive multimedia installation in which visitors can experience simultaneous live feeds of imagery from diverse urban spaces of Shenzhen, Zurich, and Barcelona.

City & Technology

An exhibition addressing the question of the implementation of Information and Communication Technologies (ICT) in different layers of the urban environment.

Future Design Education Forum

A gathering of experts and local stakeholders to discuss the character of a forward-looking education in architecture and design, related to HyperCities. Participants included the three partner university institutions, the Shenzhen Municipality and the Ministry of Education, and scientists, artists, entrepreneurs, and representatives of local youth associations, industry, and citizens.

International Call for Projects

An invitation to participants from different disciplines around the world to submit ideas, visions, and actions towards 21st-century design education models.

01 'Fragments' is an interactive, multimedia installation in which visitors can experience simultaneous live feeds of imagery from various urban spaces of Shenzhen, Zurich, and Barcelona.

Visitors can change their position in space to explore new city perspectives, connections, and juxtapositions.

NOW, THERE: SCENES FROM THE POST-GEOGRAPHIC CITY

Tim Durfee and Mimi Zeiger, Art Center College of Design

'Now, There: Scenes from the Post-Geographic City' unpacks the practices, rituals, and epistemologies that traditionally delimit the understanding of the city in terms of geographic, material, and economic parameters. Now, more than ever, urban and digital realms are inextricably linked. This exhibition presents a selection of screen-based works, objects, and texts that develop, explore, and visualise a city that is not tied to any physical locality.

'Now, There', however, understands this resulting networked city as a *place* in its own right, albeit one shaped by experiences contingent on media and devices, flows of data, and the demands of global technology. As such, it too is open to a retroactive assessment of what is now and where is there.

In looking at what we call 'Scenes from the Post-Geographic City', our perspective is neither dystopian nor boosterish. We are not interested in sci-fi moralising or video game nihilism. Rather, we take an optimistic view of this emergent urban condition and material culture, understanding that the effects of so much intimidating change can nevertheless be explored and appreciated — perhaps co-opted — with curiosity and humour in a way that designers and architects and filmmakers have been occasionally adept at in the past.

'Now, There' includes works by Besler & Sons, Walton Chu, Tim Durfee and Ben Hooker (with Jenny Rodenhouse), John Szot, m-a-u-s-e-r, and Metahaven, as well as texts by Joanne McNeil, Enrique Ramirez, and Therese Tierney.

Credits:
Curators: Tim Durfee and Mimi Zeiger, Art Center College of Design, Media Design Practices MFA Program

01 m-a-u-s-e-r posits that the Internet is a total environment in which Nature is an aesthetic obsession. *Natural Wi-Fi*, m-a-u-s-e-r, Stuttgart, Istanbul, (Los Angeles), Mixed Media, 2015

02 The boundary between pixelated flatness and approximated form marks the extent of Google's latest efforts to model the world. *Los Angeles Resolution Frontiers*, Besler & Sons, Los Angeles, Video, 2014

01

02

UNIDENTIFIED ACTS OF DESIGN

Victoria and Albert Museum (V&A)

'Unidentified Acts of Design' is an exhibition and research project that seeks out instances where design intelligence has occurred in Shenzhen and the PRD outside of the conventional notion of the design studio. The project aims to show how in a region of unprecedented growth, which has long served as the factory of the world, design acts can take on unconventional forms and occur in unpredictable places. By seeking out new definitions of what constitutes design, new actors and new objects are able to enter into the canon of the region's design history, while an expanded sense of design's relationship with the region can take shape. The display at UABB 2015 also acts as a 'test ground' for some themes and content of the V&A Gallery in Shekou, due to open in early 2017.

Tracing the history of design in Shenzhen and the PRD is a tricky task. It is often lamented that while Shenzhen and the PRD have long served as the factory of the world, very little innovation in product, industrial, and fashion design actually takes place here. Instead, design is imported from abroad direct to the factory, without design knowledge spilling out onto the streets and fostering a domestic design environment. But is this necessarily true? Surely, in a city that has grown from clusters of villages to a megalopolis in just 35 years, a mixture of social and economic forces have converged to create fertile ground for innovation and development. Indeed, in dealing with the question of Shenzhen's design history, perhaps we are too narrowly restricting our interpretation to familiar models of the design studio.

With 'Unidentified Acts of Design', the V&A looks to the broader environment of Shenzhen to seek out historical and contemporary instances that could offer alternative readings of what design is and how it is produced: from the construction methods used in the 1980s-90s that allowed for the city's unprecedented growth, to platforms that manufacture and distribute DIY technology, to the making of Shanzhai products, to the development of one of the world's largest social media platforms, WeChat. 'Unidentified Acts of Design' presents objects related to these design stories in an attempt to contribute to a renewed reading of Shenzhen and the PRD's rich and evolving design history.

Credits:

Curators: Brendan Cormier and Luisa E. Mengoni

01

02

01 **Wang Jianjun (Jasen)** is the founder of Makeblock, a start-up company providing amateur and professional DIY makers with kits for making robots of all kinds. Jasen, who considers himself primarily an engineer, was able to set up a successful company with a distinct style following his passion for DIY and through a clever use of the available manufacturing industries in the PRD region. 02 **Eric Pan**, a visionary engineer and successful entrepreneur, established Seeed, a company that provides micro-controllers for digital artists and makers as well as an open platform that allows individuals and start-ups to submit new products for prototyping and small-scale manufacture.

深圳捷炜开关电源
JIEWEI SWITCHING POWER SUPPLY
新克尔光电
华强LED交易中
祥宇通电
4F 电脑/通讯/DIY装机
华强北就上华e美食城 5F
开户有礼
平安建设为大家，建设平安
华硕ASUS MeMO Pad 8
人无信不立 业无信不兴
华硕 ASUS ZENBOOK U305 轻薄·锋芒尽显
8225 9999
Canon
SONY
DELL

03

03 **Huaqiangbei** is Shenzhen's most famous marketplace for electronics and hardware components. Widely known for Shanzhai products and fakes of all kinds, it is in fact the most visible and public expression of the open-source ecosystem characterising Shenzhen's manufacturing industries. More than just a marketplace, it spurs innovation and exchange of ideas.

REMAKE – WE MAKE: FRAMEWORKS FOR SOCIAL AND CULTURAL EXCHANGE

Lucy Bullivant with WORKSHOP architecture, Paul McHale, Xin Guo, Yan Gao, and students

Architecture as a participative process, rather than an 'a priori' abstracting regeneration framework, is the focus of 'Remake – We Make', evoking and enacting in real time principles of socially distributed urbanism. Community-engaged placemaking, embracing the handmade, the small scale and the improvisational have more positive impact on the social and political life of the city. These activities are re-evaluating architecture's social contract and organisational models, fostering fresh collaborative processes and deployments of local materials, crafts and skills. The site becomes a heart of educational interaction, overcoming the typical disconnection between the public and the processes by which spaces are made, and opening new possibilities for the building of social, ecological and health capital.

Curator Lucy Bullivant – founder and editor-in-chief of the webzine Urbanista.org, and a professor of urban design history and theory – conceived the exhibition at UABB 2015 as a space for both making and learning. WORKSHOP architecture (WSa) led a participative design-build process to make a multi-use structure using local recycled materials from urban villages and reuse facilities in Shenzhen and further afield in the Pearl River Delta, in collaboration with Assistant Professor Xin Guo, Department of Architecture, University of Shenzhen and Assistant Professor Yan Gao, Department of Architecture, University of Hong Kong.

'Remake – We Make' is a screening room for videos by film director Paul McHale about the work of various innovative practitioners working with local people, including: WSa, Assemble, Architecture 00, Studio Weave, and Carl Turner Architects. The space also serves as a design-build workshop for small craft items and a discussion and service space. The project is supported by the Norwegian Ministry of Foreign Affairs, the Norwegian Centre for Design and Architecture (DOGA) and private donors.

Credits:
Curator: Lucy Bullivant, PhD, Urbanista.org
Participatory design-build process:
WORKSHOP architecture (Clementine Blakemore, Alexander Furunes, Ivar Tutturen) in collaboration with Xin Guo, Assistant Professor, Dept. of Architecture, University of Shenzhen; and Yan Gao, Assistant Professor, Dept. of Architecture, University of Hong Kong
Video: Paul McHale
Support: the Norwegian Ministry of Foreign Affairs, the Norwegian Centre for Design and Architecture (DOGA) and private donors.

01

02

01 A farmer weaving a jute rope panel as part of Project Hariharpur, following on from the design ideas explored in the Building Community workshop and exhibition staged by WORKSHOP architecture, Delhi, India, 2013. ©WORKSHOP architecture.

02 Volunteers helping to raise the roof of the music pavilion made with WORKSHOP architecture at St John's School, Lacey Green, Buckinghamshire, UK, 2015. ©WORKSHOP architecture.

HOUSEHOLD AND CITY

Shenzhen Institute of Interior Design, Su Dan

For the many families who migrate from the countryside to Shenzhen and other growing cities, the ultimate goal is to settle into a comfortable new home. This movement also defines the task of interior designers. After the migrants have worked hard to cross all the thresholds to the city, they face the last gate to a warm nest: furniture.

Furniture defines a house as a home. In other words, the meaning of 'home' is embodied in the physical form and use of furnishings. The household is a micro-society in a big city, and the home is a carrier of tradition amidst modern surroundings. Apart from architectural narratives of plan and structure, furniture and interior design exercise an important role in shaping everyday life s. Interior design is oriented toward human and cultural values, reflecting the idea of comfort and care. The quality of a given furniture design or designer can be evaluated through function, structure, and form.

The exhibition 'Household and City' shows furniture from fifteen interior designers, who express cultural identity and their understanding of the home.

Credits:
Curator: Su Dan

01

01 Wu Gaozhong, *Home*, installation view
02 Wu Gaozhong, *Human Ladder*

02

RETHINKING URBAN RENEWAL

YIN Yujun, Projective Architecture Office

Urban space is the site of capital circulation and development pressures, sometimes to the detriment of daily life, as David Harvey has argued. This process is exemplified in recent Chinese urban renewal, which has been driven principally by the quest for economic benefit. Therefore, the position of the architect is divided between instrumental and critical practices. In serving official or capitalist development agendas, the architect's role is instrumental to power. However, by using alternative criteria to study and intervene in the city, the architect may take a critical stance.

'Rethinking Urban Renewal' at UABB 2015 exhibits a selection of projects by Chinese architects and urban designers that speak to the theme of the Biennale, Re-Living the City. Rather than simply following conventional solutions for urban development, the selected projects reflect various ideas to remake city life in innovative ways.

These practices embrace the extreme speed of the urbanisation process in China, but also provide a critical position relative to it. They question the instrumentality of architecture in defining urban form and daily life, and seek to uncover unique qualities within each urban context. The exhibition thus suggests an architecture that serves people and daily life. In addition, it offers a horizontal comparison and cross-section of possibilities throughout the country, to reveal the issues involved in Chinese urban redevelopment — and the potential for alternative solutions.

Credits:
Curator: YIN Yujun
Featuring architectural/urban design works by: Projective Architecture Office / YIN Yujun (Shenzhen), Meta Project (Beijing), Jiwu Architecture Studio (Hangzhou), Fei Architecuture (Shanghai), FCHA (Shenzhen), LanD Studio (Nanjing), and Xuhaohao Architecture Office (Guangzhou).

01 Schematic view of a commercial development designed by Projective Architecture Office, adjacent to an ecological park connected to Shenzhen Bay, now under construction.

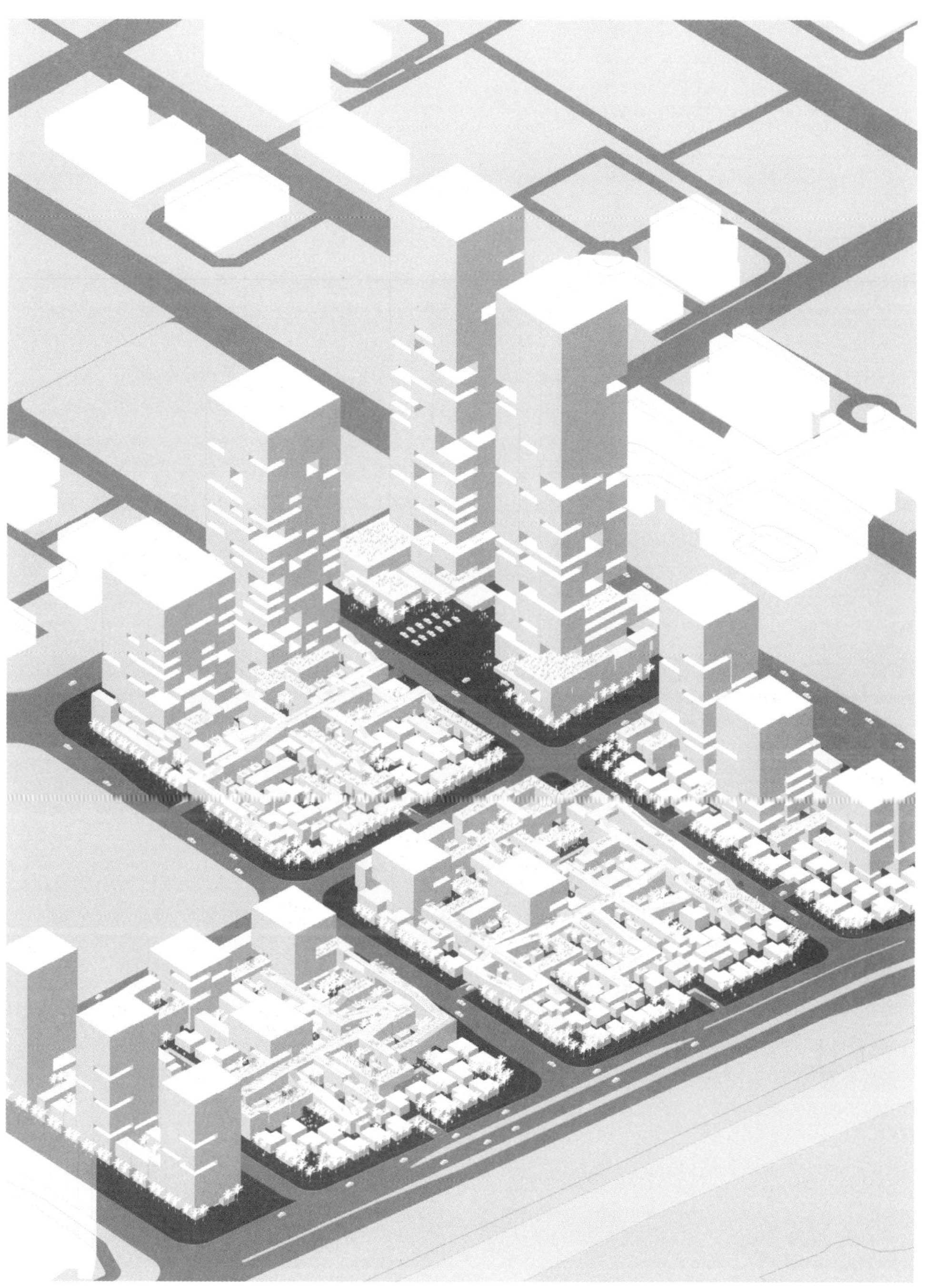

01

MY CITY

reTUMU Urban Rural Institute

During the past 35 years of urbanisation in Shenzhen, informal urban space has become more and more scarce. Massive, regularly ordered city plans by development firms have dominated the process of urban growth and change. Although informal or open-ended spaces are the starting point of urbanisation of Shenzhen, they are disappearing quickly and have not been adequately studied.

The crowdsourcing research project 'My City', launched by reTUMU with various architects, urban planners, urban scholars, artists, and software engineers, explores informal spaces in Shenzhen using digital media and emerging computational and interactive techniques. The sites in question include urban villages, spontaneous or temporary buildings, and marginal communities ignored by mainstream urban studies, which are an important part of the amazing social and economic transformation of Shenzhen since 1980.

The research encompasses several iniatives including the urban archaeology project, 'Rashomon in Gangxia', which has collected pictures, videos, and literature files including more than 550,000 words. It has attracted ten additional research groups from Sheffield University (UK), Institute for Advanced Architecture of Catalonia (Spain), Shenzhen University (China), and the Urban Planning, Land and Resources Commission of Shenzhen Municipality to join the project. 'My City' is based on crowdsourcing and spontaneous participation, to represent the urban context of Futian Central Busniess District around urban villages in Gangxia by means of research on literature, drama, novels, documentary, and VR interaction devices. The project envisions bringing the new landscapes of Shenzhen back to the informal participation of urban dwellers through historical, social, and technological perspectives.

The exhibition at UABB 2015 consists of two main components. First, the literature exhibition presents projects such as New Utopia: The Babel Village, by Di FANG, and Supermicro City, by

01 Detail of Supermicro City, a project by Fan WEN, investigates the changing scale of public space and architecture, and its effect on social relationships and economic development. 02 Flying Over Shenzhen is a virtual reality interaction device, based on the urban archaeology project 'Rashomon in Gangxia', developed by reTUMU in collaboration with the Shenzhen Public Art Center, Emax Technology, and the Shenzhen Municipal Planning & Land Real Estate Information Center.

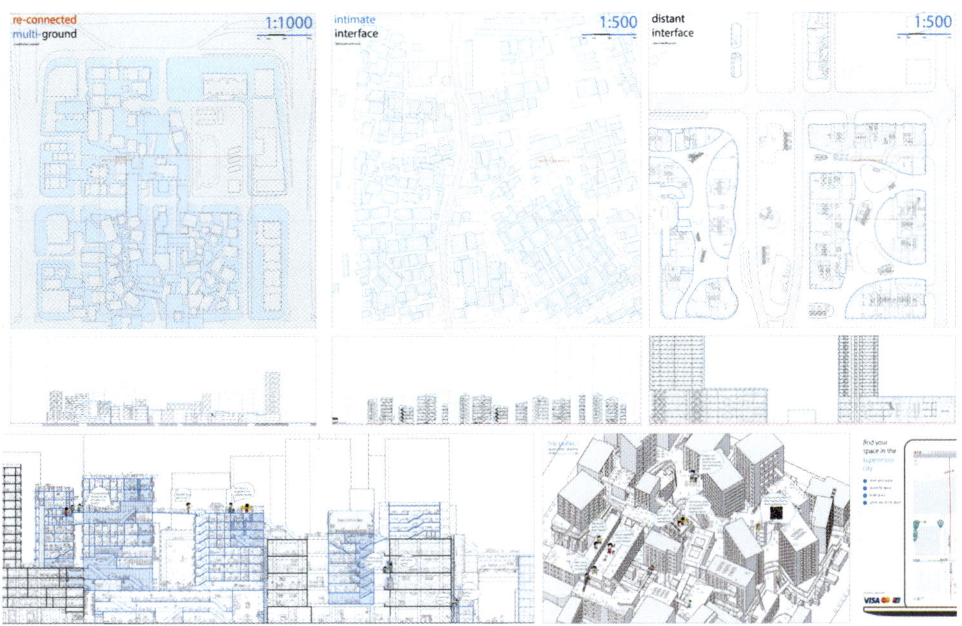

01

Fan WEN. Using cutting-edge presentation techniques, they explore openness, participation, and informal urbanism in Shenzhen. The second part of the exhibition is a virtual reality experience, 'Flying over Shenzhen', based on urban simulation data gathered in 'Rashomon in Gangxia'. Navigating this VR environment – through diachronic and synchronic virtual travelling – reveals the transitional and informal quality of the production of space, architecture, social networking, and life in the urban villages of Gangxia.

Credits:
Curator: reTUMU (Dr. REN Jue, Dr. Mary Ann O'Donnell, WANG Yan, NAI Fan, FU Na, HUANG Wei Wen)
Exhibition design: DUAN Peng and ZHANG Xue Shi
VR Interaction device: reTUMU with the Shenzhen Public Art Center, Emax Technology, and the Shenzhen Municipal Planning & Land Real Estate Information Center

富

02

CATALONIA PAVILION

Miralles Tagliabue EMBT and Enric Miralles Foundation

The Miralles Tagliabue design studio and the Miralles Foundation combine practice and research under one roof. The Foundation is an experimentation centre, a platform for investigation in collaboration with cultural centres and programs worldwide; and a research partner for the main design studio.

For UABB 2015, Miralles Tagliabue presents its competition-winning design for the Clichy-Montfermeil metro station, part of the ambitious *Grand Paris* (Greater Paris) initiative of transport infrastructure projects to connect and regenerate suburban neighbourhoods throughout an expanded metropolitan area. The design process was supported by masters student projects hosted by the Miralles Foundation, in collaboration with the Universitat Politécnica de Catalunya (UPC).

The station of Clichy-Montfermeil is located at the border of the two suburban small towns: Clichy-sous-bois and Montfermeil. It is an important node of connectivity between the metro network, the new tram line, and various bus lines. However, this rundown suburban area has been overshadowed by more robust development of other parts of the city. It earned notoriety as the scene of violent riots in 2005.

The new station will connect Paris to Clichy-sous-bois and Montfermeil, incorporating these satellite areas into the Greater Paris metro network and instigating their economic and social renewal. It will provide inhabitants with new and convenient access to places of employment and recreation throughout the Île-de-France region. Due to its relevance and location, this station serves as an emblem for the promise of Greater Paris. The design aims to give the place a new and vibrant identity. The architecture reflects the culture of the inhabitants through colour, joy, and optimism.

Credits:
Curator: Benedetta Tagliabue / Miralles Tagliabue EMBT
Exhibition design: Miralles Tagliabue EMBT
Coordinators: Elena Nedelcu, Nazaret Busto
Design team: Pablo Maal, Alexandra Antal, Cristina Marcu, Lorenzo Trucato, Wei Song
Sponsors: Enric Miralles Foundation and Institut Ramon Llul

01

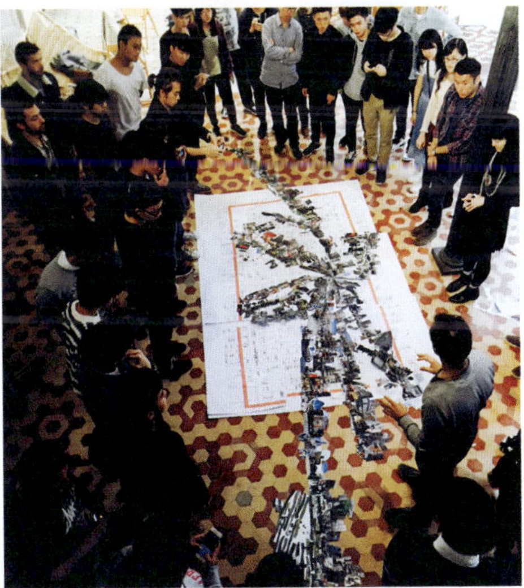

02

01, 02 The Miralles Foundation houses the archive of Enric Miralles and also hosts residency programs, workshops, courses, conferences, lectures, and international exchanges.

03, 04 Collage and drawings for the ClichyMontfermeil Metro Station Competition by Miralles Tagliabue EMBT.

03

04

INSIGHTS OF URBANISM AND ARCHITECTURE IN SHENZHEN: SHENZHEN CONTEMPORARY ARCHITECTURE

Urban Planning, Land and Resources Commission of Shenzhen Municipality; *Time + Architecture*; and URBANUS Architecture & Design

As a pilot zone of economic reforms, Shenzhen has also taken an important role in the development of Chinese contemporary architecture. In 2014, the journal *Time + Architecture* partnered with the Urban Planning, Land and Resources Commission of Shenzhen Municipality to begin research on the book, *Shenzhen Contemporary Architecture*.

Distinguished scholars and architects were invited to discuss the value and significance of Shenzhen's urbanism and architectural practice in the past 35 years. They singled out buildings representing the most pioneering architectural thought, and examined whether it was possible to identify a characteristic spatial language of Shenzhen.

The results of this research, published in a book published at the end of 2015, are presented at UABB 2015 in the form of an exhibition. It focuses on the development of Shenzhen's urbanism and architecture from multiple perspectives, including more than 30 topics in 8 series. Themes include contemporary heritage, ecological regeneration, experimentation and innovation, and the reuse of old buildings. The exhibition program also includes lectures and workshops on similar questions.

Credits:
DAI Chun, *Time + Architecture*
MENG Yan, Principal and Co-founder of URBANUS Architecture & Design Inc.
Urban Planning, Land and Resources Commission of Shenzhen Municipality

ECTIONS ON
TEMPORARY
NZHEN ARCHITE

DOMESTIC AFFAIRS: THE HOUSE IS A HOME TO A PARADOX

Bureau Europa and the Institute of Relevant Studies

The house is a home to a paradox. It houses the simultaneous desire to share private matters in the public realm and to seek privacy from the public. The house is an interface for mediating our societal relations, representing the attitude we have towards our local and global neighbours and political and economic systems. While we blur our houses on Google Street View, we invite unknown guests to rent one of our rooms for a night or two.

We live in an era of societal super-acceleration. We seem to be caught up in a restless dream that sees us stuck in an endless sequence of interiors, where fear is a given, fragmentation drifts in the slip-stream of redundant grand narratives, and a hyper-mediated 'total experience' lures us into escapism.

The exhibition 'Domestic Affairs' explores the paradox of these conditions by delving into the interior.

The work of the selected designers should be understood not as mere commodities, but as practices signifying cultural change: the incorporation of local materials and cultural narratives, a notion of context that empowers communities, aided by collective thinking and circular

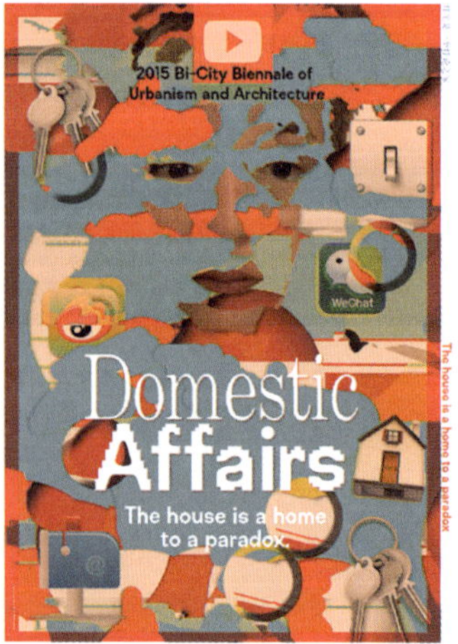

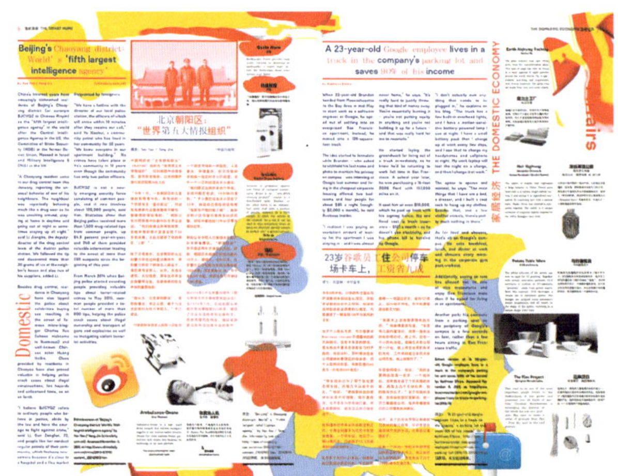

01, 02 & 03 Selected views of the newspaper accompanying the 'Domestic Affairs' exhibition.

economies, co-production schemes or the establishment of parameters for open source design tools. Further blurring the boundaries of interiority, the exhibition 'Domestic Affairs' manifests these changes as they are captured through the house and the goods and services that reach into and extended from it.

Featuring the work of: Atelier NL, Auger-Loizeau, Laura Cornet, Heather Dewey-Hagborg, Studio Droog, DUS architects, Imme van der Haak, Claire Hallewas, Ina Hollmann, Jesse Howard, Elisa van Joolen, Chris Kabel, Noortje de Keijzer, Heleen Klopper, Nicolas Maigret, Christien Meindertsma for t.e., Metahaven, MisoSoupDesign, Alec Momont, Simone C. Niquille, Ruben Pater, PinarViola, Jan Rothuizen, Helmut Smits, Studio Swine, TD, Stefania Vulpi.

Credits:
Domestic Affairs is a project by Netherlands-based Bureau Europa (Saskia van Stein, Director), curated by the Institute of Relevant Studies (Agata Jaworska and Giovanni Innella). Visual identity design by Design Displacement Group. With generous support provided by the Creative Industries Fund NL

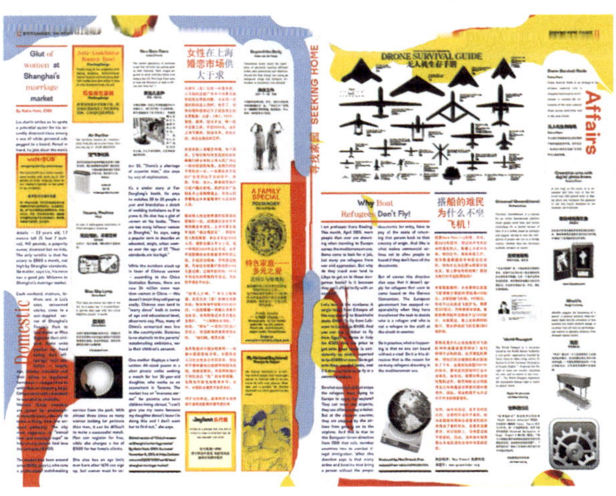

03

OUTDOOR INSTALLATIONS

FLOATING FIELDS

Thomas Chung

Floating Fields speculates on a place-based, bio-social urbanism premised on 'Re-Living the City'. It revives the poly-culture (multiple agri- and aqua-cultures) ecology that once defined the Pearl River Delta, and aspires to reinvigorate post-industrial architecture and public space with a productive edible landscape, thus positing a more organic way of life rooted in local heritage.

Centuries ago, inhabitants of the low-lying, flood-prone, delta landscape fused the cultivation of silkworm and fish with inventive engineering to develop the mulberry dyke-fish pond complex. This intensive form of eco-agriculture engendered a flourishing and sustainable water-based commerce specific to the PRD region. This year's biennale venue, the former Dacheng Flour Factory, is a product of Shenzhen's rapid urbanization, a monumental effort that covered overnight the centuries-old wetland poly-cultures with concrete and industry. The obsolete factory is now cracking up to allow sunlight, plants and water to seep through its once-impermeable surfaces, testifying to the enduring resilience of nature.

Floating Fields resuscitates the lifeless site. Concrete ground is broken up to form large, interconnected ponds for edible fish. The presence of an existing covered waterway is revealed by a filtering corridor of various water-cleansing plants and grasses for fish feed. These ponds support a complete water cycle: a contemporary version of the dyke-pond is combined with low-tech aquaponics, a life-giving waterway inspires the filtering corridor, mulberry trees are grown to feed cocoon-spinning silkworms inside a pavilion, and colourful algae is cultivated to purify the water and harvested to produce fish feed.

Floating Fields serves as a prototype for aquaponic or farming plots that could be installed on different levels of buildings, rooftops, or bodies of water. The self-sustaining ecology demonstrates the virtuous cycle of a hybrid urban-agricultural environment that can become at once a productive and leisure public space for the enjoyment of all. Returning to the roots of urban subsistence, repurposing obsolete construction, and restoring a symbiotic space for nature, Floating Fields aims to cultivate comfort and nourishment amidst the restlessness of the buoyant city.

Credits:
Concept and Design: Thomas Chung, School of Architecture, The Chinese University of Hong Kong
Executive Partner: Chi Fai Fung, Farming Consultant, Founding Member, SEED (HK)
Project and Research team: Sophia Au, Jun Kobayashi, Joshua Lam, Ng Kai Hong, Siu Man, Sylvia Siu, Wong Ming Chiu
Collaborators: Microalgae Research Team, The Open University of Hong Kong (OUHK); Prof. HO Kin Chung, Dean, School of Science & Technology, OUHK; Mr. WONG Yee Keung, Assistant Lecturer, OUHK; Mr. LEUNG Chi Chung, Research Assistant, OUHK; CHAN Ka Kwan, CHEN Jun Jie, CHEUNG Ka Yau, HO Ting Hong, LEE Yiu Lun, TSE Chun Yiu, YIU Kui Fan

Photos by Chaos.Z Courtesy of UABB Organising Committee

BAMBOO SHELTER

Laboratory for Explorative Architecture & Design Ltd. (LEAD)

The Bamboo Shelter is a temporary, light-weight, bending-active structure and habitable pavilion built on a rooftop at the UABB Shenzhen 2015 exhibition. The design highlights and gives identity to a space for public gathering. This area is located in between the auditorium and adjacent café and exhibition building.

The installation is defined by an undulating bamboo membrane that is suspended between the building edges, bent over the handrail of the walkway up, and pulled down into a central seating area. This membrane is materialised by means of a diagrid made from thin bamboo sticks. These sticks are bent onsite and manually tied together according to specific building information that was extracted from computer models. These models employ digital real-time physics simulation tools to find form that is suitable for the selected material configuration. Specific annotation and construction documentation algorithms were developed to allow easy onsite construction without the need for conventional architectural drawings such as plans, sections or elevations.

This installation is conceived as a research project within a lineage of investigations on how computational design tools can be strategically inserted into low-tech construction methods to produce innovative architecture. The thesis is that by initiating form-finding exercises from material and construction properties and restrictions, rather than from virtual speculation only, a much more practical and realistic project implementation becomes possible.

The Bamboo Shelter promotes the innovative use of natural materials which, through their symbolic and cultural associations, enforce the local identity of the project location. But most importantly it illustrates how engaging architectural alternatives are possible from the simplest of means.

Credits:
Kristof Crolla, Julien Klisz

Photos by Chaos.Z Courtesy of UABB Organising Committee

5.3449019547362E+133

Siegrun Appelt

In this outdoor, site-specific installation for the former Dacheng flour factory in Shenzhen, 72 spot lights are distributed to eight towers erected around the several buildings. The luminaires are programmed to display a precisely choreographed interplay as they slowly light up and fade away in various combinations. The light plays out beyond the physical boundaries of the place and its structures to form a spatial connection with changing constellations of light and shadow. The environment appears pictorially in the light or disappears in the dark. Passers-by become actors whilst inside the lighting cone; in the shade they become observers. The light systematically creates new, alternating perspectives of perception and is experienced as a medium which both structures and changes reality. With the lighting control set to permanent modulation, the light not only functions as a lighting medium but becomes itself discernible and observable as the source and cause of what is visible.

Thus, perception and visibility of the surrounding space prove to be functions of technoid and mediatised framework conditions. While the causes and purposes of mediatised images are usually obstructed by their omnipresence, this light installation refers precisely to the medial character of those images we have of the world and of our relationship with it.

The work's title, 5.3449019547362e+133, represents the number of possible interplay variants of the different lighting sequences. Hence, a human life span would not suffice to see and experience the entire spectrum of possibilities. By displaying the ephemeral nature of light, this installation is also about the passing of time and the transitory nature of life as a continuum, which in itself is permanently changing, and in which chance and necessity bring one another about.

Credits:
With support from Zumtobel

LIVING THE
市原点
VIP
签到处
SIGN
政务
签到处
SIGN
公众
PUBLIC
签到处
SIGN

LIVING THE
市原点
VIP
签到处
SIGN
政务
签到处
SIGN
公众
PUBLIC
签到处
SIGN

AFORMAL ACADEMY: RE-LEARNING THE CITY

Merve Bedir and
Jason Hilgefort

RE-Learning

The notion of learning, like our comprehension of cities, is undergoing a massive transition. As opposed to the classical top-down system of checking boxes of fixed units, we need to RE-read and RE-form the process of acquiring knowledge. Often people's defining educational experiences occur outside the classroom or school in the form of intense moments, encounters, and efforts. Aformal Academy: RE-Learning the City is a spatial and co-creational knowledge exchange where professors, foreign and local students, lecturers, craftsmen, visiting guests, local researchers, exhibitors, and citizens mix together in a free-flowing environment. This dynamic encounter creates a platform of multi-layered learning across disciplines, for all.

Aformal Academy

The academy starts by questioning everything, where participants RE-think the object as the core manner of perceiving architecture and urbanism. It seeks frameworks that enhance the RE-interpretation of buildings, the RE-making of our cities, and the RE-imagination of our daily lives. In the largest metropolitan region in the world, amongst some of the newest and oldest cities, in an area with an ongoing legacy of east-west co-engagement; we learn by operating within an adapting building, on a transforming city, and amongst an ongoing Biennale. The Aformal Academy is not merely a series of educational workshops parallel to the Biennale, but embodies a form of practice. It is a hybrid of learning by making, exhibition, and social space, encompassing the public at large with the evolving library of provocations and spatial archive of explorations.

Credits:
Aformal Academy: RE-Learning The City is directed by Jason Hilgefort and Merve Bedir, partners in Land+Civilization Compositions.
In cooperation with Ljubo Georgiev and Hristo Stankushev.
The Aformal Academy Online Platform was created by IRA-C and Parasite2.0 from Milan.

PARTICIPANTS AND AWARDS

RADICAL URBANISM
Curated by Alfredo Brillembourg and Hubert Klumpner

Cartographies of Planetary Urbanisation
Neil Brenner (U.S.), Christian Schmid and Milica Topalovic (Switzerland)

Autonomy & Autodigestion
Lydia Kallipoliti, Meg Studer, and Kyong Kim (U.S.)

Self-Building Processes as Critical Conscience
Recetas Urbanas (Spain)

Arsenal of Exclusion and Inclusion: The Battle for the Beach
Interboro Partners (U.S.)

Radical Cairo: From Agrarian Land to New Urban Forms
Marc Angélil and Charlotte Malterre-Barthes, MAS Urban Design – ETH Zurich (Switzerland)

Global Grids: Populations at Risk
Center for Spatial Research, GSAPP, Columbia University (U.S.)

The Medellín Diagram: The Visualisation of the Political
Teddy Cruz and Fonna Forman (U.S.) with Matthias Goerlich (Germany) and Alejandro Echeverri (Colombia)

Radical Reuse
Muck Petzet Architekten (Germany)

Urban Earthworks
Anna Heringer and Martin Rauch (Germany) with Mu Jun (China)

Collective City
Alexander Eisenschmidt / Visionary Cities Project (U.S)

Opportunity and Transformation
Wolff Architects (South Africa)

Refugee Camps of the Western Sahara
Manuel Herz Architects (Switzerland)

Do You Hear the People Sing?
Crimson Architectural Historians with Hugo Corbett (the Netherlands)

Networked Urbanism
Jose Luis Vallejo and Belinda Tato, ecosistema urbano (Spain)

Domestic Urbanism in Oroshimachi, Sendai
Atelier Hitoshi Abe with Masashige Motoe and wowlab (Japan)

Radical Temporalities (The Ephemeral City)
Rahul Mehrotra (U.S., India) and Felipe Vera (Chile) with Diego Pinochet (Chile, Hong Kong)

The Urban-Data Complex
Forensic Architecture, Goldsmiths, University of London (U.K.)

StereoTypes: Dump, Camp, and Graveyard
Ersela Kripa and Stephen Mueller, AGENCY (U.S.)

Moments In-Between
Iwan Baan (the Netherlands)

COLLAGE CITY 3D
Curated by Aaron Betsky

Symbiotic Village
Hood Design (U.S.) and Valeche Studio (Hong Kong)

Embodied Pelt
Langarita Navarro Arquitectos (Spain)

Hole In The (Window Of The) World House
Dennis Maher (U.S.)

Lost & Found
Jimenez Lai, Bureau Spectacular (U.S.)

Cacophony Collage
TOPOTEK 1 with Rebecca Saunders (Germany)

Check-In Program
Feng Feng + Fei Architect (China)

Workscape Theatre
Studio Makkink & Bey (the Netherlands)

RE–
Francesco Delogu and Maria Cristina Finucci (Italy)

Trash to Treasure Lab
Superuse Studios (the Netherlands)

Shenzhen Entropy
Rob Voerman (the Netherlands)

Ecstasies of Influences: Studiolo Wall
Lukas Feireiss (Germany) and Thomas Tsang (Hong Kong)

Power to the People
Heidelberg Project (U.S)

PRD 2.0

Curated by Doreen Heng Liu

Re-Living the Bright City
SIMA Xiao and HUANG Weidong, Urban Planning and Design Institute of Shenzhen (China)

Made In South China (MISC) – Mapping the Cultural Landscape of the PRD
Laurent Gutierrez and Valerie Portefaix, MAP Office (Hong Kong)

City of Wind
Philip YUAN, Archi-Union Architects (China)

Bay Bar
CAI Zhen and ZHU Rongyuan, China Academy of Urban Planning and Design, Shenzhen (China)

Hyper Metropolis – Speculations on Future Hybrid Lifestyle In Shenzhen
LIU Xiaodu and MENG Yan, URBANUS Architecture and Design, Inc. (China)

An Alternative Strategy for the PRD's Rural Villages
Joshua Bolchover and John Lin, Rural Urban Framework (Hong Kong)

Shenzhen Forest Island
MA Yansong, MAD Architects (China)

The City that Re-Lives Its Memories
WISE Architecture (Korea)

Spatial Economic Network
Ljubo Georgiev (Bulgaria), Hristo Stankushev (Bulgaria), Merve Bedir and Jason Hilgefort (Turkey and the Netherlands)

Wealth Architecture
FENG Yuan, Zhongshan (Sun Yat-sen) University (China)

Hong Kong Typology
Emanuel Christ and Christoph Gantenbein, Christ & Gantenbein Architects, ETH Zurich (Switzerland)

Da Lang Fever 2.0
Linda Vlassenrood, International New Town Institute (the Netherlands)

Megablock Urbanisms PRD
Jeffrey Johnson with Stephen Chou and Jiteng Yang, China Megacities Lab, Studio-X Beijing, GSAPP, Columbia University (U.S./China)

Dictionary of Mirrored Gardens
Mirrored Gardens Research Team, Vitamin Creative Space (China)

From Villages to City: the Informal History of Shenzhen
Juan DU, Univ. Hong Kong (Hong Kong)

n=distortion
Mary Ann O'Donnell, Handshake 302 (China)

Panyu: Rural Becoming Urban?
Margaret Crawford (U.S.), Max Hirsh and Dorothy Tang (Hong Kong)

Material Production – Field Practice of Zini Sugar Refinery, Panyu
Zini Sugar Refinery with TAN Hongyu (China)

PRD Revisited
Charlie Koolhaas (the Netherlands)

SOCIAL CITY
Curated by Renny Ramakers

Droog (the Netherlands)

Mark van der Net, OSCity (the Netherlands)

Jan Rothuizen (the Netherlands)

TD (Theo Deutinger and Stefanos Filippas) (the Netherlands)

Thonik (the Netherlands)

MAKER MAKER
Curated by Benjamin Ward

Bringing Fungus to China
Philip Ross (U.S)

Shwisty
Ifeanyi Oganwu, Expand Design Ltd. (U.K.)

e-white
Marina Fomenko (Russia)

Machinist Sculptor
Chris Bathgate (U.S.)

Surface II Surface
Eskayel (U.S.)

Resistor V1
Nick Puckett (U.S.)

MOBI
Sung Jang Laboratory (U.S.)

Parlay
Curtis Anthony Parlaitin (U.S.)

Hot Networks
Brandon Kruysman and Jonathan Proto (U.S.)

Here, There, Everywhere
Thing Thing (U.S.)

FABO (Fablab O)
Shenzhen Fab Lab International and Jeff Ding (China)

Smile of Iron
Yoshihito Mizuuchi (Japan)

Revolving Light
Chaihuo Maker Space (China)

Urban Assemblages: Imminence and Immanence
Olalekan Jeyifous (U.S.)

Archipelago
Ben Chang (U.S.), Young Suk Lee (U.S.) and Silvia Ruzanka (Russia)

Apartment E
Sutton Beres Culler (U.S.)

Prototypes for Dissolvable Architectures
The Bittertang Farm (U.S.)

Brick Maker
Stephen Burks Man Made (U.S.)

PAVILIONS (NATIONAL,REGIONAL, AND THEMATIC)

Macau Reframed: The City, its People and their Trace
Cultural Affairs Bureau of Macao S.A.R. Government, Architects Association of Macau, Macau Urban Planning Institute, and Center for Architecture and Urbanism (Macau)

WAY – seaWAY, railWAY, bikeWAY
Museum of Finnish Architecture, Architecture Information Center Finland, and the Helsinki City Planning Department (Finland)

Shan-Zhen: Reconnecting Shenzhen to Shannon
New Horizon_architecture from Ireland

New Industries: Positive Practices of Urban Development
Union of Architects of Russia

HyperCity: The Future of Design and Architecture Education
Harbin Institute of Technology (China), Institute for Advanced Architecture of Catalonia (Spain), and Zurich University of the Arts (Switzerland)

Now, There: Scenes from the Post-Geographic City
Art Center College of Design, Media Design Practices MFA Program (U.S.)

Unintended Acts of Design
The Victoria and Albert Museum (U.K.)

Remake – We Make: Frameworks for Social and Cultural Exchange
Lucy Bullivant (U.K.) with WORKSHOP architecture, Paul McHale, Xin Guo, Yan Gao, and students (China)

Household and City
Shenzhen Institute of Interior Design (China)

Rethinking Urban Renewal
YIN Yujun, Projective Architecture Office (China)

My City
reTUMU Urban Rural Institute (China)

Catalonia Pavilion
Miralles Tagliabue EMBT and Enric Miralles Foundation (Spain)

Domestic Affairs
Bureau Europa with the Institute of Relevant Studies (the Netherlands)

Insights of Urbanism and Architecture in Shenzhen: Shenzhen Contemporary Architecture
Urban Planning, Land and Resources Commission of Shenzhen Municipality; *Time + Architecture*; and URBANUS Architecture & Design (China)

OUTDOOR INSTALLATIONS

Floating Fields
Thomas Chung, the Chinese University of Hong Kong

Bamboo Shelter
Kristof Crolla and Julien Klisz, Laboratory for Explorative Architecture & Design Ltd. (Hong Kong)

5.3449019547362e+133
Siegrun Appelt with Zumtobel (Austria)

AFORMAL ACADEMY: RE-LEARNING THE CITY

Directed by Jason Hilgefort and Merve Bedir

Educational events, debates, workshops, readings, teach-ins, screenings, and knowledge exchange platform organised in cooperation with **Ljubo Georgiev and Hristo Stankushev** (Bulgaria).

Online platform by **IRA-C and Parasite2.0** (Italy).

AWARDS

Independent Jury Awards
Jury Members: Kristin Feireiss (Chair of Jury, Aedes Berlin), Paul Joseph Makovsky (Metropolis Magazine, New York), Aric Chen (Architecture Curator of the M+ museum, Hong Kong), Colin Fournier (The Chinese University of Hong Kong), Pedro Gadanho (Director of MAAT, Lisbon)

Gold Award: 'The National Pavilion of the Western Sahara' by Manuel Herz Architects (Radical Urbanism).

Silver Award: 'Hyper Metropolis – Speculations on Future Hybrid Lifestyle in Shenzhen' by URBANUS Architecture & Design (PRD 2.0).

Bronze Awards: 'Now, There: Scenes from the Post-Geographic City' by Art Center College of Design (Thematic Pavilion); 'Unidentified Acts of Design' by the Victoria and Albert Museum (Thematic Pavilion).

Honourable Mentions: 'Collage City 3D' exhibition curated by Aaron Betsky; '5.344901547362e+133' by Siegrun Appelt with Zumtobel (Outdoor installation); 'The City that Re-Lives its Memories' by WISE Architecture (PRD 2.0); 'Autonomy and Autodigestion' by Lydia Kallipoliti with Meg Studer and Kyong Kim (Radical Urbanism).

UABB Committee Appraisal Award
'Floating Fields' by Thomas Chung (Outdoor installation)

Academic Committee Awards
'Cartographies of Planetary Urbanisation' by Neil Brenner, Christian Schmid, and Milica Topalovic (Radical Urbanism); 'Radical Temporalities (The Ephemeral City)' by Felipe Vera and Rahul Mehrotra (Radical Urbanism); 'Cacophony Collage' by TOPOTEK 1 with Rebecca Saunders (Collage City 3D).

Public Awards
Members of the public favoured the following projects in polls conducted at UABB venues, the official website, and platforms like WeChat: 'Symbiotic Village' by Hood Design with Valeche Studio (Collage City 3D); 'City of Wind' by Philip YUAN, Archi-Union Architects (PRD 2.0); 'Social City: A Project of Design+Desires' curated by Renny Ramakers.

Best Supporting Organisation
Zumtobel Group
ETH Zurich

ABOUT UABB & COLOPHON

ABOUT UABB

Shenzhen Biennale of Urbanism\ Architecture Organising Committee

Committee Director:
YANG Hong
(Member, Standing Committee of CPC of Shenzhen Municipal Committee)

Deputy Director:
XU Chongguang
(Deputy Secretary General of Shenzhen Municipal Government),

WANG Youpeng
(Director of Urban Planning, Landing & Resources Commission of Shenzhen Municipality)

HAN Wangxi
(Director of Promotion Office of "City of Design" of Shenzhen Municipality)

Secretary General:
XUE Feng
(Deputy Director of Urban Planning, Landing & Resources Commission of Shenzhen Municipality)

Members of Organising Committee
Development and Reform Commission of Shenzhen Municipality, Financial Commission, Urban Planning, Landing & Resources Commission, Transport Commission, Education Bureau, Public Security Bureau, Culture and Tourist Bureau, Housing and Construction Bureau, Local Taxation Bureau, Urban Management Bureau, Foreign Affairs Office, Traffic Police, Government Offices Administration, The Organising Committee Office of Shenzhen "City Of Design, Shenzhen Youth Federation, Relevant District Governments, Press Group, Shenzhen Media Group, Shenzhen Customs, Shenzhen Entry-Exit Inspection and Quarantine Bureau, Shenzhen General Station of Exit and Entry Frontier Inspection".

Academic Board of Shenzhen Biennale of Urbanism\Architecture
Ole Bouman, LI Xiangning, Jeffrey Johnson, SUN Zhenhua, LU Hong, ZHU Rongyuan, SHI Jian, WANG Weijen, JIANG Jun, DU Juan, FENG Guochuan, HU Yeqiu, FU Ivan, Mary Ann O'Donnell, Roan Chingyueh

Special Fund Support
Shenzhen's Cultural Industry Development Fund

Shenzhen Biennale of Urbanism\ Architecture Organising Committee Office

Director of Shenzhen Public Art Center and Executive Director of Secretariat of Shenzhen Biennale of Urbanism\ Architecture Organising Committee:
HUANG Weiwen

Deputy Director of Shenzhen Public Art Center:
CHEN Zhen

Art Director:
SUN Zhenhua

Director of Comprehensive Department:
JIANG Peng

Director of Shenzhen Biennale of Urbanism\Architecture Organising Committee Office:
MI Lan

Exhibition and Public Programs Department
Production Coordination:
XU Liang, WANG Yixi, BU Bing, ZHOU Cong

Exhibition Coordination:
MEI Zhen, YANG Dongya

Education:
LIU He

Interns:
LI Zhaoxiong, XU Jia'er, ZOU Xueti,
HAN Lan, JIANG Jinying

Email: exhibition@szhkbiennale.org

Marketing and Branding Department
Manager:
XIE Qiongzhi

Communication and Press:
OUYANG Lingxing

Editor:
XU Tao

Business Development Officer:
WANG Yanan

Marketing Officer:
WANG Siyu

Interns:
ZHONG Jialing, LIU Bingnuan,
LV Xiaolin, XIAO Caizi

Email: Press@szhkbiennale.org

Administration Department
Manager:
LI Wen

Administration Officer:
LUO Yan, XIE Kun

Contract Management:
LI Rui, LIU Yufan

Interns:
LIN Xiaoxian, FENG Xin, ZENG Huijie,
ZHU Yanting

Accountant:
XIE Tian, YANG Li, YU Shanshan, JIANG Jie

Email: info@szhkbiennale.org

PROJECT MANAGEMENT TEAM

Project Manager:
LIU Si

Production Manager:
YIN Yujun

Preliminary Production Assistance:
Hannah Cloepfil

Production Manager (Radical Urbanism):
Andrés Ruiz Andrade

Exhibition Coordinator (Radical Urbanism):
José Castrezana López

STRATEGIC PARTNER
战略合作伙伴

招商局蛇口工业区有限公司
CHINA MERCHANTS SHEKOU INDUSTRIAL ZONE CO., LTD.

vanke万科

LONG-TERM PARTNERS
长期合作伙伴

MAIN SPONSORS
主赞助商

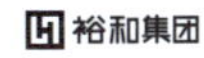

ACADEMIC SUPPORT
学术支持

ETH zürich

SUPPORTING INSTITUTION
文化机构支持

LIGHTING SUPPORT
灯光支持

ZUMTOBEL

EVENT SUPPORT
活动支持

FREE WIFI SUPPORT
免费WIFI赞助商

GRAPHIC DESIGN
平面设计

thonik

GRAPHIC DESIGN SUPPORT
平面设计支持

another design

VIDEO SUPPORT
影像支持

COUNSELOR
法律事务支持

晟典律师事务所
SD & PARTNERS

PRINTING SUPPORT
印刷支持

深圳市德信美印刷有限公司

CATERING SUPPORT
展场餐饮服务支持

DISPLAY SUPPORT
展示呈现支持

KINTO

CHIEF MEDIA PARTNERS
首席合作媒体

CHIEF NEW MEDIA PARTNERS
首席合作新媒体

MEDIA STRATEGIC PARTNER
全媒体合作

PR PARTNERS
媒体顾问

SUTTON

MEDIA STRATEGIC PARTNER
媒体战略合作伙伴

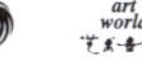

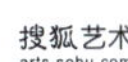

COLOPHON

Published by:
Actar Publishers, New York, Barcelona
www.actar.com

Re-Living the City: UABB 2015 Catalogue

Authors:
Aaron Betsky, Alfredo Brillembourg, Hubert Klumpner, Doreen Heng Liu

Editor:
Gideon Fink Shapiro

Graphic design and digital production:
Thonik (NL)

Photography:
Chaos.Z / UABB Organising Committee

Campaign Photography:
SWkit

Printing and binding:
Tiger Printing (Hong Kong)

Distribution
Actar D, Inc.

New York
355 Lexington Avenue, 8th Floor
New York, NY 10017, USA
+1 2129662207
salesnewyork@actar-d.com

Barcelona
Roca i Batlle 2
08023 Barcelona, SPAIN
+34 933 282 183
eurosales@actar-d.com

ISBN: 9781945150036
PCN: 2016939875
A CIP catalogue record for this book is available from Library of Congress, Washington, D.C., USA